An Anthology
of Austrian Drama

Also by DOUGLAS A. RUSSSELL:

Stage Costume Design
Theatrical Style: A Visual Approach to the Theatre

An Anthology
of Austrian Drama

Edited with a
Historical Introduction by

Douglas A. Russell

Rutherford • Madison • Teaneck
Fairleigh Dickinson University Press

London and Toronto: Associated University Presses

© 1982 by Associated University Presses, Inc.

Associated University Presses, Inc.
4 Cornwall Drive
East Brunswick, New Jersey 08816

Associated University Presses
69 Fleet Street
London EC4Y 1EU, England

Associated University Presses
Toronto M5E 1A7, Canada

Library of Congress Cataloging in Publication Data

Main entry under title:

An anthology of Austrian drama.

    CONTENTS: Nestroy, J. The talisman.—Grillparzer, F.
King Ottocar, his rise and fall.—Schnitzler, A.
La ronde.—[etc.]

    1. German drama—Austrian authors—Translations into English.
2. English drama—Translations from German.
I. Russell, Douglas A.
PT3826.D8A5   8321.008   76–19836
ISBN 0–8386–2003–5

To the Students and Staff
of Stanford in Austria

CONTENTS

Preface

This book is an outgrowth of a course in Austrian Drama and Theater History twice taught to Stanford University students studying in Austria in the Stanford Overseas Program. In 1967–68 when the program was located in a resort hotel in the Semmering and I had to bus students to Vienna to attend performances of Austrian plays, I was always dismayed to find that the translations that we studied in class were always labeled as German Drama. When I taught the course again in 1971 and the program was situated in Vienna, there was greater opportunity for my students and me to attend the theater. I became more aware of the strong Austrian theatrical tradition that set Austrian drama and theater apart from that of Germany. And yet in all anthologies and single translations of Austrian plays, the playwright and his work are treated as a sub-channel in the mainstream of German dramatic literature. With its mixture of Italian lyricism and color, Slavic fatalism, Spanish mysticism, German logic and idealism, French classicism, and native folk comedy, Austrian drama is a fascinating cross section of most of the major threads in European dramatic art. I thought that it deserved a hearing on its own, and I resolved to put together an anthology of six Austrian plays that I both enjoyed and thought typical of the distinctive Austrian traditions in the drama. I also thought that I should include a brief history of the Austrian theater to underline the distinctive elements of the Austrian theatrical tradition and give reasons for its development. This seemed particularly relevant during the year 1976, which was the bicentennial anniversary of the Burgtheater, one of the great European state theaters.

Since I am not a professor of dramatic literature but a theatrical designer and theater historian, I have not chosen the plays for their importance in the development of the individual playwright. Each play is included for its interest as a theater piece and for qualities that make it very much a part of a distinctly Austrian theater tradition or traditions. It is, of course, impossible to choose a mere six plays that will sum up a five-hundred-year history of Austrian dramatic art, and each student of Austrian theatrical art will have his or her own list. I can only hope that the plays included are interesting, and, since Vienna from the early nineteenth century through World War II was in many ways the city closest to the heart and nerve center of European psychic development, I think that the plays reflect the modern European as well as the Austrian experience of the last century and a half. The first two plays represent the patriotism and complacency of the nineteenth-century middle-class outlook; the second two, the decadence and suffering below the surface of society in the years before the first World War; and the last two plays represent the revolutionary and Fascist upheavals since World War I.

I hope that this anthology will prove useful to both students of the theater and those studying dramatic literature in German language and literature departments, but it is primarily intended for those who love Austria and its theater.

It should be quite clear that I would never have thought of editing this anthology if I had not had the opportunity to teach in the Stanford Overseas Program in Austria, and I want to thank Dr. Robert Walker, the retired director of this program, for that privilege, and to state my conviction that this is one of the most important undergraduate programs at Stanford University. I particularly want to thank Hedwig Thimig, daughter of the famed Austrian theatrical family who is currently Director of the Stanford Program in Vienna for her invaluable help, enthusiasm, and encouragement during the long period when I was seeking a publisher. I also wish to thank the Stanford University Research and Development fund and to acknowledge the encouragement of the Austrian Institute of New York in supporting publication. Thanks are also due to Joe Fabry and Max Knight, translators of the Nestroy play, for their advice and encouragement. I am deeply indebted to my wife, Marilyn, for her helpful advice and editorial assistance.

Introduction : History of
The Austrian Theater

It may be difficult for the American theater student to realize that one of the richest centers of Western theatrical art for the past three hundred years has been the city of Vienna. Americans associate opera and operetta with the city, but seldom drama. They tend to characterize even the virtuoso art of the twentieth century theatrical genius Max Reinhardt as German, and when they do see or read plays by Schnitzler and Hofmannsthal, they often think of them as examples in the richly varied development of German dramatic art. Just as Latin American theater and drama has a character that is quite different from that of Spain, and America's dramatic and theatrical development is very different from that of England, so it should not be surprising that Austrian theater and drama have a unique character that is quite distinct from developments found in the German theater and dramatic art. American students having studied the development of theater and drama in Italy, England, France, Germany, Scandinavia, and Russia have often missed the excitement of theatrical developments in Vienna or have noted them only peripherally in relation to opera and operetta. What it is important to realize is that in Austrian theatrical history, music, visual spectacle, dance, and drama have always been viewed together as essential ingredients of the art of the theater.

At the close of the medieval era, the twin foci of theatrical development in the southern part of the German-speaking area of central Europe were the cities of Munich and Vienna. In these two centers there grew up a theatrical tradition that was quite different from that in France and England. Here the Austro-Bavarian love of spectacle and gift for emotion through gesture, movement, and sound was given firm patronage by two important royal houses, Hapsburg and Wittelebach, and the result was a very popular, richly visual, strongly theatrical form of dramatic art.

11

Vienna, the capital of the Holy Roman Empire from the Middle Ages until 1806 and the cultural capital of central Europe from 1806 until 1918, was the most important of the two centers—the seat of the powerful and long-lived House of Hapsburg and the crossroads for the mingling of artistic influences from north to south and from east to west. The Hapsburg family connections alone created cultural ties with Spain, the Netherlands, Hungary, Bohemia, and northern Italy. These various cultural influences greatly influenced the development of Viennese theater.

Vienna was also heavily affected by the spiritual struggles of the Reformation, just as the city was beginning to rise out of its medieval isolation to become a center of central European culture. But the Counter-Reformation—which began in Italy in the mid-sixteenth century, took hold in Austria during the Thirty Years War, and reached its climax after the defeat of the Turks in 1683—renewed Austria's ties with Catholic Italy and Spain, and gave new power to the emperor in Vienna. The end of the Thirty Years War, which left Germany weary and exhausted, found Vienna intact, wealthy, and ready to move into the new Baroque Age with optimism and assurance. Yet one more near cultural disaster had to be averted as the Turks swept in from the east and laid siege to Vienna in an attempt to take this wealthy prize, the only major obstacle in their drive into the heart of central Europe.

With the repulsion of the Turks in 1683, Vienna both escaped cultural disaster and entered into a Golden Age of Baroque cultural and artistic development—a grand age in which theatrical entertainment seemed to be the key in all the arts. It was also a Baroque art that differed from the other national Baroque developments in Europe, since it blossomed as a fusion of Slavic, German, and Latin strains that could only have occurred in the cosmopolitan crossroad that was the imperial city of Vienna at the opening of the eighteenth century. In the theater, it was particularly the Austro-Bavarian flair for the theatrical with its equal stress on music and drama that led to the distinctive nature of Viennese theater in the later eighteenth century. Also, the grand and imperial ambitions of the House of Hapsburg in those golden years at the end of the seventeenth and the beginning of the eighteenth century played a prominent role in establishing the nature of the development of theatrical art in Vienna. In many ways from the seventeenth through the nineteenth century the history of Austrian theater is closely interwoven with the history of the House of Hapsburg, even though the popular theater certainly had nothing to do with the Imperial House. It is also interesting that Austrian drama during these three centuries—unlike German drama—was almost totally apolitical. Since the immediate power of the Imperial House made dissent seem unnatural and the Roman Catholic heritage made an acceptance of authority almost automatic, Austrian dramatists have seldom been rebels.

The first really indigenous Austrian developments in the drama came at the close of the Middle Ages when the great biblical cycles were well established at centers that included Frankfurt, Nuremberg, Lucerne, and Heidelberg. In the Austrian Tyrol in the village of Sterzing, from 1455 onward, a small Austrian reflection of the great religious dramatic festivals developed under the leadership of Stöffl Schopfer and Virgil Raber, who developed a passion play with an original native text as well as a number of dramatized tales of chivalry drawn from the heroic German legends. It was a small beginning, but its nature and quality were truly Austrian in the stress on imagination, visual display, and overt theatricality.

About the same time on a much higher literary level there developed, with the new interest in Humanism and the Classics, an academic mode of theater that was mainly the work of three men: Konrad Celtis, Joachim von Watt, and Benedictus Chelidonius. Konrad Celtis was from Franconia, but he settled in Vienna in 1497 as a professor of poetry and rhetoric at the University of Vienna. He made that university a center for classical studies and developed afternoon performances of plays by Seneca, Plautus, and Terence. He also slipped in one or two works of his own, and one bore the august title: *Rhapsodia, laudes et victoria Maxmiliani de Boemannis.* This Latin compliment to the emperor was performed before Maximilian in Vienna in 1504, and it can be seen as the seed of the later Viennese *Haupt-und Staatsaktionen* (plays about action in high places and flattering to the House of Hapsburg). In this play there is elevated style, the glorification of the ruling house, the use of music and ballet, an exchange of dialogue between the actors and the audience, and some clear instances of the business and stereotyped comic figures that were later to be so important in the *commedia dell' arte*. A pupil of Celtis, Joachim von Watt then added to these beginnings by providing in his *Gallus pugnans* (1514) an example of what was later to be the basis of Viennese farce (*posse*). In this script cocks and hens come before the court to argue about cockfighting and the rights of the sexes. Arbitrators advise the parties to fulfill their functions according to nature, and a Viennese boy, who in many ways is a prototype for the later Hanswurst comic, with his cynical down-to-earth views, says that he represents the audience point of view and tells both parties that they belong in the stewpot.

Watt and Celtis thus represent the academic Humanism of the University of Vienna as well as some of the earthy Tyrolean realism of the religious and secular folk drama. By comparison, Benedictus Chelidonius, who was Abbott of the Schottenkloster in Vienna, presented in his *Voluptatis cum virtute disceptatio* (1515) an example of a humanist drama with a completely religious outlook. He utilizes a religious-moral debate in which Greek gods and goddesses act out an allegorical tale that is resolved in completely Christian terms. Allied with him at the Schottenkloster was Wolfgang Schmetzl, a Protestant turned Catholic who, between 1541 and 1551, produced seven plays. These under the pressures of the Reformation turn against the precepts of Humanism to completely biblical subjects. But Vienna was not fruitful ground for this evangelical drama, and the very year (1551) that Schmetzl left Vienna the Jesuits arrived there to found a school and harness all the arts and especially the drama to Christian Jesuit education.

The establishment of the Austrian Province of the Society of Jesus in Vienna marks the turning of the tide against Protestantism in Austria, and one of the major tools used to win back the heretics was the vernacular interlude and the farce. The first Jesuit play to be performed in Vienna in 1555, *Euripus sive de Inanitate rerum omnium* by Lewin Brecht of Antwerp, concerns the fate of Euripus, who is assigned to perdition after being seduced by Venus and Cupid. It includes most of the qualities that make up the typical Jesuit drama until the middle of the seventeenth century. There is a humanist preference for a classical theme, a continuation of the medieval morality tradition of the play with a moral purpose, and the conclusion always includes a strong Christian message. The plays were usually presented by students at the term prize-giving, and the aim was both to give instruction in the arts of Latin grammar,, rhetoric, and behavior, and to project a strong Christian message to performers and audience. In these plays, the Baroque view of Christianity that stresses the tension between human and natural values and the incomparable and unfathomable reality of God that makes all other things a delusion is deftly and surely developed. The tension is visually worked out by showing this world as a testing ground for the next—a prelude to the grandeur of God's divine world. To present this message as vividly as possible, striking allegorical representations of the Virtues and Vices were placed on a stage divided into three parts: an upper world of Love and Nobility, a middle world of Man, and an underworld of Hate, Envy, and Adultery. The visual presentation of these worlds was rich and highly technical, combining the best in painting, landscape gardening, and architecture, and the resultant spectacle was basic to the development of both popular and court theater through the middle of the nineteenth century. The comedies of Raimund and certain early plays of Nestroy owe their structure to this Jesuit concept of man caught between an upper world of goodness and a lower one of evil, even if salvation becomes, in a more secular age, merely happiness or contentment.

Coupled with this major theme in the early Jesuit plays are three other qualities or ideas. First, there is a hierarchal view of society in which the emperor is the divinely appointed upholder of social order. Second, there is a tendency, derived from the gloomy grandeur of the Hapsburg Court in Spain, that stresses the dreamlike quality of this life when set against the reality of a heavenly existence. Calderón's *La Vida Sueño* is a superb example of this kind of theatrical thinking, and this particular play had a lasting influence on the Austrian drama. Finally, the contact with the Italian opera, whose influence was strongly felt in the early years of the seventeenth century, made music and spectacle an indispensable part of performance. This incorporation of the lyrical and the sensuous into all major Austrian dramatic works stems both from the nature of the Austrian spirit and from the historical moment in time that this uniquely Austrian drama happened to develop.

By 1620 the Jesuits had their own theater in Vienna, and gradually the use of simultaneous settings gave way to the multiple settings and grandeur of opera. In 1659 when Leopold I built his own opera house in the palace in Vienna and imported Lodovico Burnacini from Italy to do sets, costumes, and spectacular transformation effects, the local Jesuit production, *Pietas Victrix*, made use of all possible theatrical effects to underline in graphic detail the Baroque religious moral—*vanitas, vanitatis, vanitas.*

The greatest name among the writers of Jesuit drama in Austria is Nicolaus Avancinus (1612–86) who wrote *Pietas Victrix.* He held the same position at the University of Vienna that Celtis had occupied a century and a half earlier, but he also became so important a figure at the palace that he became court poet to Leopold I. Subjects culled from the classics, history, and the Bible were molded into plays that flattered the Imperial House, and in *Pietas Victrix,* Leopold is praised as the successor to Constantine the Great. Such plays were presented with great splendor and spectacle, in every way equal to the imported Italian operas also being presented at court during those years.

But this very grandeur in production led to decay in the spiritual sources that originally motivated the Jesuits to write those dramas, while the further use of the vernacular instead of Latin generated the inclusion of more and more Viennese local humor and cynical commentary on the action. Under Avancinus's successor, Johann Baptiste Adolph, the sober splendor of the Jesuit drama gradually turned to Viennese cheerfulness and gaiety, including more scenes from contemporary life and catering to lower-class tastes. Thus, during the early eighteenth century, Jesuit theater declined, and ended abruptly with the suppression of the Order in 1773.

Meanwhile, the popular theater had also been on the increase during the Baroque Age. Green's English comedians are recorded as having been in Graz, Styria, in 1608, and some of the preserved texts in the vernacular depict the customary scenes in high places (*Haupt-und Staatsaktionen*) interrupted by comic interludes that are dominated by a clown called Pickelherring. Similar wandering troupes without a permanent theater soon were seen in all German speaking areas with local actors replacing the Englishmen. By the beginning of the eighteenth century, a number of troupes that were specifically Austrian in character had developed. Especially in Vienna, the *Haupt-und Staatsaktionen* with coarse comic interludes became integrated into the developing Viennese popular theater and gained a characteristic Viennese flavor that was to remain through the great age of popular comedy in the nineteenth century.

The father of this distinctive Viennese style is undoubtedly Joseph Anton Stranitzky (1676–1726), who was from Styria and had begun his career as a wandering puppeteer. He finally settled in Vienna about 1705 and turned to the live theater while at the same time qualifying in dentistry at the University of Vienna. To the end of his career he was both a dentist and a theatrical entrepreneur. When the manager of the theatrical company for whom he had been working resigned, Stranitzky took over the troupe, and when the famous Kärntnertor Theater was built by the Vienna Corporation as the city's first permanent theater in 1710 and was given over to the imported Italian comedians, the citizenry rose up and demanded that Stranitzky's native players be given the house. In 1711 Stranitzky's group was installed, and the theater became the first permanent home of the extemporaneous German-language comedy. The nature of the plays was not that different from the popular fare of the preceding century, except for the fact that a new, specifically Austro-

Bavarian, comic type took the place of the *commedia dell' arte* or pickelherring clown. Hanswurst was his name, and he was usually a peasant pig castrator from Salzburg. He was dressed in a loose red jacket with a fool's ruff, yellow pantaloons held up by red braces, a blue heart embroidered on his chest with the initials H. W., with a tufted wig, beard, heavy eyebrows, and tall, green, pointed hat. He also had a great wooden slapstick or "pistolese" stuck in his belt, but it was his sly peasant humor and his knack for slipping unscathed past the pitfalls of the world that were his protection against life. As presented by Strasnitzky, Hanswurst was acrobatic and physical and did not play up to the audience. Only a few titles remain from the Kärntnertor repertoire, but there are fourteen other extant *Wiener Haupt-und Staatsaktionen* in which Hanswurst appears. These very probably may have been edited by Stranitzky himself and give an excellent idea of how Italian opera librettos were frequently rewritten with original songs and the character of Hanswurst integrated into the action as a commentator and go-between. He always found the actions and sentiments of his betters completely incomprehensible; his verbal humor was coarse and direct, and his visual humor was a combination of spontaneous mimicry and stereotyped tricks.

Gottfried Prehauser (1699–1769) was Stranitzky's successor, and in his hands the Hanswurst plays underwent a change comparable to the change taking place within the Viennese theater at the time. Summoned to Vienna by Stranitzky in 1725 after the latter had heard of his brilliant performances of the Hanswurst character in the provinces, Prehauser softened and changed the quality of the Hanswurst plays by making the kings and courtiers of the *Haupt-und Staatsaktion* tradition into Viennese lawyers, officers, and doctors, while Hanswurst himself became less the peasant (frequently appearing as a soldier, doctor, lawyer, etc.) and more the sentimental and rather sophisticated Viennese servant-retainer, who, unlike Stranitzky, did play up to his audience. After Prehauser died, the age of improvised comedy came to a close with Maria Theresa's edict against improvised comedy in 1752, and was replaced by the written script and a more exacting presentation of the play.

Meanwhile at court the new empress, Maria Theresa, had decided that a permanent court theater should be established, and on the 14th of March in 1741, the empress gave the use of a small badminton court close to the palace to the court chamberlain for the purpose of theatrical performance. It received the title of *Königlichestheater nächst der Burg* and much later the nickname of the Burgtheater. Both it and the earlier Kärntnertor Theater now came under royal supervision. The empress herself, however, disliked the theater for the most part, thinking that it was trivial and frivolous, and she did not appear at a performance in the Burgtheater until 1771. However, there was a direct corridor to the imperial box, and Maria Theresa appeared in nighgown and cap to announce the birth of her first grandson and offer ticket refunds so that the audience might celebrate. For almost twenty years without royal guidance the Burg went through continuous changes in personnel and policy. The plays were primarily French and Greek in the classical tradition; there was little support from the Crown and no solid theatrical development.

But as German theater in the north began to develop an artistic and national consciousness, the demand in Vienna for a higher standard of artistic and intellectual achievement in the theater increased, and this pressure was spearheaded by Josef von Sonnenfels, a professor and leader of the Enlightenment. He was a great admirer and disciple of Johann Christoph Gottsched, a professor at the University of Leipzig who, despite a stuffy and lifeless classical play-writing method based on French classical tradition, had brought German drama from popular burlesque to the level of serious dramatic writing by publicly banning Hanswurst from the German stage. Sonnenfels's aims were the same, and he greeted the death of Prehauser with the cry: "Great Pan is dead . . . the pillar of burlesque has fallen, its kingdom is destroyed." In his *Briefe über die Wienerische Schaubühne* (1767) Sonnenfels stressed the need to import the new serious drama from Germany, but he shortsightedly overlooked the native character of the Viennese theater that might lead to a new national drama in Austria. Luckily, the new emperor, Joseph II, who ruled jointly with his mother after 1765, was very interested in culture and the Enlightenment, and he too was eager to upgrade the dramatic arts.

At the same time, inside the theater itself, new forms and comic types were being developed. Josef Felix von Kurz (1717–83), whose father had been in Stranitzky's company, began his career in 1737 and contributed to the comic tradition the character of Bernardon, a restless and adventurous youth who was always becoming involved in magic and the supernatural. The interest in magic was to be central in Austrian theater for the next hundred years, representing a last reminder of Baroque universalism in its stress on the war between the forces of reality and the supernatural. The character of Bernardon moved toward the development of character comedy.

He often aged toward the end of a play while groups of children danced in a ballet as little Bernardons. Reality and the supernatural were now realized in a bourgeois form in which the adventurous hero contended with an array of good and bad spirits. *Die 33 Schelmereien des Bernardon* contained an extended series of these adventures, and Sonnenfels was furious with what he considered the absolute absence of literary and intellectual qualities in such popular fare.

Philip Hafner (1735–64), who turned to the theater as a director after a number of years as a city official, worked briefly with Prehauser before beginning to write domestic comedies and farce for the popular stage. He also admired the work of Lessing in Germany and so tried to strike a balance between the popular and the literary drama by demanding that actors stick to the script and that literary aspects of his plays be kept intact. His most famous plays are *Megära die förchterliche Hexe* (1755) and *Der Furchtsame* (1764). Hafner was the first to give supernatural characters like his witch, Megära, character frustrations, and to begin the humanization of theatrical allegory that climaxed in the work of Ferdinand Raimund. He is rightly considered the father of the typical Viennese comedy of manners or *Volksstück* in which aristocratic privilege gives way to a middle-class ethic with emphasis on honesty and civic virtue.

At this moment of cultural upheaval and change in Vienna, a famous theater was being built in the provinces. In 1766 one of the most powerful Viennese imperial families, the Schwarzenbergs, in their country seat of Česky Krumlov, 100 miles southeast of Prague, had a beautiful court theater built to replace an earlier wooden one. This theater, with its beautifully painted Rococo interior, machinery, and perspective scenery executed by Jan Wetschela and Leo Merkla from Vienna, still exists, like the Drottningholm in Sweden, as one of the most beautifully preserver of all the court theaters built in the eighteenth century.

Ten years later, in 1776, one of the great events in the history of permament repertory theaters took place. Joseph II, who viewed the theater as a powerful educational and cultural weapon for developing the national consciousness, decreed that the Burgtheater should become a national theater for the exclusive performance of serious literary drama. The theater was placed under the directorship of an intendant appointed by the Crown, and the first appointee was Sonnenfels. Sonnenfels tried with all the power at his disposal to banish the popular theater, then flourishing under the leadership of Karl Marinelli (1744–1803) at the Theater in der Leopoldstadt outside the walls of the central city. But the popular theater continued to flourish, and in 1788 the Theater in der Josefstadt, which still remains one of Vienna's most important theaters, was opened by Karl Mayer as another home for popular drama; then in 1801 the famous entrepreneur Emanuel Schikaneder (1751–1812) opened the famous Theater an der Wien.

It is thus a peculiarity of the Viennese theater of the late eighteenth and early nineteenth centuries that the regular or literary drama existed side by side with the popular drama. Though the popular drama was fully supported and accepted, it could perform only in the suburbs outside the walls of the central city, and the aristocrats who frequented those theaters attended masked.

Marinelli, the leading actor and director in the popular theater in the late eighteenth century, is given credit for introducing in *Der Ungar in Wien,* the first of a long line of characters from the non-German areas of the Hapsburg Empire. The Hungarian visitor to Vienna was seen over and over again in the next century as an exotic as well as a comic character. Schickaneder, meanwhile, was the most versatile of all the figures in the popular theater, acting in comic parts, writing a version of *Hamlet,* producing plays, writing librettos, and singing in opera and the *Singspiel.* He not only produced Mozart's *The Magic Flute,* but he wrote the libretto and played the part of Papageno to great acclaim. His productions, noted for their stress on richness and spectacle, were all supported by both the wealthy bourgeois and the court, and his work was looked on with favor by Joseph II and his successors.

At the Burgtheater the reorganization by the emperor had given the actors much more control than in the past, even though the purse strings were held by the Crown, At first, an elected representative or *wöchner* was appointed weekly by the actors to work with the intendant, but when this proved unworkable a committee of five actors was appointed for a full year to work with the representative of the Crown. One great boost in the company's fortunes during the later years of the eighteenth century came with the visit of the famous Friedrich Schröder from the Hamburg National Theatre. Franz Brockmann, who had originated the role of Hamlet for Schröder in Hamburg, had been hired by the Burgtheater, and in 1782 he was able to convince the great Schröder, hampered by his mother's interference in his management of the Hamburg Theatre, to come to Vienna as a visiting actor-director. He remained in Vienna for four years and did a great deal to strengthen discipline, tone down the ranting in tragedy and the foolery in comedy, and lay the foundations for a subtle and refined acting ensemble.

Improvements in the theatrical fare presented at the Burg continued, and a few local writers began to prepare work for the national theater. For example, Cornelius von Ayrenhoff (1733–1819) wrote under the French influence of Denis Diderot, and though popular at the time, his plays such as *Der Postzug* are completely forgotten today. One of the problems faced by would-be writers for the Burgtheater lay in the fact that the censorship rules were both rigid and ridiculous: no plays could be performed that interested only one section of the population; no play could be presented that might undermine the prestige of the House of Hapsburg; no monarch could be presented in a negative light; no crypts, cemeteries, funerals, or groups of ecclesiastics could be featured; and there was such an absolute prohibition against incest and adultery that an unmarried man and woman could not leave the stage together unless accompanied by a servant. These restrictions were so inhibiting that the truly theatrical writing was done in the popular theater, utilizing the comic types that were the successors to Hanswurst. Two very important characters were added in these years, and they continue to this day in the Viennese puppet theater. Kasperl, a German equivalent of Punch, was the creation of Johann Laroche (1745–1806) from Graz. When Laroche became the principal comedian in the Marinelli Company, he turned what had been a low-grade, second-string comic character into a brilliant new version of many of the old Hanswurst characteristics. Kasperl usually wore Tyrolean peasant dress but also appeared as servants, page boys, and so on. He spoke with a broad Viennese dialect and entertained with all manner of tricks and excessively coarse jokes. Since he did not sing, he was not included in the *Singspiel* that was being encouraged by Joseph II at this time. The other new character was Thaddädl, who was developed by Anton Hasenhut (1766–1841). This character, like Kasperl, relied not on improvisation but on a written script and was said to have been developed from Taddeo, a character in the *commedia dell' arte*. He was presented as a clumsy youth with a falsetto voice who was continuously infatuated with a girl whom he could not win. The best presentation of this character was in Kringsteiner's *Der Zwirnhändler* (1801), and though the character did not really survive intact after the death of Hasenhut, the tradition of the written script, rather than improvisations on a scenario, remained.

At this same time the native *Singspiel*, unrelated to the popular theater and comparable to British ballad opera, was developing as a native answer to imported Italian opera, and of course Mozart was the Austrian genius in both modes. *The Abduction from the Seraglio*

(1782) is a brilliant example of the *Singspiel,* just as *The Marriage of Figaro* and *Così Fan Tutte* are fine examples of the Italian comic opera tradition. But it is in *The Magic Flute* (1791) that Mozart combines the *Singspiel* with the Viennese theatrical tradition of magic and the supernatural to create a piece that links the eighteenth-century Viennese theatrical tradition to the romantic music drama of the nineteenth century. Joseph II had given permission for a season of *Singspiel* at the Burgtheater in 1788, though he disliked Mozart's operas. A musical season alternated with the dramatic season at the Burg for many years, while the imported Italian opera continued at the old Kärntnertortheater, staged by wandering troupes or *stagione*.

The Burgtheater, at the close of the eighteenth century, was leased to a Viennese count, named Palffy, with the hope that he would remove artistic problems from court consideration. Within a decade there were financial and artistic difficulties and the Burgtheater returned to the status of a court theater in the early nineteenth century under an artistic director who was to be one of the great names in the history of the Austrian theater. Joseph Schreyvogel (1768–1832), a talented, refined, well-informed, dramatic expert who was also a shrewd manager and diplomat, was able to free the theater from both court interference and the interference of muscial productions, thus paving the way for a true national dramatic theater. A writer of some reputation who had been secretary to the Burg under Count Palffy's management, Schreyvogel was equally interested in literature and theatrical art and is noted for having introduced into the repertory plays by Goethe and Schiller, lesser-known plays by Shakespeare, and the work of a complete unknown, Franz Grillparzer. Grillparzer, who was to become the Goethe of Austria, used to say that Schreyvogel was a Lessing with the gift for theatrical management.

During his management from 1814 to 1832, Schreyvogel brought Vienna the great Sophie Schröder, who was said to be the greatest tragic actress in the German-speaking world. Around her he gathered other outstanding talents such as Heinrich Anschütz, who had made a great reputation outside Vienna and was an outstanding interpreter of Wallenstein in the Schiller trilogy of the same name; Karl Ludwig Costenoble, who was an older actor noted for his character roles; Maximilian Korn, a polished leading man known for his performance of Marinelli in Lessing's *Emilia Galotti*; Ludwig Löwe and Sophie Müller, who were the handsome and talented ingenues; and, finally, for a brief period of time from 1828 until his death in 1832, the greatest actor in the German-speaking world, Ludwig Devrient. The latter's Franz Moor in *Die Rauber,* Shylock, and King Lear were considered overwhelmingly brilliant characterizations; and like Edmund Kean, his contemporary in England, he was noted for his fiery, all-consuming emotional performances. Though prematurely old and tired when he arrived in Vienna, Devrient rekindled a final splendid theatrical blaze for his new public, but it could not last. After an illness he appeared as Sheva, one of his admired roles, but the exertion was so great that, at the close of the performance, he burst into tears saying, "It is all over." He died on December 30, 1832, aged only forty-eight.

The key Viennese playwrights during this exciting period were three productive writers, Gleich, Meisl, and Bäuerle, none of whom was a playwright by profession nor wrote for the Court theater, but who prepared the ground for the later work of Raimund, Nestroy, and Grillparzer. It must be remembered that they wrote popular fare during this age of Metternich for a monarch who had lost to Napoleon and for a society now dedicated to the status quo. Strong governmental censorship demanded that all current political themes be veiled or suppressed, and thus great support was given to the *Zauberstück,* or magic play, which had originated in the Austrian Baroque Era and was now used to remove the audience and controversial themes from reality.

Joseph Alois Gleich (1772–1841) was a minor civil servant who wrote 220 plays as official playwright to the Theater in der Josefstadt and the Theater in der Leopoldstadt, ranging from comedy through magic and fairy-tale pieces to parody and moral farce. His best known work is *Der Eheteufel auf Reisen* (1822). Karl Meisl (1775–1853) was a journalist who used his adaptive and imitative qualities to turn out sophisticated and ironic parodies within the magic-theater tradition. His best known work is probably *Der Lustige Fritz* (1818). Adolphe Bäuerle (1786–1859) was the editor of *Der Wiener Zeitung* and also wrote about 80 plays both in the magic-play and bourgeois-comedy traditions. His best effort was probably *Die Bürger in Wien* (1813), in which he created a new comic character, Staberl, who now supplanted Kasperl in the public's affection.

But the great, popular, comic writer in the *Zauberstück* tradition was Ferdinand Raimund (1790–1836), who was a classic example of the comedian who wished to play Hamlet—a great comic talent who always aspired to do tragedy. He had abandoned an apprenticeship in a confectioner's shop to go into the popular theater at the Josefstadt in 1813, then transferred to the Leopoldstadt in 1817. He seemed from the beginning to know all there was to know about the character of the Viennese audience, and the mixture of tearful sentiment, gaiety, wit, and romantic charm in his performances and plays completely mirrored the taste of the times. Like Bäuerle he was a complete chauvinist about things Viennese: Vienna was the finest city in the world, its people the best, its language or dialect the most beautiful, its culture the most perfect. He also perfected a type of play pioneered by Gleich and Bäuerle, the *Besserungstück,* in which the leading character is improved through experience or dreams. For example, in Raimund's *Der Verschwender,* after the spendthrift passes through the results of his reckless spending, he finally recognizes the true values in life admired by the conservative, materialist Austrian society of the early nineteenth century (the Biedermeier period). In all of his plays his interpretation of the pathetic, gay, clever, sentimental rogue or vagabond placed against a magic theater background achieved a balance of effects not found before in the Viennese theater, while his own personal melancholic disposition captured exactly a certain naive Austrian sense of sentiment and pathos. He hit his stride as a playwright with *Das Mädchen aus der Feenwelt oder der Bauer als Millionär* (1826), was manager of the Theater in der Leopoldstadt from 1828 to 1830, and wrote his last great success, *Der Verschwender,* in 1834 as he saw himself losing the Viennese public to the newest hero of the hour, Johann Nestroy. He committed suicide in 1836 after he had been bitten by a dog that he thought had rabies.

Johann Nestroy (1801–62) already belonged to a new age. Where Raimund was sensitive, melancholy, and wistful, combining Romanticism with the earlier, stable world of the Baroque, Nestroy reflected the rising bourgeois liberal spirit that led to the Revolution of 1848. With irreverence, parody, and humorous social commentary, he appealed to thought as much as to emotion. While Raimund believed in the basic goodness of man, Nestroy was a pessimist who believed man's weak and faulty nature could be exposed but not improved. He came to the theater via a legal career and the opera, where he sang Sarastro in *The Magic Flute* in 1821, but it was after 1831 that he found his true métier at the Theater in der Josefstadt as a playwright and comic actor. With his ability for improvisation as a character actor, productivity as a playwright, ability to write in the morning for a performance that night, and his sense of how to balance realism and theatricality, he had no peer in the popular theater. He built his career on past taste and borrowed from any and all sources to find material for his strikes at the social and political targets of the day. It took courage to defy the censorship, and once he did land in jail for a few days, but he usually veiled his barbs in order to escape the censors. Though wittier than Raimund, he was less imaginative and sentimental than the playwright-actor whose traditions he inherited. His first great success was *Der böse Geist Lumpazivagabundus oder das liederlich Kleeblatt* (1833), which mixed the magic-play tradition with social criticism, but in later work he gave up the magic-play framework in favor of straight parody and comic satire. His best-known play for English-speaking audiences is *Einen Jux will er sich machen* (1842), which was the basis for Thornton Wilder's *The Merchant of Yonkers* and *The Matchmaker,* and eventually became the musical *Hello Dolly.*

Nestroy was the last playwright of importance in the native popular-theater tradition. Tastes were becoming more literary and philosophical, and industrialization, with its disruption of stable social traditions, also brought higher ticket prices and a new theater audience. After Nestroy, the divorce between actor and writer became final, attention shifted to the Burgtheater and literary drama, and what remained of the older popular theater was incorporated into the operetta. Schreyvogel had done wonders in establishing a solid but varied theatrical fare of classics and new dramas at the Burgtheater. His selections were made from Austrian, English, Spanish, and French playwrights, and from Lessing, Goethe, Schiller, and other German dramatists, and it is to his shrewd judgment that we owe the development of Austria's greatest dramatist, Franz Grillparzer (1791–1872).

Grillparzer came to the theater by way of legal studies and throughout most of his life worked in the civil service as the court archivist. He had a melancholy temperament that was afraid of making decisions and was ever fearful of the insanity that had caused the suicide of his mother and younger brother. This fear kept him from marriage and a real enjoyment of life during his long, psychologically painful career. His first major success came in 1817 when Schreyvogel produced his play, *Die Ahnfrau,* at the Theater an der Wien. It was a *schicksaltragödie* or tragedy of fate and retribution in a tradition that had been popular in the German-speaking world very early in the century but was generally out of fashion by 1817. The play already showed signs of Grillparzer's devotion to Calderón and Lope de Vega, and this attraction to Spanish literature and playwriting, as for many other Austrian artists and intellectuals, lasted throughout his life. From the beginning his work reflected the typical Austrian and Spanish preoccupation with the tragic dilemma of action versus reflection that is the core of Calderón's *Life is a Dream*. His first important drama to deal with Austrian history, *König Ottokars Glück und Ende* (1823), was performed at the Burgtheater with Heinrich Anschütz in the title role. It was a truly romantic, historical pageant honoring the founding of the Hapsburg Empire in the person of Rudolph I. For other dramas he turned to classical and even oriental settings, and in 1838 he wrote his only historical comedy, *Weh' dem, der lügt,* which failed because it was too sophisticated for an audience accustomed to the popular comic theater. Deeply hurt by this rebuff, Grillparzer, after the death of Schreyvogel, withdrew from the theater and wrote only for his own amusement. His last three plays, all published after his death, though brilliant philosophical pieces, lacked that theatrical effectiveness which came from direct contact with the stage. *Ein Bruderzwist in Habsburg* is, however, a brilliant rounding out in a pessimistic vein of the entire problem of imperial power and is frequently presented today on German-speaking stages.

Meanwhile, the Burgtheater, under the successors of Schreyvogel, went through a period of retrenchment and decline until the appointment as manager in 1849 of the German playwright-producer Heinrich Laube (1806–84), who ushered in a new era of brilliant performances, particularly with revivals of the works of Grillparzer.

Laube was a minor playwright and a respected theatrical producer who was also a prolific novelist and had been a member of the young-Germany movement, a liberal movement in the arts and literature throughout the German-speaking world. He brought to his new position a profound knowledge of the European stage and insisted on good acting, careful rehearsals, and a close adherence to the acting text. He was also a friend of Richard Wagner and of Franz Grillparzer, whom he had described in a keenly sensitive article after meeting Grillparzer as the guest speaker at a famous literary club in Vienna. It was the friendship and trust that then developed between these two men that soon brought the early and mature plays of Grillparzer back to the Burg stage in brilliant productions supervised by Laube. It is to Laube that readers also owe some of the finest written insights into the work of this dramatist whose reputation was soon to equal that of Goethe and Schiller as one of the masters of dramatic art for the German-speaking stage.

The playwrights who reached maturity at the Burgtheater after Laube became director were mostly borrowers from the past. Frederick Halm (1806–71) provided the stage with well-made tragedies upon both classical and romantic themes, but his work is thin and super-

ficial compared to the dramas of Grillparzer. Eduard Bauernfeld
(1802–90) is a better playwright whose work is still occasionally
produced in Germany and Austria. He had known both Raimund
and Grillparzer, was a protégé of the latter, and in his mature work
was able to create a true bourgeois comic realism on the stage of the
Burgtheater. He catered to the Viennese love of acid comment and
social satire, disguising his liberalism and freethinking just enough
to escape the wrath of the authorities. A good example of his work is
Der Kategorische Imperativ (1851).

But when it came to the new realism that was spreading through
Europe in the later nineteenth century, only the work of Ludwig
Anzengruber (1839–89) left its mark on the Viennese stage before
Arthur Schnitzler's brilliant dissection of Austrian society at the end
of the century. Anzengruber's peasant themes and dramatic method
ran against the Viennese love of spectacle, sentiment, and super-
naturalism, even though Anzengruber had been born there and had
toured as an actor in many typically Viennese plays. Equally successful in tragedy and comedy, he strongly stressed and underlined social
problems in the lives of the Austrian peasants through his use of
dialect and accurately realistic settings. He was at his best in the
creation of a rich array of character types and in the invention of
richly comic scenes; but to those outside the tradition of the Austrian
drama, his scenes of peasant life often seem hedonistic and lacking
in a serious moral purpose. Though it does not have a rural setting,
a good example of his work is *Das vierte Gebot* (1877), which makes
a mockery of obeying the fourth commandment when parents sacrifice
their children to their own sinful and selfish interests.

In the same tradition, but entering the theater at a much later
date, is Karl Schönherr (1896–1943), who wrote powerfully realistic
dramas of Tyrolean peasant life at a time when Schnitzler and
Hofmannsthal were at the peak of their careers. His powerful drama
Erde (1907) deals with the universal theme of the peasant's desire
to live and die close to the soil.

Before beginning a discussion of the contributions made to world
drama by Hofmannsthal and Schnitzler, mention should be made of
the brilliant contribution of the opera and operetta in Vienna to the
development of theatrical art at the close of the nineteenth century.
The great new opera house on the Ringstrasse had opened in 1869
with a gala production of *Don Giovanni,* and the old Kärntnertor
was demolished. The greatest moment for the new theater came in
1873 with the nearly simultaneous openings of the Viennese International Exhibition and the busiest opera season in the history of

Vienna. At the same moment the golden age of Viennese operetta was ushered in with the brilliant premiere of *Die Fledermaus* at the Theater an der Wien in 1874. The Vienna Opera then became a bastion of Wagnerian production under the musical directorship of Hans Richter, and Wagner himself came personally to direct *Tannhäuser*, while *Lohengrin* was staged under his expert guidance. But the really brilliant decade of operatic production came between 1897 and 1907 when Gustav Mahler was appointed general director, Alfred Roller was designer, and a great performer, Leo Slezak, achieved an international reputation. In productions like *Tristan und Isolde*, and Strauss premieres like *Elektra* and *Salome*, Mahler brought Viennese operatic performances into a position of unquestioned leadership in theatrical production. This continued in the brilliant premieres of Richard Strauss's *Der Rosenkavalier* and *Ariadne auf Naxos*. Certainly the brilliant visual presentations of these premieres and revivals made the Vienna opera the most important international center of operatic activity during the last years of the nineteenth and the first decade of the twentieth century.

During this period the Viennese theater produced two playwrights who gained international reputations: Arthur Schnitzler (1862–1931) and Hugo von Hofmannsthal (1874–1929). Schnitzler, who combined theatrical flair with a sharply realistic insight into character, was a physician whose interest in psychology led him into a series of plays in which the characters were analyzed in a subtly impressionistic manner. From Ibsen he learned the dramatic technique of slowly unfolding past crimes, but he was not a fanatical searcher, exposing social evil to bring about social change. He realized that the values in Viennese society were collapsing, and he was content to expose and underline this fact without comment and with a touch of resignation. By combining cynicism, sensuality, and refinement, he produced highly sophisticated theater pieces that reflected a distinctly fin de siècle continental manner. But there is always a touch of the impressionistic mood that one associates with Chekhov in his plays as he watches the various characters drift through life in a kind of dream state—too low-toned and will-less to be real life. The difference from Chekhov lies in tone: where Chekhov is compassionate and deeply involved on a subconscious level with his characters, Schnitzler is more sophisticated, cynical, and urbane.

Many of Schnitzler's early works still carried the influence of the Ibsen thesis play and social realism. But in *The Affairs of Anatol* (1890), a collection of playlets detailing the amorous adventures of a young Viennese gallant, he had already established the tone and style that have ever since been attached to his name. *Liebelei* (1894) and *Reigen* (1896) were also rather episodic and connected by mood and idea rather than by a continuous plot, but both project a marvelous sense of the decadent and urbane mood of late-nineteenth-century Vienna. In his last major play, *Professor Bernhardi* (1912), Schnitzler made a chief contribution to the serious problem play by probing the problem of anti-Semitism from many points of view, yet he will be remembered for his superb recording of the sexual drives and fantasies that men within a decaying society use to give themselves the illusion of youth and power.

Hofmannsthal, who was a great friend and admirer of Schnitzler, became famous at the early age of seventeen for the poetic maturity of his work in the Symbolist-neo-Romantic tradition. His lyric poems and playlets from this early period indicate an aesthetic temperament weighted down by the beauty and richness of the past—another reflection on the high imperial Austrian culture of the last years of the nineteenth century. His play *Gestern* (1891) established the theme of the young man incapable of living in the present, and this conflict between the artist and the real world, that had been used so frequently by Grillparzer, is carried forward in several other early plays. Hofmannsthal underwent a spiritual crisis about 1900 during which he seemed to awaken fully to the decadence not only in Viennese but in all European society, and he resolved to speak out directly on issues, participate in life, and use the theater as a means for probing social and personal problems. He first wrote a series of plays presenting Greek myths in terms of modern psychology; *Elektra* (1903) was the most successful. He also wrote several plays in which he examined problems of love and constancy in both a light and a serious manner, the best known of which is probably *Der Abenteurer und die Sängerin* (1898). But it was his collaboration with Richard Strauss as a librettist that established his international reputation. *Elektra* (1909), *Der Rosenkavalier* (1911), *Ariadne auf Naxos* (1912 and 1916), *Die Frau ohne Schatten* (1919), *Die Ägyptische Helena* (1928), and *Arabella* (finished by Strauss in 1933 after the playwright's death) are six monumental operatic works that made the team of Strauss-Hofmannsthal known throughout the world. These librettos were in no way incidental to his other major written work and clearly indicated his gradual return to Catholic traditions and Christian morality as he attempted to find again the ancient imperative on which European civilization could be rebuilt.

After World War I he wrote a brilliant comedy, *Der Schwierige* (1918), probing the social and personal rearrangements made necessary in the high aristocracy after the fall of the monarchy, and he collaborated with Max Reinhardt in founding the Salzburg Festival. His final work, based on the Spanish playwright Calderón's *La Vida es Sueño,* was *Der Turm* (1925 and 1927), which was meant to be his final testament to his nation and to Europe. First written with a positive ending, he finally turned it into a tragedy of the indestructible human spirit isolated and powerless in a hostile world.

In the work of both Schnitzler and Hofmannsthal there is a combination of both psychological realism and symbolic impressionism. The late Austrian imperial culture that had produced these two important playwrights also gave birth at the same historic moment to that theatrical genius and entrepreneur who was to bring these artistic trends to the public through a series of some of the most successful and publicized productions in modern times. Max Reinhardt was born near Vienna in 1873 and was a young character actor in Salzburg when he was seen and hired by Otto Brahm, the famous director of the Deutsches Theater in Berlin. He soon became a master portrayer of elderly parts, but in 1903 gave up acting for directing. It was at this time that the so-called "New Stagecraft," along with new mechanical and lighting devices, was being introduced by innovators like Gorden Craig and Adolphe Appia. Reinhardt took these new methods and trends and transformed theatrical performance with a series of theatrical productions that stressed a symbolic or impressionistic unity of style based on the director's personal view of the script. By devices such as projecting the stage into the audience, using mass crowd movements, and redesigning the entire inside of a theater, he sought to sweep the spectators into the rhythmic progression of the play. He produced *Oedipus Rex* in the gigantic Zircus Schumann in 1910, a first version of *The Miracle* in London in 1911, *The Oresteia* also in 1911, Romain Rolland's *Danton* in 1920, the huge productions in America of *The Eternal Road* and *Midsummer Night's Dream* in the early 1930s and many other smaller experiments in theatrical style. Probably his best-known production next to *The Miracle* was *Jedermann,* adapted by Hofmannsthal from the medieval morality play and presented yearly at the Salzburg Festival, which Reinhardt founded with the playwright in 1920.

Reinhardt's important contributions to Austrian theater came after World War I when he worked in Vienna at the Theater in der Josefstadt, refurnished a ballroom—the Redoutensaal—in the Hofburg Palace for eighteenth-century theatrical productions, and founded the famous Salzburg Festival. Unfortunately, when Hitler came to power, Reinhardt had to leave for the United States, and he spent the rest of his life away from his native land.

Though Reinhardt was sometimes accused of vulgarizing the theater by the size and richness of his more famous productions, it is important to remember the intimate beauty and unity of his smaller productions at the Kleines Theater in Berlin and at the Josefstadt and Redoutensaal in Vienna. Reinhardt left a legacy of artistic unity and directorial power that has influenced all Western theater to the present day.

In playwriting, Schnitzler and Hofmannsthal were the last Austrian dramatists to achieve international recognition. Richard Beer-Hoffmann (1866–1945) carried on the neo-Romantic and erotic-sensational trends pioneered by Hofmannsthal and Schnitzler, while Hermann Bahr (1863–1934), who had a distinguished career in criticism and journalism and was for a time director of the Deutches Theater in Berlin, wrote many plays in a realistic vein, the best known of which is *Das Konzert* (1910). Sometimes described as a lesser Schnitzler, he is unmistakably Austrian in his mixture of flippant gaiety, warmheartedness, and witty insight. Only Franz Werfel (1890–1945) might be said to have gained a wider recognition after moving to the United States during Hitler's rise to power. Born in Prague when it was an important intellectual center within the Austrian Empire, Werfel first gained a reputation as a poet. He spent the war years on the Italian front, then settled in Vienna, married the widow of Gustav Mahler, and beginning in 1920 gained a major reputation as a dramatist. His trilogy *Der Spiegelmensch* (1920) was an interesting reworking of the Faust-Mephistopheles theme, while *Bocksgesang* (1921) symbolized, through a monster that was half-goat and half-man and who led peasants in a revolt during the eighteenth century, the violent brutality of man in rebellion. He also received the Grillparzer prize for his historical-psychological drama, *Juarez und Maximilian* (1924), that described the tragic French interference in Mexico in the 1860s. After settling in the United States, Werfel devoted most of his time to novels, but did one last popular tragicomedy, *Jacobowsky and the Colonel* (1944), which was a great success on Broadway at the end of the war. He collaborated with the great Reinhardt only once—when he wrote *The Eternal Road,* which was presented in New York and on a U.S. tour in 1936 as a lavish spectacle with music by Kurt Weill.

Though Vienna in the 1920s seemed still to have the talent and the creative genius for high artistic work in the theater and in other arts, the diversity, richness, and national pride of the old Austrian

Empire was gone, and the small republic with its oversized capital could not sustain its sense of identity. It was foreign rather than native influences that came to predominate, and gradually over the years Vienna ceased to be a major international center of theatrical art. Yet worthwhile plays by interesting playwrights certainly con-tinued to be produced. Max Mell (1882–1971) continued the ideals of the morality play that had been developed by Hofmannsthal in *Jedermann,* and in *Apostelspiel* (1923) and *Nachfolge Christi-Spiel* (1927) this Catholic playwright developed the theme of the regen-erating power of sin. Anton Wildgans (1881–1932), who spent two short periods as Director of the Burgtheater, combined with moderate success in plays like *Armut* (1915) and *Dies Irae* (1918), naturalism with German expressionism. Alexander Lernet-Holenia (1897–   ) returned to the tradition of the *Haupt-und Staatsaktion* in plays like *Demetrius* (1926) while also practicing the traditions of Viennese comedy in *Ollapotrida* (1926) and *Die Frau des Potiphar* (1934). Franz Werfel during his years in Vienna also influenced certain writers, particularly Franz Theodor Csokor (1891–1969), who is very highly regarded in Austria today. His work as a whole represents a certain nostalgia for the bygone glory of the Austrian Empire, and his most famous play is probably *3 November 1918* (1936), which depicts the last days of the Austro-Hungarian army before it disintegrated into its various ethnic-national components. Ferdinand Bruckner (1891–1958) is another leading Austrian dramatist who developed from expressionism to the more objective style of *die neue Sachlichkeit,* which formed the early plays of Brecht and the art of George Grosz. His most successful early work was *Die Verbrecher* (1928), a courtroom drama presenting a cross section of legal cases that all end in a miscarriage of justice. Bruckner's European reputa-tion was established by *Elisabeth von England* (1930), which is a sweeping historical drama that looks at Elizabeth I in psychological terms and pioneered the technical device of having simultaneous scenes in England and Spain with complimentary dialogue. His reputation was consolidated in the years after World War II with *Der Kampf mit dem Engel* (1957), and when he died the following year he was considered Austria's most respected dramatist.

But one of the most internationally famous of Austria's dramatists since World War II has been Fritz Hochwälder (1911–   ). His Viennese background is clearly visible in his view that the theater is a mirror for showing the human race its shattered image in the hope of achieving some repair. Hochwälder's chosen field has been histor-ical drama, and in plays like *Das Heilige Experiment* (1943), which deals with attempts to establish a utopian Jesuit community in Paraguay in the eighteenth century, and in *Der Offentliche Ankläger* (1947), which deals with political persecution during the French Revolution, the playwright infuses his philosophic and political themes with true Viennese theatricality. Though no innovator in theatrical technique, Hochwälder deeply understands human weakness, passion, and injustice as these struggle with nobler instincts. By placing these human conflicts against important historical moments, he is capable of producing some gripping theatrical plays.

Two other more recent avant-garde playwrights should also be mentioned. Peter Handke (1942–   ) is a puzzle-maker with words, a master of structural linguistics whose plays have been performed in Paris, London, and New York as well as in Austria. In short works *Audience* (1966), *Selbstbezichtigung* (1966), and in a full length drama, *Kaspar* (1968), Handke uses linguistic patterns to submerge his audience in a flow of words that reach them at an instinctive rather than a rational level. Wolfgang Bauer, born in 1941, writes more conventional theater pieces with a biting wit and sometimes in a broad Austrian provincial dialect. His *Magic Afternoon* (1968) is a sensational, rather superficial description of the emptiness of pop culture in the late 60s, while *Change* (1969) is a kind of party charade of avant-garde ideas dressed up as boulevard farce. In the latter, the man who manipulates the group into encouraging a man to commit suicide, himself commits suicide at the close of the play. Both plays have English titles in German.

Still another new playwright, who is probably better known for his novels and poetry, is Thomas Bernhardt (1931–   ), whose work has an intellectual, surrealistic quality and a melancholic preoccupation with human existence in bondage to suffering. On balance, however, his work shows a profound compassion rather than an annihilating pessimism. His best known drama is probably *Ein Fest für Boris* (1970).

Today Austrian theater is still a very vital and important part of Austrian culture. In a country with a population of only 7,000,000 there are about 36 theaters, 20 of these in Vienna, which is a city of about 1,600,000. The major state theaters, all fully subsidized, are the Vienna Opera, Volksoper, Burgtheater, and Akademietheater, but there is further subsidy for other Viennese and provincial theaters. The Burgtheater is still said to have some of the finest spoken performances found in the German-speaking theater, and there is an attempt to balance the classics with occasional important contemporary plays. From time to time, cycles of plays like the tragedies of Schiller or the histories of Shakespeare are performed, but always variety and range in the selection of the repertory is stressed. The Volksoper is entrusted with keeping alive the traditions of the Viennese operetta as well as certain operas done in a popular production style. The State Opera continues a tradition of presenting international stars and a high level of production in a wide repertoire, which makes it one of the most respected opera houses in the world.

The training of actors for the Austrian theater is carried on at the Max Reinhardt Seminar, which was inaugurated by the great Austrian director in 1929. Its home is in the Palais Cumberland near Schönbrunn, but performances are frequently given in the Schlosstheater at Schönbrunn. Training stresses both acting and directing, with great emphasis placed on speech, voice, movement, fencing, dancing, character analysis, and mime. Leading teachers are frequently actors usually graduates of the Seminar. Again, it is one of the most admired and respected of the acting conservatories in Europe.

The Austrian nation since the early Renaissance has considered the theater a central institution in its cultural development, and the theater that developed had a special Austrian character that was uniquely its own and not a mere reflection of German theatrical development. In its fusion of Italian, Germanic, Slavic, Spanish, and French theatrical ideals and in its own innate love of mood, music, and spectacle, the Austrian theater created forms that had great popular appeal and wide influence outside of Austria.

An Anthology
of Austrian Drama

Johann Nestroy (1802-62)

The Talisman

Austria's greatest comic dramatist represents the last phase of the Viennese popular dramatic tradition that began in the seventeenth century, grew to adolescence with Joseph Anton Stranitzky, and fully matured with Ferdinand Raimund. But Nestroy, though only eleven years younger than Raimund, already belongs to another age. While the sensitive, delicate, melancholy humor of Raimund is a mixture of Romanticism and the stable world of the Ancien Régime, which endured longer in Austria than in the rest of Europe, Nestroy represents the move of Romanticism toward liberalism and realism. His plays have none of the elegaic pathos of his predecessor, Raimund, and his method is one of satire, irony, and parody. He uses a more direct social commentary than would have been expected under the strictures of Austrian censorship. In every way Nestroy reflects a new, bourgeois, liberal spirit that erupted in Vienna as well as in other European capitals in the Revolution of 1848. Nothing is sacred to Nestroy, and his wit is far more acerbic than is the case with Raimund, who had heart and imagination but not the temperament to attack the current social scene. Many of Nestroy's darts at the social and political targets of his day required great courage, and he was frequently fined by the government and once landed in jail for three days. Usually he was able to veil his barbs to the extent that he was able to escape the heavy hand of Count Metternich's state censors.

Nestroy came to the stage of the popular theater as an actor and singer after beginning a career in law. He made his first performance debut as an opera singer appearing in the famous role of Sarastro in *The Magic Flute* at the Kärntnertor Theater in Vienna in 1882. For the next few years he appeared in engagements outside Vienna at Amsterdam, Brünn, Pressburg, Graz, and other cities, and gradually abandoned operatic for comic and dramatic roles. While he was away from Vienna, the famous Theater in der Josefstadt was taken over by Karl Andreas von Berbrunn (Karl Carl) in 1826, and when Nestroy teamed up with this enterprising

theater manager in 1831 his personal success as an actor-playwright
began. He was obviously a born comic actor with tremendous
improvisational ability and a dazzling knack for quick, incisive,
comic characterization. He also could write a script and revise at a
moment's notice, often writing in the morning what he was to
perform the same night. His method of borrowing from existing
literature and plays reminds one of Shakespeare and his contempor-
aries. Of Nestroy's fifty major plays, only two are said to be original;
all of the others have been shown to be adaptations of novels or
plays by other authors. Since plot or story line were not Nestroy's
major interest, he borrowed quite directly from his sources and made
a piece his own through characterization, business, and dialogue.

Nestroy, like all great comic writers, saw through the sham, fraud,
and pretense of the contemporary social scene. With his own brand
of cheerful pessimism he pictured man in all his confusion and
complexity, tossed about by a fate that was unconcerned with human
welfare. He has been described as a nihilist as frequently as a comic
philosopher, and it is impossible to fix his outlook other than to
say that he sees an imperfect world of imperfect people in which
improvement, if any, will come only through individual self-criticism
preferably wrapped in humor.

Nestroy began writing his early plays within the traditions of
the magic-play or *Zauberstücke* tradition that had been so successful
for Raimund, and his first great success and still one of his most-
produced works was *Der böse Geist Lumpazivagabundus oder das
liederliche Kleeblatt (The Evil Spirit, Lumpazivagabundus;* 1833).
It was this work that established Nestroy's fame as both a writer
and a performer, and he played it 259 times. By having the King
of the fairies and the patron saint of vagabonds wager as to whether
vagabonds will remain the same if they win a fortune, he is both using
the old magic framework and parodying it at the same time. They
proceed to test three vagabonds in the persons of cobbler, tailor, and
carpenter; the first two waste their fortunes on wine, women, and
song, but the latter becomes a thrifty family man. The roots of the
play are deeply Viennese, and it has some wonderful songs and a
series of great actor-parts with an especially fine role for Nestroy as
the patron saint of all down-and-outers.

He also did classic parodies of Wagner, Meyerbeer, and an
especially deft parody of Hebbel's *Judith* (1849). He also brilliantly
exposed the pompous seriousness that abounded in plays idolizing
certain historical figures. His first major move into the world of
middle-class social commentary came with *Zu ebener Erde und im*

Ersten Stock (*On the Ground Floor and in the First Story;* 1835), and it was this vein that he exploited during his most productive years as a playwright from 1840 to 1844. In *Der Zerrissene* (*A Man Full of Nothing;* 1844), he satirized and exposed the Romantic, sentimental pessimism that plagued so many poets in the early nineteenth century. Nestroy diagnosed this early form of alienation and the existential outlook as pure boredom, and he proceeded to develop one of his most charming comedies, filled with witty dialogue, memorable characters, and comic horseplay. In *Unverhoft* (*Bolt from the Blue;* 1845), Nestroy attacked the sentimental complacency of the middle class and used his role as the disillusioned but clearheaded outsider to expose their pretensions, conventions, and sloth.

The play whose basic plot is best known to Americans, since it is the basis of Thornton Wilder's *The Matchmaker* and the musical *Hello Dolly,* is *Einen Jux will er sich machen* (*He Goes Out on a Spree;* 1842). It is a very gay farce about an apprentice who goes to the big city on a spree. It also makes use of a delightful comic staging innovation used by Nestroy in several other plays, namely seeing into two or more rooms or areas at the same time to observe two or more actions going on at the same time.

Der Talisman (*The Talisman;* 1840), included in this volume, was an immediate success, but then was forgotten, only to become popular again on the German-speaking stage in recent years because of its timely comic statement about prejudice. The play deals with the problems of being redheaded in a community in which all redheaded people are despised. In the provincial Austria of Nestroy's day, redheaded people were suspected of being "of the devil," since red hair was not a common sight and such people seemed "different" from the majority of people in a village. The leading character of Titus was a great favorite of the Viennese audience, since it allowed Nestroy a chance to disguise himself with various wigs and to play a variety of attitudes and reactions in the course of the complications that make up the play. Certainly the play is a perennially timely one in its satiric exposé of the stupidities of prejudice, especially in matters of physical coloration.

With the success of his best political satire, *Freiheit im Krähwinkel* (*Freedom in Krähwinkel;* 1848), came the brief triumph of the liberals in the Revolution of 1848, and Nestroy joined in manning the barricades. For a brief time Nestroy was able to say what he really thought about censorship, and in several plays he tried to deal with the political ferment of the times. But by the time these plays reached the stage, the old order was being restored and his work was either mutilated or suppressed. Nestroy, in his usual spirit, satirized both sides and compared the people, who had made the Revolution, to a giant—awakening in a cradle, staggering about, and then collapsing in an even more uncomfortable position than before.

After the reestablishment of the status quo, Nestroy wrote less and spent more time on theatrical management, especially after becoming manager of the Carl Theater in 1854. He finally died at Graz in 1862, loved by his audience but maligned or ignored by contemporary critics. Only twelve of his plays were published during his lifetime, and since it was thought that only Nestroy could play Nestroy, the plays were seldom produced. He was in a sense rediscovered by the Viennese critic, Karl Kraus, who, on the fiftieth anniversary of the playwright's death in 1912, launched a campaign to demonstrate the true greatness of Nestroy's comic genius. True success came when the tradition-bound Burgtheater presented its first Nestroy production.

Nestroy productions in the United States have been limited to amateur productions in translation, though there have been a number of German-language productions, beginning with a recorded performance of *Lumpazivagabundus* in New York in the early 1840s. The Liebhabartheater in New York in the years before the Civil War did a number of other Nestroy plays, as did the Altes Stadttheater, but by the early twentieth century the name of Nestroy was just another name in the theater history books, until *Einen Jux will er sich machen* was adapted by Thornton Wilder as *The Merchant of Yonkers*. It was presented in Boston and New York in 1939 in an overelaborate production directed by Max Reinhardt that, according to the critics, missed the gaiety and lightness of the play. It was not a success until later rewritten as *The Matchmaker*. The play was presented in New York in German by the Burgtheater on its U.S. tour in 1968.

Today Nestroy is popular throughout the German-speaking world, but his dialogue, dialect patterns, and subject matter are so specifically Viennese that he is very difficult to translate. However, his sense of comic satire and his use of language are so penetrating that his comic insights definitely transcend what certain critics have seen as a theatrical talent limited by a narrow background in the Viennese popular theater.

The Talisman

A Farce with Songs, in Three Acts

by

JOHANN NESTROY

Translated and adapted by Max Knight *and* Joseph Fabry

Characters

TITUS, an unemployed barber's helper
SALOME, the village gooseherd
LADY CYPRESSA, a wealthy author
EMMA, her daughter
CONSTANTIA, her lady's maid
FLORA, her chief gardener
POPONSEED, Flora's helper
MONSIEUR MARQUIS
GEORGE, servant of Lady Cypressa
SPONGE, guest of Lady Cypressa
BUNG, beer salesman and uncle of Titus
NOTARY, GUESTS, SERVANTS, PEASANTS, PEASANT BOYS
AND GIRLS, A POLICEMAN

Time and place : Mid-nineteenth-century Austria

ACT 1

(A village square. In the background a well and two stone benches. Left, a garden wall with a gate leading to the garden of Lady Cypressa.)

The Talisman is reprinted from *Johann Nestroy: Three Comedies*, translated and adapted by Max Knight and Joseph Fabry (New York: Frederick Ungar Publishing Co., 1967). By permission of publisher and translator.

scene 1

(Several country boys and girls. Dance music offstage.)

FIRST BOY. *(To a girl.)* The band has started. Let's go.

SECOND BOY. *(To another girl.)* You and me—we've been waltzing together at these village fairs for ten years.

GIRL. *(To a boy.)* I wouldn't dance with anyone in the world but you.

(They all pair off except third boy, a very ugly boy.)

FIRST BOY. *(Looking into the wings.)* Look, there goes Salome!

GIRL. With her fire-red hair!

FIRST BOY. What does *she* want at the fair?

GIRL. To set your hearts afire, what else?

scene 2

SALOME. *(Red-haired, in poor clothes, from the left.)* I hear laughter, music . . . the dancing has started, hasn't it?

FIRST BOY. *(Coldly.)* Possibly.

SALOME. Mind if I come along?

SECOND BOY. I don't see how we can prevent you.

FIRST BOY. *(Pointing at her hair.)* What about that inflammable material?

SECOND BOY. The copper over there . . .

FIRST BOY. He doesn't trust you. You were seen driving your geese past the hayloft just before it burned down.

GIRL. He thinks you did it with your fire top.

SALOME. Why do you always pick on me? Just because I'm the only person in the village with red hair?

SECOND BOY. We've never had any red-thatched girls here, and we aim to keep it that way.

GIRL. If the good Lord had wanted red-haired people he'd have made some.

SALOME. He made *me*!

FIRST BOY. Well, I don't know about that. Hot colors are more in the department of the Devil.

SALOME. I can't help it if my hair is red.

SECOND BOY. Neither can we. See if you can find a little devil to dance with you.

THIRD BOY. I'll dance with her. What do I have to lose?

FIRST BOY. Oh, come on! You can do better than that!

THIRD BOY. I suppose you're right.

SECOND BOY. Let's go. Let's dance. We've wasted enough time!

(Off-stage music plays "Let's dance.")

ALL. Let's go and dance!

(All leave except Salome.)

scene 3

SALOME. So I'm left behind again, lonesome and blue. And why? Because my hair is red. But red is a wonderful color—the most beautiful flowers are roses, and everybody knows they are red—violets are blue. The most beautiful part of the day is the morning, and it dawns red. Even dark clouds are lovely when they're touched by the fiery red of a setting sun. Why is it that what people admire in a garden and in a sky they hate in a person's head? But what's the use? None of the fellows will take me to the dance. And if I go alone, the girls will cackle. I'd rather stay with my geese . . . they cackle at me, not about me.

(Exits right foreground.)

scene 4

FLORA. *(Angrily.)* Shame on the stagecoach. The city is within spitting distance, and yet the trip takes an hour and a half.

POPONSEED. *(Slow moving, carrying a large basket.)* Oh! So that's why it's called a coach. It needs to be coached to run.

FLORA. Shut up and come on! You're so slow you'd make a pretty good stagecoach yourself.

POPONSEED. Oh, no, not me. I don't want to be a stagecoach —everybody's riding me enough as it is.

FLORA. I see this is one of your witty days, when you're even more unbearable than usual.

POPONSEED. Nag! Nag! Nag! You're the most naggative woman I know. Well, I'm glad it'll soon be over for me.

FLORA. Are you going to quit on me?

POPONSEED. No such luck, lady. But pretty soon you'll catch yourself a husband again . . . and then you'll have a new victim to pick on.

FLORA. I'll never marry again! I'm going to remain faithful to my late husband.

POPONSEED. Perhaps he believes that now. He never did when he was alive.

FLORA. *(Coquettish.)* And what if I did marry again?

POPONSEED. I wish you would! I'd even dance at your wedding. I've never found anything distasteful in seeing someone else getting married.

FLORA. Men aren't perfect but they're the best opposite sex we've got.

POPONSEED.   Marriage is a gamble. Like custard pie—you never
know whether it'll end up in your stomach or in your face.

FLORA.   Blockhead! I don't know how I can stand you—slow and
clumsy and full of foolosophy. But I've already spoken to Lady
Cypressa about hiring an assistant. A strong, capable assistant
that's what I need. *(Exits through the garden gate, right.)*

POPONSEED. *(Alone.)*.   I know what's eating her. *(Winking at the
audience.)* It isn't the garden that needs the capable assistant!

(Exits right.)

SCENE 5

TITUS *(Entering from the right.)*

SONG

You wouldn't believe what some people believe:
A piglet brings luck, a black cat makes you grieve,
A bird makes you happy, a bat makes you shiver,

If you die on a Friday, that's bad for your liver.
Some people think witches still live in this nation
And that brooms are the means of their air transportation;
But they travel by coach, drawn by one horse or two,
And coffee with schlag has replaced witch's brew.
  Superstition, superstition!
  What convenient condition!
  If a good thing or a bum thing,
  People must believe in *some*thing.

I once told a man that black cats have me scared.
The man simply shrugged and ironically stared.
He drew himself up and he said, "Oh, come on,
You know that the era of reason's begun."
I asked for a job. He would hem and would haw,
He looked at my hair, didn't like what he saw.
But he did not believe in taboos, and he said
That among his best friends there are some who are red.
  Superstition, superstition!
  What convenient condition!
  If a good thing or a bum thing,
  People must believe in *some*thing.

ENCORE

Reliance on science is always in season,
And yet we believe many things without reason.
We know we'll succeed with the opposite sex
If we just spray ourselves with deodorant X.
We think banknotes are sound if there's gold in the mint,
That something is true if we see it in print,
That no one bakes coffee cake just like our Mom,
And that problems are solved at the drop of a bomb.
 Superstition, superstition!
 What convenient condition!
 If a good thing or bum thing,
 People must believe in *some*thing.

They say that a man's chances are dealt like a card from the deck of destiny—if I could find the card sharp who dealt mine I'd club him one on the head with a spade until he cashed in his chips. On the head . . . that's my trouble. The head. My heart's as true as a diamond but to be a redhead in a world that's prejudiced against red hair is to have the deck stacked against you. Prejudice is a wall against which we can beat our heads until they're bloody, and accomplish nothing but making them redder than they are. I have red hair—so people think I'm sly and deceitful. I've red hair—so people think I'm a firebug. I've red hair—so people think. . . . Oh, prejudice! Every time I have work and make ends meet, some little bigot moves the ends. What I need is a bit of luck, but luck is too busy with the rich to bother about the poor. Luck and brains seldom go together. Fate, oh fate, deal me a joker to show me my luck has changed!

SCENE 6

POPONSEED. I'll have a beer before I water the garden—nothing like a beer to help you with the peas. *(Seeing Titus.)* Ha, what do we have here? A foreigner—and a red one, too?

TITUS. Fate, I believe you've dealt me my joker!

POPONSEED. *(To himself.)* Could this be Flora's new gardener? Strong, capable . . . yes. But the hair . . . ugh! He looks capable of anything. *(To Titus.)* Are you looking for work?

TITUS. I'd go even that far to bet a little money.

POPONSEED. *(Half to himself.)* His hair! He's a robber!

TITUS. Not yet. My talent in that field is still undeveloped.

POPONSEED. Do you know anything about gardening?

TITUS.   My qualifications lie in many directions.

POPONSEED.   You must be the capable assistant the gardener's widow is looking for.

TITUS.   Assistant to a gardener's widow? A fertile field—as I said, my qualifications lie in many directions.

POPONSEED.   Not a chance! This is a gardener's widow who doesn't like carrot tops!

(Exits, nose-in-air, through the gate.)

SCENE 7

TITUS.   *(Looking after Poponseed, furious.)* I'm profoundly confounded and confoundedly dumbfounded. This bird is so cocksure in his rudeness, he must have practiced all his life. I was a fool to expect this place to be different—it's peopled with people, and there's the rub! Studious research has shown me that you must hate people before you get to know them, and despise them afterward. Expect the worst of people, even of yourself, and you rarely guess wrong. Every human being spends most of his time being inhuman. I hate you, inhuman humanity. I'd become a hermit if I could live on roots and berries. But I'm too hungry. No, unkind mankind, you shall not lose me; appetite is the tender bond that links me with you, and reminds me three times a day that in spite of the color of my hair, I'm part of the human family. Too often I've known that bitter feeling of so much hunger that out of sheer thirst I didn't know where to sleep the next night. *(Looking to the right.)* Good gracious, there's a reddish goldilocks guiding a gaggle of geese through the gate. I have to take a gander.

SCENE 8

(Salome enters from the right, a loaf of bread and a knife in her basket.)

SALOME.   A strange young man . . . with beautiful hair!

TITUS.   *(To himself.)* I wonder if little radish-head will call me a carrot top, too. Maybe she has something eatable in that basket. *(Aloud.)* God be with you, kindred spirit!

SALOME.   I'm your servant, Sir.

TITUS. *(Half to himself.)* She's polite to me. That's the first person who ever . . .

SALOME.   Oh, Sir, I'm the least in the town. I'm the goosegirl. I'm poor. My name is Salome.

TITUS.   Poor? I'm sorry to hear it. I'm sure you rear your young geese in the most conscientious way. Your colleagues in the big city bring up their young-lady geese, year after year, without any noble end in view. You prepare yours for the benefit of all mankind—for the banquet table.

SALOME.   I can't understand you—I mean, you talk so . . . fine. You must come from a fine family. Who's your father?

TITUS.   At present he is a deceased teacher.

SALOME.   How nice. And your mother?

TITUS.   Before her untimely demise she was for a period of time the wedded wife of her nuptial spouse.

SALOME.   Ah, that's nice!

TITUS.   (To himself.)   She finds everything nice—no matter what I say.

SALOME.   And what's your name?

TITUS.   Titus.

SALOME.   That's an unusual and beautiful name. And you have no other relatives?

TITUS.   Oh, yes. My family tree shows distinct traces of an uncle. But he won't do a thing for me.

SALOME.   Maybe he hasn't got a thing.

TITUS.   He's a beer salesman, and beer is a commodity for which there is an unquenchable demand. He's foaming with money.

SALOME.   Then you must have done something he didn't like.

TITUS.   I have indeed. I've hit his most sensitive spot, his eye. Whenever he looks at me he sees red, and he doesn't like it.

SALOME.   What? His own flesh and blood?

TITUS.   The color of his blood doesn't prevent him from discriminating against my hair. And from the color of my hair he's jumped to conclusions about my character. Uncle Bung holds the world's record in conclusion jumping, and has excluded me from heart, hearth, and heritage.

SALOME.   That's not nice.

TITUS.   It's stupid. Nature gives us a gentle hint. What animal dislikes red? The bull—the more bull a man has in him the more violently he reacts to red.

SALOME.   How clever you talk. One wouldn't know just looking at you.

TITUS.   I'm not used to admiration. Uncle Bung's slap in the face was only one of many. I got it from all sides. I tried love, hoping

love was color blind—but it wasn't. Friendship? A redhead has
no friends, only people who'll tolerate him. Work? I was suspected
of everything from theft to arson. So I've thrown off love like a
topcoat, friendship like a jacket, ambition like a shirt, and here
I stand, an ideological stripteaser, in the underpants of freedom.

SALOME.   And you like that?

TITUS.   I would, if I had an umbrella to protect me against the
storms of life. It's true that the rain is falling on the rich and the
poor alike, but the rich have all the umbrellas. A poor man must
eat, too. When he smells food, all other passions disappear. He
has no anger, no emotions, no sadness, no love, no hate, not even
a soul. He has nothing but an appetite.

SALOME.   I'll tell you what. My brother works in a bakery. I'll ask
the baker. Maybe he needs another helper.

TITUS.   My only chance to roll in dough. Did your brother bake this
bread? *(Points at the bread in Salome's basket.)* Let's see how
far your brother has advanced in the science of bread-making.

SALOME.   Have a taste. But it's not the good kind. *(Cuts off a small
piece.)*

TITUS. *(Eating.)*   Hm—let me see . . .

SALOME.   My geese like it but they have no sense . . .

TITUS.   The true scientist must form his own conclusions . . .

SALOME.   Well, what do you say? It's not very good, is it?

TITUS.   Hum. To judge your brother's work I must do more research.
I need a larger sample. *(Takes the loaf and cuts off a large slice.)*
I shall give you a full report in due time. *(Puts the slice in his
pocket.)*

SALOME.   I'll go right away and see if there's a job for you at the
baker's.

TITUS.   I'm counting on your brother's nepotism.

SALOME.   I'll try. *(Looking left, frightened.)* Oh—look!

TITUS. *(Looking.)* Heavens—the carriage! The horse has gone
wild—it's running straight to the river. *(Runs off into the left
wing.)*

SCENE 9

SALOME.   Oh no! Be careful! Don't run right into the horse! My
. . . he grabs it! *(Screaming.)* Ah! The horse stands still . . . he
stopped it! What a daredevil! A man gets out of the carriage . . .
pale as a ghost . . . he can hardly stand up straight! Heavens, I
must tell the baker about this! When he hears what Titus did,
he'll give him a job for sure!

(Exits right.)

scene 10

(Titus reenters from the left, with Monsieur Marquis.)

MARQUIS. Ah! The fright's still in my bones!

TITUS. Will it please Your Honor to sit down and rest?

MARQUIS. *(Sitting down on a stone bench.)* Damned nag! It has never run away like this!

TITUS. Does it please Your Honor to feel a charley horse?

MARQUIS. No, my friend, I'm all right.

TITUS. Or perhaps a broken arm?

MARQUIS. Thank God, I'm still in one piece.

TITUS. Or a small crack in your skull?

MARQUIS. Nothing at all. I'm fine again, and all there remains to be done is to give you, as a token of my gratitude . . .

TITUS. Don't mention it.

MARQUIS. Three boys stood there, they all knew me. But all they did was shout, "Monsieur Marquis! Your carriage! It'll plunge into the water . . ."

TITUS. What? I saved a Marquis?

MARQUIS. *(Continuing.)* But they didn't lift a finger. Then you came . . . a swift savior . . .

TITUS. *(With false modesty.)* Only doing my duty . . .

MARQUIS. Just at the crucial moment . . .

TITUS. Lucky coincidence.

MARQUIS. *(Standing up.)* Your modesty embarrasses me. I don't know how I can thank you—money can never repay what you've done . . .

TITUS. Oh, money has a way of . . .

MARQUIS. Offending a man of your sensitivity.

TITUS. Well—you see . . .

MARQUIS. I see your character clearly. It would cheapen your noble deed if one would try to measure it with money.

TITUS. It all depends . . .

MARQUIS. It depends on *who* performed the deed. It reminds me of the story of . . . his name escapes me . . . who saved the life of Prince what's his name. Anyway, the Prince wanted to reward our hero with diamonds, but our hero simply said: "I find my highest reward in my conscience!" I'm sure you feel no less noble than the man whose name I forget.

TITUS. Yet, there are circumstances where a thank offering . . .

MARQUIS. Can be spoiled by many words. You're quite right. True gratitude is silent. Let's not talk about the incident.

TITUS. *(To himself.)* The Marquis has so much tact—if he were a cheapskate, the result would be the same.

MARQUIS. *(Looking at Titus's hair.)* But, friend, I've just noticed something—hum, hum! This head of yours—it must be an embarrassment to you!

TITUS. It is indeed. But it's the only head I have, I can't buy myself another one.

MARQUIS. Well, perhaps . . . let me . . . a small souvenir you must accept. I insist! Just wait here a moment!

(Exits left.)

SCENE 11

TITUS. One more minute, and he'd have called me, out of gratitude, a red beet. A fine Marquis I picked to save! *(Looking to the left.)* Look at him run to his carriage! Well, he does rummage around—maybe he'll give me a present after all. A souvenir, he said. Now he's picked up something—for heaven's sake, a hat box! Is he going to give me an old hat for saving his young life?

SCENE 12

MARQUIS. *(With a hat box.)* Here, friend, take this, and make good use of it. It will be a talisman for you *(Gives him the box.)* and I would be pleased if I'd be the architect of your good fortune. Goodbye, friend, and God bless you!

(Exits left.)

SCENE 13

TITUS. *(Alone, box in hand.)* Architect of my fortune? Talisman? Now I'm really curious about what's in here. *(Opens the box and pulls out a black wig.)* A wig! Nothing but a pitch-coal-black wig! *(Calling after Marquis.)* I'll teach you to make fun of me, you pompous penny-pincher! But—wait a minute: didn't I always want a wig to hide my red top? Hasn't it been just those lousy fifty thalers that stood between me and being one of them? Talisman, he said—he's right! I'll put on this wig, and I'll be accepted for what I really am, and not for what shows on top of my head. What do I have to lose? I'll try it! The world will open up for me, just like this gate! *(Opens the gate.)*

SCENE 14

SALOME. *(From the right.)*   Oh, Mr. Titus, I've bad news!

TITUS. *(Turning to Salome.)*   What is it?

SALOME.   The baker won't take you. When he heard about . . .
(Points to his head.)

TITUS.   Oh, it doesn't matter—I'm going to the mansion to find
work.

SALOME.   The mansion? Oh, don't even try. If Lady Cypressa sees
you she'll chase you out. *(Referring to her hair.)* I must never
be seen in the mansion.

TITUS.   The prejudices of the Lady are of no concern to me. From
now on, the most important thing is what I have in here *(Pointing at his temple.)* and not out there! *(Points at his hair.)*

SALOME.   Well, I wish you luck. I know I shouldn't feel that way
but it still hurts that another hope has dropped down the well.

TITUS.   What hope?

SALOME.   That you might stay. People would have said, "These two
are the homeliest couple in the village. The red Titus, and the
red Salome." No other girl would have looked at you, just as
no other boy looks at me.

TITUS.   We would have had a mutual monopoly on each other's
homeliness!

SALOME.   We might have become friends.

TITUS.   And from friendship to love is only one happy step.

SALOME.   I haven't dared to think that far.

TITUS.   Why not? Thoughts are free.

SALOME.   I don't know—for some you pay with sleepless nights.

TITUS.   You have to take your chances. Man proposes . . . *(To himself.)* the wig disposes, in my case. *(Aloud.)* Well, adieu, Salome.

SALOME.   Don't be so proud, Mr. Titus. Take my hand, like a
friend, and say, "See you later, Salome."

TITUS.   You are right. *(Takes her hand.)* We part as friends. See
you later.

SALOME.   Yes, and I *will* see you later.

TITUS.   You might.

SALOME.   Oh yes. You go through that gate, and through the same
gate they'll throw you out. *(Points at the bench.)* And I'll sit
here . . .

TITUS.   And wait until someone will boot me into your arms. Well,
I am accepting my fate, whatever it is.

SALOME. Are you going in there to work and get rich?

TITUS. Let's not confuse the issue. Hard and honest work is good
enough to make a living. To get rich you must use a different
approach.

(Exits through the gate.)

SCENE 15

SALOME. *(Alone.)* There he goes—and I'm left high and dry. And
yet I feel so low and my eyes are wet. I never had much luck,
and now it feels as if he'd taken even the little I had with him.
All a girl can do is sit and wait. A man can at least go out and
kick. Yes, it's a man's world.

SONG

When a girl is in love with a man who is not—
Well, what can she do? Not a heck of a lot.
She can cry, she can moan, she can hang herself, drown . . .
But look what goes on if a man is turned down:
He goes to the tavern and orders a beer,
And flirts with the waitress and whoever is near,
And he may not slow down till the field he has played—
 Yes, a man has it made, has it made, has it made!

When a girl has her first or her second affair,
Her reputation is ruined beyond all repair.
But a man with a harem of ten or a score
Will still attract girls, and the merrier the more.
In fact, they would probably fall for him good,
And if not from love, then from envy they would.
His reputation gets better with each escapade—
 Yes, a man has it made, has it made, has it made!

A woman is always a slave to her fashion,
She has to fake nature to rouse a man's passion.
With girdles and cheaters she must prove her sex:
Where she is concave she must look like convex.
And her hair—she must curl it, and braid it, and tint it,
And if she's in love, she may only just hint it.
But a man needs no girdle, no curl, and no braid—
 Yes, a man has it made, has it made, has it made!

ENCORE

The twentieth century brought on a sequel:
The woman has gained her position as equal.
Women vote, run for office, and dress up in trousers,
Become independent, divorce their dear spousers,
Or go to a school where they pick up some knowledge.
But they then take a job, put their husbands through college,
Run to work, run the house, overworked, underpaid—
Yes, men *still* have it made, have it made, have it made!

SCENE 16

*(A room in the apartment of Flora, the chief gardener.
Door in the middle and right, window left.)*

FLORA. Trouble and headaches! The pickles I get into grow like
weeds—I can't get rid of them all by myself. My dear husband,
God bless his soul, told me to stay a widow and carry on as a
chief gardener—how can a blessed soul have such a wretched
idea? The helpers have no respect, they pay no attention, they
need a man. And why fool myself—I need a man, too. Will my
husband forgive me? Sometimes I can't believe that the dead
watch us from the Beyond. How can they be in a state of bliss
if they see what's going on down here? I can see my dear
departed shake his head in the clouds. What if he decides to
appear one night—as a ghost? What if he comes down and
knocks at my door? *(There is a knock at the door. She screams.)*
Aaah! *(Supports herself on the table.)*

SCENE 17

TITUS. *(In black wig; enters at center stage.)* Sorry, lady, but do
you always scream "Aaah!" instead of saying "Come in"?
FLORA. *(Collecting herself.)* I got scared.
TITUS. *(To himself.)* Strange—she's afraid when someone knocks.
Most women of her age are afraid that no one will knock.
FLORA. You're probably surprised that my nerves are so weak!
TITUS. Surprised about the normal? Nerves made of spider webs,
hearts of wax, and heads of steel—that's the structure of the
female anatomy.
FLORA. *(To herself.)* The man has charm . . . and the romantic
dark hair . . . *(Aloud.)* What can I do for you?
TITUS. You can do a great deal for me. I'm for hire.

FLORA. Are you a gardener?

TITUS. Of sorts. I've sown prejudice, I've planted suspicion—and you should have seen how they took root and grew!

FLORA. Very clever, but . . .

TITUS. Now I'm ready to experiment with a new crop—love. The heart is said to be a fertile ground, if you cultivate it right . . .

FLORA. I must say you have a fresh approach to job hunting. *(Looks at him admiringly.)* What's your background in gardening?

TITUS. I'm an exotic plant, not native to these regions, uprooted by circumstances beyond my control, and now transplanted by fate into the flowerpot of your care, hoping to find nourishment from the sunlight of your protection.

FLORA. Your talk is flowery enough, but what do you know about plants?

TTUS. I know something about people, and that makes me an expert on plants.

FLORA. I don't see how that follows.

TITUS. Oh, but it does! Most people are like plants—they vegetate. A person who gets up day after day at the same time, clings to his office desk until he retires climbing up in slow promotion —he's an ivy, he vegetates; a person who meekly opens his store every morning, politely sells his wares to all comers, has no other recreation than his Friday night card game—he's a mashed potato, he vegetates; a person who comes joylessly home from his work bristling at his wife, has nothing but barbed answers to questions from his children, offends everyone with stinging remarks—he's a cactus, he vegetates; and a person who is so thin-skinned that he makes everyone cry who comes near him —he's an onion, he vegetates. Even the highest form of human life, the millionaire, is really only lettuce turned into man.

FLORA. You must have studied the higher fields of horticulture. Your head seems as bright inside as it is black outside.

TITUS. Don't you like my hair?

FLORA. *(Coquettish.)* You know very well how handsome dark locks look on a man!

TITUS. It's news to *me*!

FLORA. You really want a job here? All right, you're hired. But not as a helper. You have brains, manners, looks . . . *(Titus bows.)*

FLORA. You'll work directly under me. I'll make you gardener to supervise the helpers.

TITUS. I don't know how to thank you.

FLORA. We'll find a way. *(Looking at his hair.)* I've never seen such coal-black raven hair? Are you Italian?

TITUS. My mother was a gardener from Sicily. She was no wall-flower—a real bachelor's button.

FLORA. You silly man. And how vain you are! I believe you curl your hair. *(Wants to touch his hair.)*

TITUS. *(Drawing back.)* Don't touch. My head is a very ticklish problem.

FLORA. *(Dreamily.)* My husband was very ticklish, too. *(Back to reality.)* But what really is ticklish is how to present you to Lady Cypressa. You can't show yourself in this outfit!

TITUS. I don't see why a gardener shouldn't be wearing a seedy suit . . .

FLORA. Go into the next room. In the big chest you'll find the suits and shoes of my beloved husband. Try them on—I think they'll be your size.

TITUS. The suits of your beloved . . . ? And I'll be in his shoes? *(Touches his locks coquettishly.)* How can I help it if certain feelings begin to sprout . . . *(Looks at her significantly and exits right.)*

SCENE 18

FLORA. A charming man! Well, you never know—I might catch myself a second hubsand before Madam Constantia catches hers! She acts so high and mighty because she's the Lady's maid and has a lover. A lover, yes, but I bet that barber of hers hasn't said a word about marriage! I have a feeling that I'll be able to get my handsome blacktop to chase me where I want him. Right up the aisle. *(Sighing.)* To catch a husband is the perfect end of a marry chase. But now I'll have to tell the rest of my crew. *(Calls through the window.)* Poponseed, come here!

(Poponseed comes in slowly.)

FLORA. Call all the helpers together and tell them I've hired a gardener. Now he'll do the bossing, not I.

POPONSEED. Aye, aye. *Anything* will be an improvement. *(Exits.)*

FLORA. Don't be fresh! *(Looking through the window.)* Oh-oh! The Lady's maid? Coming here? That means trouble.

SCENE 19

CONSTANTIA. (Enters center stage.) Flora . . .

FLORA. *(With a curtsy.)* At your service.

CONSTANTIA. My Lady is not satisfied with the care of the garden.

FLORA. It's not my fault. The help . . . but it will be different from now on. I've hired a most promising gardener.

CONSTANTIA. Good. I'll inform the Lady.

FLORA. I'd like to take the liberty of presenting him myself.

CONSTANTIA. Are you out of your mind? Present a country clod to the Lady?

FLORA. Oh, I beg your pardon. He's not an ordinary gardener, he's a most unusual . . .

SCENE 20

(Titus enters in an old-fashioned gardener's suit, from the right, holding a bundle. He speaks to Flora without noticing Constantia.)

TITUS. Well, here I am. Does this suit bring back sweet memories?

CONSTANTIA. *(To herself.)* What a magnificent mop of hair!

TITUS. I've bundled up my own things.

FLORA. Just put them there! *(Points at a chair, left.)*

TITUS. All right. *(Turns as he sees Constantia.)* Ah! You couldn't draw a drop of blood even if you'd stick a pin in me! *(Bowing before Constantia.)* I beg of you . . . *(To Flora.)* Why didn't you tell me . . . ? *(To Constantia, with a deep bow.)* . . . not to be angry with me if I . . . *(To Flora.)* . . . that Her Ladyship is present . . . *(To Constantia, with a deep bow.)* . . . didn't pay my respects right away . . . *(To Flora.)* . . . It really is awful—in what a situation you put me!

CONSTANTIA. I'm not Her Ladyship.

FLORA. What gave you that idea?

TITUS. Your Ladyship just wants to spare my feelings . . .

FLORA. This is Constantia, the Lady's maid.

TITUS. No, I don't believe it! The noble forehead, the imperial glimmer of the eyes, the aristocratic curve of the elbow!

CONSTANTIA. *(Flattered.)* I assure you I'm only the Lady's maid.

TITUS. Really? I only believe it because I hear it from your own lips. A Lady's maid? My mother was a Lady's maid, too.

FLORA. But you said your mother was a gardener.

TITUS. She started out as a gardener, yes, but then she advanced to the position of Lady's maid.

CONSTANTIA. *(To Flora.)*   Really, an interesting, well-bred man!

FLORA.   *(To Titus, who keeps looking at Constantia.)* Just put your things there.

TITUS. *(Looking at Constantia.)*   What a waste to make a Lady's maid out of genuine Lady material!

FLORA.   Don't you hear? Put your bundle on that chair!

TITUS.   Yes, right away. *(Walks to the chair next to the door, still looking admiringly at Constantia.)*

FLORA. *(Mumbling.)*   How she throws herself at him, that slut!

SCENE 21

POPONSEED. *(Entering, center stage.)* The gardeners will be here right away.

TITUS. *(Seeing Poponseed, turns about; to himself.)* Damn it! If he recognizes me . . . *(Turns toward Constantia, with back to Poponseed.)*

POPONSEED. *(To Flora.)*   So that's the new gardener? I'd like to introduce myself. *(Steps between Titus and Constantia.)*

TITUS. *(Turns to Flora, to have his back to Poponseed again.)* Send him away. I'm no friend of ceremonies.

FLORA.   Oh, don't put on an act.

POPONSEED. *(Trying to face Titus.)*   Mr. Gardener, meet the hardest working man in your crew . . .

TITUS. *(Embarrassed.)*   That sudden draft . . . I have to . . . *(He reaches into his pocket for a handkerchief but pulls out a gray wig with a tail which he quickly holds before his face.)*

POPONSEED.   That's a funny handkerchief you have!

TITUS.   What's that?

FLORA. *(Laughing.)*   That's the wig of my former husband.

TITUS.   How former can a wig get? This one still has a tail! *(Stuffs the wig into the bundle he holds.)*

POPONSEED.   What the devil! The gardener's face looks familiar. *(To Titus.)* Don't you have a brother with red hair?

CONSTANTIA.   How dare you!

TITUS.   I have no brother at all.

POPONSEED.   Well, I guess it must have been the brother of someone else.

FLORA.   What do you mean, dumbbell?

POPONSEED.   Oh, nothing. I just saw someone with red hair. No harm done.

SCENE 22

*(Two garden helpers enter through the center stage,
carrying baskets with fruit.)*

HELPER. Here's the fruit for the Lady.

FLORA. Take it up to the mansion.

CONSTANTIA. That's not the way, to have the servants take up
the fruit.

FLORA. That's the way we've always done it.

CONSTANTIA. The new gardener will present the fruit, and that's
also a suitable occasion to present *him.*

FLORA. Present him? How so? You just told me we can't present
a country clod to the Lady.

CONSTANTIA. *(Embarrassed.)* Yes, but—that is . . .

TITUS. Country clod?

FLORA. *(Enjoying Constantia's embarrassment.)* That's what she
said!

TITUS. Country clod!

CONSTANTIA. *(Very embarrassed.)* I have . . .

TITUS. That's terrible!

FLORA. You're so right! It's . . .

TITUS. . . . a mystery to me *(To Flora.)* how you can think the
words "country clod" refer to me.

FLORA. These were Madame Constantia's words.

TITUS. *To Flora.)* Let me tell you, there are plenty of country clods
around. I'm not such an egoist that I would claim the words only
for myself.

CONSTANTIA. *(Recovering.)* I just meant . . .

TITUS. *(Pointing at Constantia.)* If Madame really brought such
words over her beautiful lips, she must have meant one of the
helpers. *(Pointing at the servants.)* She hadn't met me yet, so
how could she appraise my cloddishness? *(To Constantia.)* Am
I not right?

CONSTANTIA. Absolutely.

FLORA. *(Very angry.)* You want to call me a liar?

TITUS. No. Merely a slanderer.

CONSTANTIA. *(To Titus.)* You come with me now.

FLORA. What's the rush? The Lady isn't home yet.

CONSTANTIA. That's why. I—uh—mean it's more appropriate for
the gardener to wait for her, than for her to wait for him.

TITUS. That's obvious. *(To Constantia, referring to Flora.)* She
knows nothing of etiquette. The most proper place to wait for

Her Ladyship is with the Lady's maid.

FLORA. *(To herself.)*   I could tear her to pieces, the bitch!

TITUS.   And it's also proper that I present myself, as a garden supervisor, in a manner that—ah, here we are! *(Goes to the window and pulls flowers from the flowerpots.)*

FLORA.   My flowers!

TITUS.   Just the thing for a bouquet. Now for a ribbon . . . *(Takes a wide satin ribbon from the table and wraps it around the flowers.)*

FLORA.   Heavens! The new satin ribbon I bought for my evening gown!

TITUS.   For such an occasion the best is barely good enough. *(To Constantia, pointing at Flora.)* She knows nothing of etiquette.

SCENE 23

(Several helpers enter at center stage.)

HELPERS.   We came to welcome the new gardener!

TITUS.   Greetings, my good fellows. You're just in time. Come on, carry the baskets.

HELPERS.   Yes, Sir.

CONSTANTIA. *(To Titus.)*   This is the occasion to establish your place and earn the loyalty of your crew. The best way to do it is to circulate a little money. At least that's what I've found . . .

TITUS.   I've found that, too, Madame, but *(fingering his vest pocket.)* . . . what I don't find . . .

CONSTANTIA.   Oh, it will be my pleasure . . . *(Wants to give him a purse.)*

FLORA.   Excuse me, that's my business. Here. *(Wants to give him a purse.)*

CONSTANTIA. *(Preventing it.)*   No, this won't do. It's a matter of honor for the house, and the Lady will want me to handle it.

FLORA.   I'll put it on the Lady's bill. It's up to me as chief gardener . . .

TITUS. Excuse me, ladies, but this matter can easily be disposed of without any hurt feelings. I'll take the liberty . . . *(Takes the purse from Constantia.)* Just hand it over . . . *(Takes the money from Flora.)* There! Avoid all friction, that's my motto. *(To the helpers.)* I'll treat you all!

HELPERS.   Hooray!

TITUS.   And now, on to the mansion!

(Exits with Constantia, followed by the helpers carrying the baskets. Flora glares after them, and Poponseed watches her with amusement. The helpers cheer.)

(Curtain.)

ACT 2

(Lady Cypressa's garden. In the right foreground the gardener's cottage of Flora, with entrance. Table and garden chairs. In the background a wing of the mansion.)

SCENE 1

(Poponseed and several helpers are sitting around the table, drinking.)

HELPERS.   Come on! Another round of wine!

POPONSEED.   That's right. We still have half the money left, it must be spent on drinks! We can't quit now.

HELPER.   "Don't quit now"—that's what Flora always says.

POPONSEED.   Just remember, a gardener is a plant that's always thirsty. It must be wetted!

HELPER.   But not with water!

(All laugh and drink.)

HELPERS.   Hooray for the new supervisor! A generous man! Hooray for the new gardener!

POPONSEED.   Horsemanure! He's a lazy lout, I know the type. He'll put his hands in his pockets, his feet on the table, and will make us work, work, work!

HELPERS.   Well in that case we'll . . .

POPONSEED.   Not now. Let's not spoil our party. Later, when we're back at work we can take time out to fret about him. Everything at the proper time!

SCENE 2

FLORA. *(With a basket, from the house.)*   Now be off with your glasses. I need the table.

HELPERS.   We were about to quit anyway.

POPONSEED.   It's a party in honor of your gardener.

FLORA. *(To helpers.)*   Go back to work!
HELPERS. *(Leaving.)*   All right, we're going.

(Helpers leave.)

SCENE 3

POPONSEED.   I don't see how you can have the heart to break up a garden party.

FLORA. *(Has taken a tablecloth from the basket and spreads it over the table.)*   Shut up and help me set the table for dinner.

POPONSEED.   Aye, aye, you don't have to order me twice to do *that* job. *(Takes plates and silver from the basket.)* Only for two?

FLORA.   A dinner for two.

POPONSEED.   Does the new gardener take his meal in the mansion, with the Lady's maid?

FLORA.   Dummkopf. He'll eat here with me.

POPONSEED.   Now, let's see—he, you, and me—that makes three.

FLORA.   I've let you eat here in the past because I didn't want to sit all by myself. Now I have the gardener to keep me company. You will disappear when the meal is served.

POPONSEED.   Now? It'll get cold. God knows when he'll show up.

FLORA. *(Looking impatiently toward the mansion.)*   He'll be here any moment. I don't understand what's keeping him.

POPONSEED.   I'm beginning to understand.

FLORA.   Hush, and do as you're told.

POPONSEED.   The capable assistant must be busy in the mansion, taking care of tu-lips—that's what's keeping him.

(Exits into the gardener's cottage.)

SCENE 4

FLORA. *(Alone.)*   That's the last time I'll let him go up there! The way Constantia digs her hooks into him, it's disgusting!

TITUS. *(From the mansion, napkin tied around his neck, a chicken leg in his hand.)*   Ah, you there, good to see you . . .

FLORA.   Upon my word, what's keeping you? The dinner's waiting.

TITUS.   I'm not. I've been waited on.

FLORA.   At the mansion.

TITUS.   In the Lady's maid's chamber. Dined and wined. Look at this chicken—that's the last leg of his journey on earth.

FLORA.   It's quite improper for you to sponge off Constantia. I won't hear of it! *(Snaps her fingers.)*

TITUS. You're damn right, you won't hear of it. On account of it's none of your business. I'm no longer under your green thumb, I have slipped through your fingers, you snapdragon. I've accepted a better position.

FLORA. What?

TITUS. But I do owe you something, so wait a moment. I'll be back. *(Withdraws into the house.)*

FLORA. *(Alone.)* Constantia, this is your work! A widow with a lover of her own who snatches someone's else's beau—in my book that's a human spittoon.

SCENE 5

POPONSEED. *(Carrying a pot.)* Here's the soup.

TITUS. *(Coming back.)* And here's the suit. The late lamented gardener's garb. Compliments of the new management! *(Tosses the bundle at Poponseed and withdraws.)*

POPONSEED. Missed me! What is it?

FLORA. *(To Poponseed.)* Oh, go jump in the lake!

POPONSEED. Won't you eat?

FLORA. No! If you don't lose your appetite over this, then you've got no appetite to lose!

POPONSEED. Won't you eat?

POPONSEED. Well, I thought this was to be the cozy dinner for two where I wasn't wanted.

FLORA. Go to hell! *(Exits.)*

POPONSEED. *(Alone.)* What do you know! He doesn't dine here, she doesn't dine here, and I—who was sent packing—I dine for the two of them. Oh Fate, shrouded in mystery, you surprise me with such an unexpected fit of justice! *(Sits down; eats the soup.)*

SCENE 6

(Room in the mansion. Center and two side doors. Titus enters in an elegant gamekeeper's uniform.)

TITUS. *(Alone.)* History repeats itself in a hurry: one widow acts like the other, offers me the defunct clothes of the departed husband. Now this one wants me to be Lady Cypressa's gamekeeper. Well, if that means nothing more than opening the carriage door and hopping onto the running board—that's as much of gamekeeping as I know. Oh, wig, you have done wonders—the food is delicious, the wine exquisite. I really don't know whether it's my changing luck or the Tokay that's gone to my head.

SCENE 7

CONSTANTIA. *(Entering.)* Ah, that's the way to be dressed! Your countenance is much better suited to a gamekeeper's uniform than to a gardener's outfit.

TITUS. I hope Madame will share your views about my countenance. Or in the end I'll be back with shovel and spade.

CONSTANTIA. You don't have much confidence in my influence around here, do you? My late husband was the gamekeeper, and the Lady certainly won't expect me to remain a widow forever.

TITUS. Such divine features must not be condemned to widowhood for life.

CONSTANTIA. Suppose I'd marry again. Do you doubt that Lady Cypressa would give my husband a position in the mansion?

TITUS. Any such doubt would be blasphemy.

CONSTANTIA. I don't say this because I have designs on you . . .

TITUS. Of course not. You're entirely undesigned.

CONSTANTIA. My interest in a gamekeeper is strictly professional.

TITUS. I realize that. I'm game.

CONSTANTIA. I'm not the kind of animal that shops around for a husband, but I do need a man trained in animal husbandry.

TITUS. I get the difference.

CONSTANTIA. I only mention it to show you that I do carry weight around here . . .

TITUS. *(Ogling her.)* You do carry quite a little. Around here.

CONSTANTIA. . . . and can get a man in the position I want him in when I throw that weight around.

TITUS. *(To himself.)* Oh raven-black skull, you're performing red-letter-day miracles!

CONSTANTIA. My husband, God bless him . . .

TITUS. God blessed him at the time He placed him in your arms, not now, when the poor wretch has to look down on his divine widow from a mere heaven. Oh, Constantia, one pays marriage a poor compliment by calling only those husbands "blessed" who have departed!

CONSTANTIA. So you think that one could, at my side . . .

TITUS. . . . walk on clouds and look into all sorts of heavens!

CONSTANTIA. Flatterer!

TITUS. *(To himself.)* Metaphysics is a good place to dip for apple-sauce. *(Aloud.)* I think I hear voices.

SCENE 8

SALOME. *(Shyly entering through the middle.)* Excuse me . . .

TITUS. *(Scared, to himself.)* What the devil—Salome! *(Throws himself nonchalantly into a chair, so she can't see his face.)*

CONSTANTIA. How did you get in here?

SALOME. There was no one outside, so I thought it was the entry to the hall . . . I never realized . . . please, Madame, come outside with me . . . I can't even talk properly standing in the midst of such luxury . . .

CONSTANTIA. Stop fussing. What do you want?

SALOME. I'm looking for someone I've already looked for at the gardener's—but he wasn't there, so I came here.

CONSTANTIA. *(Suspiciously.)* Whom are you looking for?

SALOME. For a man with red hair.

CONSTANTIA. *(Relieved).* Well, you'll easily find *him.* He'll glow in the dark. *(Titus winces.)*

CONSTANTIA. You won't find him here, that is certain. I would not tolerate such a being—nor would my Lady—we share a justifiable prejudice against both scarlet men and scarlet women.

SALOME. Well, if you happen to run into him, tell him that there are people from the city here who've asked me all sorts of funny questions about him . . .

TITUS. *(Forgetting himself, turning.)* And what did you tell them?

SALOME. *(Frightened.)* What's that? *(Recognizes Titus.)* Ah! *(She faints in Constantia's arms.)*

CONSTANTIA. What's the matter with her? *(To Titus.)* Go on, bring a chair, I can't hold her forever.

TITUS. *(Bringing a chair.)* There. Set her down.

CONSTANTIA. *(Sets her down.)* Look at her. She doesn't move. *(To Titus.)* That's strange. She fainted when she saw you.

TITUS. *(Embarrassed.)* I'm not that much of a knockout.

CONSTANTIA. But you see she doesn't move.

TITUS. *(Very embarrassed.)* Yes, I see that.

CONSTANTIA. Now . . . it seems . . . yes, she moved!

TITUS. Yes, I see that, too. I'll go and get her a glass of water. *(Wants to leave.)*

CONSTANTIA. You stay. Or do you have reasons to sneak off?

TITUS. Why should I? I don't know the person.

CONSTANTIA. Then you need not be afraid that she'd wake up.

SALOME. *(Recuperating.)* Oh, Madame . . . I'm beginning to feel better . . .

CONSTANTIA. What's the matter with you?

SALOME. This man . . .

CONSTANTIA. So you know him?

SALOME. No, oh no, I don't. I don't know him at all. *(Getting up.)* It's just . . . when he so suddenly spoke to me . . .

CONSTANTIA. Is that why you fainted?

SALOME. It's silly, isn't . . . city nerves in a country girl! *(To Titus, who watches her in amazement.)* Don't be angry with me, Sir, and if you happen to see the one with the red hair tell him I meant well, I just wanted to warn him. I certainly won't tell anything to the people who're asking about him. Tell him I surely won't stand in his way if he wants to make his fortune . . . *(Suppressing her tears.)* Tell him that, if you happen to see the one with the red hair. *(To Constantia.)* And again, forgive me for fainting in rooms that are out of my class and God bless you, both of you, and . . . *(Breaking into tears.)* now I'm beginning to cry . . . that's not proper . . . please forgive me, I'm such a silly goose.

(Hurries out the middle, crying.)

SCENE 9

CONSTANTIA. *(Looking after her, surprised.)* I daresay, I find the whole episode highly suspicious.

TITUS. *(Recovering.)* Why?

CONSTANTIA. She was so moved, so stirred up . . .

TITUS. About someone with red hair. She said so.

CONSTANTIA. She spoke of him, yes, but it was you who seemed to affect her.

TITUS. Now how can I affect her?

CONSTANTIA. You can't deny that she was moved.

TITUS. That's not my fault. First you blame me that she didn't move, then that she was moved. I really don't know—

CONSTANTIA. Now don't be angry. I may be wrong to connect you with such a common person—it would be unbelievable!

TITUS. It would indeed. I'm a man set on his career. *(Crudely hinting.)* My romantic ideas float in regions high above the riffraff.

CONSTANTIA. *(Coquettishly.)* Oh? Well, it was lucky that the Lady wasn't present at that disgusting scene. She hates the common. Her interests are intellectual—just as mine. She is an author.

TITUS. An author? She writes?

CONSTANTIA. Poetry. We have many literary teas in the mansion —you know something about literature, don't you?

TITUS. I know more about tea, but it doesn't matter. I know all about writers. If she'll read her stuff to me and I tell her that I find it divine, she'll say, "Ah, this man has judgment . . . insight . . . a fine education!"

CONSTANTIA. You're a fox! *(To herself.)* Quite a different caliber of man from my hairdresser!

SCENE 10

MARQUIS. *(Entering through the center.)* My darling Constantia . . .

TITUS. *(To himself.)* What the devil! My illustrious wig donor! If he talks, my career is wrecked before it started! *(Retires to the side of the stage.)*

MARQUIS. I almost missed this happy opportunity to press your lovely hand to my lips. *(Kisses her hand.)*

TITUS. *(To himself.)* A marquis kissing the hand of a Lady's maid? Is that broadmindedness or dirtymindedness?

CONSTANTIA. It's so late—I didn't think you'd show up today.

MARQUIS. Believe me, only an extraordinary emergency could have prevented me—who's this? *(Notices Titus, who quickly grabs a piece of cloth from a chair and begins to dust the furniture busily.)* A new gamekeeper?

CONSTANTIA. Hired today. A man of many talents.

MARQUIS. How can you judge the talents of a gamekeeper? And anyway, what is the Lady's game that needs a keeper?

CONSTANTIA. You see how he keeps busy.

MARQUIS. *(Trying unsuccessfully to examine Titus's face.)* Yes, but what's his game?

CONSTANTIA. *(To Marquis.)* You haven't told me what happened to you.

MARQUIS. *(With occasional glances at Titus.)* Oh yes. I was in a double accident: I might have drowned or broken my neck—if by a stroke of good luck a brave young man had not checked my horse . . .

CONSTANTIA. I never trusted that horse with its red mane! *Titus winces.)*

MARQUIS. I shall believe your judgment forever, my wise Constantia. This young man then . . . *(Looking sharply at Titus.)* my savior *(Turning Titus around.)* I was not mistaken—it's him!

TITUS. *(Bowing deeply.)*　Monsieur . . . please . . . you mistake me for someone else . . . *(Wants to leave.)*

MARQUIS. *(Holding him back.)*　Why deny it, my brave man? It's you—the figure, the voice, and—humph—the color of your hair . . .

TITUS.　The color of my hair has nothing to do with it.

MARQUIS.　Yes, it has.

CONSTANTIA.　That's right. Once you have seen these locks you don't easily forget them. A remarkable head of hair!

MARQUIS. *(Flattered.)*　Oh, thank you.

CONSTANTIA. *(Laughing.)*　You act as if you'd made it yourself. But you do know something about hair—have you ever seen such brilliance, such miraculous growth? *(Points at Titus's head as if she wanted to touch it.)*

TITUS. *(Drawing back.)*　Don't touch! It's my sensitive spot.

MARQUIS. *(Softly to Constantia, irritated.)*　You seem to take a special interest in the new servant . . .

CONSTANTIA. *(A little embarrassed.)*　Oh, a little encouragement for the newcomer . . .

MARQUIS. *(As above.)*　. . . which, in my opinion, is out of place in the relationship between a Lady's maid and a fellow domestic.

CONSTANTIA. *(Softly but sharply.)*　Thanks for the lesson, but I can very well judge what is and isn't out of place between me and my "fellow domestic."

MARQUIS. *(To Constantia in conciliatory tone.)*　My dear Constantia, I merely wanted . . .

CONSTANTIA.　You wanted to comb the blond page wig that the Lady is going to wear at the masquerade. You'll find it on the table in the next room. Go and do your work!

TITUS. *(To Marquis.)*　What? You are a hairdresser? I thought you were a marquis—a cross between a baron and a duke.

MARQUIS.　Marquis is my name, and I'm a wigmaker.

TITUS.　Well, that's a wig of a different color! The abyss between us is quickly filling up with combs and scissors, and we can be friends. *(Offers him a hand.)*

MARQUIS. *(Taking his hand.)*　I owe you thanks . . . *(Softly.)* but you owe me something, too, and don't forget it!

TITUS.　I never forget a kind deed—if I did it.

CONSTANTIA.　Madame will be back soon. I'll go and lay out her clothes for the evening. *(Exits center.)*

TITUS. *(Calling after her.)*　So long, charming layer outer of clothes!

SCENE 11

MARQUIS. My good man, that was uncalled for. . . .Constantia is my fiancée and I won't stand for such familiarities.

TITUS. Are you threatening me?

MARQUIS. I'm warning you. Don't forget your fate hangs on a hair—on a pretty bunch of dark hair.

TITUS. Could you be ungrateful enough to reveal our secret?

MARQUIS. I might be smart enough to get rid of a competitor that way.

TITUS. May I remind you that, without my intervention, you would not be the lucky fiancé of an affectionate woman but the unfortunate victim of some frigid water nymph?

MARQUIS. I owe you thanks but not an option on my bride.

TITUS. I'm not in the market for brides. I'm being pleasant to the Lady's maid not to win her heart but her patronage.

MARQUIS. Now, that's better. In that case you can count on my cooperation and, what's more, on my keeping my mouth shut. But keep your hands off my girl—or else! Just remember, your head is in my hands!

(Exits right.)

SCENE 12

TITUS. *(Alone.)* My poor head! So much has come over it today, and into it, too. The Tokay went to my head, and that this wigmaker is Constantia's fiancé also goes around *(Pointing at his head.)* in here. *(Throws himself into an easy chair.)* It's really a matter of the heart but all the heart does is flutter and dump problems into the lap of the head even if the head is up to its neck in trouble. I'm done in. *(Yawns.)* It'll be a while until Lady Cypressa comes home . . . *(His head drops.)* meanwhile . . . I could . . . *(Yawning.)* rest . . . a little . . . not fall asleep . . . just . . . rest . . . a . . . little . . . *(Falls asleep.)*

SCENE 13

MARQUIS. *(Coming back after a short while.)* It's too dark in there to work on the wig—I have to find a light . . . maybe the gamekeeper can help me. Where did he go? Has he sneaked off to my Constantia? Now just you wait till I . . . *(Wants to run out the center door, sees Titus in the easy chair.)* Oh, there he is, resting like a baby . . . my silly jealousy! That's not the way a man sleeps who's madly in love . . .

TITUS. *(Stammering in his sleep.)* Con — stan — stan — tia!

MARQUIS. What was that? *(Steps carefully closer.)*

TITUS. *(In sleep.)* One — more — ki — ki — kiss!

MARQUIS. Hell's peckerneck, I don't allow such dreams! *(Is about to grab Titus, then reconsiders.)* Wait—I have a better idea! We'll see if she'll give a ki-ki-kiss to a red mop! *(Cautiously takes off Titus's wig.)*

TITUS. *(Still asleep.)* Don't Stan—stantia . . . I'm ticklish on . . . my head . . .

MARQUIS. Now try your luck, you red Casanova! Your talisman is gone forever! *(Puts wig in his pocket and exits through center.)*

SCENE 14

TITUS. *(Talking in his sleep.)* Ah—your—tender—hands— *(Noise of a carriage outside, then the sharp sound of a doorbell. Titus wakes up.)* What was that? I must have . . . *(Runs to the center door.)* A servant is running out . . . the Lady is coming home . . . this is *it!* Now I'm going to be presented. *(Straightens his uniform.)* My uniform is all crumpled . . . my tie slipped . . . I need a mirror . . . *(Runs to a mirror at left, looks at himself, startled.)* For God's sake, my wig's gone! It must have dropped off while I had dropped off. *(Runs to the easy chair, looks around.)* No, it's gone, lost, stolen! Who could be so mean as to . . . oh, of course, the jealous pomade peddler, the sneaky hair curler, the oiley Othello. He has stolen my talisman! Now, at this decisive, this most promising moment, I stand here, a flickering candle at the coffin of my young career! But wait—he's in there, working on the Lady's hair piece . . . he won't get away! You'll give me back my wig, dandruff chaser, or I'll shake your brilliantined slick soul out of your body!

(Exits right.)

SCENE 15

(Exits right.)

CYPRESSA. I must say I find it rather impertinent of Constantia to hire a new servant without my permission.

EMMA. Don't be mad at her, Mamma, I've always wanted a game-keeper. He will be so much more fun to have around than our two wobbly-kneed servants in their old-fashioned uniforms.

CYPRESSA. We don't really need a gamekeeper.

EMMA. But Constantia says he's such a militant-looking black-top. He has no moustache, she says, but you must order him to grow one. And I want him to grow whiskers, too, black and all over his face so you can't see anything but two blazing black eyes. Oooh! He will look magnificent standing on the back of our carriage!

CYPRESSA. I'll send the man away again, and that'll be the end of it. Where is he, anyway? Titus is his name, she said. I say, Titus—Titus!

SCENE 16

TITUS. *(In a blond wig, from the right.)* Here I am, Your Ladyship, paying my humblest respects to the illustrious Lady I am to serve.

EMMA. *(To her mother.)* What's that? That's no blacktop!

CYPRESSA. *(To Emma.)* But he has manners, the blondie.

TITUS. *(To himself.)* Blondie? Did she say blondie?

CYPRESSA. *(To Titus.)* My maid hired you without my permission —however . . . *(To Emma.)* Emma!

TITUS. *(To himself.)* Blondie, she said! *(Looks around and moves so he can see himself in the mirror.)* Holy thunder, I *am* a blond! It was so dark in there—I must have grabbed the wrong wig from the barber's table. What if Constantia sees me now?

CYPRESSA. *(Continuing her instructions to Emma.)* And tell Constantia . . .

TITUS. *Oh-oh!* She's already calling for her.

CYPRESSA. . . . to prepare my evening gown . . .

TITUS. *(To himself.)* At least that will keep her busy for a while.

EMMA. Yes, Mama. *(Mumbling while leaving.)* That silly Constantia . . . trying to tease me . . . she knows my weakness for black hair!

SCENE 17

TITUS. *(To himself.)* She's an author—now, everyday words won't do . . . I'll have to dress up my speech in Sunday clothes . . .

CYPRESSA. And now for you, my good man . . .

TITUS. *(Bowing deeply.)* This is the moment I've anticipated and dreaded at the same time. I face it, if I may say so, with knee-shaking bravado and bold trembling.

CYPRESSA. You have little reason to be afraid. You seem to know how to behave, you have a passable appearance, and if you do your work . . . Tell me, where have you served before?

TITUS. My record is untarnished—I have served nowhere. This uniform contains an independent spirit ready to place itself in voluntary servitude for the first time.

CYPRESSA. And your father? Is he a gamekeeper, too?

TITUS. No, he has a quiet and peaceful occupation, the unbusiest of all business. His duties are heavenly, yet he is earthbound. He's held in bondage by the strictest master, yet he's free and independent, for he is the molder of his own existence—in short: he's dead.

CYPRESSA. *(To herself.)* How lavishly he expresses in forty words what can be said in one—he's obviously gifted as an author. *(Aloud.)* What is your education?

TITUS. I'm a product of the school of life. My education is tenuous but extremely widespread: a smattering of geography, a fraction of mathematics, a molecule of physics, just an idea of philosophy, a germ of medicine, and a pinch of the law.

CYPRESSA. How charming! You have learned much but not lost yourself in details. The mark of the true genius!

TITUS. *(To himself.)* Ah, this explains why there are so many geniuses!

CYPRESSA. Your blond locks indicate a poetic soul. Did you get your hair from your mother's or your father's side?

TITUS. Neither. It's sheer coincidence.

CYPRESSA. The longer we talk the more I'm convinced that you're meant to wear a uniform. You're not cut out to be my servant.

TITUS. What? Dashed? Quashed? Smashed?

CYPRESSA. Not at all. I'm a writer and need someone to help me, not as a mere copyist but as a secretary, a consultant. That will be your job.

TITUS. *(Happily surprised.)* Mine? Does Your Ladyship really think I have it in me, this intellectual midwifery?

CYPRESSA. I have no doubts. The position happens to be open . . . I just had to let a young man go—a scholar, highly recommended, but unfortunately he had a touch of red in his hair. It gave me the shivers—I couldn't help it.

TITUS. I can't help it either . . . *(Quickly)* that I'm blond, I mean.

CYPRESSA. Well, a head of hair like yours certainly won't harm your career, young man. Now you take off that servant uniform. I expect company tonight and want to present you as my new secretary.

TITUS. If I take off this uniform I'll have to put on my old clothes which are a uniform, too—the uniform of poverty: a patched coat with worn cuffs.

CYPRESSA. That can easily be helped. Go in there . . . *(Pointing to the right.)* you will find the wardrobe of my late husband. He had about your figure. Select what you need.

TITUS. *(To himself.)* Again the suit of a late lamented! *(Bowing.)* Thank you, Your Ladyship! *(To himself, while leaving.)* Today I'm dressing my way through an entire rummage sale.

(Exits right.)

SCENE 18

CYPRESSA. The young man is dizzy from the heights to which I've lifted him. What will he say when I open for him the gates of heaven itself by reading him my poetry!

CONSTANTIA. *(Entering excitedly, through the center.)* Shameful! That's what I call it: shameful!

CYPRESSA. What is it?

CONSTANTIA. I must complain about Mademoiselle Emma. It's shameful to carry a joke that far. She said I lied to her about the new gamekeeper's hair. First I thought she was having sport with me; but in the end she called me a dumbbell.

CYPRESSA. I'll reprimand her. By the way, the young man no longer is a gamekeeper. I made him my personal secretary, and expect everyone to show him the respect that goes with that position.

CONSTANTIA. Secretary! I'm delighted that he has pleased Your Ladyship. The black dress-coat of a secretary will beautifully match his hair.

CYPRESSA. What are you talking about?

CONSTANTIA. About his gorgeous black hair.

CYPRESSA. Don't be silly. I never saw a more beautiful blond.

CONSTANTIA. It pleases Your Ladyship to jest, too. I saw with my own eyes . . .

CYPRESSA. My eyes are just as own as yours.

CONSTANTIA. And Your Ladyship calls *that* blond?

CYPRESSA. What else?

CONSTANTIA. I beg your pardon, Your Ladyship, but I call it the pitchest pitch black I ever saw.

CYPRESSA. Don't be ridiculous. He's as blond as an angel.

CONSTANTIA. Heaven save us! Someone has bewitched us all!

CYPRESSA. Here he comes. See for yourself—is that dark or fair?

SCENE 19

TITUS. *(From right, in black dress-coat, breeches, silk stockings, and shoes.)* Here I am, Your Ladyship. *(Sees Constantia and shrinks back.)*

CONSTANTIA. *(Astonished.)* How is that possible?

CYPRESSA. *(To Constantia.)* In the future I won't stand for such nonsense.

CONSTANTIA. But I only said what . . .

CYPRESSA. *Enough.* I want to hear no more.

TITUS. *(To Cypressa.)* Your Ladyship is upset? May I be of help?

CYPRESSA. Imagine—my maid here said your hair was black.

TITUS. Blackest slander and of the deepest dye!

CONSTANTIA. I'm losing my mind!

CYPRESSA. Never mind your mind. What counts is that I'm losing my patience. Go and lay out my clothes!

CONSTANTIA. I can only repeat . . .

CYPRESSA. *(Angrily.)* And I repeat: go!

CONSTANTIA. *(As if swallowing a big lump.)* Mercy on us! Now the roosters will start laying eggs!

(Exits center.)

SCENE 20

CYPRESSA. The person has gone mad!

TITUS. *(To himself.)* I feel like a shipwrecked sailor on a plank: to survive, I have to push off the others. *(Aloud.)* Your Ladyship, I'm not surprised.

CYPRESSA. Why? Has she given you other indications?

TITUS. Well, indications is a weak word for what she's given me. I don't care to talk about it, but I dislike that sort of thing. She always looks at me as if . . . she talks to me as though . . . she behaves like . . . well, I just dislike that sort of thing.

CYPRESSA. She'll pack up, today!

TITUS. But what really shocks me is that all this time she and this wigmaker . . . it reflects on the good reputation of the house.

CYPRESSA. Is he chasing her?

TITUS. Yes, and I'd have thought that at her age the only one who'd chase her was Father Time.

CYPRESSA. What? How dare you — ?

TITUS. Oh, everybody knows that a woman is in her declining years only before she's thirty—after that she seldom declines.

CYPRESSA. How very clever. So, Constantia and that hairdresser . . .

TITUS. I don't want to talk about it.

CYPRESSA. I don't want to hear about it. What is it? It's my duty to know.

TITUS. It's my sad duty to tell. He . . . *Looks around, then steps forward and whispers in her ear.)*

CYPRESSA. *(Thrilled.)* No!

TITUS. Yes!

CYPRESSA. Anything else?

TITUS. Well, he also . . . *(Whispers again.)*

CYPRESSA. (Gaping.) I'll never let this man touch my hair again!

TITUS. I'm sorry to see him go. But what I really didn't want to talk about is Flora, the gardener.

CYPRESSA. Is she immoral, too?

TITUS. Oh, no, on the contrary—she proposed marriage to me.

CYPRESSA. She'll leave today.

TITUS. I don't like to tattle like this, but . . .

CYPRESSA. I'm glad you told me. Write the three notes of dismissal right away.

TITUS. No, I can't do that. My first duty must not be so cruel.

CYPRESSA. Young man, your noble heart does you honor!

SCENE 21

EMMA. *(Entering from the left.)* Mama, I have to complain about Constantia. She forced me, by her stubborn behavior, to call her a dumbbell.

CYPRESSA. You will dismiss her today. Constantia in person, Flora and the wigmaker in writing.

EMMA. Yes, Mama.

TITUS. *(Pretending to be surprised.)* Mama?

CYPRESSA. Yes, this is my daughter Emma.

TITUS. No—that's not possible!

CYPRESSA. Why not?

TITUS. It doesn't add up in years.

CYPRESSA. *(Very flattered.)* Oh yes, it does.

TITUS. Such a young lady—and a grown-up daughter? No, I can't believe it—a distant sister, perhaps, a remote cousin twice removed. If Your Ladyship did have a daughter she could be only—at the very most—about that big. *(Indicates the size of a baby.)*

CYPRESSA. Yet, it's true. One conserves oneself.

TITUS.   Oh, I know what conservation can do. But that would be ultra-conservatism!

CYPRESSA. *(Smiling benevolently.)*   Well, my droll young man, I now have to go and get ready for my guests. Come with me, Emma . . . *(To Titus.)*   See you soon.

TITUS. *(As if overcome by emotion.)*   Oh yes, soon! *(Pretends to be upset by this outburst, bowing, in submissive tone.)*   Soon, I mean to say, to start out with my duties . . .

CYPRESSA. *(Smiling.)*   Adieu!

(Exits left with Emma.)

SCENE 22

TITUS. *(Alone.)*   I'm in luck! All of a sudden I'm in luck. I'm not used to people liking me. If all your life people slap you down and suddenly you're able to charm them, that's a new experience that changes not only you but the whole world—human beings begin to look human and you can't help suspect that some of them may have a heart, hidden somewhere, and perhaps even a soul which is even harder to find because it's behind the heart. Imagine—I'm now one of them: I can talk to them, joke with them, work for them, live in the same house with them—it's hard to believe. I was used to hiding my feelings when my luck was bad—but it's not so easy to hide good luck—every breath becomes a trumpet, every motion a drumbeat: "Look here, see this colossal bliss!" And all this change took place since this morning—within the span of four or five hours! Yes, time is a busy tailor who is doing all the alterations in the shop of life. Sometimes the work goes fast, sometimes slow, but it gets done, all the same—everything in the world gets altered.

SONG

A beauty turns down twelve proposals of marriage,
Including eight owners of horses with carriage.
Two string themselves up by their necks, for her sake,
Three blow out their brains, four jump in a lake,
And one Japanese commits harakiri.
But eighteen years later our dearie is weary:
Now *she* wants to marry, her boyfriends do not—
Time changes a lot, yes, time changes a lot.

A rich man is fussy, has a cook and a valet,
And nothing is quite good enough for his palate.
He goes to the Alps for his milk and his trout,
Even Brussels will *not* do for *his* Brussels sprout.
He travels, in search of fried ants and frogs' legs,
And, in Africa, looking for crocodile eggs,
He ends up in the pot of the chief Hottentot—
    Yes, time changes a lot.

An opera singer—a smash hit was she,
Even hearing her hiccups they paid her a fee.
The envy left all of her colleagues depressed,
Even nightingales sometimes turned green in their nest.
Her C was so high it could shatter a glass
But seven years later it sounded like brass.
Her bust is still opera, but her voice is now shot—
    Yes, time changes a lot.

In the golden old days when a boyfriend felt brave,
He dragged his true love by her hair to his cave.
In the best of tradition of Adam's and Eve's
He gave her a wardrobe of newly-picked leaves.
"Mind the kids and the fire, and do all that I say,
While I go with the fellows a-hunting today."
"I'll obey you, my master," she said, "to the dot."
    Yes, times sure have changed—and a hell of a lot.
                            (Exits.)

SCENE 23

SPONGE. *(Entering with several ladies and gentlemen.)* Oh yes, I'm looking forward to this evening. A literary tea is my favorite beverage—it's the most nourishing brand of all teas.
GUEST. Every caramel comes with an ode, every fudge is wrapped in a sonnet . . .

SCENE 24

CYPRESSA. *(Entering.)* Welcome, ladies and gentlemen.
SPONGE. *(Bowing.)* And the Muse herself is pouring . . .
GUEST. The air is fragrant—with poetry.
CYPRESSA. Please be seated.

    (All sit down at the table.)

TITUS. *(Entering from the right.)*   Is it all right if I . . . ?

CYPRESSA. You're just in time. *(Presenting him.)* My new secretary.

GUESTS. Delighted . . . enchanted . . .

CYPRESSA. *(To Titus.)* Please sit down. *(Titus sits down.)* This young man is going to read to you from my memoirs at our next soirée.

GUESTS. Ah . . . charming . . .

SPONGE. It's a pity Your Ladyship didn't write for the theater . . .

CYPRESSA. Who knows—I might try it sometime.

TITUS. I hear it's very simple—if you pick the right subject.

CYPRESSA. And what would that be?

TITUS. Love. It's the most original subject for a play, and I happen to know how it all got started. Creation, after creating man, which was a tragedy, tried its hand in a little comedy called "Love." It was an immediate smash hit, with many curtain calls and rave notices—so, the inevitable happened.

CYPRESSA. What was that?

TITUS. Creation got carried away and wrote a sequel called "Marriage." But as often happens with sequels, there just wasn't the interest.

SPONGE. How true!

TITUS. And consider the practical side: Love is cheap to produce —only two characters, no extras, any scenery will do, and the less lighting the better. But Marriage—just think of the cast of characters: a wife, a husband, a maid, a cook, servants, children, and a lot of extras, particularly if the wife is pretty. And the scenery: a salon, a ballroom, expensive restaurants . . . And the wardrobe—you know the bill a wife can run up! The language, too, is much coarser here—no, no, stay away from the sequel!

CYPRESSA. *(To the lady next to her.)*   Well, what do you think of my new secretary?

SCENE 25

FLORA. *(Enters from middle, crying.)*   Your Ladyship, please excuse me, but . . .

GUESTS. What happened? The gardener! She's crying!

TITUS. *(Alarmed.)*   How can I wiggle out of this?

FLORA. *(To Cypressa.)*   I can't believe that I'm dismissed. I haven't done anything . . .

CYPRESSA. I don't have to account to you for my decisions.

FLORA. *(Seeing Titus.)* What's this? He's blond?

CYPRESSA. The hair of my secretary is no concern of yours.

SCENE 26

CONSTANTIA. *(Entering weeping with Emma, through the middle.)* No, it can't be.

EMMA. I only carried out Mama's orders.

CONSTANTIA. Am I dismissed?

GUESTS. What? She, too?

CONSTANTIA. Your Ladyship, I'd never have expected that. Without a reason . . .

SPONGE. What did she do?

CONSTANTIA. It's all because of the secretary's hair.

CYPRESSA. Nonsense. That has nothing to do with it. *(To her guests.)* By the way, what do you think of a person who insists on calling this man's hair black? I ask you : is it blond or isn't it?

CONSTANTIA. He is black.

FLORA. Yes, I know he's black.

SCENE 27

MARQUIS. *(Entering through the center.)* And I tell you he's neither black nor blond. He's red!

GUESTS. Red?

TITUS. *(Desperate.)* Well, hell! Now all is lost! *(Getting up and tossing his wig into the middle of the stage.)* Yes, I'm red!

GUESTS. *(In confusion.)* What? Red? Oh, no!

CYPRESSA. Heaven forbid!

CONSTANTIA. (To Titus) How disgusting you look!

FLORA. *(To Titus.)* And this beetroot wanted to marry me?

MARQUIS. *(To Titus.)* Wanted to get us all fired—eh?

CYPRESSA. *(To Titus.)* You are a fraud who spread falsehoods about my most faithful servants! Out, go, or I'll call the police!

TITUS. *(To Cypressa.)* Don't worry, I'm going . . .

GUESTS. Out!

TITUS. *(Resigned.)* The rise and fall of the Roman Emperor Titus! *(Exits slowly with lowered head. Guests in disarray; Lady Cypressa affects a fainting spell; Mr. Sponge fans her. Scene ends in general confusion.)*

(Curtain.)

ACT 3

(Lady Cypressa's garden. Same scene as at the beginning of Act 2)

SCENE 1

(Titus enters alone from behind the wing of the mansion.)

TITUS. *(Gloomily.)* The sweet home of my hopes has burned down, without insurance, my shares of good luck have dropped out of sight, and the figure of my cash is the fattest and roundest of all digits—zero. I'm back to my old belief that earth is a heavenly body on which most of us lead a hellish life. And why? Because people have no imagination—or they would realize how a man feels who is a man just like everybody else except that he has a different color of hair. They are not bad people—most of them are not, yet there is so much misery in the world because all of these millions of good people are nothing more than just good people. Well, I'm no worse off than when I started out—in fact, I profited by a good suit.

SCENE 2

GEORGE. *(Coming quickly from behind the mansion.)* The Lady sent me after you. She wants you to leave all her things here —coat, breeches, shoes, everything.

TITUS. My dear man, you're on a most unpopular mission.

GEORGE. Never mind. Just leave the clothes here.

TITUS. Suppose I had skipped town?

GEORGE. We have laws. Our coppers catch all the tramps.

TITUS. Or suppose, my dear man, I forgot about laws and lammed you one . . .

GEORGE. Help! Help!

TITUS. I said, "suppose." If you say suppose it's not against any laws.

GEORGE. *(Calling into the gardener's cottage.)* Poponseed!

POPONSEED. *(From inside.)* What is it?

GEORGE. *(Opening the door and calling inside.)* This tramp here . . . see that he puts on his old clothes.

POPONSEED. *(As above.)* Aye, aye.

TITUS. *(To George.)* You're a charming fellow.

GEORGE. Flattery won't get you anywhere. Off with you, and leave the good clothes in here. Understand?

(Exits.)

SCENE 3

TITUS. *(Alone.)* Oh yes, I understand it all. I had a little success, and it not only turned my head, it wrung my neck, and now bad luck is coming for a visit. I meant to receive it in a black coat and silken stockings but bad luck says: "I've known you all your life, don't bother dressing up, your old clothes will do."

POPONSEED. *(From inside.)* What's keeping you?

TITUS. I'm coming.

(Exits into the cottage.)

SCENE 4

SALOME. *(Entering from left with Bung.)* You promise you won't do him any harm?

BUNG. I told you a thousand times, I'm only doing what the master brewer told me. He speaks for the entire guild and he's the only man I listen to.

SALOME. And what did he tell you?

BUNG. He told me, "That's what you get for not paying any attention to the boy. Now he's taken off and will disgrace your family." That's why I'm looking for him.

SALOME. You don't want to get him arrested?

BUNG. I'd love to, but the master brewer told me, "That would disgrace your family.

SALOME. Oh, come now, your own flesh and blood—

BUNG. Your flesh and blood can be a pain in the neck if it sprouts red hair.

SALOME. Is that a crime?

BUNG. Red hair is the sign of a sly temperament, a slippery character—and it spoils the image of the family. Of course, everybody in the family is dead except me and him, but they all had brown hair, there wasn't a spark of fire in them—and then this boy had the nerve to be born a redhead.

SALOME. That's no reason to let your own nephew starve. If you have something yourself, that is.

BUNG. What I have, I owe to my brains. My parents didn't leave me a penny? But I figured things out.

SALOME. How's that?

BUNG. It wasn't simple. First, Cousin Alois died and left me ten thousand thalers. That set me thinking. I figured, if more of my family would pay their last debt, I'd be sitting pretty. And what do you know? Four weeks later, Aunt Mitzi cashes in her chips and comes across with thirty thousand. The next summer Uncle Fritz calls it quits to the tune of twenty thousand, and the winter after that, Cousin August gets his everlasting and treats me to forty thousand more—just as I figured it. And then I won eighteen thousand in the lottery.

SALOME. What? That, too?

BUNG. Yes, you mustn't get the idea that inheriting money is all there is to it. You must try other ways, too. That's using the old noddle.

SALOME. If you're so good at figuring, don't you figure that your day will come, too, and that Titus will inherit everything?

BUNG. Oh no, he won't. I can always find people more to my taste, so the redhead doesn't have to disgrace me by doing *me* the last honor.

SALOME. Then you'll do nothing for Titus?

BUNG. I'll do what the master brewer told me. I'm going to buy him a barber shop in Vienna, that will keep him out of mischief, give him a few thousand thalers so he'll not disgrace the family, then I'll call him a few names for being a redtop, and tell him to keep out of my hair.

SALOME.. *(Sadly.)* I'm happy for him but when he's no longer poor he'll really be lost to me. *(Sighing.)* He is, anyway.

BUNG. What does he do up there in the mansion?

SALOME. I don't know for certain but he's wearing a pretty uniform all covered with gold braid.

BUNG. A servant's uniform! It's a disgrace for the family—a nephew of a beer salesman wearing a servant's uniform! Show me the way to him and I'll shake him out of it—quickly!

SALOME. But I'm telling you . . .

BUNG. *(Agitated.)* Quick, I said. I owe a lot to my family!

   (Exits, driving Salome ahead of him across the stage.)

SCENE 5

FLORA. *(Entering, left.)* Holla, Poponseed! Poponseed!

POPONSEED. *(Entering, from cottage.)* What is it?

FLORA. The tramp is gone, I hope?

POPONSEED. No, he's putting on his old clothes.

FLORA. Tell him to hurry.

POPONSEED. *(Maliciously.)* Do you want to invite him to one of those cozy dinners for two where I'm not wanted?

FLORA. Go get lost!

POPONSEED. Now you can have him all to yourself. The Lady's maid will let you have him.

FLORA. Shut up and send him on his way.

POPONSEED. *(Calling into the cottage.)* You there, hurry up and get on your way.

TITUS. *(From inside.)* I'm done.

SCENE 6

TITUS. *(Enters in old clothes from cottage.)* Here I am.

FLORA. That's the wrong place for you to be.

TITUS. The gardener lady who gave me the brush! How would you like to give me a little something else on my way?

FLORA. What? For the dirty trick you played on me you want me to *give* you something? I'd rather check to see you haven't *taken* anything! *(Looks at him with contempt and exits into the cottage.)*

POPONSEED. Yes, one never knows! *(Also looks at Titus contemptuously.)* You red blockhead!

(Exits to the cottage.)

SCENE 7

TITUS. *(Alone.)* Impertinent folk! I shouldn't be surprised if illusions leave the heart only slowly, in single droplets. I deserve to be trampled on—I did the same thing to others when I was on top. I stabbed Flora in the back, that wigmaker who tried to help me, and even Constantia. I never did more than talk about them—but I should have known from my own experience that the tongue is the deadliest of all blunt instruments. A few hours ago I had a whole mansion at my disposal, and for tonight I don't even have a bundle of hay to sleep on.

GEORGE. *(From behind the mansion, politely.)* Mr. Titus! Mr. Titus!

TITUS. I'm going.

GEORGE. I'm glad I still caught you. You're wanted at the mansion.

TITUS. I—wanted? For what?

GEORGE. I don't know but the Lady's maid wishes to talk to you.

TITUS. What? Constantia?

GEORGE. The Lady, too, wants to see you once more. Be up there in half an hour.

TITUS. I'll be there. What do I have to lose?

GEORGE. Very well, Mr. Titus, the Lady will be expecting you.

(Bows and leaves.)

SCENE 8

TITUS. *(Alone.)*   Is he pulling my leg? Or did Lady Cypressa get a conscience indigestion after she chewed me to pieces? Conscience is a funny material . . . very elastic—today it's hardly big enough to cover a molehill, and tomorrow it will spread over a whole mountain. Has the Lady's conscience forced her to tolerate my hed-headed presence? What . . . ? I'll make it easier on her eyes . . . *(Reaching into his pocket.)*   I still have the gray wig of the departed gardener . . . *(Pulls it out.)*   I'll put it on for my last visit. Black and blond and red people have at least that much in common that they all turn gray in the end. I'm not cheating, just giving them a glimpse of things to come. Maybe the gray wig will bring more lasting luck.

(Exits left.)

SCENE 9

FLORA. *(Running from the cottage, to Poponseed.)*   I saw it, he took it. Stop, thief! Come, Poponseed, run after him!

POPONSEED.   It's not worth the bother.

FLORA.   He stole the wig of my beloved husband—to me it's full of memories!

POPONSEED.   Oh, come on, it's full of moths!

FLORA.   Don't argue—what's the idea?

POPONSEED.   I haven't had an idea in years.

FLORA.   Run, I tell you! Quick!

POPONSEED. *(Walking off slowly.)*   I'll do my best but I doubt if I can catch him.

SCENE 10

FLORA. *(Alone, angrily.)*   I have a good mind to have him arrested, that bummell!

GEORGE. *(Entering from the left.)*   What's bothering you!

FLORA.   Oh, that good-for-nothing, Titus.

GEORGE.   Well—wait a minute. Respect where respect is due. I called him names too, but now it turns out that he has a filthy rich uncle who'll buy him a barber shop in the city and give him a heap of money.

FLORA.   You don't say!

GEORGE.   The Lady sent me after him, to ask him back to the mansion—and I had to say "Mister" to him. Respect where respect is due.

(Exits.)

SCENE 11

FLORA. *(Alone.)* Well, well—that throws a different light on every-thing. I bet Constantia is reconsidering and has asked Lady Cypressa to help her land him. I know Constantia—she'll take a second look at that redtop now that he has a rich uncle. I may have been a little rough on Titus myself for something over which, after all, he has no control. *(Looking to the left.)* There he is still! Hey, Titus, Titus!

TITUS. *(From the left, the gray wig in his hand.)* Yes, I know, it has sentimental value for you. There, you can have it back, your gray wig.

FLORA. Oh, not at all, keep it. Although I don't know why you want to be gray at your age.

TITUS. Woman, if you'd been a redtop all your life, you'd consider any color an improvement.

FLORA. I'm afraid I was a bit rude before.

TITUS. It wasn't so bad, you only called me a tramp and a thief.

FLORA. I could kick myself.

TITUS. Say, how about this sudden rash of sisterly love?

FLORA. Well, the way I see it, it's the duty of a Christian to do good deeds, even to his enemies. But that doesn't mean you can't call people names and wish them a little bad luck—it doesn't follow that it'll turn out that way. No one is without faults, you know. You have to take the good with the bad.

TITUS. That's true. Even a person who has one leg too short, also has a longer leg—and, I guess, everyone who has a shortage in his character must also have some bigness in him, somewhere.

FLORA. I was just thinking the same thing about your hair, too. After all, no men are without faults, so the choice is between having no man or taking one with faults.

TITUS. Flora, gardener, you're giving me back my faith in mankind! I've got to pinch myself : I'm Titus, the beetroot, with no talisman to cover up my head—and yet I'm being treated like a human being!

DUET

TITUS. Madame Flora!

FLORA. Mister Titus!

TITUS. What's the bond that may unite us?

FLORA. Never underestimate
Any woman, keep this straight.

TITUS. *(Bowing to her.)*   If I underestimate
It's her age, perhaps her weight.

FLORA. A girl who is clever looks over the field.

TITUS. A man with red hair—may he hope he appealed?

FLORA. The chances are slim that they'll get intertwined.

TITUS. I already had lost all my faith in mankind

FLORA. A girl has to pick the best deal she can find.

TITUS. I already had lost all my faith in mankind.

FLORA. But there are exceptions to every rule.

TITUS. I've heard this before, I learned it in school.

FLORA. A girl is entitled to changing her mind.

TITUS. Are you giving me back now my faith in mankind?

FLORA. Our love, on occasion, can be colorblind.

TITUS. You're giving me back all my faith in mankind!

FLORA. Mister Titus!

TITUS. Madame Flora!
Come and be my faith restorer.

FLORA. Conscience has turned on the heat,
Tells me that I musn't cheat.

TITUS. Is it conscience and the heat?
Or did Flora get cold feet?

FLORA. Your mind is like lightning—it's quick but it's crooked.

TITUS. *(Clawing the air to scare her.)*
I'm a blackheaded monster—although I don't look it.
I'm a redheaded devil with a vampire mind.

FLORA. O horror, I'm losing my faith in mankind.

TITUS. I am growing a tail sprouting out from behind—

FLORA. I'm done for—I've lost all my faith in mankind.

TITUS. It may not be true—was perhaps I maligned?

FLORA. That indeed would restore all my faith in mankind.

TITUS. On beer, not on blood, I have wined and have dined.

FLORA. You're giving me back all my faith in mankind.

TITUS. Madame Flora!

FLORA.   Mister Titus!
Singing gives me tonsillitis.

TITUS. But in our day and age
Opera is the greatest rage.

FLORA. Everybody sings like birdies
Wagner's arias or Verdi's.

TITUS. *(Parodying opera style.)*
O villainous woman, accursèd and wretchèd!

FLORA.   I'm a victim of lechery, I swear, I was lechèd.
        The King himself was it who after me pined.
TITUS.   The King made me lose all my faith in mankind.
        If His Majesty ordered, obedience is blind.
FLORA.   My hero has lost all his faith in mankind.
        But hark, my beloved, and please stop your barking.
TITUS.   Speak up, cursèd woman, speak up—I am harking.
FLORA.   A purse full of ducats the King left behind.
TITUS.   Such a gift gives me back all my faith in mankind.
        The ducats are gold and you haven't declined?
FLORA.   Thank heavens, he's recaptured his faith in mankind!
FLORA.   Mister Titus!
TITUS.   Madame Flora!
        Times have changed, my dear signora.
FLORA.   Modern music blasts and blares.
TITUS.   Opera is reserved for squares.
FLORA.   Radio, hi-fi, and TV
        Bring us cacosymphony.
TITUS.   The boys bang the drum and they strum the guitar.
FLORA.   The audience—it screams and it faints—it's bizarre.
TITUS.   They sing "yeah, yeah, yeah," all go out of their mind.
FLORA.   It's enough to lose faith in the whole of mankind.
TITUS.   The musicians' long hair makes them practically blind.
FLORA.   I already have lost all my faith in mankind.
TITUS.   But the Viennese waltz is still king of the ball.
FLORA.   My faith in mankind is restored after all.
FLORA.   My faith in mankind is again very strong.

ENCORE

FLORA.   Mister Titus!
TITUS.   Madame Flora!
        Come, and let's sing an encora.
FLORA.   *(To the audience.)*
        Your applause, this must delight us,
        Even goes to redhead Titus.
TITUS.   Yes, this makes a man feel good:
        Superstition's dead, touch wood.
FLORA.   No longer will prejudice hang on a hair.
TITUS.   It has become skin-deep, that's progress, I swear.
FLORA.   A prejudiced man finds it hard to unwind.
TITUS.   I'd already lost all my faith in mankind.

FLORA. A man who looks different is still left behind.
TITUS. It sure makes me lose all my faith in mankind.
FLORA. Today all the redheads can work where they wish.
TITUS. A redheaded girl is considered a dish.
FLORA. That's progress since Nestroy's time, keep that in mind.
TITUS. You've given me back all my faith in mankind.
FLORA. We've made a good start, let's not keep it confined.
TITUS. You've given me back all my faith in mankind.

SCENE 12

(Room in the mansion with arches and glass doors in the center leading to a terrace and moonlit garden. Doors left and right. Lights on tables on both sides.)

CONSTANTIA. *(Alone.)* I didn't think that wigmaker had it in him. All of a sudden he turns up his nose at me and says goodbye forever. This could crush a ordinary widow but I, thank heavens, only need to cast a glance, and another man, Mr. Titus, is at my feet. I only hope the Lady can get that old beerocrat of an uncle to make Titus his heir.

SCENE 13

CYPRESSA. *(Entering from left.)* Constantia!
CONSTANTIA. Your Ladyship?
CYPRESSA. It won't work.
CONSTANTIA. He won't do it?
CYPRESSA. I spent half an hour with the man but his watertight soul is impenetrable. He'll buy Titus a shop but he won't make him his heir.
CONSTANTIA. What a miserable miser!
CYPRESSA. Don't look down on a miser—misers make wonderful persons to inherit from.
CONSTANTIA. I didn't think he would give Your Ladyship any trouble. I even called in the notary to draft the papers. Let's try again, together.
CYPRESSA. If you want to . . . I've done you an injustice this morning and would like to make it up to you by an act of motherly guidance.
CONSTANTIA. *(Kissing her hand.)* Your Ladyship is extremely good to me.

CYPRESSA. *(Leaving with Constantia at left.)* I have little hope,
though. Unless a meeting with his nephew will make a dent . . .
CONSTANTIA. Titus ought to be here at any moment.

(Both leave left.)

SCENE 14

*(Titus enters through the glass door with George. He wears the
gray wig with an old-fashioned queue.)*

TITUS. Can't you tell me . . . ?
GEORGE. Strict orders. *(Staring at him.)* Why are you wearing a
gray wig?
TITUS. If you don't tell me anything, I won't tell you anything.
I was asked to come here, so I'm here. Go and announce me
to Her Ladyship.
GEORGE. All right, all right. I will.

(Exits left.)

SCENE 15

TITUS. *(Alone.)* It'll sting a little here . . . *(Pointing at his heart.)*
to see Constantia again. But I only need to recall when she said
"How disgusting you look!" Such a recollection is the best medicine for a soft spot in your head. The Lady's maid can remain
an old maid, for all I care—I'm through with women! *(Enter
George.)* Have you announced me?
GEORGE. No, Her Ladyship is in conference and must not be disturbed.
TITUS. *(Mimics him.)* Her Ladyship is in conference . . .
GEORGE. You'll just have to wait. After a while I'll go and see if
it's time to announce you.

(Exits right.)

SCENE 16

TITUS. Oh, fiddledeedee, you uniformed serving machine! The Lady
in conference? I should live so long! People all over the place
get the silliest excuses thrown into their faces, and they're expected
to swallow them politely.

SONG

A man comes to see me, makes a touch for a buck.
He says: "I am starving, I've had such bad luck.
I'm looking for work but there's *no* vacancy.
My mother needs care and my wife has TB."
His breath smells of wine, and my feeling is strong:
    I should live so long!

"This thing has to stop," shouts the husband in rage.
Her eyelashes flutter like birds in a cage.
"You're jealous," she stammers, "and this makes you blind.
The man is in love with my soul and my mind.
We only read Shakespeare, we just play mah-jong."
    I should live so long!

A cigarette firm has found out by research
That to smoke is as safe as to sit in a church.
It is true, they acknowledge: some doctors believe
That smoking is harmful—but this is naïve:
For ten million customers cannot be wrong!
    They should live so long!

ENCORE

Three generals I see in my bright crystal ball
Who have moved from the front to the conference hall.
They've sent home the soldiers of their last platoon
And are taking together a trip to the moon.
Their names are Kotchenko, Jim Smith, and Li Wong—
    . . . so long!

(Exits.)

SCENE 17

CYPRESSA. *(Entering from left with Constantia.)* I wonder what's keeping him . . .
CONSTANTIA. George said he'd be here . . .
TITUS. *(Entering right.)* Your Ladyship is referring to me?
CYPRESSA. Ah, there you are. You'll be surprised to hear the news . . .
CONSTANTIA. *(To Cypressa.)* Your Ladyship . . . look—his hair!
CYPRESSA. What kind of masquerade is this?
TITUS. *(Pointing to his wig.)* That's the only wig I could get my hands on. I'm wearing it to save Your Ladyship the upsetting

experience of having to talk to a redhead.

CYPRESSA.   Oh well, your shade of red is not too offensive . . .

TITUS.   But the way you carried on . . .

CONSTANTIA.   *(Noticing Bung entering from the left.)*   Too late. He's here.

CYPRESSA.   *(To Bung.)*   Here's your nephew, Mr. Bung.

CONSTANTIA.   *(To Cypressa.)*   I don't have much hope for this cement-head—he's all mixed up and hardened to a rock!

(Both leave.)

SCENE 18

TITUS.   *(Surprised.)*   Uncle Bung! How did you get here?

BUNG.   In a more honest way than you. Vanishing into thin air is not my way of travelling.

TITUS.   Would be hard to do, anyway, for a man of your tonnage.

BUNG.   You disgrace of the family! You black sheep! *(Peers at Titus' hair.).*   What's that? Gray hair?

TITUS.   *(Embarrassed.)*   Well . . . you see . . .

BUNG.   But you are a paprikahead!

TITUS.   I was.

BUNG.   And now?

TITUS.   I'm gray.

BUNG.   But that's impossible . . .

TITUS.   Reality is the best proof of the possible.

BUNG.   You're only twenty-six!

TITUS.   I was, yesterday. But being abandoned by my only kinsman, and having to wander alone through the world, has aged me a thousand years. I've become gray overnight.

BUNG.   Overnight?

TITUS.   At seven sharp I leave home, an hour later I look into the mirror of the desperate, the river, and my hair is like a radish sprinkled with salt. I think it's the twilight, select my night's quarters—a ditch, with the fog for a blanket—and fall asleep again. In the morning, I look in the river again with a handful of my hair—it's gray. I blame the silvery moon and fall asleep again. In the morning, I look in the river again and the bright flame of yesterday has burned to ashes—I recognize the hair as mine only by the face that's hanging from it.

BUNG.   That's unbelievable!

TITUS.   Oh no, it's happened before. For instance, to a certain Belisarius—have you heard of him?

BUNG. Was he a beer salesman?

TITUS. No, he was a Roman general. His wife had the Senate scratch out his eyes.

BUNG. Women usually do that themselves.

TITUS. Well, this one used the legislative branch for it. Belisarius took it hard, and in three times twenty-four hours he was gray. Just think of it, Uncle, a Roman general needed three days for what I accomplished overnight—and you, Uncle, are the cause of this historical event!

BUNG. *(Very moved.)* Titus, lad, flesh-and-blood . . . I don't know what's coming over me—I am the uncle of an historical event! *(Sobbing.)* Nineteen years I haven't shed a tear, and now they come by the bucket. *(Dries his eyes.)*

TITUS. It's good for the old beer to come out!

BUNG. *(Spreading his arms.)* Come here, ash colored boy! *(Embraces Titus.)*

TITUS. *(Embracing Bung.)* Uncle Bung! *(Suddenly draws back.)*

BUNG. Why are you bouncing off like a barrel on a staircase?

TITUS. *(Embarrassed, trying to keep the wig's tail out of Bung's reach.)* You . . . eh . . . hurt me . . . with your ring.

BUNG. Don't be a sissy, lad! Back to your uncle's heart! *(Titus lifts the tail of the wig during the embrace with his right hand, to prevent it from being pulled by Bung.)* That's better. *(Letting Titus go.)* I'll tell you what: so this ring won't hurt you any more . . . *(Pulls off a heavy signet ring from his finger and hands it to Titus.)* There you are. Now I want you to know that I'm going to take you back to Vienna, buy you a fine barber shop, and . . .

TITUS. *(Happily.)* Uncle Bung!

BUNG. Look at your clothes . . . this coat . . . it's a disgrace. And I'll have to present you as my nephew to the Lady . . . and this other person . . .

TITUS. *(Scared.)* What other person? A hairdresser?

BUNG. Hairdresser? *(Laughs with heavy-handed waggishness.)* No, lad, don't play tricks with me! My eyes are poor but I could see that she wasn't after your *hair*, that person. *(Takes a brush from the table.)* Let me clean you up a bit . . .

TITUS. What are you doing?

BUNG. I'm tidying up a natural phenomenon that slept in a ditch. I'm dusting a historical event—that's no disgrace, not even for a beer salesman. Turn around!

TITUS. No, no! Start in front!

BUNG. *(Brushing in front.)*   Just imagine! Getting all gray worrying about the family. *(Moved.)* I'm getting all flabby hearted. It was I who left you in the ditch . . . Now turn.

TITUS. *(In desperation.)*   Uncle, would you believe that my worries about the family not only made my hair gray but also made me grow a queue?

> *(Bung has stopped brushing and taken out a handkerchief to blow his nose. He hasn't heard Titus's last remark.)*

BUNG.   Look, Titus, lad. I've never had a boy to take care of . . . you are a good lad . . . you've taken it to heart because I was such a cold-hearted uncle. And why was I cold-hearted? Because you had red hair. But now you don't have red hair any more, so there's no reason to be cold-hearted. Even the master brewer would agree to that. You are my only kinsman, you are my nephew—you are as much as my son . . . I'll make you my sole heir!

TITUS.   What?!

SCENE 19

CYPRESSA. *(Entering with Constantia and notary.)*   "Sole heir" . . . these are the words we've been waiting for.

CONSTANTIA.   We knew your heart would tell you what to do. That's why we brought the notary along.

CYPRESSA.   And he has brought the necessary papers.

BUNG.   Good. Where are they?

> *(Notary pulls out papers and discusses them with Bung in the background.)*

TITUS. *(To Cypressa, referring to Constantia.)*   She's pushing my inheritance faster than I.

CYPRESSA. *(To Titus.)*   You see how much this unselfish woman *(Pointing to Constantia.)* acts in your best interest? She has confided in me and I'm ready to bless the bond which love has tied and gratitude will strengthen.

TITUS. *(Bows before her.)*   Women's styles may change but their designs remain the same.

BUNG.   Everything's fine. Roll out the barrel!

> *(Constantia and the notary lead him to the table with inkstand and quills. He sits down to sign.)*

TITUS. *(To Constantia.)*   That he buys me a barber shop I can

accept—he's my uncle. But to become his heir on a fraud—no!
(To Bung.) One moment, Uncle, let me . . .

BUNG. What? Are you still not satisfied?

SCENE 20

FLORA. *(Entering through the center.)* Your Ladyship, I've come . . .

CYPRESSA. At the wrong time.

FLORA. . . . to settle my account.

CYPRESSA. Didn't I tell you that you may stay?

FLORA. Yes but . . . I'm not sure now . . . I may marry and move
to the city.

CYPRESSA. Marry? Whom?

FLORA. It's too early to say, but Mr. Titus . . .

CYPRESSA. What?

CONSTANTIA. *(At the same time.)* What impertinence!

BUNG. *(To Titus.)* To how many womenfolk have you promised
marriage, in your desperation?

TITUS. Promised? None.

BUNG. Oh, I don't care. Marry who you want. You're my sole heir,
you can support them all.

SCENE 21

SALOME. *(Rushing in through the center.)* Mr. Titus! Mr. Titus!
*(She sees the crowd of people and freezes at the doorway, without
noticing Flora.)*

CYPRESSA. What do *you* want?

SALOME. *(Shyly.)* I beg your pardon . . .

CYPRESSA. How dare you break in here?

SALOME. I have a message from Madame gardener for Mr. Titus . . .

CYPRESSA. Flora needs no messenger. She's here.

SALOME. *(Noticing Flora.)* Oh, yes, then she can tell him herself.

CYPRESSA. Tell what?

SALOME. Nothing. She's signaling me not to tell.

CYPRESSA. Come out with it. Speak up!

SALOME. Not as long as Madame gardener is signaling me . . .

CYPRESSA. *(To Flora.)* You stop that. *(To Salome.)* Well . . . ?

SALOME. *(Embarrassed.)*. Madame gardener told Poponseed, and
Poponseed told me to tell Mr. Titus . . .

CYPRESSA. *(Impatiently.)* What?

SALOME. To give back her wi . . . *(Cypressa and Constantia try to
restrain her.)* . . . her wig.

BUNG. What wig?

TITUS. *(Taking off the gray wig.)* This one.

BUNG. *(Angrily.)* What? You've had the nerve . . .

CONSTANTIA. *(To Cypressa.)* Now all is lost!

CYPRESS. *(To Constantia.)* Quiet! *(To Titus.)* That was a childish prank you tried to play on your distinguished uncle. But you didn't really think that a man of his brains would fall for it? He would have to be a real nitwit not to have seen through it right away. But as a man of wit . . .

TITUS. He played along and played a prank on *me*!

CYPRESSA. *(To Bung.)* Isn't that so?

BUNG. *(Perplexed.)* Huh? Oh yes, yes, of course. I fooled him good, didn't I?

CYPRESSA. *(To Titus.)* And now it's up to you to ask his forgiveness.

CONSTANTIA. *(To Titus.)* A smart man like your uncle certainly won't deny you the inheritance just because the color of your hair happens to be red. *(To Bung.)* Am I right?

BUNG. *(As above.)* Of course, oh yes.

TITUS. *(To Constantia and Flora.)* Now, wait a minute . . . there are a few things I have to say about this, too. If he will buy me a barber shop—fine, that's all I need. I'll be very grateful for it. I need no inheritance, and I wish him a long and happy life of about three hundred years!

BUNG. *(Moved.)* A person can sell a lot of beer in that time! You're a good lad, in spite of your red hair!

TITUS. *(Referring to Constantia and Flora.)* Secondly, I will not marry anyone who will pardon red hair only when it's growing on the head of a sole heir. Neither will I marry anyone who looks at my fiery hair and sees it grow paler with every thousand thalers I inherit. I'll stick with the girl who cared for Titus before he had a talisman either on his head or in his pocketbook—and that, I believe, was the case with this one. *(Embraces the surprised Salome.)*

SALOME. What? Mr. Titus?

TITUS. Is yours, if you want him.

CYPRESSA. *(Icily cold.)* Adieu! *(Exits indignantly at the left, followed by the notary.)*

CONSTANTIA. Her Ladyship wishes not to be disturbed any further! *(Exits.)*

FLORA. *(To Titus, maliciously.)* Congratulations! Birds of a feather flock together! *(Exits.)*

BUNG. *(To Titus.)*   What about me? Don't I have any say about whom you marry?

TITUS. *(With reference to Salome.)*   I know, Uncle, you don't like redheads. Almost no one likes them. And why? Because there are so few of them, because they're in the minority, because they're different. If there were lots of redheads, people wouldn't even notice them, they'd be acceptable. But we shall overcome: The solution to the problem is for redheads to multiply like rabbits, and you can be sure, Uncle, that Salome and I will do our share.

(Curtain.)

Franz Grillparzer (1791-1872)

King Ottocar, His Rise and Fall

Most modern critics would place Franz Grillparzer, Austria's greatest dramatist, second only to Goethe and Schiller in his influence on the German Romantic drama of the nineteenth century. In many ways it was the production of his plays at the Burgtheater in Vienna by Schreyvogel and Laube that made the Austrian capital the center of the German theatrical world throughout the nineteenth century. The plays of this melancholy genius have tended, however, to remain virtually unknown outside the German-speaking world because of the gloomy pessimism and inaction of his leading characters.

Born in Vienna in 1791, Grillparzer prepared for a career in law, but a shy, indecisive, melancholy disposition led him gradually to retire from life into a civil service position in the bureaucracy of Prince Metternich, prime minister to the Hapsburg emperors in the early nineteenth century. This melancholy strain was deepened by overpowering hypochondria that increased after the deaths of his mother and younger brother by suicide. It was one of the primary reasons that he never married, though he had a number of love affairs and a lifelong devotion to Kathi Frölich. A few journeys from Vienna, during one of which he met the great Goethe, were the only breaks from the stifling atmosphere of theatrical censorship and the deadly routine of an imperial archivist. His indecisiveness led to a writing technique that wavered between Classic and Romantic models for his plays, although his devotion to the Spanish playwright Calderón remained a constant inspiration throughout his playwriting career.

His first play, *Die Ahnfrau (The Ancestress*; 1817), was based directly on the mood he loved in Calderón's *Life is a Dream*. It was a highly effective dramatic treatment of the genre known as fate-tragedy, combining scenes of terror and horror with verse of great power and beauty. The play was an enormous success with the public when it was produced by his close friend and mentor, Joseph Schreyvogel, at the Theater an der Wien in 1817. Upset at being classed as a fate-tragedian, Grillparzer turned to a classic theme for *Sappho*

(1818), which concerned the dilemma of the artist caught between a poetic temperament and the demands of the everyday world. Sappho represents the artist and, by analogy, Grillparzer himself, who must pay for poetic achievements with the renunciation of all normal human relationships. Then came his most ambitious undertaking in the Classical manner, *Das Goldene Vliess (The Golden Fleece;* 1820), a trilogy based on the story of Jason and Medea. Instead of concentrating on the final revenge of Medea as in Euripides, he attempted to stage the entire legend. But the final play, *Medea,* is still the best of the three parts, exquisitely weaving together, until the disastrous conclusion, the threads of antagonism between the passionate and barbaric Eastern woman and the ambitious, civilized Western man.

Next Grillparzer turned from Classical sources to write his first historical drama, *König Ottokars Glück und Ende (King Ottocar's Fortune and Death;* 1823), included in this volume, about the rise to power of Rudolf I, the first Hapsburg emperor. Despite the complimentary attitude toward the Hapsburgs, the play ran into censorship problems because of the parallel between the person of Ottocar and that of Napoleon. This kept the play off the stage until 1825. Rudolf is presented as a direct and unassuming person dedicated to the state, while Ottocar has some of the qualities of Shakespeare's Richard III. Though very successful in evoking period and delineating character, it suffers from the looseness of structure found in most chronicle plays. Its force derives from the brilliantly etched conflict between the unscrupulous Ottocar and the righteous and self-possessed Rudolf. That the play has a very special place in the hearts of the Viennese is witnessed by the fact that the play was chosen for the postwar reopening of the rebuilt Burgtheater, and was chosen during the 1976 bicentennial observance of the founding of the theater as the premiere for the anniversary season.

This play was followed by an inferior piece entitled *Ein treuer Diener seines Herrn (A Faithful Servant of His Lord; 1826),* which was very self-revealing in its attempt to depict in a historical setting the conflict between duty and a weak will in the devotion of a servant to his king.

Grillparzer once again returned to Greek sources to tell the story of Hero and Leander within the same psychological context that he had used in *Medea. Des Meeres und der Liebe Wellen (Waves of the Sea and of Love;* 1829) is concerned primarily with Hero's betrayal of her vocation as a priestess of Diana. In surrendering to the experience of human love, which Grillparzer saw as natural and inevitable, she also exposed herself to life and so, like Sappho, must die. It was his favorite melancholy theme of the artist killed by exposure to love and life, and once again there was a brilliant analysis of the female psychology.

For his next play Grillparzer turned to Spain and his favorite playwright, Calderón. In *Der Traum ein Leben (The Dream, A Life;* 1834) he retells the dramatic legend of Rustan, who rises to power by treachery and violence. Seeing his base ambitions discovered, he flees for his life, awakening to realize that all has been a dream. It is a play deeply indebted to the traditions of the Viennese popular theater as well as expressive of the listless passivity of dying Romanticism. The hero only dreams of greatness, and, awakening to reality, he prefers to remain safely at home. Following this very Austrian play, Grillparzer attempted his only comedy, *Weh' dem, der lügt (Woe to Him Who Lies;* 1838), which was much too sophisticated and philosophical to please the Viennese audience, who thought themselves connoisseurs in this field. The play, laid in the seventh century, was amusing but earnest in tone, and told the story of a humble but witty kitchen boy whose invariable truthfulness finally freed his master's nephew from the barbarians. Embittered by the reception of this ill-fated comedy at the Burgtheater, Grillparzer. at this point, withdrew from the theater to write only for his own amusement.

All of his last three plays, published only after his death, lack the theatrical effectiveness of his earlier work, since there was no longer day-to-day contact with the theater. *Ein Bruderzwist in Habsburg (Family Strife in Hapsburg;* n.d.) the first of these later closet dramas, was a brilliant statement of the need for passivity rather than active ambition in political leaders at certain moments in history. It was the tale of the events that led to the Thirty Years War. The leading character, the inward and passive Rudolf II, was depicted as an aging philosopher with a humanistic outlook who foresaw the tragedy of the coming struggle between Protestants and Catholics while wearily cognizant that it could not be averted. Again it was a theme similar to the one Grillparzer had borrowed from Calderón for earlier dramas, and it brilliantly reflected the impotence and passivity that marked many artists and intellectuals in the repressive age of Metternich. Though not written for the stage, *Ein Bruderzwist in Habsburg* has proved to be one of Grillparzer's most interesting plays in the modern theater because of the searching psychological interpretation of the eccentric Rudolf.

To this same period also belonged *Libussa* (n.d.), posthumously published and performed to great acclaim at the Burgtheater with the famous Austrian actress Charlotte Wolter in the title role. It was the story of an ancient Bohemian princess who renounced her supernatural gifts in order to marry a peasant and become part of the world. But this was impossible, and only a child remained as a synthesis between diety and humanity. Finally, *Die Jüdin von Toledo* (*The Jewess of Toledo;* n.d.) is an adaptation of Lope de Vega's *Las Paces de los Reyes y Judiá de Toledo*. It depects with vivid realism the spell exercised by a wayward Jewess over Alphonso VIII of Castile. The King was only brought back to a sense of his responsibilities after the Jewess had been killed at the Queen's command.

Grillparzer was deeply Austrian in his borrowings from the past as well as very *Biedermeier* in his outlook on the present. (*Biedermeier* is the name used to describe the complacent, self-satisfied, middle-class attitude of Viennese society during the early nineteenth century.) He both admired and utilized great Romantic and Classical sources from the past while pessimistically showing the disillusionment that came from excessive idealism and the necessity for a compromise with reality. The influence of Lope de Vega, Calderón, Shakespeare, and popular Viennese theater is clearly seen in his work. Unlike Goethe and Schiller, he was able to create various cultural levels in his use of speech, while using many colloquialisms, bits of humor, and characterizations from the Viennese farce. Though his central dramatic conflicts were usually rooted in personal problems and his solution was almost always renunciation rather than action, he managed to present his themes objectively. He was at his best a master of dramatic technique and psychological insight, who might have achieved more had he lived in a less-bureaucratic state.

Due to the great influx of German immigration to the United States in the nineteenth century, there is evidence of more than a hundred performances of seven of Grillparzer's dramas in all parts of the country from New York to San Francisco, from St. Paul to New Orleans, before World War I. Probably the ealiest play performed was *Die Ahnfrau* in New York in the early 1840s, and both *Medea* and *Der Traum ein Leben* were also performed at New York's first dignified house of German drama, the Altes Stadttheater, in the later 40s and 50s. Undoubtedly, the most publicized performances of Grillparzer in the nineteenth century were those of the Czech actress Fanny Janauschek, who presented *Medea* in both English and German all across America in the years after her debut in New York in 1867. Blanche Bates starred in Thomas Broadhurst's version of *Medea* in San Francisco, and there have been a number of other academic and amateur productions of Grillparzer's plays both in English and in German in the years since World War I. Unfortunately, Grillparzer has never received in the United States the attention accorded Goethe and Schiller, his German romantic predecessors.

King Ottercar, His Rise and Fall

by

FRANZ GRILLPARZER

Translated by Arthur Burkhard

Characters

PRIMISLAUS OTTOCAR, King of Bohemia

MARGARET OF AUSTRIA, widow of Henry Hohenstaufen, his wife

BENESH OF DIEDITZ
MILOTA, his brother } The Rosenbergs
ZAVISH, their nephew

BERTA, daughter of Benesh

BRAUN OF OLMUETZ, the King's Chancellor

BELA, King of Hungary

CUNIGUNDA OF MASSOVIA, his granddaughter

RUDOLPH OF HAPSBURG

ALBRECHT and RUDOLPH, his sons

FREDERICK OF ZOLLERN, Burgrave of Nuremberg

HENRY OF LICHTENSTEIN } Austrian knights
BERTOLD OF EMERBERG

THE ELDER MERENBERG
SEYFRIED MERENBERG } Styrian knights
FREDERICK PETTAUER

HERBOTT OF FUELLENSTEIN

ORTOLF OF WINDISCHGRAETZ

OTTOCAR OF HORNECK

LADY MERENBERG

PALTRAM VATZO, Burgomaster of Vienna

THE BURGOMASTER of Prague

THE IMPERIAL HERALD

THE SEXTON of Goetzendorf

THE CHANCELLOR of the Archbishop of Mainz

ELIZABETH, lady-in-waiting to Margaret

LADY-IN-WAITING to Cunigunda

ENVOYS of the German Electoral Assembly

NOBLES and CLERGY of Bohemia, Austria, Styria, Carinthia

SOLDIERS

This play is reprinted from Franz Grillparzer, *King Ottocar, His Rise and Fall*, translated by Arthur Burkhard (Yarmouth Port, Mass.: The Register Press, 1962). Single copies of this edition may be obtained from Mary S. Rosenberg, 100 West Street, New York, N.Y. 10023.

ACT 1

(The castle at Prague: Queen Margaret's antechamber. Doors right and left; the one at the right leads to the inner rooms. Before this door Seyfried Merenberg stands guard, leaning on his halberd; enter Lady Elizabeth and another lady-in-waiting from the Queen's chamber.)

ELIZABETH. Quick, Barbara, be off! Fetch Master Niklas!
 The Queen seems well but I still feel concern.
 (To a servant who enters.)
 Have you the balm? Give it to me, my friend.
 O most unhappy day! My poor, poor lady!
MERENBERG. *(Enters.)* How fares the Queen?
ELIZABETH.   She keeps her courage up;
 But not without some cost, as one can see.
MERENBERG. Who stays with her?
ELIZABETH.   The Count of Hapsburg, sir.
 That I must live to see this day!
 (Exit into the Queen's chamber.)
MERENBERG.   My son!
SEYFRIED. *(Has been standing leaning on his halberd lost in thought.)*
 Yes, father?
MERENBERG.   Yes, and have you heard?
SEYFRIED.   I have.
MERENBERG. And say to it?
SEYFRIED.   It is not true.
MERENBERG.   Not true?
SEYFRIED. No father. And it makes me so enraged
 That with this halberd I should like to crush
 The heads of those who say it, liars all.
MERENBERG. *(Steps back.)* You would, alas, then strike your father,
 son; I too believe it.
SEYFRIED.   You?
MERENBERG.   My son, I know!
SEYFRIED. How could a knight, a noble, such a king as he,
 So sin against his plighted word,
 Forsaking her, the woman pledged to him?
 Did I not serve him in my days as page,
 And was he not the model and the mould
 Of conduct and of form?
MERENBERG.   No one turns bad.
 That was not good before he took the turn.

SEYFRIED.   No valiant deed, no virtuous thought of mine
But I compared with him, his noble bearing,
Ashamed to find the contrast all too great.
He latterly dealt me a grievous blow;
He fought the Magyars, leaving me behind.
He thinks, perhaps, that some regard remains
For Berta, her of Rosenberg, you know.—
Oh, that this blot were taken from his life,
The only stain; in all else he is clean!—
But surely it was they that led him on,
Those Rosenbergs! The father—shameless pander!

MERENBERG.   Think as you like, but know this much is true:
The Queen must go, and she and those who serve her,
They have the very worst, the uttermost to fear.
I shall go home to Merenberg today,
Where I belong. You also must be off.

SEYFRIED.   I, father?

MERENBERG.   You! Your foolish confidence
Shall not, if I can help it, wreck your life.
You do, as if to follow; but in Bruck
Pick up fresh horses from our trusted servant,
And while they still assume you safe at home,
You will in secret head for Germany.
The Queen will not, though great her need, address
The Empire; I, God willing, so intend.
I cannot see the daughter of my lord,
Expelled from home and country, lacking aid.
Make straight for Frankfurt and this letter give
(Opens his jacket and shows where the letter is hidden.)
The Archbishop of Mainz. I hear a step,
Someone approaches.
(Moves away from him.)
Secrecy and haste!
One day now lost means losing thirty years!
(Enter Benesh of Dieditz and Milota.)

BENESH.   Was not Lord Zavish here?

SEYFRIED.   *(Turns away.)*   I have not seen him.

BENESH.   But he just passed you!

MILOTA.   Brother, do be calm!

BENESH.   Be calm? I am. The King will never dare!
Am I not Rosenberg? Is not our house
In all the land by far the mightiest?

And he would dare? Disgrace like this? Why, nonsense!
But I will learn who started this report;
Find him and smite him; thus, and thus, and thus!
Him, and his son and heirs!
(Enter Berta.)

BENESH. You, foolish creature?
What brings you here? Go home, stay in your room.

BERTA. I cannot stay. I feel I am pursued.
Men scurry through the halls, fright in their eyes,
And whisper things too terrible to bear.
Say, father, is it true?

BENESH. You ask of me?
Away, be off!

BERTA. Is no one human near?
(Walks toward Seyfried but starts back as she sees who it is.)
You, Merenberg! You, whom I should avoid,
Of all men, you! And yet you have a heart.
I wronged you past endurance, Merenberg.
But wreak no vengeance now. See, I shall kneel.
(She kneels.)
Say, is it true?

SEYFRIED. What, Berta?

BERTA. Is it true?
The King casts her aside?

SEYFRIED. So father says.

BERTA. The others say so, too—and now he weds—
Too late comes shame; is this a time for shame?
And he now weds anew, and whom?—

SEYFRIED. *(Pityingly.)* Not Berta
Of Rosenberg.
(With a cry Berta presses her face to the ground.)

BENESH. *(To Seyfried.)* Who says so?—Girl, come here!

MILOTA. *(Goes toward Berta.)* My niece, pray come; this is no
place for you.

BERTA. O Seyfried, save me!

SEYFRIED. By your leave, Lord Milota!
If you but dare to touch her with your hand,
I promise you, my pike will pierce you through.
(Lowers his halberd.)

BENESH. And if I—

SEYFRIED. Even so!

BENESH. Would you deny a father
   His child?
SEYFRIED. If only then you had denied her
   She would not now be groaning at our feet
   The heart within me shattered, as I look.
BENESH. You mean we should have wedded her to you?
SEYFRIED. Far better, sir, than have such shame as now.
BENESH. My child!
SEYFRIED. Hands off! She placed her trust in me,
   And I keep faith with someone so entrusted.
BENESH. Then shall my sword—
SEYFRIED. Put by!—No cause to fear, my dear!
   (Enter Zavish; he pauses at the door and laughs loudly.)
ZAVISH. Ha, ha, ha, ha!
BENESH. *(Turns around quickly as he sees Zavish.)* You, Zavish?
   God has sent you.
ZAVISH. What show of heat, you noble-minded hunters,
   About a bearskin of a bear unslain?
   Sir Bruin cheerily jogs down the slope
   And will, as suits him, let you feel his paws.
   Fair cousin, my regards! *(To Seyfried.)*
   And you, my huntsman,
   Put by your spear and your forbidding frown;
   I am no game for you!
BENESH. Now tell us all.
MILOTA. Yes, nephew, speak.
ZAVISH. Tell, speak; what would you have?
BENESH. The King—
ZAVISH. Engaged and trounched the Magyar troops
   At Croissenbrunn; *(To Milota.)*
   Why, uncle, you were there!
BENESH. Who asks you that?
ZAVISH. The treaty has been signed:
   In Austria—
BENESH. Not that!
ZAVISH. In Styria—
BENESH. You mock at me?
ZAVISH. What is it you would have?
BENESH. The King's—
ZAVISH. Ah, yes; his marriage is dissolved.
BENESH. The document is signed?
ZAVISH. Yes, signed and sealed.

The Queen will leave today; go to Vienna,
And then—

BENESH.   Is there no talk?—Curse you!—with whom—
(Turns to Berta.)
Be quiet, you—With whom the King?—

ZAVISH.   Oh, that!
With whom the King will wed this second time?
With whom else could he, pray, if not with her,
Your daughter? Craftily you played your cards!
You first presented her without a word,
Decked out she was as fair as fair can be;
Then you supplied the poor thing's lack of wit
With wisdom of your own. How she did talk!
The Queen of Sheba talks not half so well.
At last—well, how can I know all you did?
In short, enamoured as he is, you'll see
He soon will come and sue for Berta's hand.

BERTA.   *(Leaps to her feet.)*
To her, the Queen! To clasp her knees and die!
(Exit into the Queen's chamber.)

ZAVISH.   Ha, ha, ha, ha!

MERENBERG.   Lord Zavish!

ZAVISH.   Let us dance.
Make merry at the wedding of the King!
(To Seyfried.)
You, too, were once a suitor for her hand?
Why even I myself. God knows, one night
At wine was tempted by her rosy cheeks!
Give me your hand, my friend; comrade-at-arms!
(Seyfried turns away.)

MILOTA.   Why play the silly fool? Speak out, be brief:
Who is it that the King will wed?

ZAVISH.   As brief
As is your question shall my answer be:
One Cunigunda of Massovia,
Niece of the Magyar King.

BENESH.   Damnation, no!

ZAVISH.   You wished yourselves to have the band dissolved,
Worked years on end to have it come about:
It is dissolved—and he weds Bela's niece.

BENESH.   *(Beats his forehead.)*
Betrayed; deceived, defrauded! Shameful, shameful!

ZAVISH.   Knock not so loudly at the gate of thought!
  If it closed then, it will not open now!
BENESH.   You mock today, and yet you once approved.
ZAVISH.   I once approved? This senseless, crazy scheme?
BENESH.   You did, and you!
MILOTA.   By promising success.—
BENESH.   Bring her to me, bring me the girl, you hear?
  She shall not live! Not she, nor I! Oh!—Oh!—
SEYFRIED. *(Calls across to them.)*
  Why blame the girl? The blame rests on yourselves.
  What grounds were there to think that for your daughter
  A sovereign's hand, the hand of her own King—
ZAVISH.   Sufficient grounds to entertain such thoughts!
  A Merenberg were mad to aim so high;
  But we, descended from imperial Rome,
  From those patricians who subdued the world,
  And, called Orsini now, still stand beside that throne,
  From which Saint Peter's might rules over rulers;
  We may, in truth, reach out for royal crowns,
  And girls, born Rosenberg, can make so bold
  To wed the noblest men our world affords!
  And—ha, ha, ha, ha, ha!
MILOTA. *(Has sat down.)*   Cursed be his laughter!
ZAVISH.   The daughter raves, the father tears his hair,
  And we are mindful of our ancient line!
  And were it older than the angels' fall,
  The King can nod, and crash, it lies in ruin.
BENESH.   Before I fall, revenge! *(Seizes Milota.)*
  Brother, revenge!
MILOTA.   I gave it thought, and now intend to act.
ZAVISH.   Are you roused too, slow-moving Milota?
  Well, then the King must surely shake with fear!
BENESH.   If you—if you refuse us your support,
  You are no Rosenberg; You are a knave!
MILOTA.   Quite so.
ZAVISH.   Well, then? And how shall we proceed?
  Next time at church, crowd close beside the King
  And step upon his toe; how that can hurt!
  And so you are avenged!
BENESH.   He mocks at us?
  My head, my head!—He is no Rosenberg!
MILOTA.   Come, brother, let us go. A man who laughs

When shame is on his house, deserves—
ZAVISH.   Stop, friend!
How comes it that the two of you complain?
When you shout openly your scheme of vengeance
To walls that do not hear—and ears that do!
Forge plans in public places, and rebel at home!
Bright people, Merenberg, you must admit
If drunk with fury or if drunk with wine,
In either case, fresh air provides a cure.
So let us seek the open, worthy sirs.
We may not quench the flames that burn our house,
But we at least can get our fingers warm.
The King, he is my lord, and so hurrah!
MILOTA. *(Approaches him.)*
I wonder, do you tell us all you think.
What do you take us for?
ZAVISH. *(Loudly.)*   Well-meaning folk:
Things one withholds, you nevermore can guess;
And if you guessed, they would not be withheld.
See where the Queen, her door now opened wide,
Steps out. With her, the Lord High Almoner,
The Count of Hapsburg. Let us leave,
Not to intrude upon their hour of prayer.
*(They move away as the Queen comes out of her chamber;
with her is Rudolph of Hapsburg; she is followed by two servants
who are carrying the unconscious form of Berta Rosenberg in a
chair; Lady Elizabeth supports her.)*
MARGARET. *(Enters; turns toward the Rosenbergs as they withdraw.)*
They draw away; like lowering thunder-clouds,
Which after bursting, seek the rising sun.
(Turns toward Berta.)
See she is taken home and cared for there;
I shall myself come by, once I am free.
RUDOLPH.   Too much concern almost, your Majesty.
*(Berta, surrounded by her relatives, is borne away. The two
Merenbergs also leave the stage.)*
MARGARET.   She is not bad herself, but slow of wit.
And vain beyond belief, and so misled.
Her cousins, though, those relatives of hers,
Huge stubborn Milota, explosive Benesh
And Zavish, most contemptible of all,
With talk of riches, power, the very throne—

Their proud ambition craved no less than that—
They led the poor distracted girl astray.
For long I watched, as stealthily those three,
Bad angels of my Lord, the King, had worked
At loosening those bonds, already weak,
Which still kept Ottocar attached to me.
I heard them nourishing his wish for heirs.
Sons born of him to follow on the throne.
As with feigned sympathy they led him on.—
A wish one may well pardon in a King!
What good, though, is a birthright sprung from wrong?
They were the ones who worked unceasingly,
Almost without the sanction of the King,
To have this marriage speedily annulled;
For one of their own house, they fondly hoped,
To seat upon Bohemia's royal throne:
This poor thing, tortured by a mind deranged.
I often watched her at affairs of state,
Decked out in style, as courtiers crowded round,
While I was left alone with my despair.
The King had eyes for nothing but her charm,
And ears for what she wished; his mouth's command
Was changed for her to gentle flattery.
She, gay and proud, with happy smiles of bliss,
Perhaps with some contempt, looked down on me.
My heart felt pity for the hapless victim,
And I resolved, upon her fall from grace,
To be of help and generous in her need.
O Ottocar, how great the guilt you bear!

RUDOLPH.   Do not forget, because of wrongs done her,
The greater wrong inflicted on yourself.

MARGARET.   Do not believe that I excuse the King;
May I stay far from ever praising wrong!
His actions are improper and unjust,
And I will so inform him, when we meet.
I am not young nor did I make believe.
That grief effaced what charm my features had,
He must have seen before he sought my hand.
He may deplore my lack of cheer and jest;
But why did one so cheerful come to woo
The ill-starred, melancholy queen of tears,
Crushed to the grave by loss of those she loved?

Since with these eyes I saw him dead
In that Apulian prison's dreary walls,
Saw him, my husband Henry, King of Rome,
Hard-hearted Frederick's all too gentle son,
Where he lay slain by hands of his own kin,
And dead both sons that were our only hope,
Whom I had borne before my womb was closed,
Since then, no joy but shuns my barren breast,
And smiles have fled in terror from these lips,
Upon which grief and pain have placed their seal.

What reasons are alleged to break our bond?
I know the first: I have not borne an heir,
And am not like to bear another child;
I will not, even though it be, I could!
That Ottocar knew well before we wed.
I told him so and he seemed in accord;
My Austrian inheritance it was
On which he fixed his greedy eye, both he
And his land-hungry father, Wenzeslav.
What does the King demand? Some children, heirs?
A foundling would be better on the throne,
Than royal sons whom wrong had brought to birth.

What further reasons are advanced, what more?
RUDOLPH.   You are related; much too close of kin.
MARGARET.   I did hear tell, when I was still a child,
About some Bela; yes, a Geysa, too,
Two brothers who had daughters that were wed,
One with an Austrian, one with a Czech,
In days of long ago. The King but jests!
The royal houses all are close akin
And dispensations easily procured.
Nor was such mention made, when we were wed.
RUDOLPH.   Now opportunely recollection comes.
MARGARET.   Do not believe that I am loath to leave,
That I regret the honors of the court.
If only at this moment I might go,
All regal pomp and glory left behind,
Go straight to Haimburg, my ancestral home,
There, where I stayed upon my husband's death,

And wept to think of him and our dead sons;
If but the King would send me off today,
I should owe thanks I never owed before.
Our marriage vows I bid him not to touch,
And not to soil the bonds that made us one,
And so make of the years we lately passed
A grievous memory and an offense!

I never wished nor sought to wear the crown.
In Haimburg, troubled as I was with grief,
I scarcely heard the misery round about,
Where fire and pillage laid my country waste.
Hungarians here, Bavarians there, and Czechs,
These ravaged Austria with ruthless sword,
Destroying all my family's proud domains.
They then convened, the Lords at Triebensee,
Considering what man to put in charge;
Their messengers they sent to Saxon lands,
To get a prince from there, Constantia's son,
Who had been born a Babenberg, like me.
The messengers were captured by the King,
Who ruled Bohemia then, called Wenzeslav,
The Wily; he began, and never ceased
His threats, requests, his promises and presents
Until his son, until this Ottocar,
Was chosen by the Lords to rule the land.
One man agreed, another not; anew
Came war with hotter flames to scorch my earth.
Then in my Castle Haimburg there appeared
My country's Lords, complaining of their need;
One cure they mentioned as the only one:
To give the mightiest my added might,
By marrying this Ottocar to me,
So making Austria and Bohemia one.
I answered: No, remembering the faith
I owed my husband, lying in his grave.
They led me to my castle's battlements,
And bade me look upon my charred domain;
The barren fields, the vanished homes, their owners dead.
Dense throngs of women, children, bleeding, bruised,
Surged round as, horror-struck, I heard their cries,
Entreating me to save them, for I could.

I would have risked my all, and so I promised.
Soon after they brought Ottocar to me,
The man whom I was destined soon to wed.
His black eyes peering out from blackest brows,
He stood, reflecting and abashed, apart,
A lad, appraising me, already old.
I, ever mindful of my country's woes,
Walked up to him and spoke in friendly terms;
So I became his wife. I never loved him, no;
Nor did I ever wonder if I could.
I served him quietly, and as I served,
A feeling came to birth within my breast,
That knows the anguish love can bring, but not
The happiness of love. Such was our life.
Judge for yourself if leaving frightens me.
Yes, I shall leave; our marriage, though, must stand.
No grounds exist that it should be dissolved.

RUDOLPH. They argue one point more : that you at Trier,
King Henry, he, your husband, having died,
Vowed solemnly that you would never wed again.—
Mere rumor, I suppose.

MARGARET. No; it is true.
It was no solemn vow; at least not one
The Church could use to call our marriage void;
And yet I made a promise—one I should have kept!

At Trier I lay before our God in prayer,
And faith forever, lasting widowhood
I promised him, King Henry, then deceased.
I vowed no hand of man should ever touch
A finger of my own, my garment's hem,
Nor even woman ever kiss the lips,
That once had been my husband's very own.
Yes, that I vowed, and bade disaster come,
Should ever I forget, upon my head.
Disaster, I now see, does what was asked.—
Let me repeat, it was no solemn vow;
A promise made to me and Henry's spirit,
And yet a promise; one I should have kept!

RUDOLPH. What word, my Lady, shall I take the King?

MARGARET. How quick we are to criticize in others
What we, in lesser measure, do ourselves!

Lord Duke of Hapsburg, tell King Ottocar,
The matter I leave wholly to his conscience;
I give assent to what he may decide.

RUDOLPH. You will agree, then?

MARGARET. I will not protest.

RUDOLPH. But they intend to ask that you concede.
The lands of Austria and Styria,
Your family's domain.

MARGARET. I have so done.

RUDOLPH. The marriage contract had it so arranged,
Now, with that bond dissolved, the deed is void.

MARGARET. I can again affirm it.

RUDOLPH. Keep in mind,
Those lands are both imperial fiefs,
The Empire's own, and so not yours to give.

MARGARET. I will surrender what by right is mine.
So tell the King, and tell him too:
He should beware of doing what is wrong;
No misdeed goes unpunished. So fare well.

(Trumpets and noise in the street. Enter the elder Merenberg.)

MERENBERG. The King!

MARGARET. O God in Heaven—I shall go
To seek new strength to bear me up through prayer.

(Dismisses the two men with a gesture and goes to her chamber. Exeunt Rudolph and Merenberg, left.)

(Throne room with Gothic arches and columns; throne halfway back, right. In the foreground on each side, a table with rich covering, and an armchair. Martial music, blaring of trumpets, and cheers of the populace outside. Enter Bohemian magnates and knights, rear. They arrange themselves in rows, some beside the throne and some opposite it. Left, forward, a deputation of the City of Prague, the Burgomaster at its head. Rear center, a group of Tartar envoys. Enter the Chancellor.)

CHANCELLOR. The King, the King!

ALL. Long live King Ottocar!

OTTOCAR. *(Enters hastily at the rear. He is in full armor but without his helmet.)*
My thanks to you, good sirs.

(Pauses before the Tartar envoys who have knelt.)
Who are these men?

CHANCELLOR.   Sire, envoys of the Khan of Tartary;
    He greets you and makes offer of alliance.
OTTOCAR.   Bid them stand up!—You hear? Up from the floor!
    Strange people, I must say, and no less strange their arms.
    Show me your sabre. *(Takes it and tests its balance.)*
    Much too sharply curved.
    (Swings it once in the air.)
    That robs the blow of force. That should be changed.
    A curved blade has its uses, but the weight
    Should balance near the point. One man of mine,
    Flat sword in hand, could deal with ten of you.
    Returns the sabre.)
    What of your other arms? That hank of hair,
    What purpose does it serve? To aid your foe,
    So he can seize you, drag you from your horse,
    And carry off your scalp. Were I their king,
    Their heads would all be shaved within the hour.
    Tell them to go and come again tomorrow.
    (Exeunt tartars.)
OTTOCAR. *(Comes forward.)* Well, gentlemen, we trust you are content.
    The Magyars will no more disturb your rest;
    We chased them out.—And now, what is there else?
    (To the deputation of the City of Prague who have come forward.)
    And who are you?
BURGOMASTER.   The Council, Sire, and Mayor.
    Of your devoted, loyal town of Prague.
OTTOCAR.   What do you want?—Ah!
    (Throws himself in an arm-chair, left front.)
    Gentlemen, speak up!
    (To the servants.)
    I am fatigued; do get this armor off.
    (Two servants set to work to remove his armor.)
BURGOMASTER.   Most high, invincible and mighty King!
    Fame spreads the aura of your victory,
    And—
OTTOCAR.   Fuellenstein!
FUELLENSTEIN. *(Comes forward.)*   My lord, at your command!
OTTOCAR.   Where was it we dispersed the Magyar force?
FUELLENSTEIN.   At Croissenbrunn.
OTTOCAR.   Tom Fool, that was our camp!
    Think you, I have forgot where we encamped?
    I mean where last our horsemen made the charge
    That won the day?

FUELLENSTEIN.   They call the place Marchegg:
    The river March there makes an edge-like turn.
OTTOCAR.   Marchegg, so will I have the city called
    That I shall build to mark our victory.
    Marchegg shall be the landmark of my fortune;
    From then on forward; who can hold me back?
    And all who later happen on this town,
    Shall tell how Ottocar here won renown.
    (Has arisen; to the servants.)
    Why such delay?—Ah, yes; now comes the leg.
    (Sits down again.)
    You Burgomaster, lend a hand and pull;
    Not that way, no! Why hesitate so long?
    (Rips the greave off and throws it into the center of the room.)
    Right at the river's bend, across it, on a hill
    King Bela sat, perched high upon a knoll
    With Heinrich Preussel near, as I could see;
    He would explain, as in a puppet play,
    The battle-field, the way the fighting went,
    The changing sides, which troops were which, and so on.
    At first success seemed sure; but then when Hapsburg
    Charged of a sudden with his heavy horse,
    And all who cursed in Magyar turned to flee
    And floundered in the March, their matted beards,
    Protruding much like reeds in stagnant water—
    Where is this Hapsburg? He, good God above,
    How he did fight! A modest fellow, really,
    But when he charges, Devil is his name.
    Where is Count Hapsburg?
SERVANT.   Shall we summon him?
OTTOCAR.   Pray, do not!—When King Bela saw the rout,
    He did not need an expert to explain.
    He raised his hands and wildly clutched his hair,
    At war with his own self. Old man, thought I,
    You need not trouble; we can do it better.
    But he is now our friend and our ally,
    And so we speak of him in kindest terms.
    Well, are you done at last? *(Arises.)*
    My cloak and hat!
    And what has been accomplished, Burgomaster?
    Or have you been asleep?
    This hat is tight!

(To a servant who is at a loss what to do.)

Damn you, another hat!—Well, out with it!
The wall upon the Visherad is built?
BURGOMASTER. It is.
OTTOCAR. The bridge across the Moldau, too?
BURGOMASTER. The last stone yesterday was put in place.
OTTOCAR. Yes, since you knew I would be here today.
And have you, for those Germans that I sent,
Made room by clearing out the lower town?
BURGOMASTER. Your pardon—
OTTOCAR. Is it done?
BURGOMASTER. Your Highness—
OTTOCAR. Well?
BURGOMASTER. Not yet.
OTTOCAR. Why not? In Heaven's name, why not?
BURGOMASTER. We wished to ask your Highness once again,
Before so many loyal Czechs were driven—
OTTOCAR. What, driven! Who said drive? Why, no such thing!
I said to send them to Chrudim, where fields
And building-sites, three-fold, had been reserved,
And three-fold payment promised for the move.
But they shall leave the quarter where they are.
They shall, they must! You hear me, must! Good God!
I know what you Bohemians prefer:
To squat in corners, heaped with age-old trash,
Where light can scarcely pierce the clouded panes,
Consuming what the day before has sown,
And reaping what tomorrow will consume,
On Sundays, feasts; at Kermis, dancing brawls,
For other things both deaf and blind;
So you would do; I would not have it so.
For as one takes the drowning by the hair,
I shall at your most tender spot take you:
The Germans I shall set upon your heels,
To snap at you, until the pain and rage
Will rouse your sluggish limbs, and you will jump,
As horses do when spurred. You dream of times,
When princes of your land crouched at the hearth,
And wore a kettle on their shameful coat of arms;
I am not one of them, God knows!

(Shows the cloak the servants have put over his shoulders.)

See here!
In Augsburg cloaks like this are made and sold.
The velvet, gold, the needlework, the cut;
Can you in this your land produce the like?
You shall, by God, you shall! And I will teach you!—
With London, Paris, Vienna and Cologne,
This Prague of yours shall stand as proud as they,
The lands that once looked down on you with scorn,
I have laid low and humbled with my sword:
The Magyar flees, Bavaria is tamed,
And Austria, stout-hearted Styria,
The Adriatic lands and German soil,
All these have I united in my realm.
To distant parts I bore Bohemia's name;
From distant parts her glory echoes back.
I might have slept in peace as did my fathers,
And let you sleep the way your fathers did:
Whom have I done this for? For you!
Now you must do your part, I pledge my word.
I dragged you half-way up the mountain side;
Now climb the other half or break your necks.
(Turns away from them.)
See that the Germans settle where I said!

(The Chancellor enters and approaches the King.)

OTTOCAR.   Who comes?
CHANCELLOR.   The Queen as you commanded, Sire.
OTTOCAR. *(Turns back again to the burghers.)*
And also this, this too, on your account.
What is the dearest thing to every man,
Accord and peace at home, I have disturbed,
To give you peace and give your children peace.
Lest I should die and leave no heir behind,
And civil strife undo what I have done,
I have put Margaret, my wife, aside,
Who has no hope of giving me an heir,
And entered on a union that is new.
(Turns to the whole assemblage.)
Indeed, my Lords, that you be all informed:
To seal the terms of peace agreed upon,
King Bela offers me his grandchild's hand,
The hand of Cunigunda, only daughter

Of Michael, Lord Duke of Massovia.
Now since for long, the Bishops of the Realm
Condemn my marriage with Queen Margaret;
And other reasons can be urged besides:
First, she is old; yes, old and barren, too,
No hope exists that she will bear a son;
And then she is my kin—I never know
In what degree, or how, and finally—
But why insist on all this one-two-three;
For first and last and always it must be!—
The Queen will come officially to sign the deed
That reaffirms bestowal of her lands;
As witnesses you are assembled here. *(Ascends the throne.)*

CHANCELLOR.   *(Has spread his papers on the table at which the King
has been seated and now advances to the center of the room
holding an official document in his hands.)*
Respect and silence; this the King commands!
*(Queen Margaret, clad in a cloak with a long train and wearing
a crown, enters, extreme front, left. She is escorted by Hapsburg
and Merenberg, and is followed by her ladies-in-waiting.)*

CHANCELLOR.   Illustrious Queen and Lady, Margaret,
Duchess of Austria, of Styria,
Widow of Henry, lately King of Rome,
Now consort of Bohemia's Majesty:
Who serves as spokesman in your royal cause?

MARGARET.   I! *(With a gesture of refusal to Merenberg as he steps
forward.)*
Speak not, Merenberg!—I shall, myself!
Alone to bear the stigma of his wrath,
To speak and suffer as I must, alone.

CHANCELLOR.   You are informed?

MARGARET.   I know.

CHANCELLOR.   Let us proceed.
A holy synod, assembled in Vienna,
With Guido, cardinal-legate, in the chair,
His title from San Lorenzo in Lucina,
Has given judgment on the marriage bond
That joined you to our gracious lord and liege;
Whereas you are, within the fourth degree,
Through Bela, King of Hungary, and Geysa,
Blood brothers, grandsires of the two of you,
To our aforesaid monarch thus akin;

And whereas further, as has come to light,
Upon the death of him you wedded first,
Of Henry, King of Rome, whom all revere,
You swore that you would never wed again;
A vow made at Saint Catherine's in Trier—

MARGARET.   It was no solemn vow.

OTTOCAR.   Here is the proof!
Continue.

CHANCELLOR.   Therefore—
(Blare of trumpets outside.)

OTTOCAR.   What is this?

SERVANT.   The Estates.
Of Austria have come to pay respects;
They bring to you their country's ducal crown.

OTTOCAR.   My welcome. They are witnesses well met.
*(Nobles and Clergy of Austria enter bearing before them the
ducal crown on a cushion.)*

LICHTENSTEIN. *(As spokesman.)*   Your valiant sword, exalted Prince,
has shown,
By putting Magyar forces to defeat,
Who shall be King and rule our fair domain.
The baneful, blood-stained strife is at an end.
And, light of heart, we come again to pay
Our homage, unencumbered now and free.
(Turns to Margaret.)
To you, above all others, gracious Lady,
The noble heir of that heroic line,
That gloriously ruled Austria for long—

OTTOCAR.   Leave off your speech and fall in line to wait.
Old loyalty outweighs oaths sworn anew.
And faith kept once says more than promises twice made.
(To the Chancellor.)
Continue!

CHANCELLOR.   Therefore they have so decreed,
That such a union cannot be upheld;
In fine, they have declared it null and void.

The grants you once bestowed upon your husband,
Together with your family heritage,
Remain in force, and you are hereby charged,
To reaffirm them for the sake of form.
To you will be assigned, as life estate,

The town of Krems and Polan near by Horn
And Grevenberg, by Ottocar, our Liege.
MARGARET.   You reached the end?
CHANCELLOR.   I did, most gracious lady.
MARGARET.   I think of several things I might reply.
OTTOCAR.   But why? The judgment still will hold.
MARGARET.   Yet I submit.
OTTOCAR. *(Descends from the throne.)*   Well then, what is there else?
MARGARET.   And take my leave as it is asked of me—
OTTOCAR. *(Coming up to her.)*   How good to find you reasonable
   and wise;
   So Margaret has always been, I know,
   And always I respected her as such.
   It is not youth's impulsive, wild desire,
   The turbulent and fiery urge for change
   That bids me part from you. It is my land,
   Which weds me, then unweds, weds me again.
   As high as any man can raise his might,
   So high has Ottocar now raised his own.
   Bohemia is mine, Moravia feels my strength;
   Wars won me Austria and Styria,
   My uncle at his death will leave me Carnten.
   (Lowers his voice so that Margaret alone can hear.)
   In nearby Hungary I have a hand,
   The nobles look to me, the discontented;
   Silesia shows good will, and Poland rolls,
   A storm-tossed ship, to safety in my port.
   (Raises his voice again.)
   From Baltic straits to Adriatic shores,
   From sunny Inn to ice-bound Vistula,
   All men must bow to Ottocar's command;
   The world since Charles the Great has never looked
   Upon a realm that could with mine compare.
   Indeed, the crown of Charles himself,
   It seems not for this brow of mine too high.
   One thing alone I lack; one thing yet—all;
   An heir who could receive what I have won.
   I aim to crown the edifice I built;
   Margaret, I know, would wish to grant me this.
MARGARET.   I grant you all; more than I grant myself.
   Nor is it my advantage, rather yours,
   That bids me speak a warning once again.

Shall we withdraw where we can be alone—
OTTOCAR.   Stay here and speak; in company of kings
Your Ottocar remains another king.
These here are subjects—
MARGARET. *(Quickly.)*   They are, sir; but how long?
It is of this my warning words would speak.
(Comes closer to him.)
These very lands, my family's heritage,
Have been conveyed to you by Margaret's hand.
God knows, I gladly leave. But when I leave,
New riots will with hissing torch flare up,
And then your foes—
OTTOCAR.   Are you some baker's wife,
Whose shop came to her foreman whom she wed,
And fear the bailiffs now will come from town,
And dispossess me, once my wife has gone?
(Turns halfway round toward the Austrian estates.)
I hold them, do you see, with this my hand;
I dare them; let them try the slightest move!
MARGARET.   You are beset by evil men and traitors.
OTTOCAR.   Would you teach Ottocar to know his men?
I go my even way; what blocks it, falls.
MARGARET.   You face destruction, hear me, Ottocar!
(Repeated blasts of trumpets.)
SERVANT.   The Styrian estates wait at the door,
And ask for audience, if it should so please.
OTTOCAR.   Bid them come in!—You see now, Margaret,
Your gloomy prophecy is not fulfilled.
(The Styrian Estates enter, preceded by the ducal crown on a cushion.)
SPOKESMAN.   *(Kneels before Margaret.)*   My Lady—
MARGARET. *(Motions him away.)*   Not to me!
OTTOCAR.   To me, good sirs!
The King it is who makes his wife a Queen.
No need to speak; I know why you have come.
I wrested your domain from Magyar hands,
And mean to keep it safe from every one;
Safe, too, from you, should any need arise.
Stand over yonder and await your turn.
You might, before you go, inspect me well,
So next time you will know at once on coming in,
To whom you have to kneel.

(The Styrians take their places in the same row with the Austrians, opposite the throne; those who carry the crown in front.)

OTTOCAR. Now for the last!
You have the pact at hand, Lord Chancellor,
The covenant of gift of Margaret's lands?

CHANCELLOR. Not I. Her Majesty—

OTTOCAR. You have it, Margaret?

MARGARET. I keep it in my chapel in a shrine,
And there locked up.

OTTOCAR. Well then, let someone go.

MARGARET. No eye has ever looked within the shrine,
Nor seen the treasures which its lock protects.
Beside my husband's counterfeit it lies,
Beside the funeral shrouds of my dead sons,
Beside the blood-stained arrowhead that pierced
On River Leitha's shores, my brother's heart.
May I myself not go?

OTTOCAR. As you prefer.

(Trumpets and cheers outside.)

SERVANT. *(Enters.)* Oh sir!

OTTOCAR. What now?

(Enter the Estates of Carinthia, knights and peasants, all together, with the ducal crown before them on a cushion.)

OTTOCAR. Who is it?

MARGARET. Shall I go?

OTTOCAR. I ask you, do.—You see. I am engaged.
What, more crowns still?

(Exit Margaret.)

SERVANT. Most gracious Sire, the King
Of Hungary is here—

OTTOCAR. *(Goes to the men who are carrying the crown.)*
What men are you?

SPOKESMAN. The Duke of Carnten, uncle of your Grace—

OTTOCAR. And has he died?

SPOKESMAN. He has, Your Majesty;
And as the contract with your Grace provides,
His land and ducal crown now go to you.

OTTOCAR. Let those who don't inherit mourn his death!
I bid you welcome, worthy men of Carnten.
Your crown, arrayed beside those others there,
Provides a regal treat to please my eye.

(The Carinthians take their places in a row with the Austrians and Styrians.)

OTTOCAR.   Still shouts persist. Why that?

SERVANT.   Let me repeat:
The King of Hungary has ridden in,
With him are envoys of the Imperial Diet,
Who bear the double eagle held on high
With shouts—

VOICES. *(Outside.)*   Ottocar, the German Emperor!

VOICES. *(Inside the hall.)*   Hail Ottocar, the German Emperor, hail!

OTTOCAR. *(In the foreground.)*   I bid you, Earth, stand fast!
You never yet have borne a greater man!
(Hurries to the rear to welcome the King of Hungary. While Ottocar is so occupied, Merenberg walks over to Bertold Emerberg who is in the extreme foreground, left, the first of the Austrian nobles.)

MERENBERG. *(Whispers.)*   This kerchief hides a letter in its folds;
Convey it to my son. He understands.
I leave for Merenberg. And bid him hasten.
(Drops the handerkerchief and moves away; Emerberg picks it up. Enter the King of Hungary with his retinue and accompanied by Ladislaus and by Cunigunda in a cloak and an Hungarian cap.)

OTTOCAR. *(Goes to welcome him.)*   Illustrious Sire and Father, if God wills!

BELA. *(Steps back.)*   Before I answer, let these men proceed!

(The Embassy of the Imperial Diet moves forward.)

FIRST AMBASSADOR.   The Princes of the Holy Roman Empire,
At Frankfurt met to choose an Emperor,
Send us to you, esteemed Bohemian Prince.
The eyes that seek a man to guide the realm,
As Emperor, have now been turned toward you.
Since it does not befit us to elect,
As liege, a man who might refuse our choice,
We here appear, to ask, exalted King,
If, should the Council offer you the crown,
You would assume the burden of the realm.
Do not refuse! You know the old remark:
The Imperial Eagle must seek the lion's lair,
If he would come to rest. Large-minded lion,
(Seizes a shield with the figure of a lion upon it that stood beside

the steps of the throne, and raises it high in the air.)
Take up the Eagle as it flies forlorn,
And give him shelter from his many foes!
OTTOCAR.   What do I see? Who is it tricks me so?
No, that is not Bohemia's white lion!
This one is red!
RUDOLPH. *(Comes toward the center of the stage from where he has*
been standing beside the throne, right front.)
It's Hapsburg's lion, sir!
The shield is mine. I left it when I came.
SECOND AMBASSADOR.   You are the Count of Hapsburg?
RUDOLPH.   I am he.
SECOND AMBASSADOR.   Why in Bohemia?
RUDOLPH.   Back from the Holy Wars.
OTTOCAR.   Enough!—You wait, my Lord Ambassador,
Until we summon you. *(Turns to King Bela.)*
Most noble Prince,
My duty calls me doubly now to you.
BELA.   Let me present my children; first of all,
Here Ladislaus, my heir on my demise,
And here another.
OTTOCAR.   Do you have, King Bela,
More than the one?
BELA.   You still do not suspect?
(To Cunigunda.)
You are not welcome here.
CUNIGUNDA.   Yet it was I,
Who hoped that I might please you most of all!
Will you make room for me among your troops?

(Throws off her horseman's cloak and Hungarian cap and stands
there, dressed as a woman.)

ZAVISH. *(Stands not far from her, left; loudly.)*
How fair a trooper!
CUNIGUNDA. *(Turns in his direction.)*   Ha, who speaks?
OTTOCAR. *(Angrily.)*   Who speaks?
ZAVISH. *(Also turns to look.)*   It seemed to come from there, from
over there.
CUNIGUNDA. *(Quickly.)*   It was—
not you. Else you had never said
To me, who stood so close, that it was not!

Your Highness will forgive me this surprise.
They wanted me at first to wait outside;
But I wished to be present, so I came.

RUDOLPH. *(Who has taken his old position, right front.)*
What inconsiderate and ruthless haste!
(Queen Margaret returns with the documents.)

OTTOCAR. *(Motions her back.)* Not now!

MARGARET. *(Supports herself by a chair.)* O God! Will none help
me away?

MERENBERG. *(Steps forward.)* The Queen needs help!

OTTOCAR. Who was it summoned you?
Who was it gave you leave to quit your place?
You meddled in our business once before.
Step back! *(Merenberg returns to his place.)*

MARGARET. *(In a faint voice.)* Away from here!—Will no one help?

RUDOLPH. Here is my arm, revered and gracious Queen!
No Hapsburg but gives refuge to the wronged.

OTTOCAR. Who bade you interfere?

RUDOLPH. Does one bid him,
Whom no one can forbid?

OTTOCAR. You are, you know,
In lands I rule.

RUDOLPH. No longer than I wish.
I fought your battles as a volunteer,
Not for rewards, and I refuse your thanks.
I am not bound to you.

OTTOCAR. Stay where you are,
First let him speak who has the right to speak.

SECOND AMBASSADOR. *(Steps forward.)* Then I will give this Princess
my protection,
I, Chancellor of the Archbishop of Mainz,
By him sent with the Electoral Legation,
A silent listener, while others speak.
You still remember me, Count Hapsburg?

RUDOLPH. I?

SECOND AMBASSADOR. Do you recall once in a wood near Basel
A priest, with sacrament in hand, who sought
A sick man's bed and, stopped by raging floods,
Strayed helplessly beside the River Aar,
To whom you gave your horse to ford the stream?

RUDOLPH. That priest?

SECOND AMBASSADOR. And did you, later, not escort

The Archbishop of Mainz upon his way,
Through hostile lands, through wars and flame and death,
As he set out to find the Pope in Rome?
The bishop's clerk, it was, at his request,
Who often did approach and speak with you;
Do you begin to recognize this clerk?

RUDOLPH. You, sir?

SECOND AMBASSADOR. *(Turns to the assembly.)* For her, a Princess
of the Realm,
I ask safe conduct, such as is her due.
Lord Count of Hapsburg, let her have your arm,
She shall be taken where she feels secure.
In the Holy Roman Empire's august name,
Make way for Margaret, Duchess of Austria!
(They escort Queen Margaret out of the hall.)

OTTOCAR. Once I am Emperor, your tone will change!

FIRST AMBASSADOR. Would you now deign to make us answer, sir?

ZAVISH. *(Pushes his way forward.)* And would you rob us of our
King, our liege?
Is he not mighty? Why should he need you?
As God in Heaven, he rules here on earth;
The Empire brings him cares but no rewards.
Leave him and offer Germans what you will.
You give to get returns. Leave us our King!

OTTOCAR. I find some truth in what he says, good sirs.
Much in the Empire needs a guiding hand,
Much stubbornness there is to bend or break;
Your master up to now has been your slave.
But I, I am a rich Bohemian prince, God forbid,
I should become an Emperor in need.
But you can wait in case I be induced
To look with greater favor on your plan.
(Turns to Cunigunda.)
Now I am yours, completely and alone.

ZAVISH. Long live King Ottocar!
(Cheers and blare of trumpets.)

VOICES. *(On all sides.)* Bohemia's King!
The Duke of Austria!
Styria!
Carnten!
Cran!
The German Emperor! Long live Ottocar!
                    (The curtain falls.)

ACT 2

(Verandah with a marble balustrade some three feet high at the back; it is assumed that beyond this balustrade the garden descends in a series of terraces. Front, both sides, doors; and beside them, statues. The main entrance is between the columns at the left side of the balustrade.)

ZAVISH. *(Enters laughing.)*   I am in love! Alas! my heart is lost!
Good people, help! come rescue me! Ha, ha!
What sharp reproof her black eyes shot at me;
Hungarian and proud! To no avail!
And by the God of miracles, how fair!
A full-blood filly, wild and saddle-shy,
That fights the bridle that would hold her in.

All else progresses much as God would wish.
The Austrians deserted to a man,
As soon as Margaret, their Queen, had gone;
One to the right, one left, but every one
To Frankfurt for election time. Well, well!
Of course, to have their wish recorded there,
That Ottocar be chosen after all!
MILOTA. *(Off-stage.)*   In here, for now.
ZAVISH.   Whom do they bring?

(Enter a troop of armed men with a prisoner, Seyfried Merenberg. Milota, in full armor follows; he has a sealed letter in his hand.)
MILOTA.   The King is at the tourney still?
ZAVISH.   He is.
Well, well, Young Merenberg! And so escorted!
MILOTA.   His father, yes, that traitor, sent him off
To take this letter to the Archbishop
Of Mainz. He counselled him to go in haste—
SEYFRIED.   Yes, that he did.
MILOTA.   The young man, none the less,
On finding that his way led past the door,
Where brother Benesh and his daughter dwell,
Wished once again to see his former love;
There he was captured and sent here to us.
ZAVISH.   What? With our pretty cousin? With Fair Berta?
SEYFRIED.   Delirious with fever and half crazed,

They said she was. I only wished to see,
To learn if she still lived, and so I put
My father's head and mine in hostile hands.
Fool that I was! A blind, accursèd fool!

MILOTA. Here is the letter, marked for him of Mainz.

SEYFRIED. Lord Zavish, know, I never cared for you,
I thought you false; yes, false and double-tongued,
Yet father says, I am no judge of men.
Do show how wrong my judgment was of you,
Let us destroy this letter, you and I;
Thereafter do, as you would like, with me.
I also did a favor once for you:
When you, you know, with relatives and friends,
Before the ante-chamber of the Queen,
Let rather curious words escape your lips;
I did not run and give the King the news,
As well I might, perhaps I should have done;
For then I honored still and loved the King,
As consort of the princess we revered,
And as my true and righteous-minded liege.

ZAVISH. Hear that, friend Milota?

MILOTA. Who marks his words?

ZAVISH. The letter is inscribed—*(Reads.)*
To the Archbishop
Of Mainz. Your life is forfeit, good my friend,
Should such a letter ever reach the King.

SEYFRIED. Oh save me, sir!

ZAVISH. Yes, yes, I know.
These people are informed? *(Points to the soldiers.)*

MILOTA. They are, why ask?

ZAVISH. *(Weighs the letter in his hand.)* This letter may hold
little—may hold much.
A poisonous small drop—
(Quickly puts the letter behind his back.)
A sea of doubt.
(Turns toward the guards.)
Go home and give our cousin Benesh greetings.

MILOTA. What would you do?

ZAVISH Be off!
(Exeunt the guards.)

ZAVISH. And you, my friend
What will you give me, should I spare you now?

SEYFRIED. My life—

ZAVISH. Oh that, my friend, keep for yourself.
Would you mind jumping?

MILOTA. Zavish!

ZAVISH. Well, come on!
Here is your letter, take it!
(Leads him to the balustrade.)
Now jump!
(Seyfried leaps from the balustrade.)

MILOTA. You must be mad!

ZAVISH. See how the lad can run!

MILOTA. Pursue him!

ZAVISH. No! You placed your trust in me;
Well, having done so, why distrust me now?
For I know best what should be done, what not;
In time, it may disclose itself to you.
And then—a lad so young, my heart so soft!
Ha, ha!—Speak not, and go! Prospects arise
At which I would not welcome lookers-on.
You gave your word that I might have my way:
Then, go!

MILOTA. *(Turns as he is about to leave.)* You will not see the
tourney out?

ZAVISH. My arms I have already laid aside;
The prize is mine. Now go! The hour has struck,
And like a creditor, demands its due.
(Exit Milota.)

ZAVISH.   I see her coming down the garden path.
One only maiden-in-waiting at her side,
Now quick to work!
*(Turns toward a statue of the Goddess of Love which stands
left front.)*
Chaste Goddess, Thou, of love,
True spouse to that fair God thou has espoused,
I do beseech thee, lend me thy support.
*(Takes from his doublet a sheet of paper, climbs up to the statue
on a ledge of the pedestal and puts the paper under the half-
raised foot of the goddess.)*
This paper keep, until it finds its place.
They come!—I must delay a little!—Now!

(Jumps down and hurries away as if ashamed. At the same moment enter Queen Cunigunda and her lady-in-waiting, left rear.)

CUNIGUNDA. Was that not Rosenberg? The shameless fellow!
  Bid him, come back.

LADY-IN-WAITING. *(Calls into the wings.)* Lord Zavish, will you come?
  The Queen commands you to return. You must!
  (Zavish returns, twisting his cap in embarrassment.)

CUNIGUNDA. I do not know, sir, has my mind been lost,
  Have feverish dreams of late unbalanced me,
  Or are you so completely unashamed,
  So raving mad—No, language lacks the word,
  Derangement it might possibly be called—
  So shamelessly deranged as you pretend?
  The day I came you shouted out aloud—
  Yes, you! I stood three steps away and know it!
  And ever since you challenge me with glances,
  With glances that I choose not to describe;
  My temper seethes, do I but think of them.
  (Comes nearer to him.)
  At dancing, now, when I held out my hand,
  You dared to press it, forward as you are!
  Who am I, sir, and who are you?

ZAVISH. Forgive!

CUNIGUNDA. Do people in your land so treat a queen?
  If I were not too proud to stir to wrath
  My husband in affairs that are my own;
  If here one counted as at home with us,
  Where woman also has a right, a voice,
  The power to carry out what she conceives,
  And where a queen is not plain consort of a king,
  But really rules; you would regret your acts.

ZAVISH. Forgive!

CUNIGUNDA. Forgive! First impudent and bold.
  And now so servile that it sickens me.
  What have you hidden at the statue's base?

ZAVISH. The statue's base? Is something there?

CUNIGUNDA. A paper.

ZAVISH. A paper? So there is!

CUNIGUNDA. *(To lady-in-waiting who obeys.)* Take down the thing.
  What does this writing mean?

ZAVISH. I do not know.

CUNIGUNDA. You put it up yourself.

ZAVISH. I did? Oh, no!

CUNIGUNDA. You did, as I approached.

ZAVISH. I was not here;
    I came from over there.

CUNIGUNDA. In Heaven's name,
    I must be mad; my head is all awhirl.
    Are these things trees, and is this earth and air?
    I saw it plainly, not three steps away,
    When you concealed the paper by the statue.

ZAVISH. If you so say, my most exalted Lady,
    It must be so, though it has never been.

CUNIGUNDA. What does the sheet contain?

ZAVISH. Mere fantasies;
    Outpourings of a poet's fervent heart.

CUNIGUNDA. *(To lady-in-waiting.)*   Bring it! *(Unfolds the paper and
    reads the heading.)*
    "To Her, the Fairest One"
    You devil,
    Take back this witness of your shame-faced folly,
    (Throws the paper at his feet.)
    And should you dare to make one more advance,
    The outrage will be punished by the King.

ZAVISH. *(Picks up the paper and kneels with it before the lady-in-
    waiting.)*
    My lady, know, I serve you as a knight,
    The secret now for long has burned my breast.
    In these bold lines I finally confess,
    I cannot longer live if I am spurned.
    (Rises and leaves.)

CUNIGUNDA. Laugh, I really must at one so mad!

LADY-IN-WAITING. Look, Majesty, before I turn a hand,
    I win myself a knight and troubadour.

CUNIGUNDA. You truly think his words were meant for you?
    He has his shameless eyes on me—the villain!

LADY-IN-WAITING. Yes, gracious Queen, in all Bohemia
    None can compare with Rosenberg, this man
    Called Zavish. How he holds himself, his bearing,
    The many graces of his nobel frame,
    You saw them, Majesty, no less than I:
    In valor, too, heroic enterprise,

He heads all those who bear the name of knight,
In Padua he studied many years,
And he makes rhymes and sings them to the lute.
CUNIGUNDA. So much the worse!
LADY-IN-WAITING.   The worse, Your Majesty?
CUNIGUNDA. At home we pay such players of the lute
  With coins and with contempt.
LADY-IN-WAITING. Not so with us.
  Here many nobles vie with troubadours,
  And Zavish has himself won maidens' hearts
  With songs sung to the music of his lute.
  You soon shall see.
  (Unfolds the paper.)
CUNIGUNDA. *(Has sat down.)*
  He shall be made to pay.
LADY-IN-WAITING. *(Reads.)*
  "To Her, the Fairest one."—My thanks for that.
  O hand of snow—
CUNIGUNDA. 'O hand of snow,' What does that mean?
LADY-IN-WAITING. Snow-white.
CUNIGUNDA. *(Takes off her glove and looks at her hand.)*
  I think he never yet has seen my hand;
  My glove at most.
LADY-IN-WAITING. *(Continues reading.)*
  O hand of snow,
  Yet warm to hold—
  (Cunigunda stamps her foot.)
LADY-IN-WAITING. Your Majesty?
CUNIGUNDA. Read on for all of me;
That is, I mean to say, do as you please.
LADY-IN-WAITING. O hand of snow,
  Yet warm to hold;
  O fiery eyes
  Yet icy cold:
CUNIGUNDA. Would that it were a brand and burned you up;
  Then could I torture him to taste revenge.
LADY-IN-WAITING. Those sweetest lips
  Can harshly chide;
  This breast that breathes
  Is stone inside.
CUNIGUNDA. Be still!

LADY-IN-WAITING.   O eyes, grow warm,
   O breast, be soft,
   O hand—
CUNIGUNDA.   I tell you, you shall hold your tongue!
LADY-IN-WAITING.   Would you deny me pleasure in my conquest?
CUNIGUNDA.   The little fool thinks it was meant for her!
   (Rises.)
   If only I could leave this land again.
   Be with my own, in Hungary, at home!
   There I had worth, was free to stray afield,
   Here, there and yonder, as my fancy chose.
   My agèd father served my beck and call,
   So did the princes, all his retinue,
   And each and every man from far and wide.
   And life there was and fire, warmth and strength!
   Then I was called away to distant Prague:
   A king, who ruled there, was, so people said,
   Still full of force, bound to an older wife.
   Athirst, was he, to have a fiery mate,
   With zest to match his own so zestful breast.
   I come and find—a man grown old; yes, old!
   Is not his hair already grizzled grey?
   They say: the trials of war, but none the less!
   Or is he not short-tempered as with age,
   And domineering, uncontrolled? God knows,
   I cannot sit in silence and obey.
   But all the others flatter, beg and fawn;
   Their blood is slow, their hearts bled white and cold.
   Except this Rosenberg. In Hungary,
   With us, he would have held his head up high,
   Like that intrepid captain of the Cumans,
   Whom he is also like in face and form,
   The first and best of Hungary's strong men!
   But he was brave, a gay and gallant knight,
   Straightforward, open in his aim and acts;
   While this Bohemian creeps on bended knee,
   Degrades himself and sullies all his worth.
   (Sound of trumpets outside.)
CUNIGUNDA.   What noise?
LADY-IN-WAITING.   The tournament is over now,
   And winners will be given their awards.
   The prizes are bestowed by you, the Queen.

CUNIGUNDA. We will be called.—Give me that written page,
  From hearing it, I scarcely caught the sense.
  (Takes the paper.)
LADY-IN-WAITING. My Lady, see, His Majesty draws near,
  With him his court, all those who saw the jousts.
  (Enter Ottocar with Milota and Fuellenstein; behind them are
  knights and ladies coming from the tourney, among them the
  First Imperial Ambassador.)
OTTOCAR. *(To those behind him.)* If he insists upon it, bring him
  here.
  (To Cunigunda as he comes up.)
  The winner of the tournament has said
  He will accept the prize from none but you.
  Well, Gunda, how are you?
  (Starts to stroke her chin, but she steps back.)
CUNIGUNDA. Quite well.
OTTOCAR. Good Lord!
  Ill-tempered, as I live:
  Oh, Milota!
  (Walks with Milota to the other side of the stage, front.)
OTTOCAR. Young Merenberg escaped?
MILOTA. Yes, Sire, he did.
OTTOCAR. Bad luck! How could the letter then be known?
MILOTA. He boasted of it, as young people will;
  Then, too, some claim the letter has been seen.
OTTOCAR. Directed to the Archbishop of Mainz?
MILOTA. To him, they say.
OTTOCAR, So Wolkersdorf has left?
MILOTA. And Hartneid Wildon. All the Austrians,
  Now that Queen Margaret is gone for good,
  Are ill-disposed, and steal away from court.
OTTOCAR. Had I the letter, I should know the traitors,
  Then I could I crush the rabble under foot:
  But now I feel distrust of every one,
  And must keep watching all of them; yes all!
  Suspicion, bloodhound to join your chase?
  (While Ottocar is speaking, Zavish Rosenberg, as winner of the
  tournament, has entered with an escort and stands before the
  King.)
OTTOCAR. And now?—Ah, yes, you won the tournament.
  Your valor has been always known to me;

Go where the Queen will grant you your award.
Oh, Fuellenstein!

FUELLENSTEIN.   My lord, at your command.

OTTOCAR.   Equip some men and post them fully armed
At every doorway leading from the castle;
Then at the time our guests set out for home,
Arrest the persons I shall single out,
And keep them under guard as hostages.
Him now, I do not trust—Nor Lichtenstein,
That crafty Ulrich—

FUELLENSTEIN.   Sir, but Henry, too?

OTTOCAR.   Why shout? Come here and listen while I speak.
*(Withdraws somewhat with Fuellenstein and whispers to him.
While listening to Fuellenstein, Ottocar turns his eyes toward
Zavish and Cunigunda who are talking together. Zavish stands
before the Queen who sits with fixed gaze, lost in thought.)*

LADY-IN-WAITING.   *(Tries to get the Queen's attention.)*   But, madam!

CUNIGUNDA.   *(Notices that Zavish is standing in front of her.)*   What,
you rashly here intrude?
(Springs to her feet.)

LADY-IN-WAITING.   *(Points to the richly embroidered sash which a
page is holding on a cushion.)*
The guerdon, ma'am! *(Cunigunda takes the sash and the page
puts the cushion on the floor at her feet.)*

ZAVISH.   *(To the lady-in-waiting.)*   Do let me have the paper,
I did entrust to you a while ago;
I want it for another's hand.

LADY-IN-WAITBING.   But sir!—

ZAVISH.   Return it! *(Holds out his hands.)*

LADY-IN-WAITING.   Please!

ZAVISH.   *(Still holds his hands out.)*   It was not meant for you!

LADY-IN-WAITING.   I—do not have it!

ZAVISH.   Do not have it?—Good!
Then it has found the hand where it belongs.
(Throws himself on the cushion before the Queen; ardently.)
O Queen, accept a thousand, thousand thanks —
(Slowly.)
For the award you are about to give.

OTTOCAR.   *(Breaks off his conversation.)*
Why not bestow the prize now, Cunigunda?

CUNIGUNDA. *(Offended.)* I started to, before you gave command!
(Approaches Zavish with the sash.)
Sir Knight!
ZAVISH. What favors you bestow, my Queen!
A vassal humbly bows his servile head. *(Whispers.)*
O hand of snow,
Yet warm to hold!
CUNIGUNDA. *(Whispers.)* Be quiet, else—
ZAVISH. *(Aloud.)* Girt with this precious pledge,
Without my armor and without all arms,
I shall crusading traverse sea and earth,
And so proclaim your glory and my King's,
Proclaim them and defend them everywhere;
My life is yours and his!
*(Whispers rapidly as Cunigunda bends over to put the sash
around his neck.)*
Old men like him,
They ought to woo and wed old women. Youth
Belongs to youth! *(Cunigunda throws the sash on the floor.)*
OTTOCAR. *(Calls over to her.)* Are you finished yet?
ZAVISH. *(Whispers.)* The hangman have my head, if you so wish!
OTTOCAR. What now?
ZAVISH. The sash fell down.
CUNIGUNDA. *(To the lady-in-waiting.)* Hand me the sash!
Forbearance finally must reach an end,
Presumption also ought to stay in bounds.
Here is the sash; take it and fare you well.
*(She puts the sash around his neck; as she is bending over him,
Zavish seizes the ribbon on her sleeve. It falls to the ground and
he stoops quickly to pick it up.)*
CUNIGUNDA. My husband, hear! *(Ottocar turns toward her.)*
ZAVISH. *(Rises and withdraws to the center.)*
My King, see to the Queen!
OTTOCAR. Your wish? What is it, Cunigunda?
*(Pause. While it lasts, Cunigunda looks at Zavish who stands
quietly with his eyes fixed straight ahead of him; she gives him
one more glance, then addresses the King.)*
CUNIGUNDA. You planned the hunt at Ribnik for today?
OTTOCAR. Why do you ask? Today, so it was planned.
But you look troubled. What has taken place?
Bestowing prizes seems to tax you so

That in the future you shall be relieved.
(Turns away from her.)

CUNIGUNDA. *(Whispers to the lady-in-waiting.)*
He must give back my ribbon; go, tell him that.
(Ottocar has moved to the center of the hall. The assembly forms a half-circle: the Queen is at the left end, Zavish at the right where he has come to the front in efforts to avoid the lady-in-waiting.)

OTTOCAR.   Which one of you would free me from a care,
A care which, gentlemen, oppresses me?
The Lord of Merenberg, in Styria,
To me has shown himself to be a traitor,
To me and to his country ruled by me.
With letters to the Archbishop of Mainz
He sent his son to Frankfurt days ago;
No doubt to harm my prospects of election,
When they proceed to choose an Emperor,
And to promote sedition, mutiny.
The son, alas, escaped; the father, though,
Shall nevermore evade the penalty,
Nor his accomplices avoid detention.
This miscreant sought refuge in his home,
His castle, well protected from attack;
Whoso will bring him, bring me him alive,
Shall have as his reward the traitor's lands,
All his possessions forfeit by his treason.
Ortolf of Windischgraetz, you seem disposed?

FUELLENSTEIN.   Then let me be the second, gracious Lord.

OTTOCAR.   Among my men you may select the best;
This one—and that—
(Points out certain armed men at the rear.)

LADY-IN-WAITING. *(Reaches Zavish's side after passing behind the others.)*
The Princess is enraged;
She bids me say you must return the ribbon.

ZAVISH.   The ribbon? Now and nevermore, my lass!
I won it fairly, it is mine; my life.
This head I yield, but not the ribbon.
(Takes the ribbon out of his doublet.)
Look you, how fair! Red as your radiant lips,
And white, white, as your silver shoulder.
(Touches her shoulder with his finger.)

No; it is mine to keep, and on my bier
Next shield and helmet it shall proudly lie.
Did I not venture life and blood to have it?
You, blood-red ribbon, I shall have and hold!
(Holds the ribbon aloft.)

CUNIGUNDA. *(At the other side of the stage.)*
But this is madness! Heavens, if the King—!

LADY-IN-WAITING. *(To Zavish.)* The Queen is making signs. Put
it away.
Here comes the King.

OTTOCAR. *(Returns.)* What have you, Rosenberg?

ZAVISH. *(Puts the ribbon in his doublet.)*
I? Nothing, Sire.

OTTOCAR. How?

ZAVISH. Sire, there are things
One rightly hides, and even from the King.

OTTOCAR. A pledge of love?

ZAVISH. A pledge one loves, my lord.

OTTOCAR. *(Studies the Queen for a moment.)*
Who was it helped the Queen today to dress?

LADY-IN-WAITING. I, Majesty.

OTTOCAR. Are you so careless, wench,
That you put bows upon one arm alone,
And leave the other plain?

LADY-IN-WAITING. Most surely—lost!

ZAVISH. *(Bends over as if to look.)*
One must make search.

OTTOCAR. No need of that, Lord Zavish;
It will be easier, with people gone.
I hope to see it though, when evening comes.
To him, who shall have found it, give this ring
(Takes a ring from his finger and gives it to Zavish.)
From her, who is his lady and my wife:
For queens may well give diamonds as gifts,
Not bows, though, from their bodice. You, my Queen,
I pray you take more care another time,
(To Zavish.)
Do not forget the message for the finder.

CUNIGUNDA. From me and in my name, however, tell him:
That he may keep whatever he has found;
For what I give, a diamond or a bow,
In that I give it, undergoes a change,

And is, and stays, a present from the Queen,
And let him also understand my right
To give what I desire, though it be more
Than ribbons, more than diamonds and gold.
(Exit.)

OTTOCAR. *(Walks up and down once or twice and then halts in front of Rosenberg.)*
Explain this, Rosenberg.

ZAVISH. *(Sinks on one knee.)*   Is my King angry?

OTTOCAR. *(Looks at him steadily.)*
Could you be fool enough to draw my wrath,
The wrath of Ottocar upon your head
For idle fancy, nothing but a whim?
Who are you, that you foolishly would dare?
I need but breathe—and where was Rosenberg?
I never thought you slow of wit—Get up!

ZAVISH.   Not if you harbor wrath.

OTTOCAR.   I say: Arise!
(Zavish rises.)

OTTOCAR. *(To a servant who obeys.)*
Will you seek out my wife and say to her:
That as the hostess she should not deprive
Our guests of pleasure by continued absence.—
You, Ortolf, get the preparations made
You promised; your reward I guarantee.—
What fools to have the Empire interfere!
(Strikes his breast.)
Here is the Empire!

SERVANT. *(Returns.)*   The Queen is indisposed.

OTTOCAR.   Oh, such an illness can be quickly cured:
Go back again and beg her to return.
(Exit servant.)

OTTOCAR.   Now, gentlemen, come join me in the hall
And there let dance and feasting be resumed
That revelry hold sway till morning dawns.
(To Fuellenstein.)
Do not forget my orders.

FUELLENSTEIN.   Never fear.
(Enter Servant.)

OTTOCAR.   Well, will the Queen appear?

SERVANT.   She will not, Sire.

OTTOCAR. She will not, will not, when I say she shall?
  Tell her—But no. She will herself reflect:
  Treat women's whims with patience and with time.
  I pray you, gentlemen!
FIRST AMBASSADOR. My Lord and King!
OTTOCAR. How now, Ambassador! You still are here?
FIRST AMBASSADOR. Still waiting for an answer, if you please.
  To those who sent me, to the Prince Electors
  Of the Holy Roman Empire.
OTTOCAR. Gracious Sir,
  An answer cannot easily be made.
  I am a monarch over many lands.
  Too many almost for one man alone.
  You seek to load me with another care,
  Care for another land, a land besides,
  That means to share the rule and council seat.
  But I am used, when I have once said: yes!
  Tho have him lose his head who dares say: no!
  What have you after all to give your Prince?
  Your revenues and custom dues are pledged;
  And what the Emperor had, with thieving hands,
  In that long interregnum, these, then those
  Took for themselves, dividing up the loot.
  Am I to risk my rich inheritance,
  Its life-blood, in so hazardous a game?
  It would no doubt be pleasant, if you could,
  With what I have, assuage your crying needs;
  But I would rather stay here in Bohemia
  And laugh that German Emperors are poor.
  Than be an Emperor and poor, myself.
  Not that I would disdain the chance to crown
  The highest power with this, the highest honor,
  To sit upon the throne of Charles the Great,
  A second Charles, and wield imperial sway:
  But they must first themselves bring me the crown,
  And place it on the cushion at my side,
  Before I shall decide what is to be.

  I sent my chancellor, Lord Braun of Olmuetz,
  To Frankfurt where the Diet has convened,
  And see, he writes me *(Produces the letter.)* that before too long
  We shall have news. The Palsgrave of the Rhine

Will be the man who casts the vote for all.
He is no friend of mine; he and that man
From Mainz intrigue, my Chancellor reports;
These German princes, though, will never risk
A frown upon the brow of Ottocar.
The crown is mine, provided I accept.
But first it must be here, then I shall speak.

SERVANT. *(Enters.)* The chancellor, Lord Braun of Olmuetz, Sire.

OTTOCAR. You see, he has returned.

SERVANT. With him a knight
In shining armor, such as princes wear,
Two heralds also, black and red and gold,
An eagle on their coats, who sound their horns.
(Sound of trumpets outside.)

ZAVISH. Permit us, Sire, our King and Emperor,
To be the first of your new servitors—
(The whole assemblage starts to move toward Ottocar.)

OTTOCAR. Stand back! The Diet's messenger might think
The news he brings comes as a great surprise.
Nor do you know as yet if I accept.
(To the Ambassadors as they start to withdraw.)
Why go away? You have not been dismissed!
There is no need to interrupt our plans.
That bishop, he of Mainz, had best beware;
Once I am on the Rhine, and that is soon,
In payment for his many crafty moves,
I shall have him removed and driven out.
*(The Chancellor has entered meanwhile. All surround him with
questioning gestures. He remains far back, wringing his hands.)*

OTTOCAR. *(As before.)* The Rhenish Palsgrave too, is not my man;
His office I shall give his closest kin.
And I will rid your land of other things,
And all of those whose names are mentioned here—

ZAVISH. *(At rear: excitedly, but not too loudly.)*
You mean they did not vote for Ottocar?
(The Chancellor, his hands folded, shakes his head.)

ZAVISH For whom, then, else?

CHANCELLOR. For Rudolph, Count of Hapsburg.

OTTOCAR. *(Meanwhile has been showing the Ambassador the letter,
pointing to several passages.)*
All these must go—He, too!—

(At the Chancellor's first speech he listens in keenest suspense but without changing his position, to what is being said behind him. When the Chancellor pronounces the name of Hapsburg, Ottocar starts up suddenly; the hand with which he had been pointing to the letter, begins to tremble; he stammers a few further words.)

OTTOCAR.   And he—must go!

(The hand which holds the letter sinks; he stands with trembling knees for a moment longer, his eyes staring into the distance, then pulls himself together and walks with firm tread to his chamber.)

ZAVISH.   But Chancellor, say, is it really true?

CHANCELLOR.   Yes, all too true; Hapsburg is Emperor.

ZAVISH.   How did it happen?

CHANCELLOR.   Things were going well,
Most of the Princes voting for the King,
When suddenly appeared the Chancellor
Of the Archbishop of Mainz—he who was here—
With him one Wolkersdorf from Austria
And Hartneid Wildon, he a Styrian.
They brought complaints—But hush, the King returns.

OTTOCAR. *(Enters from his chamber.)*
Go tell my wife to hold herself prepared;
I plan to hunt before the evening falls.
(Walks up and down with heavy tread.)

CHANCELLOR. *(After a pause.)*   Your Majesty!

OTTOCAR. *(Startled.)*   Yes? You?—And were you here
A moment since?

CHANCELLOR.   Ah, yes.

OTTOCAR.   And did you speak?

CHANCELLOR.   I did, Sire.

OTTOCAR.   Damn!
(Throws his glove in the Chancellor's face; then leads him by the hand to the front of the stage.)
What was that crazy talk
Of Diet and of votes?

CHANCELLOR.   Hear for yourself!
(Enter the Burgrave of Nuremberg preceded by two heralds and followed by his retinue.)

OTTOCAR. *(Advances with heavy step as far as the center of the hall to meet him.)*
And who are you?

BURGRAVE.   Frederick of Zollern, sir.
Burgrave of Nuremberg, sent by the Emperor.

OTTOCAR. God speed you!
(Turns his back on him and comes forward again.)
BURGRAVE. Rudolph, Emperor by God's grace—
OTTOCAR. It seems the Empire would make sport of me;
    Here stand the envoys still who had arrived
    To offer me the crown, and you elect
    Another man before I answer?
BURGRAVE. The Chancellor of the Archbishop of Mainz
    Brought back report with what unseemly words
    You had rejected both the crown and realm.
OTTOCAR. A brazen breach of faith by German barons!
BURGRAVE. You charge the German princes broke their faith?
    Let me explain what turned their choice from you :
    We sought a gracious lord who would be just,
    And offered you the crown as such a man.
    Then came the word, then witnesses arrived.
    Who poured complaints in the Electors' ears
    Of wrongs inflicted on Queen Margaret,
    Your lawful wedded wife whom you cast off;
    How you curtail the rights of lands which you
    Control and have unrightfully withheld;
    How your disfavor costs a person's neck;
    And men get punishment but not a trial.
    Such ways displease in Swabia and on the Rhine;
    The Prince we choose must be a gracious man,
    And in addition we would have him just.
    With this in mind, they moved to cast their votes—
LICHTENSTEIN. *(Behind the scene.)*
    We are betrayed!
OTTOCAR. Who calls us?
    (Murmurs among the assembled company.)
    Lichtenstein?
LICHTENSTEIN. *(Enters and comes forward.)*
    Those who are Austrian had best beware!
    For castle bailiffs stand at every gate,
    And challenge all except Bohemians.
FUELLENSTEIN. *(Enters after him with drawn sword.)*
    Lay down your arms!
OTTOCAR. *(Comes forward.)* Give me your weapons, Henry.
    You Ulrich Lichtenstein, Count Bernhard Pfannberg,
    Chol Seldenhoven, Wulfing Stubenberg,
    Surrender first your swords and then yourselves.

LICHENSTEIN. What have we done?

OTTOCAR. So you do nothing, friend,
I hold you fast. So you do not escape
To join the newly risen Majesty,
Like Wolkersdorf and Wildon, those two traitors,
And Merenberg—*(Stamps his foot.)*
Who gets me Merenberg?
Once we have dragged him from his craggy nest,
The judges shall confront you, each with all,
And lucky he, who has no guilt to fear.
(Turning to Zollern.)
And now let us continue our concern.
(The hostages are led off.)

BURGRAVE. This scene spares me the need of explanation
Why you, my Lord, were not the princes' choice.
And now my message for Bohemia's King:
Rudolph, by grace of God the German Emperor,
Enjoins you soon to come to Nuremberg
To do cup-bearer's service for a day—
Your office as Elector of the Empire—
And there receive investment with the fiefs,
Bohemia and Moravia, yours by right.

OTTOCAR. How so? No more? And Austria, Styria?

BURGRAVE. And Austria and Styria, Carnten and Cran.
With Eger, Portenau, the Wendish March,
You shall surrender to the Emperor,
As lands now wrongfully withheld from him.

OTTOCAR. Ha, ha, ha! A merry tale, indeed!
And he, the Emperor, asks nothing more?

BURGRAVE. The Empire's lands alone.

OTTOCAR. But they are mine!
Styria I won from Hungary in battle,
With blood, my own, and my Bohemians' blood;
Carnten I hold as heritage from my uncle
By wills we made for mutual exchange;
And Austria was dowry brought to me,
When Margaret became my wife and queen.

BURGRAVE. But where is Margaret now?

OTTOCAR. Although we parted,
She reaffirmed bestowal of her lands;
And everything is mine that then was hers.

BURGRAVE. The fiefs of Austria and Styria,

Pursuant to the Emperor Frederick's grant,
May rightly fall to the last tenant's daughter,
But not his sisters; and Margaret is sister
To Frederick, the Duke of Babenberg,
Who died, last of his line, without an heir.
Imperial fiefs are not passed on to heirs,
And by no marriage may they be transferred;
Give back, therefore, imperial lands you hold.

OTTOCAR.   I can believe, he would be quite content,
Your new-made liege, were I to send to him,
In Swabia, these rich domains to swell
His empty purse and fill his pauper's hands;
He hopes in vain. I am now old enough
To realize which side is profit, which is loss.
So get you gone and tell the German Empire,—
A German Emperor I do not know—
That many a crow shall stuff his crop, before
They get what is Bohemia's and mine.
He bids me come to him? Well, I shall come,
And bring along some guests to join the dance,
Whose stamping feet will shake the very earth,
For miles around up to the River Rhine.
So fare you well and tell your master that.
(Exit Burgrave.)

ZAVISH.   And we meanwhile will buckle on our arms,
To fight for life and limb for our great King.
(Exit; the others start to follow.)

OTTOCAR.   Halt, You! For what? For whom? Against what foe?
Throughout the land you are to go and come,
As though deep peace prevailed. When comes the time,
I shall myself decide what guests to choose.

Now, come with me. This new impoverished king
Shall not protect a single doe from death!
We go to Ribnik for tomorrow's hunt.
You all must come. Be merry and rejoice!
Bring lights, for it grows dark. Bring torches here!
Come, follow me! The hunt is on! Away!
(Exit; the rest follow tumultuously.)
(It grows darker. A short pause. Then the notes of a zither are heard.)

LADY-IN-WAITING. *(Enters through the door leading to the Queen's chamber.)*
Now, they are gone! Who plays the lute, I wonder.
CUNIGUNDA. What sounds? Who plays?
LADY-IN-WAITING. *(On the balcony.)* I cannot say, my Lady.
Hark! Words? 'O hand like snow yet warm to hold!'
It is Lord Zavish Rosenberg. He sings.
Shall I tell him to go?
CUNIGUNDA. *(Seated.)* No need of that.
I find it pleasant in the cool of evening.
(Rests her head on her hand, lost in revery.)

(The curtain falls.)

ACT 3

(Hall in Merenberg's castle in Styria. The elder Merenberg stands at the open window, his cap in his folded hands.)

MERENBERG. See where the sun arises. Thanks, O God,
An old man's thanks for yet another day,
And for the day Thou hast vouchsafed our land,
When Thou didst summon from the dark abyss,
The smiling rays of Hapsburg's radiant sun,
That once more makes our trampled meadows green,
And once more mild the penetrating air.
Oh, grant that we, the Germans most removed,
Partake of bliss our countrymen enjoy;
That all those Austrian by birth and name,
Freed from a foreign tyrant's harsh constraint,
Return like brothers to their parents' house,
Watched by one father's all-embracing care.
Amen, so be it!—Yes, who knocks?
LADY MERENBERG. *(Outside.)* I, Father.
MERENBERG. Well, then, come in!
LADY MERENBERG. *(Enters with food and wine.)*
I bring your morning meal.
MERENBERG. Do put it down. What voices in the court?
LADY MERENBERG. Two horsemen, asking after you.
MERENBERG. Well, then,
Why were they not brought up?

LADY MERENBERG. I thought—

MERENBERG. Yes, what?

Am I at feud with any of my neighbors?
Is Merenberg not loved by those close by,
That I should fear two horsemen who arrive?
Who knows what news of import they may bring;
News of my son, perhaps. Go, show them up.
(Exit Lady Merenberg.)
I should, moreover, seem to be suspicious,
Were I to close my doors to news and guests;
Though, to be sure, the evil times today
Urge caution, even justify distrust;
Yet I have twenty sturdy guards below.
(Herbott Fuellenstein and Ortolf Windischgraetz enter, led by Lady Merenberg. They are both armed and have their visors closed.)

MERENBERG. Good morrow, gentlemen! Wife, bring more wine!
(Exit Lady Merenberg.)
What brings you here to me. Before you speak,
Be seated, pray, and share this food with me;
That is our custom here in Styria. *(They sit down.)*
You would not care to put your helmets off? *(Both shake their heads.)*
A vow, perhaps, forbids?—But as you please.
You wish to join the army of the King,
King Ottocar?—His camp is by the Danube,
A goodly stretch away, not far from Tulln,
The left bank of the river, I am told.
And Emperor Rudolph—Hapsburg, I mean to say—
Hopes to besiege Vienna from the right.
To cross the stream seems venturesome to both.
But you refuse to speak, refuse to eat!
(Fuellenstein and Windischgraetz rise to their feet.)

FUELLENSTEIN AND WINDISCHGRAETZ. We don't break bread with traitors!

MERENBERG. *(Leaps up.)* Take that back!

FUELLENSTEIN. *(Draws his sword, takes his stand before the door, and opens his visor.)*
You know me now?

MERENBERG. Herbott of Fuellenstein.
The other knight opens his visor.)
And Ortolf Windischgraetz!—Why are you here?

(Ortolf steps to the window and sounds his horn.)

FUELLENSTEIN. In the name of Ottocar, our King, I take
You into custody, charged with high treason.

MERENBERG. How so?

FUELLENSTEIN. Did you not send your son to bring
Complaints before the Princes and the Empire?

MERENBERG. The careless fellow; caught!—No, not complaints,
Requests, they were, to help Queen Margaret
To hold what should be hers by right of birth.

FUELLENSTEIN. But is your son not serving with the Emperor?

MERENBERG. I am undone!

FUELLENSTEIN. Yes, that you are! Now follow!

MERENBERG. Where to?

FUELLENSTEIN. Where you will be so close confined
That every intrigue will be strangled dead.

SQUIRE. *(Outside.)* Let me come in!

FUELLENSTEIN. You, Ortolf, guard the door.

SQUIRE. *(Outside.)* For God's sake, let me in!

WINDISCHGRAETZ. It is your squire,
That young Bohemian boy!

FUELLENSTEIN. What can he want?

(Windischgraetz opens the door.)

SQUIRE. *(Enters.)* Imperial troops have been reported near.

FUELLENSTEIN. Damnation!

SQUIRE. They have taken Graz, it seems.
Have captured Milota, the governor,
And occupy the land in Rudolph's name.

FUELLENSTEIN. How can this be?

SQUIRE. They further say that Meinhard,
The Count of Goerz, has joined the German side
And devastates the land with fire and sword.

MERENBERG. Thank God for that!

FUELLENSTEIN. It shall not help you, sir!
Away with him! See that your naked swords
Point at his breast and if his courtyard guards
Dare lift a finger, strike him down at once.
I know the way about here; let me lead you.

MERENBERG. *(As he is led off.)*
My son is free, the Queen with friends abides;
And as for me, why care? The Lord provides.

(Exeunt all.)

*(Bohemian camp on the left bank of the Danube. The king's
tent; a table with a map of the locality, in the foreground.
Enter Ottocar, the Chancellor, and several others.)*

OTTOCAR. *(As he enters to his companions.)*
 If he deserted, have the rascal hanged.
 If thieves must hang, then surely he; Good God!
 I find a coward worse than any thief.
 (Comes forward, the Chancellor following him.)
 You dog my every step, Lord Chancellor?
CHANCELLOR. Yes, every step, my master and my King,
 Till you give heed and grant me a reply.
 Sire, our state is bad!
OTTOCAR. *(Paces up and down.)* Our state is good!
CHANCELLOR. Is good,
 When sickness and when want prevail in camp?
OTTOCAR. The sickness fear; the want, a lack of courage,
 But only with a few of us, I hope,
 And of those very few one hangs outside!
 Is this a time for sickness, or for hunger?
 My only hunger is for victory!
CHANCELLOR. Bohemia sends no news for five days past,
 Perhaps—
OTTOCAR. Perhaps I am as ill served there
 As I am here!
CHANCELLOR. Here you are well served!
 (Strikes his breast.)
 Or here, at least, you are well served, my King.
OTTOCAR. May be, may be!
CHANCELLOR. Austrians and Styrians
 Desert in crowds each night to join the foe.
OTTOCAR. *(Arrests his step.)*
 They shall be punished!—This broad expanse of land
 Shall be a desert where no man can dwell,
 Where only wolves and foxes have their lairs,
 And idle travellers in times to come
 Shall ask where Neuburg stood, and where Vienna.
CHANCELLOR. Upon the left bank where we are entrenched,
 Some men assert that Rudolph's troops were seen.
OTTOCAR. I almost think that some there are who wish it;
 It cannot be.
CHANCELLOR. But yet the sentries saw.

OTTOCAR. Send out a brave man, one who will not see!
CHANCELLOR. Near Wolkersdorf—
OTTOCAR. Do not tell me: I know!
  If any troops were seen, they are Moravians.
  (Stands by the table, looking at the map.)
  That was the plan. Moravians coming down,
  Then Milota, our rear guard, pushing up,
  While we, like eels, slip through the Danube and,
  Across, step out like lions; then—
  Strike hard!
  (Strikes the table with his hand.)
  I have them, they are mine. *(Resumes his pacing.)*
CHANCELLOR. Oh God, have mercy!
  While I keep thinking how we could be saved,
  You still predict a victory.—I wonder
  At news that comes from Styria at times.
OTTOCAR. Aye, wonder all you will, Lord Chancellor.
  There I have Milota, an able man;
  No brains, but with a fist of stone and steel.
  The sort who strikes one spot some twenty times
  And never stops to ask.
CHANCELLOR. So be it, then.
  I have protested. Once before I warned:
  Trust not Bavaria. You trusted, though.
  And now he lets the Emperor cross his land.
OTTOCAR. Fear has a nose expert at smelling fear;
  You caught Bavaria's scent, I grant you that.
CHANCELLOR. The Swabian Councils' alliance is dispersed.
OTTOCAR. They never were such very close allies.
CHANCELLOR. To make it short: The Emperor Rudolph, Sire—
OTTOCAR. Emperor?
CHANCELLOR. Well, call him Hapsburg, then.
  He is not such a man, as once we thought.
OTTOCAR. I should be sorry, were he even less;
  A soldier and a man, perhaps; no king.
CHANCELLOR. So not a few believed who helped elect him.
  Events, some unforeseen, show otherwise.
  In Aix, when for bestowal of the fiefs,
  No scepter could be found—they thought to plague him—
  He calmly strode ahead, took from the altar
  A crucifix—

OTTOCAR. And so gave out the fiefs?
　Who wants to give, can readily find means;
　But taking needs a tougher coat of mail.
CHANCELLOR. Peace now prevails throughout the German lands,
　The robbers have been punished, feuds allayed;
　Through marriages, through words of stern command
　The Princes are at one and leagued with him;
　The Pope is for him; with one common voice
　All praise and bless the man who saved their lives.
　When he sailed down the Danube with his troops,
　Exultantly to where Vienna lay,
　The sound of bells rang out from either shore,
　From either shore came shouts of joyful praise,
　From crowds who gaped amazed and knelt in prayer,
　On seeing where, in modest dress of grey,
　He stood alone, far forward in the boat,
　His head inclined in thanks for their salute.
　Sire, call him Emperor, for that he is!
OTTOCAR. So warm your praise?
CHANCELLOR. For you much warmer still:
　Have I pledged him my faith, as I did you?
　But that two kings, both eminent and high,
　Should stand opposed, when but one spoken word,
　A single word could make them reconciled—
　Yes, Sire, I said it, and it must be said!
　What I must now announce may anger you:
　The Emperor has sent a herald here,
　And asks that you and he confer as friends.
OTTOCAR. Be still!
CHANCELLOR. The Isle of Kaumberg, he suggests,
　Be occupied by both of you alike;
　You would not go to him, nor he to you,
　But meet on equally divided soil,
　There to arrange what benefits us all.
OTTOCAR. My wrath—
CHANCELLOR. Your wrath, sir, yes; but even so!
　I cannot help but speak when duty bids.
　(Enter Zavish Rosenberg.)
OTTOCAR. How good you come: do stop this raven's croak!
ZAVISH. What does he wish?
OTTOCAR. He says to compromise.
ZAVISH. To compromise? The doddering old fool!

This very morning when a troop of Cumans,
By wading through a ford, approached our camp;
I gave them chase with my Bohemian men,
And, though they scattered, not a one got back.
OTTOCAR. *(To the Chancellor.)* You see?
CHANCELLOR. That some should fall, does not decide.
ZAVISH. But many falls will fell the foe at last!
The axe is at the roots; come, drive it home!
(To the Chancellor.)
Where is a force that can with ours compare?
Such strength and courage, confidence and pride,
Pride in itself and pride in him, their chief.
CHANCELLOR. You well know, Zavish, things are different now.
ZAVISH. *(Continues.)* And you can talk of compromise and peace?
Though they are many, we are hardly less;
Though they are brave, who can compete with us?
Their Emperor? The German Emperor is here!
This battle won, and then it will be he.
CHANCELLOR. Oh, Rosenberg, the game you play is false.
I think you are not honest, Rosenberg.
A wrong once done your house in days gone by
By him, our monarch, commonly so just,
Has taken root, I fear me, in your heart,
And makes you speak as you have spoken now.
Trust me, my King; your interests are mine.
ZAVISH. They have the disadvantage, that is clear.
OTTOCAR. That is not clear; they have the upper hand.
The sole advantage—the decisive one!—
Is this: That Ottocar leads you, and Hapsburg them.
(Goes to the table and, supporting himself with his right hand, studies the map spread out before him.)
ZAVISH. The day is ours; believe me, Chancellor.
CHANCELLOR. And even so, what gains accrue to us?
Defeat the Emperor today, next year,
His army reassembled, he returns.
Your lands, you must agree, are discontent,
And ripe for insurrection and revolt;
They may at any time call Germans in.
Should Rudolph die, or in the wars be slain,
Another will make similar demands,
And conflict with the Empire never cease.
ZAVISH. What more?

CHANCELLOR.   What more?—You think it matters not
That war and horrors overrun our land?
That crops are trampled down, that homes are burned,
And human beings slaughtered like—Oh God!
For shame, Lord Rosenberg, to speak such thoughts!
Was it for this our King risked gold and goods
To raise Bohemia to its present state?
Ploughs turn the sod, the weaver works his loom,
The spinner twists his thread, mines yield their wealth;
And you would have his own, his princely hands,
Destroy the structure he himself has reared?
Come, come! You say what is not so, Lord Zavish;
The King is better versed than you suppose.

OTTOCAR. *(To himself.)*   In fact, they were the ones who first
aproached me.

CHANCELLOR.   They were!

OTTOCAR. *(Resumes his pacing.)*   Disgrace, if any, falls on them.

CHANCELLOR. *(Folds his hands in thanks.)*   He gives it thought!

OTTOCAR.   Men compromise from weakness!—
Not if the recompense had been the world,
Would I have made the first approach to him!

CHANCELLOR.   Your honor stays intact; your fame increased.

OTTOCAR.   Forgive your foes; but first, have them chastised!
Men compromise from weakness!

CHANCELLOR.   Gracious Sire—

OTTOCAR.   And really, Zavish, I want so much to know
How he will act, when he sees Ottocar—
This pauper Hapsburg in the Emperor's cloak—
What he will say, when in the self-same tone,
In which I ordered him at Croissenbrunn—
"On, Hapsburg, march!"—I now demand my fiefs,
That Austria and Styria be returned.—
Without my troops, a single-handed triumph!

ZAVISH.   Suppose, he should, with sly and cunning ways—

OTTOCAR.   Agreed, I'll take your offer, Chancellor!

CHANCELLOR.   A thousand thanks!

OTTOCAR.   Do not give thanks too soon.
I go but not for reasons you assume.—
While he stands shyly there and gropes for words,
I shall begin: Keep your imperial cloak,
Continue wearing it for all of me.
But you are not to trifle with my lands;

And so be on your way and go in peace.
We might at most give him a patch of ground,
So he can plume himself and boast at home :
Look you, what we have conquered for the realm.
That joy we grant him. Now, Lord Chancellor,
We go in quest of peace and compromise;
You are the leader; you, we shall obey!
Let every man in camp, high rank or low,
(Turns toward the entrance at which some men come in.)
Bestir himself, adjust his best attire.
Have shields and armor glow with gold and jewels;
And woe to any page whose coat does not
Outshine the Emperor's a hundred fold.
(Exit, the others following him.)

(Isle of Kaumberg in the Danube. The Camp of the Imperial army. In the background, elevated a few steps, a costly tent decorated with the Imperial eagle. Enter a Captain; after him several armed men who, with crossed pikes, try to hold back the on-crowding populace.)

CAPTAIN.   Let them come in; the Emperor so commands.
(Crowds of people come streaming in.)
FIRST CITIZEN. *(Has made his way with a companion to the front of the crowd.)*
Here, look, this place is good, here, let us stay.
SECOND CITIZEN.   If only he comes out, where we can see.
A WOMAN. *(To her little girl.)*   Keep close to me, mind your flowers, child!
SWISS SOLDIER.   Where is our Rudi? Sir, my countryman.
We have some questions for the Emperor.
CAPTAIN.   Have patience, wait! The tent must open soon.

(The tent opens. Emperor Rudolph, clad in a leather shirt, is seated at a camp table. He holds a helmet in his hand and is busy hammering out some dents in it. As he finishes his work, he looks at it with satisfaction.)

RUDOLPH.   That ought to hold; at least, a little while.
(Looks around.)
What, people here?—George, come and lend a hand!
(Puts on his coat with the help of the servant.)
FIRST CITIZEN. *(Well forward.)*
Good Neighbor Tin-Smith, did you see? The Emperor,

A hammer in his hand! Vivat Rudolphus!

SECOND CITIZEN.   Be quiet, quiet now! He comes this way.

(The Emperor descends the steps.)

SEYFRIED. *(Kneels.)*   Most gracious Lord!

RUDOLPH.   Ah, Merenberg, you here?

Have no concern: your father shall be freed,

I promised you, he shall. Throughout the realm,

With God's assistance, peace has been restored,

And soon will bless your provinces as well.

Today Bohemia's Prince comes to confer;

Before all else we shall consider you.

(Seyfried retires; a little girl with a bouquet of flowers runs up to the Emperor.)

RUDOLPH.   Whose child is this? Your name is—

WOMAN.   Katharina,

Katharina Froehlich, born a Viennese.

RUDOLPH.   Take care, Katharina! What a winsome child!

Can eyes so brown make such a shy appeal?

Yet roguish, too. She knows her charm, the minx!

Good woman, yes, what is it?

WOMAN.   Oh, Your Highness,

Bohemian troops set fire to our house;

My husband lies abed, his hope destroyed.

RUDOLPH. *(To one of his followers.)*

Take down the name, and see what can be done.

(To the woman.)

Yes, we shall help, where help can still avail.

SWISS SOLDIER. *(Comes forward followed by two or three others.)*

Your pardon, sir, most gracious countryman!

RUDOLPH.   Well, Walter Stuessi from Lucerne? You wish?

(To the little girl.)

You, run and join your mother, Katharina;

Your father will be helped, go tell her that.

(The little girl runs to her mother's side.)

SWISS SOLDIER.   I and these others here from Switzerland,

We come to ask, would you be good enough

And let us have some money?

RUDOLPH.   Money, friend,

Yes, money; what a thing it is to have!

SWISS SOLDIER.   You mean; you have none? How?—And still wage war?

RUDOLPH.   Look, friend, you must remember this from home.
   A farmer often has enough stored up
   Of food and feed to last the winter through,
   And well on into spring. But spring, at times,
   Will come not late in March, but early May,
   When snow still covers fields where grain should be;
   If then supplies run short, do you condemn
   The man for planning badly?
SWISS SOLDIER.   God forbid!
   A few of us have had such luck ourselves!
   —And you?—Ah, yes! *(To other Swiss.)*
   You see, he is the farmer,
   And if the winter lasts,—the war, he means,—
   And foodstuffs, he means money, get used up,—
   Well, sir, we shall content ourselves a while;
   Meantime, we can explore the peasant's larder,
RUDOLPH.   Stay, if you like; if not, then go.
   But anyone who scorns our army fare,
   And dares lay hand on any peasant's store,
   He'll hang, no matter who!
SWISS SOLDIER.   It does no harm,
   We thought, to ask. We now know where we stand.
   We shall remain three days, or may be, four;
   Perhaps things may improve by then.
RUDOLPH.   So do!
   My greetings to your townsmen in Lucerne.
   (The Emperor turns to go.)
OTTOCAR OF HORNECK. *(Steps out of the crowd, forward.)*
   Illustrious Sire and Emperor, give heed!
RUDOLPH.   Who are you?
OTTOCAR OF HORNECK.   Ottocar of Horneck, liegeman
   To Ott, the noble knight of Lichtenstein,
   Whom Ottocar, the King, with other knights,
   Without a trial, unjustly holds in gaol.
   Oh, look upon him, look upon our land!
   Well worthy that a prince think of its weal.
   Where lies a land that can with this compare?
   Look round, whichever way your glances turn,
   It smiles as on a bridegroom smiles the bride.
   With meadows shining green and grain like gold,
   Made gay with saffron's yellow, flaxen blue,
   Spiced fragrantly with flowers, precious herbs,

It sweeps through ample valleys, broad and vast—
A rich bouquet, so far as eye can see,
Held in the Danube's silvery embrace!—
Then climbs aloft to vineyards on the slopes,
Where serried rows of lustrous grapes ascend,
Full-ripened under Heaven's radiant sky;
While forests dark for hunting rise on high,
And God's own gentle breath suffuses all,
And warms, matures and makes the pulses throb,
As no man's pulse can throb on chilly plains.
And so the Austrian is free and frank,
He bears life's pain, life's pleasures openly,
Not envious, oft though he envied be!!
And what he does is done with cheerful mien.
Perhaps in Saxony or on the Rhine,
There may be folk more versed in bookish lore;
But in what counts before the sight of God:
An open eye, straightforward common sense;
In these the Austrian outstrips his brothers,
Thinks his own thoughts and leaves the talk to others.

My native land! No child like Italy,
Nor yet like Germany a man; instead,
Between these two, a lad, cheeks flushed with life:
May God protect, preserve your youthful zest,
And so restore what others brought to ruin.

RUDOLPH.   A man of worth!

FIRST CITIZEN.   Aye, sir; a scholar, too.
He rhymed a chronicle in which you, Sire,
Are also mentioned.

RUDOLPH.   Favorably, I trust!
I promise you, your master shall be freed.
And you—in memory of this hour—pray, accept
This chain of mine which you shall proudly wear:
Let knowledge be rewarded and achievement!
(*Takes a chain from his neck and hangs it about Horneck who
has knelt. To one of the knights standing near.*)
To you, such favor may appear too high?
Were I to touch this man, Sir, with my sword,
He would arise a knight, like all the rest;
With what, however, shall I touch a man
To make him write a chronicle like his?—

But nothing of this in your record, friend,
Lest I appear to praise myself through you.

CAPTAIN. *(Enters.)* The King, he of Bohemia, sir, draws near.

RUDOLPH. Almighty God, my comfort on my way;
Complete the mission I began with Thee!

(A camp-chair is brought and set up, right front. The Emperor sits down and his retinue stand about him. Enter King Ottocar, clad in splendid armor over which he wears a richly embroidered mantle that reaches to his feet; he has a crown, not a helmet, on his head. After him the Chancellor, and his retinue.)

OTTOCAR. *(As he makes his way forward.)*
I have for some time now looked right and left;
Where do you keep your Emperor, good sirs?
  Ah, Merenberg, I hit upon you here?
I plan to hit upon you later elsewhere!
Well, where is Rudolph? Oh!
(Catches sight of him and goes up to him.)
Good morrow, Hapsburg!

RUDOLPH. *(Rises: to his retinue.)*
What makes you stand here with uncovered heads?
When Ottocar meets Hapsburg, man to man,
Then Tom and Dick can keep their bonnets on,
He is, like them, a man.—On with your caps!
But when a vassal comes to greet his liege,
Bohemia paying homage to the Empire, *(Steps among them.)*
Then woe to him who fails to show respect!
(Walks firmly up to Ottocar.)
How are you, Ottocar? What brings you here?

OTTOCAR. *(Taken aback, retreats a step.)*
For—conference, I thought I had been asked!

RUDOLPH. Well then, you would confer about affairs?
I thought you meant to visit, friend with friend.
To work! How is it, my Bohemian Prince,
That up to now you did not heed my call?
I summoned you before, three different times,
At Nuremberg, at Wuerzburg and at Augsburg,
That you do homage and receive your fiefs;
You never did appear. When last I called,
The worthy Bishop Seckau came instead,
Whose acts were far less worthy than his name.

OTTOCAR. Bohemia has been mine since Richard's day.

RUDOLPH. The King of Cornwall. Yes, there was a time,

When one in Germany, with coin in hand,
Could get control of more than fiefs and land;
Those times are past. I swore a solemn oath,
I swore to my almighty, gracious God,
That right and justice should prevail, and law
In German lands. They shall and must prevail!
You have done wrong, as an imperial prince,
To flout the Empire and the Emperor;
You fell on Salzburg, the Archbishop's lands,
With death and with destruction in your wake,
And your brute soldiers wrought such havoc there
As heathen folk would fear to look upon.

OTTOCAR.   I gave him ample notice of the feud.

RUDOLPH.   Now, no more feuds, what we want now is peace!
The lands of Austria and Styria,
With Carnten and with Cran, the Wendish March,
As fiefs illegally withheld by you,
You will return to me where they belong.
There must be pen and paper here; we can
Draw up and sign the deed without delay.

OTTOCAR.   Almighty God above! Am I myself?
Is this not Ottocar, this not his sword,
That one presumes to speak in such a tone?

How would it be, sir, if my sole reply
Were to recross the Danube, as I came,
And then ask questions at my army's head?

RUDOLPH.   Twelve months ago you had been well advised
To let battle-field and blood decide.
You are a prince well-versed in war, no doubt,
As for your army, it has often won;
Your coffers teem with silver and with gold:
I lack in much, or, truth to tell, lack all,
And yet, believe me, I feel so secure:
If every man about foresook my side,
My last remaining squire had decamped;
The crown upon my head, the scepter in my hand,
I should alone breach your rebellious walls,
And call: Sir, give the Empire what is due!
I am not he whom formerly you knew:
No longer Hapsburg and not Rudolph more;
The blood of Germany flows through these veins,

The pulse of Germany throbs in this breast.
All that was mortal, I have laid aside;
To be the Emperor who never dies.
When I was chosen for this high estate,
When I, to whom such fortune seemed a dream,
Upon my humble head received from Him,
Who rules all worlds, the crown of this, His realm,
While still the oil was moist upon my brow,
I felt a miracle had come to pass,
And learned to trust in miracles to come!
No prince there was not mightier than I;
Yet it is I these princes now obey!
War-mongers fled before my voice;
Not I, but God it was, that gave them fright.
Five paltry coins lay in my money-pouch,
When I took ship in Ulm for this campaign;
Bavaria's duke rebelled, he soon succumbed;
My troops were few with which I reached your land,
The land itself supplied me troops unasked;
Deserters from your ranks, they joined with mine,
And Austria conquers Austria for me.
I swore that peace and justice be secured;
And by the Triune, our all-seeing God,
Not so much as the breadth of this small hair,
Shall you retain of property not yours;
And so in sight of Heaven I step forth
And cry: Give back the lands you have withheld!

OTTOCAR.   These lands are mine, I say!

RUDOLPH.   They never were!

OTTOCAR.   Queen Margaret brought them me, when we were wed.

RUDOLPH.   But where is Margaret now?

OTTOCAR.   No matter where;
   She gave her lands to me.

RUDOLPH.   Shall I appeal
To her to judge between us?—She is here!

OTTOCAR.   Here in the camp?

RUDOLPH. *(In a different tone.)*   She whom you injured so,
   And cruelly robbed of rights and happiness;
   This morning she appeared, and pled with us
   To show him mercy, him the man that showed her none.

OTTOCAR.   The woman might have spared herself the task;
   There is no need of pleas for Ottocar.

RUDOLPH. *(Sternly.)* You, my Bohemian prince, may well need pleas;
  One single word from me and you are lost.
OTTOCAR. I, lost?
RUDOLPH. Your access to Bohemia, cut off.
OTTOCAR. You may besiege, but I shall free Vienna.
RUDOLPH. Too late for that!
OTTOCAR. How so?
RUDOLPH. *(Turns around.)* Paltram Vatzo!
  Bring him! He asked for audience with me;
  The Mayor and the Council of Vienna.
  *(Enter Paltram Vatzo, Burgomaster of Vienna, with members of
  the Council; they bear the keys of the city on a cushion.)*
PALTRAM VATSO. In all humility, my lord, I bring
  The keys of our Vienna here to you,
  And do implore you not to harbor wrath,
  That I, through loyalty I pledged my King,
  Have held the town from you until today;
  And might, perhaps, have held it longer still,
  Had not the citizens forced me to yield,
  Worn by the long blockade and deprivation.
  (Lays the keys at the Emperor's feet.)
  My office, with these keys, I here give up;
  Your loyal subject I intend to be. *(Rises.)*
OTTOCAR. Damn them, these Viennese! A fickle folk,
  Atremble for your dainty palates, were you?
  You will repent. Provisions will be cut
  From Klosterneuburg, where my fortress holds.
RUDOLPH. Your fortress, Neuburg, has surrendered, too;
  Across the Danube, nothing more is yours.
  You, Friedrich Pettau, come!
  (Pettau advances with downcast eyes.)
OTTOCAR. You shameless traitor, you!
  You let them have my fortress?
PETTAU. No, not I.
  Attacked without a warning, late last night—
OTTOCAR. Enough! I know that I have been betrayed.
  Yet do not triumph! I will mock you yet!
  A well staffed army comes from Styria
  With Milota, a leader tried and true;
  He will attack your hirelings from the rear,
  While, like black clouds of thunder, Ottocar
  Knocks down the feeble reeds that form your front,

And laughs to see the Danube swallow them!
RUDOLPH. I beg you, speak no more, impulsive prince!
OTTOCAR. Do you now see how distant is your goal?
RUDOLPH. Nor should you base your hopes on Milota.
OTTOCAR. My base is firm; your turn it is to tremble;
We next shall meet in battle.
RUDOLPH. You would leave
And will not yield the lands?
OTTOCAR. *(As he turns to leave.)* Why should I yield?
RUDOLPH. Will you then learn from Milota yourself,
How good your reasons are for trusting him?
(Enters Milota in chains.)
RUDOLPH. The men of Styria brought him to me, bound
In chains, because he had oppressed them so.
Remove the fetters from him! Here is the banner
Of Styria, and here is Austria's banner,
*(The Estates of Austria and Styria come forward on the side of
the stage where the Emperor stands, carrying the banners and
flags of their lands.)*
RUDOLPH. They freely came and begged us for protection.

Why be so saddened, my Bohemian Prince?
Look round about! The clouds are blown away,
And you can see conditions as they are.
If Austria is lost—
OTTOCAR. Lost, by no means lost!
RUDOLPH. Do not delude yourself! Your heart must know
That it is lost, and lost it is for good!

You were a powerful monarch, mighty king,
Before the chance of adding to your realm
Bred craving in your breast for more and more,
And you will still be mighty, rich and great,
Though that be lost which could not be retained.
For God forbid that I should stretch my hand
To reach for lands that rightfully are yours.
Nor could I so. Your army still is strong,
Equipped for battle and prepared for war,
And fickle are the fortunes of the field.
Refrain from strife. Accept the hand of God
Which clearly pointed out His holy will.

The futile urge for honors once drove me,
As it has driven you, when I was young.
On aliens, closest kin, on friends and foes
My youthful arms essayed its hasty strength,
As though the world were one broad practice-field
For Rudolph and his sword. On being banned,
I joined with you in heathen Prussia's war,
Aud fought the Magyars, battling at your side,
Yet chafed within because of limits set,
By over-anxious acts of Church and State,
On courage rashly craving greater scope.
Then God laid hold on me with mighty hand,
And raised me to the towering throne whose steps
Rise high above all else to rule the world.
And like the pilgrim who has scaled a height,
And looks upon the valleys far below,
And on the walls that lately penned him in;
I felt the blinding scales fall from my eyes,
And my ambition suddenly was cured.
The world was given us that all may live,
And great is He alone, the only God!
The earth no longer dreams its early dreams,
And when the giants and the dragons went,
The titans and the tyrants disappeared.
No more do hordes descend like avalanches
On other hordes; the cloudy liquor clears;
And by the signs it almost seems to me
We stand before an era that is new:
The peasant walks behind his plough in peace,
In towns the busy workmen ply their trades,
New industries and guilds lift up their heads,
Swiss towns and Swabian plan to organize,
Its speedy ships the active Hansa sends
To North and East for commerce and for gain.
You always labored for your people's good;
Let them have peace; there is no better gift!

O Ottocar, how good a time it was,
When we, returned from Prussia's war, looked out
From fortress walls upon the high Hradschin,
And talked of deeds the days to come would bring!

Beside us, in those days, Queen Margaret sat—
Will you not see her? Not see Margaret?

OTTOCAR. Sir!

RUDOLPH. How could you cast this guardian angel off,
Who always gently reconciled your foes,
With blessings charmed away your rash distempers,
And, like a loyal sister, cared for you.
You banished her and with her banished fortune—
Your home can offer you no solace, Ottocar!—
Would you see Margaret? Shall she be called?

OTTOCAR. That, no! I will do homage for the fiefs.

RUDOLPH. Bohemia and Moravia?

OTTOCAR. Yes, for those!

RUDOLPH. Restoring—

OTTOCAR. Austria and Styria,
Both yours again; both have deserted me.
How much I did for them! Ingratitude
And human wickedness—how they revolt me!

RUDOLPH. Come to the tent.

OTTOCAR. And why not here?

RUDOLPH. Vassals
Do homage to the Empire on their knees.

OTTOCAR. I kneel?

RUDOLPH. The tent shuts out all prying eyes.
You there shall kneel to God and to the Empire,
And not before a mortal such as we.

OTTOCAR. Lead on!

RUDOLPH. Agreed? Then blessèd be this hour!
Do you go first; I shall be glad to follow,
To celebrate a triumph shared by both.
(They enter the tent, the curtains close.)

MILOTA. *(Crosses the stage and joins the Bohemians.)*
Well, God be praised! That makes me free again.
These days just passed will always haunt my mind.
(Enter Zavish Rosenberg.)

ZAVISH. Where is the King?

MILOTA. Within the Emperor's tent;
He does him homage.

ZAVISH. Oho! And hides away?
A sight for all of loyal heart to see!

(Draws his sword and at one stroke cuts the tentcords so that the curtains fall to the ground. Ottocar is seen kneeling before Rudolph who has just invested him with the fief of Bohemia.)

ZAVISH.   The King is on his knees!

BOHEMIANS.   *(In consternation.)*   His knees!

OTTOCAR.   *(Leaps to his feet and hurries to the front of the stage.)*

RUDOLPH.   *(Follows him with the flag of Moravia in his hand.)*

Will you do homage for Moravia also?

(Ottocar sinks on one knee.)

RUDOLPH.   *(Gives him the flag of Moravia.)*

I name you Margrave of Moravia,
And do accept your solemn plight and pledge
To me as Emperor, in the name of God.

Arise King Ottocar, and with this kiss
I welcome you as vassal and as brother.
But all of you who are of Austria,
And hold your lands in fief to Austria's lord,
Come to Vienna, there to take the oath
Of loyalty as vassals at my hand.
Do you come, too, respected King and Monarch?

(Ottocar bows his head.)

RUDOLPH.   I shall await you, if it should so please.

You, swing your flags, and let the bells peal forth
The bloodless victory of sweet accord.

(Exit with his retinue. Ottocar still stands with bowed head. Seyfried Merenberg has remained behind; after a little hesitation he advances to Ottocar with pleading gestures.)

SEYFRIED.   Illustrious King, I come to ask—

OTTOCAR.   *(Raises his head quickly and looks at him fiercely. With one hand he rips apart the buckle that fastens his mantle; the mantle slips to the ground. With the other hand he tears the crown from his head, letting it fall behind him, and rushes off the stage exclaiming):*

Away!

(As the others follow him, the curtain falls.)

ACT 4

(Before the castle at Prague. The great gateway with a portcullis, rear center, leads into it. Beside that, a small postern to which some steps ascend. It is closed. At the right, halfway forward, is the porter's lodge with a stone table and a bench. Before it is a bed of flowers. Enter Milota and Fuellenstein from opposite sides.)

MILOTA. You saw the King?

FUELLENSTEIN. I did not.

MILOTA. Nor did I.

FUELLENSTEIN. In Znaim he left his followers and vanished,
A single servant may have gone with him,
And since then strays about Moravian lands.
In Kraliz he was seen, in Hradish, Lukow;
And last in Kostelez, not far from Stip,
Where flows a little wonder-working spring,
To which from far off pious pilgrims come.
A wretched hut for bathers in a valley,
Remote from man and any sign of life,
Is where, a fortnight long, he stayed concealed;
A place to die in, rather than to live.
And as the pilgrims of the region do,
Who, mindful of desires unfulfilled,
Throw in the wishing-well a cross of twigs,
And prophecy the future as it sinks or swims,
So he did days on end, and seemed perturbed.
When finally word reached the magistrate,
He straightway went to take the King away;
But found him gone to regions far afield.

MILOTA. Have you as yet discovered where he is?

FUELLENSTEIN. Some men report they saw him on the road
To Prague.

MILOTA. To us?—I hope now he will rest.
His wings so proudly spread are somewhat clipped;
The land that kept on luring him away,
He has relinquished with a solemn pledge.
If he will rule here as his fathers did,
Will have no Germans living in his realm,
And with Czech nobles lending him support
Consider his own people's fortune first:
I may, perhaps, forgive the wrong he did
To me and mine.—Go find the Chancellor,
And let him know that an imperial herald,

Demanding that the treaty's terms be met,
That first of all those hostages be freed
From Austria and Styria who still
Are kept imprisoned here throughout the land,
Has made his entry in our town of Prague.
He should at once comply with these demands,
Before the King comes, causing a delay.

FUELLENSTEIN. But if the King—

MILOTA. Do now as I have said.

(Exit Fuellenstein.)

MILOTA. If all our land were not disgraced with him,
I too would laugh, as once our Zavish laughed.
Have every thing arranged before he comes,
Then he has only to approve and—sleep.

(Exit into the castle. Short pause. Enter one of the King's servants
who looks cautiously around and then calls off-stage.)

SERVANT. Now, there is no one here, my gracious master.

(Enter Ottocar, wrapped in a dark cloak and with his black cap,
that has a black feather on it, pulled far down over his eyes.)

SERVANT. You wish the chancellor to come?
Good sir,
Would you not rather wait inside the castle?

(Ottocar shakes his head.)

SERVANT. These two days past you have not slept nor eaten,
You must give heed; protect your precious self.

(Ottocar laughs in bitter mockery.)

SERVANT. I do entreat you, sir, to go within.

(Ottocar impatiently stamps his foot.)

SERVANT. Well, I shall go; but you, sir, do be seated.

(Exit into the castle.)

OTTOCAR. How could I venture in, home of my fathers?
And desecrate your threshold with my step?
When I, triumphant, flushed with victory,
Rode through the cheering streets to reach your walls,
Held out the banners I had won in battle;
You welcomed me with portals opened wide,
And from your battlements my forebears watched.
Your vaulting walls were arched to harbor heroes,
And none, who was disgraced, has gone within.
Here will I sit, a keeper of the gates,
And ward off shame from entering my house.

(Seats himself on the steps of the postern and covers his head.
Enter the Burgomaster of Prague and several burghers.)

BURGOMASTER. Nay, keep me not, I hasten to the meeting.
A herald from the Emperor himself
Has lately come, so we must not delay;
For now Bohemia has joined the realm.
The King with solemn oath did so attest,
Affirming loyalty on bended knee.

BURGHER. On bended knee?

BURGOMASTER. Aye, in the Emperor's camp.
He kneeling down, the Emperor enthroned;
The army to a man looked on, amazed.
Is someone there?

BURGHER. A man crouched on the steps.

BURGOMASTER. Pride comes before a fall, I often said.
Do go and see who could be sitting there:
Suspicious folk now roam the countryside;
These shiftless mercenaries should be shunned.

BURGHER. *(Returns.)* Oh sir!

BURGOMASTER. Why tremble so?

BURGHER. It is the King!

BURGOMASTER. That person on the steps? You must be mad!

BURGHER. I saw his face. See for yourself!

BURGOMASTER. The King!
Could he have given heed to our remarks?
Should I bow down?—It would be best, perhaps,
That we withdraw. He seems to meditate.
(Draws away to right front. Enter Benesh Rosenberg and Berta,
right rear.)

BENESH. *(With a staff; leads Berta.)*
But see how bright the sunshine is today.
Come out, out in the open. Berta, come!
Closed in, the stifling air will do you harm.
And will you not, to please me, try to speak?
Speak, Berta, speak! Say but a single word,
Say, yes or no. For your old father's sake.
Come next Midsummer's Day—who knows how long,
By then, that you sit silently, and stare.
How sad that is! Will you not talk to me?
Much rather would I have you madly rage,
Than hear no single word the whole day long.

We must remember what is past, is past;
No longer think of it, then all is well.
BURGOMASTER. Be still!
BENESH. She has, alas, been still for long.
Day in, day out, she will not make a sound.
BURGOMASTER. *(Whispers.)* There sits the King!
BENESH. Sits where?
BURGOMASTER. There on the steps.
BENESH. Look, Berta; there he sits, the wicked king
Who brought such suffering to you, poor child!
Do speak for once and let him hear you scold.
Say: Evil man, how glad your misery makes me;
It serves you right for wrongs you did us both.
*(Berta picks up a handful of earth and throws it, aimlessly, as
children, in front of her.)*
BENESH. Yes, throw it, do; would that it were a dagger!
Throw, Berta, throw. That wicked, evil man.
But God has undertaken our revenge:
He had to kneel to his most hated foe,
Before a man whom he had once despised;
In sight of all his army, he knelt down.
Aye, toss your head! I am no more afraid.
One higher has your destiny in hand.
See to it that my daughter speaks again;
Then have me killed, so little do I care.
(Enter Cunigunda with Zavish and servants.)
CUNIGUNDA. How comes it that this crazy girl goes free?
Were you not told to keep her under guard?
BENESH. *(As he is led away.)*
Well, Berta, come. He has enough to bear. *(Exit.)*
CUNIGUNDA. Go, all of you, all who have eyes to see!
(Exeunt all but Cunigunda and Zavish.)
CUNIGUNDA. We are alone! Alone with our disgrace:
Will you not now rise, you almighty King,
And give out mighty words, as was your way?

See where he sits, that overstrong, proud man,
For whose great self the world once seemed too small;
See where he sits, a beggar at the door,
And get a scant 'God bless you' and contempt.
The man who wore his crowns like idle wreaths;
And when one withered, wove another one

Of flowers plucked afresh from foreign gardens.
Who, holding lives of thousands in his hands,
Set them, as for a playful game of chess,
Upon a field, marked off by blood and dust,
And cried out 'Check' as if they were but pawns,
By artists rudely formed of lifeless stone,
And nick-named knight and charger as a jest.
Who even challenged Nature as a foe;
And when he rode forth mornings for a hunt
And saw the heavens overcast with clouds,
He halted, had his master-mason come,
And bade him not to hurry over much
With work upon the church at Gueldenkron.
Now see him staring glumly at the ground,
He used to stamp so proudly underfoot!

ZAVISH. Well, gracious Lady; luck, you see, is round!

CUNIGUNDA. Bonds other men respect to him are sport:
He cast his wife, Queen Margaret, aside—
Her years, God knows, made her the mate for him,
The Queen of Sorrows was a fitting spouse!—
In far off Hungary he woos himself a maid.
For what cares he if she, perhaps, long since
Had let her choice fall on another man?
If at that time a lover, ranking less,
But greater far, was suing for her hand!—
An unsubdued Cumanian prince can match
In worth a grovelling Bohemian king!—
But what cares he? He wants a wife and heirs,
Let break what must; and there an end!
I came here, spirited and fancy free,
Well worthy of a partner, young in years,
And found—Why now, I found King Ottocar!
Not quite the sorry sight sits brooding there,
Yet not much better, God will bear me out!
He kept his thoughts and counsels to himself,
Kept me as handmaid rather than as queen;
He wished to be the ruler, he alone.

ZAVISH. Ah, good my Queen, to rule is sweet, as sweet
Almost as—to obey, and none will share it.

CUNIGUNDA. How he has ruled, and ruled he has, indeed!
A bubble nothing more, now burst and gone.

And he could talk, with great and princely talk!
What never yet had been and could not be
Was fact upon his lips! When first he heard
The Emperor's message brought from Nuremberg,
How he did talk and with what royal airs!
No town, no house; no, not a single clod
Would he give up of Austria's broad domains;
And though a hundred times the doctors swore
It might well cost the Emperor's life,
No smallest saffron leaf would he release!
Upon our plains we have a beast, called mule;
When from afar it sees a wolf approach,
It loudly brays, kicks out on every side
And scatters clouds of flying dust and dirt.
But once the wolf comes close, it shakes with fright
And calmly lets itself be swallowed up:
The King has acted much the self-same way!
With boastful words he marched against his foes,
Assembling in his army half the world;
With Poles and Cumans, Tartars, Germans, Czechs
Discoursing in his camp in different tongues,
And Austria too small to hold the host;
But when the battle's fateful hour had struck,
There was no heart to move these sturdy arms;
And in the enemy camp, he—Rosenberg!

ZAVISH. Your Majesty?

CUNIGUNDA. Say, have you ever knelt?
Knelt, not to women—ever knelt to men?
For pay, for hire, for fear, before your peers?

ZAVISH. Not I!

CUNIGUNDA. And never should?

ZAVISH. Not in my life!

CUNIGUNDA. But he, he did! Knelt down before his foe,
Knelt down before the man whom he despised,
His man, his henchman once; when that man said:
Come here! he came, and when he told him: Go!
He went, and almost with unseemly haste.

ZAVISH. Your Royal Highness, it was but a jest!
A jest among good friends. You see, the Emperor,
He wished to have the people see his strength;
And so he asked our King, and he complied.

CUNIGUNDA. I will not have me called a bondsman's wife,

No longer share a vassal's shameful bed;
Nor on the Emperor's summons to Vienna,
Help bear his lowly housewife's courtly train;
Nor will I kneel to Rudolph, as you did.
(The King leaps to his feet.)
CUNIGUNDA. Yes, rise up, do! You cannot cause me fright!
Shall I alone, of women or of men,
Still shake in fear of Ottocar, the King?
Escort me; I'll go home to Hungary,
Where kings can live with honor unimpaired.
Come, Rosenberg, your arm! And now no more
Of that disgrace your eyes have shared with mine.
ZAVISH. *(Gives the queen his arm.)*
It was a jest. We all were much amused;
Not only Rudolph; he, of course, the most.
And good it was to see, I must confess.
(Is about to leave.)
OTTOCAR. Zavish!
ZAVISH. *(Turns back.)* What is your wish, sir?
OTTOCAR. Your sword!
(Hands it to him.) It's yours.
OTTOCAR. *(Draws back for the thrust.)*
You, traitor!
CUNIGUNDA. *(Calls off-stage.)* Rosenberg!
OTTOCAR. Here, take your sword and go.
ZAVISH. Ah, many thanks! This is no place to tarry.
(Exit in search of the Queen.)
OTTOCAR. *(Stares fixedly for a while at the ground.)*
Is that my shadow?—Well, two kings, it seems!
(Trumpets off-stage.)
OTTOCAR. They come, draw near! Where can I hide myself?
*(Wraps his cloak about him and steps to one side. Enter an
Imperial Herald with two trumpeters; after him the Austrian
hostages who have been released, Merenberg among them. Jostling
crowds follow; the Chancellor in argument with the Herald.)*
CHANCELLOR. I enter protest in my monarch's name.
HERALD. *(Holds the treaty in his hands.)*
This solemn treaty, here in section three,
Declares that hostages should be released!
Wherefore with legal powers accorded me,
I claim full freedom for these several men
Of Austria and Styria, all now

Leal vassals of the Emperor and his realm.
And likewise, I demand, the terms of peace,
Till now but half-fulfilled, be fully met.
Bohemian garrisons are quartered still
In districts, here and there, on Austrian soil;
And Heinrich Kuenring, loyal to your cause,
Is ravaging the lands beyond the Danube,
Helped quietly by neighboring Moravians.
Such acts must cease, my Emperor commands!
To stop these forays, I have come to Prague.

CHANCELLOR.   We first will have to notify the King.

HERALD.   But why? Is not the Emperor sovereign?
Such acts are covered by the vassal's oath.

CHANCELLOR.   The Emperor, on his part, has not yet fulfilled
The treaty's terms, as were agreed upon;
Imperial troops patrol Moravia's still.

HERALD.   They will withdraw, as soon as you comply.

CHANCELLOR.   Why should Bohemia be the first to yield?

HERALD.   "To him that hath,"—an old law, as you know.

CHANCELLOR.   You call that law? I call it Might, not Right!

HERALD.   I grant you choice of words, no choice of acts.

CHANCELLOR.   I can refuse you nothing, nor agree.
The King, they say, is here in Prague. From him
Must come concessions touching your demands.

HERALD.   Why not take me to him?

CHANCELLOR.   I cannot, now.
He is in Prague, but more we do not know.

HERALD.   Well then, you must let trumpets sound the call,
That echoes shall resound throughout the town
And Ottocar, the King, be so informed,
That messengers his sovereign sent are here.

(*Ottocar steps out of the crowd. He has cast his cloak aside.*)

OTTOCAR.   Here is the King. What is it you demand?

HERALD.   Sir, they refuse to set these prisoners free.

OTTOCAR.   Refused? Who?

HERALD. (*Pointing to the Chancellor.*)   He!

CHANCELLOR.   Only till you approved, Sire.

OTTOCAR.   These men were surety for their country's debt;
The debt is cancelled, those who pledged are yours!
But one face I discern among the rest
That almost makes me rue my promised word.
I mean you, Merenberg! You are no hostage,

An undisputed traitor, that you are,
The first, you were, that led them on to crime.
Away, I say! Within me hatred boils
And longs to let your blood to cool itself!
(Merenberg retires behind two other hostages.)
OTTOCAR. What else?
HERALD. Withdraw your troops from Austria.
OTTOCAR. They have withdrawn.
HERALD. Not all.
OTTOCAR. It shall be done.
The treaty so provides; so let it be.
HERALD. *(Makes proclamation.)*
Who still has claims against Bohemia's crown,
For rights infringed or damage done to him,
Whoso would swear allegiance to the Realm,
Is bidden to the Council Room to court,
The Palsgrave there presides and gives out fiefs.
Vivat Rudolphus, Roman-German Emperor!
*(Exit, the crowds following in a tumult; the Chancellor alone
remains behind with the King.)*
OTTOCAR. All rush to follow! Leave me here alone!
(To the Chancellor.)
My one-man retinue?—Ha, Ottocar!
Made mock of by the lowest of my servants,
Scorned by my wife and with good reason scorned,
Chased like a beast, dislodged from house and bed—
I cannot bear it, cannot so exist!
My name is stricken from the roll of princes,
A servitor to him I used to scorn;
Unpunished, laughing in my face, those knaves
Who played me false, go out my prison free.
Hark! *(In the distance the herald can be heard repeating the
proclamations.)*
OTTOCAR. Vivat Rudolphus? May he live in Hell!
Call back the herald!
CHANCELLOR. O my gracious lord!
OTTOCAR. Call him, I say, or, varlet, dread my wrath!
(Exit the Chancellor.)
OTTOCAR. Much better had I found my death in battle,
The last one of my soldiers next to me.
They have betrayed me, stolen up by stealth.
A bank of fog has lifted from my brow;

I have been dreaming: like cool morning air
Remembrance comes and wakes me back to life.
I led my army to the Danube's shores,
And pitched my camp, so far does memory serve:
From there on, night! What further happened then,
How they enticed me to the Emperor's tent,
And there—O God Almighty! I will kill
Each one and all who shared the sight!
Yes, kill myself, if I can not blot out
The memory of that indign disgrace!
(Re-enter the Herald, with hostages; after them, Milota.)

HERALD.   You had me summoned, asked for my return?

OTTOCAR.   First, mark me well, that in no name but mine
Shall anyone make public proclamation
In Prague where I am King.

HERALD.   But, sir—

OTTOCAR.   Enough!
Next have the hostages fall in line,
One must investigate so no one else,
Some prisoner escaped, has joined their ranks.

HERALD.   The Empire vouches for them, as you know;
Still, may I ask you, sirs, to fall in line.

OTTOCAR. *(Reviews the ranks.)*
You go along, and you—How smug you look
Sir Ulrich Lichtenstein. You must be glad
Now you are free? I shall not wish you ill.
You never cared for me, nor I for you.
That makes us quits. Go then, for all of me.
But there stands one with whom I need a word.
Good morrow to you, Merenberg, you knave and traitor!

CHANCELLOR.   May he keep quiet, never contradict!

OTTOCAR.   How does the Emperor's service suit your son?
A lad of promise, with his father's traits!
You rescued him before it was too late,
When signs appeared of Ottocar's decline.
When last we met, we two, I promised him
To give him news of me, and also you;
How would it be, were I to send this word;
Your father, that old scoundrel, lives no more!
(To the Herald.)
A hostage, no; one guilty of high treason;
He cannot with those other men go free.

HERALD.   He is the very man my lord, the Emperor—
OTTOCAR.   He is the very man his lord, the King— *(To Merenberg.)*
   You were the first, the man who made the start,
   You led the other. traitors on their way,
   To Frankfurt you sent charges and complaints,
   Then they elected Hapsburg, him, my foe.
MERENBERG.   I wrote no charges!
OTTOCAR.   Scarcely praise, though, either!
   When once your son was in the hostile camp,
   The other Austrians soon joined him there,
   And by the Danube they did play me false,
   Abandoned me, their rightful liege and lord.

   You know, perhaps, where last I saw your son?
   It was near Tulln in the imperial camp,
   There where King Ottocar—Death and Damnation!—
   Before his foe—as vassals do—in dust—
   Remembrance, fade away and leave no trace,
   Come, Madness, settle down upon my brow,
   And veil in misty clouds what there occurred,
   There where King Ottocar—why not speak out
   What all the world has seen—knelt before his foe.
   And this man's son, he stood close by to watch
   And laughed!—Because of that, man, you must die.

   The others may go free; this man remains!
MERENBERG.   O God in Heaven!
HERALD.   Think, sir, what you do!
OTTOCAR.   Think rather what you say, imprudent sir!
   Think that your welcome here is at an end—
   No; go in peace and leave me free to act;
   I still am master in this land of mine!
MERENBERG.   But Styria owes allegiance to the Realm!
OTTOCAR *(To the herald.)*
   He was my subject at the time he did me wrong,
   And as my subject I shall punish him.
   Imprison him, and he who brings me word
   That Merenberg is dead, bears welcome news.
HERALD.   The Emperor, though—
OTTOCAR.   Sir, tell your Emperor
   To rule in Germany as he sees fit.
   The promises I made him I have kept;

Although betrayed, defrauded, shamelessly deceived,
I kept my promise, for I gave my word.
But tell him, in my bosom beats an urge
That ever cries: Take what they stole from you!
Your royal honor save! A king's good name
Has worth beyond a thousand human lives.
They used their wits to dupe you at the Danube,
Now see if they will triumph over force.
Go, tell him that and tell him this beside;
The treaty's terms are met, he has the lands,
The hostages will go, he has his due;
But in Bohemia he had best beware
And speak no word which I might disapprove,
Nor interfere in matters that are mine;
Or I will teach—no, rather say to him:
Do all these things, defy me to my face,
March his assembled forces in my land;
That I may cool my wrath, the boiling hate,
In blood that issues next his very heart!
For my sake tell him lies! Say I reviled him,
Called him a tyrant who usurped my place,
Who stole from me possessions that were mine,
Laughed down the herald whom he sent to me,
Condemned to death the man he tried to save—

HERALD.   You cannot, no!
OTTOCAR.   I can, for it is done.
HERALD.   The treaty's terms—
OTTOCAR.   The treaty's terms be damned!
Would you with treaties master me, with words?
I still have swords, an army still is mine,
Unvanquished, too; you triumph with mere tricks!
And tear these tricks I will, as I now tear
The treaty you obtained from me by guile.
(Snatches the treaty from the herald.)
Watch this! *(As he is about to tear up the paper, he pauses suddenly.)*

CHANCELLOR.   Oh, God! What will he do? Oh, good my Lord!
OTTOCAR. *(To a servant who obeys.)*
Now call my wife to me, the Queen.
Where all could see, was Ottocar defiled,
Where all can see, he washes out the stain.
She shot the poisoned shaft and rammed it home

Within my breast; she shall be present now,
When I withdraw it, or in my attempt,
Drive it deep down where rests the source of life.
(Enter the Queen.)
CUNIGUNDA.   You wish?
OTTOCAR.   But now, you harshly chided me;
That I, to keep from shedding blood, gave in
And to the Emperor relinquished my domain.
CUNIGUNDA.   I chide you still!
OTTOCAR.   Look, in my hands I hold
The pact that bound me to the Emperor.
Were I to tear it, then the bond is broken,
That holds me now; I should be free once more.
Tear it, shall I?
CUNIGUNDA.   No brave man would have doubts!
OTTOCAR.   But think! The demon, war, will rage anew,
Anew the land will reek with smoke and blood:
Some morning, Fortune well may so decide,
Your husband will be brought you on his shield.
CUNIGUNDA.   Far better I should stand beside your bier,
Than lie beside you covered in with shame.
OTTOCAR.   So hard? A drop of kindness would be sweet.
CUNIGUNDA.   Until you have been cleansed of this disgrace,
You shall not share my chamber nor my couch.
(Turns to go.)
OTTOCAR.   Remain! Look here! The treaty torn in two!
(Tears the treaty.)
My honor, whole! our future's door unclosed;
What will result, shall be our common burden.
God grant you something of what moves me here
(Points to his breast.)
And give to me the strength you have displayed.
CUNIGUNDA.   I now can welcome you!
OTTOCAR.   Not so! Not so!
I seem to see on your white fingers blood,
Blood still to flow; so keep your hands from me!
God fashioned woman out of softer clay
And named her Mercy; what, I ask, are you?
Should memory at last awake to tell
How you received the King on his return,
And welcomed him, your husband to his home—
Be gone! I seem to feel my eyesight growing dim,

A sign that it is time for you to go.
Away, I say away! *(Exit Cunigunda.)*
OTTOCAR. *(To the Chancellor whom he had grasped for support.)*
　　Do I seem hard? Nor was she kind to me!
　　So goes it, give and take; God strikes the balance!

　　　　You, Herald, will I now no more detain.
　　Go, tell your master things you witnessed here.
　　(Turning toward Merenberg.)
　　To prison take him! What protects from treason
　　If not prompt punishment of former traitors?
　　If you would sow, you first uproot the weeds;
　　Off with this evil vine, this poisoned creeper!
MERENBERG.   Hot-headed King, why make me out a traitor?
　　Those are the traitors who stand next your throne,
　　The Rosenbergs—
OTTOCAR.   So you would slander, too?
MERENBERG.   The man who holds me, leads me off to gaol,
　　He merits prison more, alas, than I.
OTTOCAR.   No Czech has ever yet betrayed his King!
　　Now I am fully certain of your guilt.
　　Lock up this liar!
MERENBERG. *(As he is led away.)*
　　Regret will come, alas, too late!
OTTOCAR.   To prison!
MILOTA.   If he prattles, stop his mouth!
　　(Merenberg is led away; the herald follows.)
OTTOCAR. *(Steps out among his men.)*
　　No Czech has ever yet betrayed his King;
　　Despite that liar's word, I am convinced!
　　As we engage now in another war
　　To bring our country fame and added strength,
　　I trust you much as I do trust myself.
　　Who is opposed, who disapproves my plan,
　　Is free to hold aloof and take no part;
　　He will remain unharmed nor be reproached.
　　But he who joins by choice, and thinks as I,
　　That man will I embrace and call him brother.
　　The oath I swore, when I became your King,
　　Beside my father's grave, I swear anew:
　　True unto Death! Do you the same!

The world holds many evil, wicked men;
Renew the oath upon your sovereign's sword.
(Takes a sword from one of the bystanders; the men in front row kneel.)
Kneel not! Arise! I cannot see men kneel!—
And do not swear!—A man can kneel and swear
And yet not keep the promise that he made.
I trust you as you stand, without an oath!—

And now to work! You go to Breslau, there
Duke Henry, him and Prinik, Duke of Glogau,
Invite to come officially to Prague.
You, off to Germany; in Dresden, Meissen,
From Madgeburg, the Margrave with the Dart,
Bespeak as much support as they will grant.
(To the Chancellor.)
You will address the other lords and princes.
We shall assemble such an ample force
The Emperor will not believe his eyes.
I am still Ottocar, the world will see.
And all of you must lend your lusty strength.
The holdings and the castles you have lost,
Lands that I forced you to assign the Crown,
I shall give back, and give you more besides.
The Rosenbergs get Frauenberg returned,
With Aussig, Falkenstein; to Lar goes Neuhaus;
To Zierotin and Krushina, their old estates!
Take back your lands again, rejoice in them!
United, we shall resolutely stand.
Moravia goes to Milota to guard;
An upright soldier, he will keep it safe.
(Enter Zavish Rosenberg.)
OTTOCAR. Look you, Lord Rosenberg! Well met, we two!
You will, I trust, make common cause with us?
One of the foremost men of all my realm,
On whom, more than on others, I can count.
ZAVISH. That which my brothers do, I also shall;
Like them, I shall not fail to serve the common need. *(Exit.)*
OTTOCAR. *(Follows him with his eyes; with a gesture.)*
He keeps things up his sleeve; not one to trust!
You, Milota, you are my man.
I well believe that you can also hate

But not deceive. I trust myself to you.
Sir Chancellor, have you finished?

CHANCELLOR. *(Where he sits writing.)* Yes, my King!

OTTOCAR. Much have we lost by actions over-rash.
We must now see if caution will avail.
So you would have it, would you not, old man?

CHANCELLOR. O King, chide rashly as you did before;
More pleasing to my taste than gentleness.

OTTOCAR. Write to the Captain in command of Znaim
To send a thousand men—too many, no!
The fortress would meanwhile have no defense.
Five hundred men could make the frontier safe—
But still five hundred are too few. *(Turns toward Milota.)*
Not so?
Write rather than from Iglau—wrong again!
I am confused; no rest the past two nights,
Nor any food.—
Lend me your wooden bench
That I may try to get some rest.

CHANCELLOR. Out here,
Why not the castle, sir—?

OTTOCAR. No, no, no, no!
Pray have my wife come back; she left in anger.
She shall sit down beside me, speak with me,
Until sleep comes to close my heavy lids.
My friend, do be so kind to bring her here.
(Exit the servant.)

OTTOCAR. How good it is to stretch out weary limbs!
And one gets tired! See to Merenberg;
The man is old and prison beds are hard.
Though he has erred, they must not torture him.
But give him treatment as befits a knight.
(Exit Fuellenstein; the servant returns.)

OTTOCAR. The Queen will come?

SERVANT. She is not coming, Sire.

OTTOCAR. Then let her be! Old Chancellor, you come
And lend your knees to me tonight for rest.
Once I have rested—you shall see—
I am the Ottocar I was before. *(Sleeps.)*
(Enter Fuellenstein.)

CHANCELLOR. He sleeps, the King!

FUELLENSTEIN. Soon Merenberg will, too.

When he went ranting on and would not stop
Some guard or other kicked him down the stairs;
They rather think that he will not survive.
OTTOCAR. *(Sits up.)* Ha, Merenberg you come?
CHANCELLOR. He is not here.
OTTOCAR. I thought I saw him.—Sleep, come let me sleep!
(Sinks back asleep. The Chancellor, commanding silence, lays his fingers on his lips.)

(The curtain falls.)

ACT 5

The churchyard at Goetzendorf. Three quarters of the mid-stage is closed in by the sexton's house on which there is a bell tower. Vanguard of the Bohemian army. A bivouac fire with soldiers lying around it. Ottocar sits back of it on an elevation, his chin in his two hands which are supported on the hilt of his sword. Right forward, Milota and Fuellenstein lying on the ground. Before daybreak. It is dark. Enter a Messenger.

MESSENGER. The King is here?
MILOTA. He is, what news?
MESSENGER. *(in a low voice)* Some Magyars
And Cumans from the hostile ranks are roving
Along the River March behind our lines;
Some few were seen in Droesing, people say.
Shall I inform the King?
MILOTA. I should not now.
He is already in an ugly mood;
Besides, the Poles are there and troops of mine,
These two will teach them how to get back home.
MESSENGER. Well, if you think—
MILOTA. Be off; I soon shall follow.
(Exit the messenger.)
FUELLENSTEIN.*(In a low voice.)* This endless waiting, endless wavering!
And always in retreat. A curse upon it!
The King has changed, no more the man he was.
God knows that things were bad enough before;
The Queen's desertion dealt the final blow.
If soldiering were not the life I love,
I should long since have left the army ranks.

A fortnight he besieges Drosendorf,
And gives the Emperor time to gather strength;
And when at last we think he will attack,
As we stand fully armed and ready at Marchegg,
Comes orders to withdraw and we withdraw.
And every town and hamlet that we held,
And every stream and river where we stood entrenched,
Are given up, almost without a blow.

MILOTA. Things soon will be decided, rest assured.

FUELLENSTEIN. He calls it caution; cowardice, I say!
Unlike our earlier days when fight we did.
Now we are cowards.

MILOTA. Hush! The King awakens.

FUELLENSTEIN. High time!

OTTOCAR. *(At the camp fire.)* Bad luck pursued us yesterday.
The enemy gains ground. But what of that?
I still hold Drosendorf; the rear is safe.

FUELLENSTEIN. *(Loudly.)* The rear is safer, almost, than the front.

OTTOCAR. My methods do not suit you, Fuellenstein?

FUELLENSTEIN. To tell the truth, sir, no. We used to fight!

OTTOCAR. You would have struck already at Marchegg?

FUELLENSTEIN. I should have, sir; and so would you have done
Two years ago. When we fought Hungary
On this same spot, you did not hesitate.
Swords out and at the foe. That won the day.

OTTOCAR. It won the day for fortune favored us.
Oh, then I was a rash, imprudent fool,
As you are still. Time comes and ripens men.

FUELLENSTEIN. The Emperor, when we met him at Marchegg,
Had under his command a thousand men;
Now he has thirty thousand, if not more.

OTTOCAR. God only could have known — What is the hour?

SERVANT. Past midnight, almost three.

OTTOCAR. The battle must be fought.
We face the enemy. Today decides.
What town can this be?

SERVANT. Goetzendorf, my King!

OTTOCAR. What stream?

SERVANT. The Sulz.

OTTOCAR. I thought I was in Stillfried.

SERVANT. We rode through Stillfried in the dark of night.
The Emperor camps there now.

OTTOCAR. Well, God decides.

SERVANT. You ought to go indoors, Your Majesty.

OTTOCAR. And see that none attack till I command.
I lured him hither to this mountain pass,
Deluding him with my pretended flight;
Should he advance, my center will retreat,
My flanks move in and close—then Emperor, Goodbye!
I have him cornered like a mouse. Ha, ha!
(Breaks out in a hoarse laugh that turns into a fit of coughing; rubs his hands.) How cold! Has no one here a mantle?
Before day breaks the wind is at its worst.
(As a cloak is put around him.) Is this a summer night? The grain uncut,
And yet so cold. The summers once were warm,
The winters cold; the seasons have exchanged.
Times also change and we are changed with them.
Has no one any word which way the Queen
Has gone?

SERVANT. We have as yet heard nothing, Sire.

OTTOCAR. And Zavish with her still?

SERVANT. Yes, Sire, he is.

OTTOCAR. I hope in course of time to come upon them!—
Will morning never dawn?

SERVANT. Across the March
The sky is grey; day soon must break.

OTTOCAR. *(Leaps to his feet.)* I hail thee, fateful and portentous sun!
Ere thou hast set, fate will decide my doom,
If peace through war or peace within the tomb.
(Throws the cloak aside.)
Put out the fires and have the bugles sound,
Prepare for battle, men; do now or die!

MESSENGER. *(Enters.)* Sir, Droesing is in flames!

OTTOCAR. Behind my lines?
Are not your men there stationed, Milota?

MILOTA. A casual troop of Cumans, it may be;
As yet we do not know.

OTTOCAR. Is there no hill
That we can see what flames there are and where?

SERVANT. The tower, perhaps?

OTTOCAR. Climb quickly up and look!

(Several men go and pound on the door.)

OTTOCAR. How should Hungarians be in Droesing? God above!

The men to blame shall hang!–Hurry!

SERVANT. Sir,
They would not let us in.

OTTOCAR. They; who are they?

SERVANT. Some women in the tower.

OTTOCAR. Women? Nonsense!

SEXTON. *(Comes out of the house.)* Yes, women who attend Bohemia's
Queen.

OTTOCAR. *(Seizes him.)* Attend Bohemia's Queen?–Her retinue?
She too, no doubt?–Ha, knave!–And Zavish also?
What pleasure now for me to cool my wrath!

SEXTON. Consider, Sire.

OTTOCAR. Aside!

SEXTON. Oh, sir!

OTTOCAR. Make way!

(Forces his way into the house, the Sexton after him.)

MILOTA. What chance has Zavish, should he there be found!
I must preserve him at whatever cost!
Stand back, and if I call to summon aid,
Force in the doors and do what I command;
The King when angered loses self-control!

(Goes into the house; the others withdraw.)

(A shallow room: at the back, a Gothic arch before which a dark curtain falls to the floor. Ottocar rushes in; Lady Elizabeth steps in his path.)

OTTOCAR. Away, you bawd! Where have you hid your patrons?

ELIZABETH. Oh, gracious sir, do grant her peace at last!

OTTOCAR. That curtain, I suppose, conceals the secret?
Come, come, my sweet! Up with the curtain; off!

(Tears the curtain open and recoils. On an elevation, covered with black, and with candles at her head and feet, lies Queen Margaret dead in her coffin, the arms of Austria at her feet.)

OTTOCAR. *(At front; in a hollow voice.)*
But this is not the Queen, Bohemia's Queen!

ELIZABETH. She was!

OTTOCAR. Here, Margaret of Austria,
My former wife, but kin of fourth degree,
Hence parted by the Church and through the law,
–God grant her rest eternal!

ELIZABETH. Aye: Amen!

OTTOCAR. When did she die?

ELIZABETH. But yestermorning, Sire.

OTTOCAR. How came she here?

ELIZABETH. Forced from her seat at Krems,
    By your marauding troops, she hoped to reach
    Marchegg, and find the Emperor, when she
    Was overtaken there by Death.
OTTOCAR. Why to the Emperor?
ELIZABETH. Sir, she never said;
    I think to serve as maker of the peace.
OTTOCAR. Peace-maker, that she was!–What caused her death?
ELIZABETH. It commonly is called, a broken heart;
    For weeping night and day–
OTTOCAR. Enough, enough.
    And now, what will you do?
ELIZABETH. We think to wait
    Until the fighting ends, this way or that.
OTTOCAR. This way or that!
ELIZABETH. And then to Lilienfeld
    To bury her in her ancestral tomb,
    Where lies Duke Leopold who was her father;
    And he, the last male heir of Babenberg,
    Her brother Frederick, whom they call the Fighter.
OTTOCAR. That do;–this ring–
MILOTA. *(Enters.)* The enemy draws near!
OTTOCAR. This ring I leave
    To rest beside her body in the grave.
ELIZABETH. Oh, Sire!
OTTOCAR. And when hostilities have ceased,
    And so be I survive, then come to Prague
    That I reward the loyal way you served.
    Now I must go. *(Moves toward the door).*
ELIZABETH. *(Opens the door for him.)* God bless you!
OTTOCAR. *(Halts at the door.)* Margaret,
    Now you are dead, and I am unforgiven? *(returns.)*
    You met your death, god-fearing, loyal soul,
    The feeling of injustice in your breast;
    And now before the judgement-seat of God,
    You make complaint, call vengeance down on me!
    Oh, do not, Margaret, pray, do not!
    You are avenged. What I gave you for, gave up all,
    Is fallen from me like sear autumn leaves,
    All that I gathered, scattered in the sky,
    Without the fruitful blessing from on high;
    And I now stand alone, bowed down by grief,

And none to comfort, none to lend me ear. *(Comes up closer.)*
They wickedly misused me, Margareta;
Ingratitude reared up its loathsome head.
Those next to me conspired behind my back,
Those whom I lifted up have cast me down.
And she, for whom I sacrificed your worth,
That woman cleft my heart within my breast,
Sold my fair honor to a serving man;
And when I came from battle, bruised and bleeding,
She poured not balm but venom on my wounds.
With mock and taunt she knew to goad me on,
Till I ran blindly in the fatal net,
Whose threads draw tight and close about my brow.
(Kneels beside the coffin.)
You often comforted; give comfort now!
Stretch out your icy hand and bless me, do.
One thing I feel is sure: that Death is nigh,
Today, it may be, Ottocar will die;
So bless me now as you yourself are blessed.
(Lays his head on the cushions)

ELIZABETH. He must be praying. Thou, kind God above,
Forgive him, too. And oh, how great a joy
For her, who here lies dead. Did I not say
He would return? And now you are together,
You see? *(Looks upward.)*

VOICE. *(From without.)*   The King is here?

ELIZABETH. *(At the door.)*   He asks to be alone,
That no one shall disturb him. *(Lets the curtain fall.)*
Strife and conflict,
For those kings always seem to find the time,
Not always do they find the time for prayer.
What? Noise again? What heathen disrespect!

(New alarms outside. Elizabeth goes out the door with her finger on her lips, commanding silence.)

(Place before the house as at the beginning of the act. Milota leads a Squire to the front of the stage. The rest remain at the rear. At intervals, the blare of trumpets and uproar outside.)

MILOTA. What! Zavish Rosenberg? He sent you on?
SQUIRE. He did.

MILOTA. And from the Emperor's camp?

SQUIRE. Yes, he is there.

MILOTA. What letter do you bring?

SQUIRE. He gave me none.
　　He told me only–laughable it seems–
　　He told me to remind you of the song:
　　"The winter comes again, the roses wither".

MILOTA. What can he mean?–Roses?–Rosenberg!–
　　Tell him the roses shall not cease to bloom,
　　The snows will melt and winter not return.
　　(Exit the Squire.)

FUELLENSTEIN. *(Enters.)*　Where is the King?

MILOTA. Within.

FUELLENSTEIN. He should not be;
　　The fight's already on.

KNIGHT. *(Enters hastily.)*　The King is here?
　　The vanguard has been forced to yield. Send aid!

MILOTA. He still delays.

FUELLENSTEIN. See there, at last he comes.
　　(Enter Ottocar with Sexton from the house; Lady Elizabeth follows.)

OTTOCAR. *(To the Sexton.)* Your house, should things go badly,
　　will be spared.
　　Be on your way; include me in your prayers.
　　Herbott, what news?

FUELLENSTEIN. Troops fighting hand to hand.

OTTOCAR. Give me my helmet.

FUELLENSTEIN. One of Salzburg's men
　　Could not control his frightened horse; it shied
　　And ran away, the others galloped after.

OTTOCAR. *(Has his helmet on, draws his sword.)*
　　Well then, with God!

SEXTON. And may he bless you, Sire!

ELIZABETH. A thousand times; and bring you safely home.

OTTOCAR. *(Trumpets without.)*　Our hope it is!
　　We hear you and will come.
　　Where are the horses?

FUELLENSTEIN. Out, beyond the gate.

OTTOCAR. *(As he leaves.)*　Men, come!

ELIZABETH. God bless your Highness!

ELIZABETH AND SEXTON. Success and triumph!

(Exeunt all.)

(Open field along the March: broad daylight. Enter Emperor Rudolph with his two sons, accompanied by other Knights with banners.)

RUDOLPH. The sun in splendor rises from the mists;
    The day it brings is fair. My son, when now
    Today you first set foot on Austria's soil,
    Look round about. The land you see is yours!
    The plain surrounding us is known as Marchfeld,
    A battle-field no other can surpass,
    A harvest-field as well, thanks be to God!
    Which it may ever prove to be for you!
    There flows the March; there, swathed in river mist,
    Vienna lies; the Danube dances by,
    With many islands cutting through its course.
    There shall you dwell, if God grant victory.
    But first we have to fight, and so shall you.
    This standard is for you to hold on high,
    To bear before me in our glorious fight.
    (Gives him the flag; to his younger son.)
    Your arm is not yet equal to a sword,
    You stay by me, close at your father's side.

    You, Margrave Hochberg, bear the Empire's eagle;
    And as the eagle strikes live prey alone,
    Smite him who fights, and spare the one who flees.
    (Gives him the eagle.)
    You, Conrad Haslau, although old and grey,
    I will entrust with Austria's glorious banner,
    Borne honorably by you these twenty times.
    You, Henry, Lord of Lichtenstein, stand by,
    And guard the man and what it is he bears.
    Well guarded, yes! Were I to seek a guard
    For this, my head, I should not know a better,
    Than one of Lichtenstein. And now my lords,
    Take up the flag and bear it on before;
    That stripe of white of noble Austria;
    And as it, gleaming, cuts the field of red,
    So may her army move its white-flagged rows
    Between the blood-stained corpses of her foes.

    Now on, with God! And, Christ, our battle cry.
    and as He died for us upon the cross.

So will we die for justice and for right,
Though wrong should offer wealth to us, and life.
Most Reverend Lord of Basel, lead the way,
Intone the battle song: Hail Mary, pure of heart!
SERVANT. *(Enters)* The Queen of Bohemia, Your
    Imperial Highness!
RUDOLPH. Why does she come to me?

(Enter Cunigunda with Zavish; Berta is led in behind them; attendants, who remain at rear.)

CUNIGUNDA. I shall explain;
    To seek protection I have come to you.
RUDOLPH. Protection, Madame, from your husband's foe?
CUNIGUNDA. Because my grimmest foe is he, that husband!
    His rage most often strikes those close to him;
    By fleeing could I barely save my life.
RUDOLPH. How great the confidence you place in me, my Queen!
    I know of women, some of courage, too,
    Preferring death, though by a husband's hand,
    To life with those who seek the husband's death.
    You may, however, stay within my tents,
    Awaiting what relief the future brings.
    (To an attendant.)
    See that Her Majesty is well bestowed.
CUNIGUNDA. I thank Your Highness—Zavish, come with me.
    (Exit)
RUDOLPH. You do not serve, Sir, at your sovereign's side?
ZAVISH. The King has grievously insulted me.
RUDOLPH. Insulted, Sir? And you consider that,
    When he goes out, perhaps to meet his death?
    You may thank God, you are no man of mine,
    Else I should teach you: chapter, first; then verse!
    Go follow her, your Queen, who now must do as King.
    (Exit Zavish.)
RUDOLPH. One matter more before we go. I learn
    That some of those I yesterday made knights,
    And who because of wrongs, or other cause,
    Now harbor hatred of Bohemia's king,
    Men mostly from the Austrian domain,
    Have pledged themselves to seek him on the field,
    And let the finder slay him on the spot;

As Emperor, I here declare such oaths as void,
And I demand that no one lay his hand
Upon King Ottocar to do him harm;
Unless, of course, it be in self defense.
(To Seyfried Merenberg who stands next to him.)
You understand me, sir? Then on, with God.
(Enter a soldier running.)
SOLDIER. Bohemian troops approach!
RUDOLPH. The Austrians have arrived!
Do you imagine we should be afraid?
A single troop; pray, follow me, my lords.
(Enter Fuellenstein with soldiers.)
FUELLENSTEIN. *(Rushes in)* Where is the Emperor? I challenge him!
RUDOLPH. Here, friend, he is!
FUELLENSTEIN. Or rather say, he was.
RUDOLPH. Are you so certain? Let him come, my lords,
I should not like to lose my fencing skills!
Lay on, my friend!
FUELLENSTEIN. Come after; slay them all!
(Exeunt all, fighting.)

(Another part of the battlefield. Left front, the slope of a little hill running down upon the stage. Close by, a tree. Enter Ottocar, helped by a servant; two other servants and Milota follow.)

OTTOCAR. Lord Milota, your men do not attack!
And your Moravians, where are they? Hell!
I fear you are a knave, Lord Milota,
And if you are, because I trusted you
You are a knave ten and a hundred fold!

They killed my horse beneath me as I rode;
My leg still pains me from the sudden fall.
Go, find a mount; I shall await you here.
(Exit the servant.)
You, Milota, ride quickly to your troop—
But no; stay here!
(To a servant)
Go you, and tell the guard
To move to the attack, else I will move on them!
(Exit the servant.)
Look toward me, Milota. Straight in my eyes!

You look with hate. I hope meant for the foe;
If meant for me, then on your death-bed, sir,
A Milota would front you; face to face,
And glare with hatred in your dying eyes.

Mount to the top of yonder hill and see
To Fuellenstein, and how the battle goes.
(Exit Milota.)
OTTOCAR. And you, give me your hand to reach that tree,
To hold me up until I have a mount,
Keep watch and warn me, should a foe approach.
(Stands beside the tree and holds on to a dry low-hanging branch for support.)
The Czechs fight lamely, much as people would
For one they do not like, because they must.
The Austrians and Styrians, however,
Men usually so slow at my command,
Seem changed to devilish messengers of death,
And each one is a hero fighting me.
Pay day is here, and they deal out the pay!

My ways upon Thy earth have not been good,
Almighty God! Like tempests, like a storm,
I swept across Thy peaceful fields.
But Thou alone canst ride upon the whirlwind
For Thou alone, Great God, canst heal its harm.
And though my aim was in itself not bad
How could a grovelling worm like me presume
To play the role of Him who rules the worlds
And seek a path that leads to good through evil?

And Man, whom Thou hast put here for his joy,
A unit, end, a world within the world—
Him, Thou hast made a wonder of Thy hand;
His forehead, high; his neck, erect and proud,
And robed him fair in beauty's festal robe,
With wonders wondrously encircling him.
He hears and sees and feels, knows pleasure.
Once food and drink have furnished him with strength,
Creative energies begin their work,
And weave untiringly through tissues, nerves and veins
To build his house, his frame. No king's abode

Can be compared with such a human form!
But I threw them away by thousands at a time,
To satisfy a folly, please a whim,
As one would scatter refuse from a door.
No single one of all those left for dead,
But had a mother who, on bearing him in pain,
Pressed him with pleasure to her mother breast,
A father who regarded him with pride,
And brought him up, instructed him for years.
When he did merely graze his finger-tip,
They ran to him and washed and bound the cut,
And watched that it would surely heal aright.
All for a finger-tip, a bit of skin!
But I cast them aside like wisps of straw,
And for unbending iron cleared a path
Straight through their pulsing warmth. If Thou dost mean
To summon and to sentence Ottocar,
Then punish me but spare, I pray, my folk.

My eyes were dazzled; so it was I sinned.
Not consciously have I committed wrong.
Yes; once I did!–and once again: O God,
I have, and consciously, committed wrong.

It is not fear of death that bids me so to speak;
And Thou to whom no heart is closed,
Thou knowest whether fear impels this heart.
But if repentance pleases Thee of one,
Moved not by punishment but by his wrong,
Then look on me who kneel before Thy face,   (Kneels.)
And hear me pray as, praying, I implore:
Be Thou a God of mercy, not a judge! (Bows his head.)
(Enter Seyfried Merenberg fully armed, at rear.)

SEYFRIED. Ottocar!

OTTOCAR. Who calls?

SEYFRIED. (Remains at rear)   Where is my father?

OTTOCAR. (Mutters in a muffled voice.)   When God put Cain to question,
   He replied:
   Thou didst not give him unto me to keep!

SEYFRIED. I gave him unto you by my own folly!
   And now I stand before you clad in steel
   And ask for his return: Give me my father!

OTTOCAR. You well know where he is.

SEYFRIED. I well know: Dead!

OTTOCAR. He paid as traitors pay.

SEYFRIED. A traitor, he?
> Too true he was, to you, to me, to all the world.
> He did not know I served the Emperor;
> The letter he dispatched contained requests
> For your rejected wife.

OTTOCAR. He is with God!

SEYFRIED. Where you will be! To Him commend your soul!
> *(Runs at him with drawn sword. Enter Emerberg.)*

EMERBERG. Seyfried, what is that?

SEYFRIED. Thanks for warning me!
> The Emperor forbade that you be slain
> With weapons; let me like a basilisk,
> They try to slay you with an evil eye.
> Look in my face and hear me: Merenberg!
> A call that Hell will echo: Merenberg!

OTTOCAR. Give way; I must rejoin my troops.

SEYFRIED. Stand back!
> You were my teacher, model, my ideal;
> I honored you as no one else that lived;
> The fame of earth is dimmed by what you did,
> Its happiness, my father's death destroyed.
> Give back to me my confidence in man;
> My father give, whom I myself surrendered
> For you to seize. Cold-blooded murderer,
> Look close, this is the face of Merenberg.
> Come, slay him once again in slaying me.

OTTOCAR. Your visor close; then combat can begin.

SEYFRIED. No, no! Come, King, come battle with the dead!
> Well valiant Ottocar! For once afraid?
> *(Enter Ottocar's Servant.)*

SERVANT. Lord Milota! Come, help! The enemy!

SEYFRIED. *(To Emerberg.)* Hold back that man! He must cross swords
> with me,
> That I may tell the Emperor: Majesty,
> I did not slay him, he himself attacked:
> We might fight back, you said, in self-defense.
> *(Emerberg fights with the Servant.)*

SERVANT. Lord Milota!

EMERBERG. Give way!

SERVANT. God help me now!

(Falls dead at the King's feet.)

OTTOCAR. *(Takes the sword he had laid beside the tree.)* So be it!

(Enter Milota.)

OTTOCAR. Milota, come aid your King!

SEYFRIED. Halt; friend or foe?

MILOTA. No foe of yours, my lords!
   Which road will lead me homeward?

OTTOCAR. Milota!

MILOTA. My brother, Benesh, sends his last regards;
   He died, his reason lost, his mind diseased,
   And cousin Berta raves beside his grave.
   Make way, my lords; Good luck and fare you well!
   (Passes by them, wrapped in his cloak; exit.)

OTTOCAR. You would desert and not hear my reproach?
   To leave your sovereign, though, makes you a knave forever.

SEYFRIED. Give in!

OTTOCAR. You think to capture Ottocar?
   First you must fight! *(Stamps his wounded foot.)*
   Now, Foot, hold firm!
   This is no time for pain.–And you, make way!

EMERBERG. Look, you are lost; your men have taken flight.
   (Bohemians in flight fill the back of the stage.)

OTTOCAR. You lie. No Czech would flee. Come, let me go.

SEYFRIED and EMERBERG. *(Hold him back with their swords)*
   You, stay!
   (Enter Henry of Lichtenstein, center, with a band in pursuit of the Bohemians; he hurries to the rear with the Austrian banner in his hand.)

LICHTENSTEIN. Our foes take flight! Hail Austria!

OTTOCAR. Halt, cowards, halt!
   And you make way!

SEYFRIED. When dead,
   Not else!

OTTOCAR. *(Makes a thrust.)*   Bohemia here!

SEYFRIED. *(Thrusts also.)*   Here Austria!

OTTOCAR. *(With a second thrust.)*   Here Ottocar!

SEYFRIED. Here Merenberg and God! *(Cuts him down.)*
   (Ottocar falls, quickly gets up again, stumbles a few steps and then falls dead beside the little hill.)

EMERBERG. What have you done? Transgressed the Emperor's order!
   (Seyfried stands motionless, his hands hanging at his side.)

LICHTENSTEIN. *(Returns.)*   Triumph and victory! Hail Austria!
   (Enter Rudolph with his retinue.)

RUDOLPH. A truce to slaughter! Spare the vanquished foe!
What happened here? What turned you into ice?
Ha, Ottocar! Struck down, blood-covered, dead!
You did it! Flee, like Cain, the first to kill
And let me nevermore behold your face!
(Exit Merenberg in flight.)
RUDOLPH. Allow Bohemians now to leave for home;
Announce that he for whom they fought is dead.
ELIZABETH. *(Off-stage.)* Help, help!
RUDOLPH. Who calls?
ELIZABETH. *(Falls at the Emperor's feet.)* Oh, gracious Majesty,
Marauders have come in; they steal, they burn,
They do not even leave the dead in peace.
Protect us, Sire!
RUDOLPH. See that they are helped!
Who are you?
ELIZABETH. Lady-in-Waiting to my Queen,
Queen Margaret of Austria, now deceased,
Those men are bearers of my lady's body.
(Four men, accompanied by women, dressed in black, carry in the coffin.)
RUDOLPH. And there the body of your master!
ELIZABETH. Oh, God!
So he is dead, the moment he grew kind!
My poor, poor master! Put the body down,
Then they may lie together, joined in death.
*(The coffin is set on the mound at Ottocar's head.
Enter Cunigunda, followed by Zavish and Berta.)*
CUNIGUNDA. The King is captured, so the people say.
RUDOLPH. See, woman, here your husband lies!
*(Cunigunda sinks trembling to her knees with a cry; Zavish stands with
bowed head.)*
RUDOLPH. *(Continues.)* At his wife's feet;
That she remained his wife, she proved in death.
BERTA. *(Has taken her position on the mound behind the
coffin and leans upon it with both elbows;
she raps on the coffin and speaks.)*
Come, open, Margaret. See, your husband here!
*(Enter the Chancellor with several other prisoners;
he throws himself down beside Ottocar.)*
CHANCELLOR. Oh Sire! You, my mistaken, valiant Master!
(Lays Ottocar's head upon his knees.)

RUDOLPH. You lie here, bare and unadorned, great King,
  Your head reposing in your servant's lap,
  Of all the robes and riches you once had,
  Not even one poor coverlet remains
  To serve your lifeless body as a shroud.
  The Emperor's mantle you so much desired,
  I take it off and with it cover you, (*Does so.*)
  That like an Emperor you be interred,
  Who died alone and wretched beggar's death.
  Take him to Laa, and have him lie in state,
  Until they bear him where his fathers rest.
  (*Bares his head and prays silently; the others
  do likewise. Cunigunda covers her face with her veil; Zavish stares fixedly
  in front of him.*)
                    (*Pause.*)
BERTA. (*Still leans on the cover of Margaret's coffin.*)
  Forgive us, as we too forgive,
  And lead us not into temptation.
RUDOLPH. Aye, lead us not into temptation, Lord!—
  And now, my son, here where this body lies.
  Of one now dead but who in life was King,
  I here invest you with the fief of Austria.
  (*At a sign from him, both his sons kneel; he addresses his remarks mainly to
  the elder one.*)
RUDOLPH. Be great and strong; increase your race and line,
  Make it extend to regions near and far,
  With Hapsburg's name emblazoned like a star!
  Stand by your brother, lend him your support.
  Should you by arrogance be led astray,
  With pride in governing raise up your head,
  Think of this overweening man here dead,
  Whose misdeeds God will punish, one and all,
  Of Ottocar, his rise and of his fall!
  Stand up! And you! You nevermore need kneel;
  I hail you, sovereign now of this your land.
  And hail him also, you, with welcome cry.
  That, thunder-like, it echo through the sky:
  Hail Austria's first Hapsburg; Hapsburg, hail!
ALL. Hail! Hail!
  Austria, hail! Hapsburg for ever!
  (*All keel to do him homage. Trumpets and cheers.*)

                    (*The curtain falls.*)

A scene from the Vienna Akademietheater's production of Johann Nestroy's The Talisman, 1937, directed by Herbert Waniek, designed by Stefan Hlawa, with Hermann Thimig as Titus and Alma Seidler as Salome. (COURTESY OF THE AUSTRIAN NATIONAL LIBRARY, VIENNA)

A scene from the Vienna Burgtheater's production of Franz Grill-parzer's King Ottocar's Fortune and Death, 1955, directed by Adolph Rott, settings by Fritz Judtmann, and costumes by Elli Rolf, with Albert Rueprecht as Seyfried Merenberg, Attilia Hörbiger as Rudolph of Hapsburg, Ewald Balser as King Ottocar of Bohemia, and Albin Skoda as Zawisch. (COURTESY OF THE AUSTRIAN NATIONAL LIBRARY, VIENNA)

A scene from the Salzburg Festival Theatre production of Hugo von Hofmannsthal's Elektra, 1964, *directed by Herbert von Karajan with M. Mode as Clytemnestra.* (COURTESY OF PHOTO ELLINGER, SALZBURG)

A scene from the Linz Landestheater production of Fritz Hoch-wälder's The Raspberry Picker, *1975, directed by Hermann Molzer, designed by Heinz Köttel, wih Willy Meyer-Fürst A. G. as the Factory Director, Walter Sofka as Doctor Schnopf, Ernst Zeller as Conrad Steisshäuptl, Engelbert Jirak as Contractor Ybbsgruber, Hubert Mann as the Police Inspector, and Dieter Naumann as the Headmaster.*
(COURTESY OF THE LANDESTHEATER, LINZ)

A scene from the Carnegie-Mellon University Drama Department production of Arthur Schnitzler's La Ronde, *1967, directed by James Rosenberg, settings by Stanley Thomas, costumes by Richard Lang.* (COURTESY OF WILLIAM NELSON AND THE CARNEGIE-MELLON UNIVERSITY DRAMA DEPARTMENT)

A scene from the Theatre Guild production of Franz Werfel's **Goat** Song, *New York, 1926, directed by Jacob Ben-Ami, designed by Lee Simonson.* (PHOTO BY VANDAMM, COURTESY OF THE PERFORMING ARTS RESEARCH CENTER OF THE NEW YORK PUBLIC LIBRARY)

Arthur Schnitzler (1862-1931)

La Ronde

In the history of the Austrian drama Arthur Schnitzler, a doctor by profession as was Anton Chekhov, stands firmly within the modern world of psychological dissection of personality and culture. His dramatic technique stems from Ibsen and the realists, yet it was also imbued with *fin de siècle* impressionism and a deep sense of the psychological problems that lay at the heart of the ancient and decaying Hapsburg culture of Vienna. Only a physician-playwright attempting to dissect his own work in relation to all of the forces that were in motion at the end of the nineteenth century would self-consciously say, as Schnitzler did, that a writer is at once a realist and an idealist, an impressionist and an expressionist, a naturalist and a symbolist. At that moment in time all these trends were jostling for position in the battle of the styles, and there was no cohesive cultural style in western Europe except the secondhand, diluted Romanticism of middle-class tastes that was then more than a century old. Especially in Vienna, where the weight of the past was very strong, the struggle to say something valid in a meaningful style was at the forefront of every writer's consciousness. As a physician-playwright who was making many of the same discoveries as Freud, Schnitzler combined the dispassionate attitude of the consulting room with wistful charm and a pessimistic sense of the political and cultural decay that lay at the heart of the Austrian Empire. However, his cynicism and skepticism were of a very different order from Chekhov's sensitive, spiritual probings of his characters. The difference in spirit was due not only to the difference of temperament between the two physicians, but in large part to the specific cultural atmosphere prevailing in Vienna at the turn of the century.

The son of a prominent physician, Schnitzler studied medicine in Vienna where he spent most of the remainder of his life. He became a practicing physician in 1885 and wrote medical reviews on such subjects as psychotherapy and hypnotism at a time when Freud was researching many of the same subjects. But Schnitzler soon gave up medicine to become a writer—a connoisseur of the delicate variations and many shaded emotions connected with love. His earliest works were signed with the name *Anatol,* and his first collection of one-act plays that appeared in 1893 was called *The Affairs of Anatol,* which related the amours and intrigues of a worldly man-about-town with rather cynical commentary by an interested friend. In these early one-acts, Schnitzler already embodied the major theatrical tone for which he is famous: the spirit of gaiety and sensuality of *fin de siècle* Vienna–the fleeting moment, the passage of time, the amoral adventures tinged with a melancholy sadness, the ultimate emptiness that lay beneath the fun and charm of the sensual life. *Liebelei (Light-o-Love)*, published in 1895, further established his reputation, and despite a superficial sentimentality, it was again a subtle and deft dissection of contemporary Viennese society including one of the playwright's most winning portrayals of the *süsse Mädel*,—sweet maiden, in the character of Christine. It depicts the darker side of the social scene, in which this young working girl kills herself on learning of the death in a duel of the young aristocrat who had been trifling with her affections.

Probably the best known play by Schnitzler, at least to the American theater and moviegoing public, is *Reigen (La Ronde* in French and *Hands Around* or *Round Dance* in English). This play, which is reprinted here, was written in 1896, privately printed in 1900, and published in 1903. It was not produced until 1912. It has since been produced and filmed many times and has become the play most securely linked in people's minds with the name and playwriting style of Arthur Schnitzler.

It is a fast-moving comedy in ten scenes, a sprightly and erotic dance involving a chain of sexual partners that finally comes full circle when the Prostitute who has seduced the Soldier in the opening scene turns up in a brothel next to the Count in the final scene. The sequence of scenes has led from the lowest levels of Viennese society to the highest, and none of the escapades or seductions has led to either fulfillment or lasting relationships. Each has been a moment of mere physical contact, and the audience is left at the end with a gnawing emptiness and a deep sense of the foolishness and elusiveness of the quest for true human relationships through random sexual encounters.

Schnitzler, in this play as in many others, is a moralist who never moralizes, a judge who disguises his insights with a mask of sophisticated urbanity. Underneath the glossy surface of his Viennese society, he brilliantly probes with psychological accuracy the discontent, disillusionment, and boredom that result from random "affairs", and yet he does not resort to casebook details. Schnitzler seemed innately aware that sex was an escape from the felt decadence and decline in Viennese society for a people trying to maintain a former grandeur while the world of nineteenth-century Romanticism was crumbling about them.

His other plays of this early period are *Freiwild (Free Game;* 1896), *Die überspannte Person (The Extravagant One;* 1896), and *Der Schleier der Beatrice (The Veil of Beatrice;* 1900). Of the one-act plays from this period, *Der Grüne Kakadu (The Green Cockatoo;* 1899) is the best known.

It is a colorful philosophic drama set on the eve of the French Revolution, which ironically represents man's obliviousness to the great events around him. There are many other one-acts during the next dozen years, several puppet plays, and two pantomimes, one of which was later set to music.

Der Einsame Weg (The Lonely Way; 1904), another distinguished work in its tone and ideas, also underlines what critics have come to recognize as Schnitzler's strong limitations as a dramatist and one of the reasons that he was often happier with the one-act form. This play, like so many others, has essentially static characters, a lack of plot development, and an overall lack of unity and form. The play has a kind of autumnal half-light in its sensitive portrayal of man's lonely path from birth to death. The central character of Sala, who is both sentimental and sarcastic in his response to life and wants to live to the fullest, is also deeply aware of its sadness, transience, loneliness, and death.

Other less-successful plays were *Zwischenspiel (Intermezzo;* 1905), *Der Ruf des Lebens (The Call of Life;* 1906), *Der junge Medardus (Young Medardus;* 1910), and *Das weite Land (The Distant Land;* 1911). His last important drama, *Professor Bernhardi* (1912), is an atypical and rather autobiographical study of anti-Semitism, which had been spreading in Vienna throughout the late-nineteenth and early twentieth century. Though he labeled the play a comedy in five acts, it is basically a subtle problem play about ethics and religion as they relate to a situation in a Viennese hospital. Schnitzler attempts to canvas objectively from all angles the repercussions to an anti-Semitic incident in the hospital without coming to any simple answers or sharply drawn conclusions.

Schnitzler's final plays were three comedies—*Fink und Fliederbush (The Finch and the Elder Tree;* 1917), *Die Schwestern, oder Casanova in Spa (The Sisters or Casanova at the Spa;* 1919), and *Die Komödie der Verführung (The Comedy of Seduction;* 1924), and two wistfully nostalgic plays, *Der Gang zum Weiher (The Walk to the Pond; 1925) and Im Spiel der Sommer Lüfte (Play in the Summer Air; 1930).* The year after his death, three one-acts were published: *Anatol's Grossenwahn (Anatol's Great Delusion), Die Mörderin (The Murderess),* and *Die Gleitenden (The Decline).*

Basically his talent represented prewar Vienna, and his work and spirit suffered under the new Austrian Republic. Schnitzler was a true son of the Austrian theatrical tradition, despite superficial borrowings from both French writers and earlier realists. His plays beautifully expressed the dying fall of one of Europe's great cultures and one of its most sophisticated and cosmopolitan cities. He also expressed the great themes and traditions of the Austrian theater: sentiment edged with cynicism, reality clouded by illusion, sweetness and charm tinged with sadness, and romanticism ringed with melancholy.

In the United States, Schnitzler has been most fully represented on the stage in various adaptations of *The Affairs of Anatol*. A very successful production of five of the seven playlets opened in New York in 1912, with John Barrymore as Anatol, and the *New York Dramatic Mirror* for October 16, 1912, admired Anatol's "geniality and utter detestation of hypocrisy. He runs the whole gamut of possible 'affairs' without once besmirching his honor." In Chicago, *The Record Herald* for December 18, 1912, was not interested in matters of honor: "The intention of the thing is deplorable, its effect is tedious and insipid." Six of the Anatol playlets were revived in 1931 with Joseph Schildkraut in the title role, and again in 1946 Mady Christians, who had played in Max Reinhardt's production of 1924, revived six of the plays for the Equity Library Theatre. Selections from the Anatol playlets have also long been presented by schools and amateur groups, while *avante-garde* theaters used to feel very daring in presenting *La Ronde*. But as Brooks Atkinson said of the Theatre Marquee revival of 1960 in the *New York Times* for May 10: "The Freudian attitude toward sex has tempered the audacity of the material. Now we can hardly avoid regarding the ten episodes as repetitious, each being less interesting than its precedessor . . . not so incendiary now as it was in a polite society."

The play that has received the most serious attention abroad in recent years is *Professor Bernhardi*, which was included in the Burgtheater tour to the United States in 1968. In the May 20 issue of the *New York Times*, Dan Sullivan commented that it was a fascinating play in which the performers "remind you . . . of a great, mellow European orchestra. . . . The Company itself is the star."

La Ronde

Ten Dialogues

by

ARTHUR SCHNITZLER

Translated by Carl Richard Mueller

Characters

THE PROSTITUTE

THE SOLDIER

THE PARLOR MAID

THE YOUNG GENTLEMAN

THE YOUNG WIFE

THE HUSBAND

THE SWEET YOUNG THING

THE POET

THE ACTRESS

THE COUNT

Time and place: Vienna of the 1890s

SCENE 1

(The Prostitute and the Soldier. Late evening. On the Augarten Bridge. The Soldier comes along on his way home. He whistles.)
PROSTITUTE. Hey there, honey. Come here.

(The Soldier turns to look, then continues on.)

PROSTITUTE. Don't you want to come with me?

SOLDIER. You uh-talking to me?

PROSTITUTE. Sure. See anybody else around? Come on. I live right around here.

SOLDIER. I don't have time. Got to get back to the barracks.

PROSTITUTE. You'll get back to the barracks okay. It's nicer here with me.

SOLDIER. *(Near her.)* You think so, uh?

PROSTITUTE. Pst! A policeman could come by anytime.

SOLDIER. Ah, you're crazy! A policeman! Anyway, I'm armed!

PROSTITUTE. Come on, what do you say?

SOLDIER. Cut it out! I haven't got any money.

PROSTITUTE. So who needs money?

SOLDIER. *(Stops; they are at a street light.)* Who needs money?! Who the hell are you?

PROSTITUTE. I only make these civilians pay. But a guy like you can get it free anytime he wants.

SOLDIER. I'll bet you're the one Huber was talking about.

PROSTITUTE. I don't know any Huber.

SOLDIER. Sure, you're the one. You know—the coffeehouse in Schiff Gasse? He went home with you from there.

PROSTITUTE. I've gone home with more guys than him from that coffeehouse. Eh! Eh!

SOLDIER. Okay, let's go, let's go.

PROSTITUTE. What's the rush, you can't wait now?

SOLDIER. Well for Christ's sake, what's there to wait for? Besides, I gotta be back at the barracks by ten.

PROSTITUTE. How long you been in?

SOLDIER. None of your business! You live far?

PROSTITUTE. About ten minutes' walk.

SOLDIER. Ah hell, that's too far. Give me a kiss.

PROSTITUTE. *(Kisses him.)* I figure that's the best part of it when you really like a guy.

SOLDIER. You think so, uh? Ah hell, I can't go with you, it's too far.

PROSTITUTE. Well, then why not come tomorrow afternoon?

SOLDIER. Okay. What's the address?

PROSTITUTE. Ah, but you won't come.

SOLDIER. If I promise?

PROSTITUTE. Hey, you know what? If you don't want to go all the way home with me tonight . . . what about . . . over there? *(She points toward the Danube.)*

SOLDIER. What's over there?

PROSTITUTE. It's nice and quiet there too. Nobody around this time of night.

SOLDIER. Ah, that's no good.

PROSTITUTE. Everything I got's good. Come on, stay awhile with me. Who knows, we might be dead tomorrow.

SOLDIER. All right, come on—but make it quick!

PROSTITUTE. Careful, it's dark over here. One slip and you end up in the Danube.

SOLDIER. That might be the best bet after all.

PROSTITUTE. Pst, not so fast. We'll come to a bench soon.

SOLDIER. You're right at home, aren't you?

PROSTITUTE. I'd like one like you for a sweetheart.

SOLDIER. I'd only make you jealous.

PROSTITUTE. I could take care of that.

SOLDIER. Ha—

PROSTITUTE. Not so loud. Sometimes these policemen get lost down here. Who'd ever think us in the middle of Vienna?

SOLDIER. Come over here, come on.

PROSTITUTE. What's the matter with you? If we slip we end up in the river.

SOLDIER. *(Takes hold of her)* There, that's better . . .

PROSTITUTE. You just hold tight.

SOLDIER. Don't worry . . .

. . . . .

PROSTITUTE. It would have been better on the bench.

SOLDIER. Hell, what's the difference!—Well, come on, get up.

PROSTITUTE. What are you running for?

SOLDIER. I've gotta get back to the barracks, I'll be late as it is.

PROSTITUTE. Hey, uh, what's your name?

SOLDIER. What's it to you what my name is?

PROSTITUTE. My name's Leocadia.

SOLDIER. Ha!—Who ever heard of a name like that!

PROSTITUTE. You!

SOLDIER. Well, what do you want?

PROSTITUTE. Well, uh, how about a little something for the janitor?

SOLDIER. Ha! What do you think I am! So long! Leocadia . . .

PROSTITUTE. Tightwad! Son-of-a-bitch!

(He has disappeared.)

SCENE 2

(The Soldier and the Parlor Maid. The Prater. Sunday evening. A path leading from the Wurstelprater Park out into the dark avenues. The confused sounds of the Park are still audible, along with the music of the Fünfkreuzertanz, a banal polka, played by a brass band.)

(The Soldier. The Parlor Maid.)

PARLOR MAID. Tell me, why did we have to leave just now?
(The Soldier laughs stupidly; he is embarrassed.)

PARLOR MAID. It was so nice in there. And I just love to dance.
(The Soldier takes her by the waist.)

PARLOR MAID. *(Letting him.)*   But we're not dancing now. Why are you holding me so tight?

SOLDIER. What's your name? Kathi?

PARLOR MAID. You must have Kathi on the brain!

SOLDIER. I know, I know, don't tell me . . . Marie.

PARLOR MAID. Oh, it's so dark here. I'm going to be afraid.

SOLDIER. As long as I'm here you don't have to be afraid. You just leave it to me!

PARLOR MAID. But where are we going now? There are no people around. Come on, let's go back!–And it's so dark!

SOLDIER. *(Draws on his Virginia cigar, making the tip glow red.)*   How's that for light? Haha! Oh, you beautiful . . .

PARLOR MAID. Hey, what are you doing! If I had only known!

SOLDIER. I'll be damned if you aren't the softest one of the bunch, Fräulein Marie.

PARLOR MAID. I suppose you tried them all.

SOLDIER. You notice things like that, dancing. You notice a lot of things! Ha!

PARLOR MAID. You sure danced more with that pie-faced blonde than with me.

SOLDIER. She's a friend of a friend of mine.

PARLOR MAID. The corporal with the turned-up mustache?

SOLDIER. No, the civilian at the table with me earlier, the one with the big mouth.

PARLOR MAID. Oh, I remember. He sure is fresh.

SOLDIER. Did he do anything to you? I'll teach him a . . . What did he do to you?

PARLOR MAID. Oh, nothing–I only watched him with the others.

SOLDIER. Tell me something, Fräulein Marie . . .

PARLOR MAID. You'll burn me with that cigar.

SOLDIER. Sorry!–Fräulein Marie, why are we being so formal?

PARLOR MAID. Because we aren't acquainted yet.

SOLDIER. A lot of people who can't stand each other aren't as formal as us.

PARLOR MAID. Maybe the next time, when we . . . oh, Herr Franz–

SOLDIER. So . . . you do know my name.

PARLOR MAID. But, Herr Franz. . .

SOLDIER. Just call me Franz, Fräulein Marie.

PARLOR MAID. Then don't be so fresh–Come on, what if somebody sees us!

SOLDIER. So let them look. They couldn't see two feet in front of their own faces out here.

PARLOR MAID. But, Herr Franz, where are you taking me?

SOLDIER. Look there–two others just like us.

PARLOR MAID. Where? I can't see a thing.

SOLDIER. There–right in front of us.

PARLOR MAID. Why did you say "two others just like us"?–

SOLDIER. Well, what I meant was, they like each other too.

PARLOR MAID. Oh, be careful there! What is it? I almost fell.

SOLDIER. Just the railing around the grass.

PARLOR MAID. Stop pushing me like that, I'll fall.

SOLDIER. Pst, not so loud.

PARLOR MAID. I'm really going to scream in a minute.–Why, what are you doing . . . why–

SOLDIER. There's not a soul in sight out here.

PARLOR MAID. Then let's go back where there are.

SOLDIER. What do we need people for, Marie . . . what we need is . . . come on . . . come on.

PARLOR MAID. Oh, but, Herr Franz, please, for heaven's sake, listen to me, if I'd only . . . known . . . oh . . . oh . . . yes! . . .

. . . . .

SOLDIER. *(Blissfully)* My God, don't . . . don't stop . . . ah . . .

PARLOR MAID. . . . I can't even see your face.

SOLDIER. My God . . . my face . . .

. . . . .

SOLDIER. Well, are you going to lay there all night, Fräulein Marie?

PARLOR MAID. Please, Franz, help me.

SOLDIER. Oh, come on.

PARLOR MAID. Oh, God, Franz.

SOLDIER. Well, what's all this with Franz all of a sudden?

PARLOR MAID. You're a terrible man, Franz.

SOLDIER. Sure, sure. Hey, wait for me.

PARLOR MAID. Why did you let go of me?

SOLDIER. Do you mind if I light my cigar again!

PARLOR MAID. It's so dark.

SOLDIER. It'll be light again tomorrow.

PARLOR MAID. At least tell me if you like me.

SOLDIER. What's the matter, Fräulein Marie, didn't you feel anything? Ha!

PARLOR MAID. Where are we going?

SOLDIER. Back.

PARLOR MAID. Please, not so fast!

SOLDIER. What's the matter now? Do you think I like walking in the dark?

PARLOR MAID. Tell me, Franz–do you like me?

SOLDIER. But I just told you I liked you!

PARLOR MAID. Don't you want to give me a kiss?

SOLDIER. *(Kindly.)* There . . . Listen–you can hear the music again now.,

PARLOR MAID. You mean you want to go back dancing again?

SOLDIER. Sure, why not?

PARLOR MAID. Well, Franz, I've got to get home. They'll be angry with me, as it is, my mistress is such a . . . she's rather . . . we never go out.

SOLDIER. All right, then go home.

PARLOR MAID. Well, I was thinking, Herr Franz, that you would walk home with me.

SOLDIER. Walk home with you? Ah!

PARLOR MAID. Well, you see, it always so lonely walking home alone.

SOLDIER. Where do you live?

PARLOR MAID. Not at all far–in Porzellan Gasse.

SOLDIER. I see! We've got quite a little walk ahead of us . . . but it's too early now . . . I want to have some fun. I've got a late pass tonight . . . don't have to be back before twelve. I'm going to dance some more.

PARLOR MAID. Sure, I know. Now it's the blonde's turn—
with the pie-face!

SOLDIER. Ha!–She's no pie-face.

PARLOR MAID. Oh, God, why are men so terrible! I'll bet you
treat all of them that way.

SOLDIER. Oh, I wouldn't say that!–

PARLOR MAID. Franz, please, not tonight again–stay with me
tonight, won't you–?

SOLDIER. All right, all right. But I'm still going back in dancing.

PARLOR MAID. I wouldn't dance with another soul tonight!

SOLDIER. We're almost there.

PARLOR MAID. Where?

SOLDIER. The Swoboda! We made good time. Listen, they're
still playing it . . . tatatatum tatatatum . . . *(He sings along.)*
. . . Okay, if you want to wait for me, I'll take you home
. . . if not . . . so long!

PARLOR MAID. I'll wait.

(They enter the dancehall.)

SOLDIER. I'll tell you what, Fräulein Marie—why not buy yourself a glass
of beer?
  (Turning to a blond as she dances past in the arms of a young man.)
  May I have this dance?–

SCENE 3

*(The Parlor Maid and the Young Gentleman. A hot summer afternoon. His
parents are already off to the country. The cook is having her day off. The Parlor
Maid is in the kitchen writing a letter to the soldier who is her lover. A bell rings
from the room of the Young Gentleman. She rises and goes to the room of the
Young Gentleman—The Young Gentleman is lying on the divan, smoking and
reading a French novel.)*

PARLOR MAID. Did the young gentleman ring?

YOUNG GENTLEMAN. Oh, yes, Marie, yes, I, uh, rang. Yes,
now what was it I . . .? Oh, yes, of course, the blinds,
would you let them down, Marie? Its cooler with the blinds
down . . . yes . . .

(The Parlor Maid goes to the window and lowers the blinds.)

YOUNG GENTLEMAN. *(Continues reading.)* What are you doing,
Marie? Oh, yes, well, now it's too dark to read, isn't it?

PARLOR MAID. The young gentleman is always so studious.

YOUNG GENTLEMAN. *(Ignores this genteelly.)*   There, that's fine.
*(Marie goes out. The Young Gentleman tries to continue reading; soon,
however, he drops his book and rings again. The Parlor Maid appears.)*
YOUNG GENTLEMAN. Oh, Marie . . . what I wanted to say was
      . . . uh . . . would you have any cognac in the house?
PARLOR MAID. Yes, but it would be locked up.
YOUNG GENTLEMAN. Well, who has the key?
PARLOR MAID. Lini has the key.
YOUNG GENTLEMAN. Who is Lini?
PARLOR MAID. The cook, Herr Alfred.
YOUNG GENTLEMAN. Well then, tell Lini to get it.
PARLOR MAID. Yes, but she's on her day off.
YOUNG GENTLEMAN. I see . . .
PARLOR MAID. Shall I run down to the café for the young
      gentleman?
YOUNG GENTLEMAN. No, no . . . it's warm enough as is. I
      don't think I'll need the cognac. But, Marie . . . you might
      bring me a glass of water. And, Marie . . . let it run so it
      will be nice and cold.

*(The Parlor Maid goes out. The Young Gentleman watches her leave. At the
door she turns around to him—the Young Gentleman looks into space.—The
Parlor Maid turns the handle on the tap and lets the water run. Meanwhile she
goes into her little room, washes her hands, and arranges her curls in front of the
mirror. Then she brings the Young Gentleman his glass of water. She goes to the
divan. The Young Gentleman gets up halfway, the Parlor Maid hands him the
glass of water, their fingers touch.)*

YOUNG GENTLEMAN. Thank you– Well, what is it?–Be careful;
      put the glass back on the saucer . . . *(He lies down again
      and stretches himself out.)* What time is it?–
PARLOR MAID. Five o'clock, sir.
YOUNG GENTLEMAN. Oh, five o'clock.–Good.

*The Parlor Maid goes out; she turns around at the door; the Young Gentleman
has followed her with his eyes; she notices this and smiles. The Young Gentleman
remains on the divan for a while, then rises suddenly. He walks as far as the door,
then comes back, lies down again on the divan. He tries to continue reading.
After a few moments he rings again. The Parlor Maid appears with a smile
which she does not try to hide.*

YOUNG GENTLEMAN. Oh, Marie, what I meant to ask you—
did Doctor Schüller come by this morning?

PARLOR MAID. No, there was no one here this morning.

YOUNG GENTLEMAN. How strange. You're certain he didn't
come? Would you know him if you saw him?

PARLOR MAID. Yes. He's the tall man with the black beard.

YOUNG GENTLEMAN. That's right. Was he here?

PARLOR MAID. No, sir, there was no one here.

YOUNG GENTLEMAN. *(Having decided.)* Come here, Marie.

PARLOR MAID. *(Steps a bit closer.)* Yes, sir?

YOUNG GENTLEMAN. Closer . . . there . . . why . . . I always
thought . . .

PARLOR MAID. What is it, sir?

YOUNG GENTLEMAN. I thought . . . I always thought . . .
About that blouse . . What's it made of . . . Well, come
on, come closer. I won't bite.

PARLOR MAID. *(Goes to him.)* What about my blouse? Doesn't
the young gentleman like it?

YOUNG GENTLEMAN. *(Takes hold of her blouse and pulls her
down to him.)* Blue? It's quite a lovely blue, isn't it? *(Simply.)*
You're very nicely dressed, Marie.

PARLOR MAID. Oh, but the young gentleman . . .

YOUNG GENTLEMAN. Why, what is it? *(He has opened her
blouse. Pertinently.)* You have such lovely white skin, Marie.

PARLOR MAID. The young gentleman flatters me.

YOUNG GENTLEMAN. *(Kisses her breast.)* That can't hurt you,
can it?

PARLOR MAID. No.

YOUNG GENTLEMAN. It's your sighing! Why are you sighing
so, Marie?

PARLOR MAID. Oh, Herr Alfred . . .

YOUNG GENTLEMAN. And what nice slippers you have on . . .

PARLOR MAID. . . . But, Herr Alfred . . . what if someone
rings!

YOUNG GENTLEMAN. Who would ring at a time like this?

PARLOR MAID. But doesn't the young gentleman . . . look . . .
how light it is . . .

YOUNG GENTLEMAN. You needn't be ashamed in front of me.
You needn't be ashamed in front of anyone . . . not as
lovely as you are. My God, Marie, you're so . . . Even
your hair smells wonderful.

PARLOR MAID. Herr Alfred . . .

YOUNG GENTLEMAN. Don't be silly, Marie . . . I've seen you
    –look quite different. One night just after I came home I
    went to the kitchen for a glass of water; the door to your
    room was open . . . well . . .
PARLOR MAID. *(Hides her face.)*   Oh, God, I never thought you
    would do such a terrible thing, Herr Alfred!
YOUNG GENTLEMAN. I saw everything, Marie . . . here . . .
    and here . . . and here . . . and–
PARLOR MAID. Oh, Herr Alfred!
YOUNG GENTLEMAN. Come here, come here . . . come . . .
    there, that's right . . .
PARLOR MAID. But someone might ring!
YOUNG GENTLEMAN. Now you stop that . . . we simply won't
    answer . . .

           · · · · ·

(The bell rings)
YOUNG GENTLEMAN. Goddamn! . . . Couldn't he make a little
    more noise!–He probably rang earlier and we didn't hear
    him.
PARLOR MAID. Oh, I was listening the whole time.
YOUNG GENTLEMAN. Well, go and see who it is–through the
    peephole.
PARLOR MAID. Herr Alfred . . . you're . . . no . . . you're a
    terrible man.
YOUNG GENTLEMAN.   Please, go see who it is . . .
(The Parlor Maid goes out. The Young Gentleman opens the blinds.)
PARLOR MAID. *(Appears again.)*   He must have left again. There's
    no one there now. It might have been Doctor Schüller.
YOUNG GENTLEMAN. *(Unfavorably moved.)*   That will be all.
(The Parlor Maid draws nearer to him.)
YOUNG GENTLEMAN. *(Avoids her.)* Oh Marie–I'm going to the
    coffeehouse now.
PARLOR MAID. *(Tenderly.)*   So soon . . . Herr Alfred?
YOUNG GENTLEMAN. *(Sternly.)*   I'm going to the coffeehouse. If
    Doctor Schüller should call–
PARLOR MAID.. He won't come anymore today.
YOUNG GENTLEMAN. *(More sternly.)*   If Doctor Schüller should
    come, I'll . . . I'll be in the coffeehouse. *(He goes into the
    other room.)*

*(The Parlor Maid takes a cigar from the smoking table, puts it in her pocket and
goes off.)*

(The Young Gentleman and the Young Wife. Evening. A salon in the house on the Schwind Gasse, furnished with cheap elegance. The Young Gentleman has just entered, and, while still wearing his topcoat and with hat still in hand, lights the candles. He then opens the door to the adjoining room and looks in. The light from the candles in the salon falls across the inlaid floor to the four-poster against the back wall. The reddish glow from a fireplace in the corner of the room diffuses itself on the curtains of the bed. The Young Gentleman also inspects the bedroom. He takes the atomizer from the dressing table and sprays the pillows on the bed with a fine mist of violet perfume. He then goes through both rooms with the atomizer, pressing continuously on the little bulb, until both rooms smell of violet. He then removes his topcoat and hat, sits in a blue velvet armchair, and smokes. After a short while he rises again and assures himself that the green shutters are down. Suddenly he goes back into the bedroom, opens the drawer of the night table. He feels around in it for a tortoise-shell hairpin. He looks for a place to hide it, then finally puts it in the pocket of his topcoat. Then he opens a cabinet in the salon, removes a tray with a bottle of cognac on it and two small liqueur glasses which he places on the table. He goes to his topcoat and removes a small white package from the pocket. He opens it and places it beside the cognac, returns to the cabinet, and takes out two small plates and eating utensils. From the small package he takes a marron glacé *and eats it. He then pours himself a cognac and drinks it. He looks at his watch. He paces the room, back and forth. He stops in front of the large wall mirror and combs his hair and small mustache with a pocket comb.—He now goes to the door of the hallway and listens. Not a sound. The bell rings. The Young Gentleman starts suddenly. He then seats himself in the armchair and rises only when the door is opened and the Young Wife enters. She is heavily veiled, closes the door behind her, remains standing there for a moment while she brings her left hand to her heart as though to master an overwhelming emotion. The Young Gentleman goes to her, takes her left hand in his and imprints a kiss on the white black-rimmed glove.)*

YOUNG GENTLEMAN. *(Softly.)* Thank you.

YOUNG WIFE. Alfred—Alfred!

YOUNG GENTLEMAN. Come in, gracious lady . . . come in, Frau Emma.

YOUNG WIFE. *(Still standing at the door.)* Please, leave me alone here for a while—please . . . please, Alfred!

(The Young Gentleman stands in front of her, holding her hand.)

YOUNG WIFE. Where am I?

YOUNG GENTLEMAN. With me.

YOUNG WIFE. This house is a fright, Alfred!

YOUNG GENTLEMAN. But why? It's a very distinguished house.

YOUNG WIFE. I passed two gentlemen on the stairs.

YOUNG GENTLEMAN. Did you know them?

YOUNG WIFE. I'm not sure. It's possible though.

YOUNG GENTLEMAN. But, my dear lady, you must know your own friends.

YOUNG WIFE. I couldn't see a thing.

YOUNG GENTLEMAN. Even if they had been your best friends —they could never have recognised you. With that veil on I would never have recognised you myself, unless I knew.

YOUNG WIFE. There are two of them.

YOUNG GENTLEMAN. Won't you come in? And you must at least take your hat off.

YOUNG WIFE. Oh, but, Alfred, I couldn't possibly! I told you before I came; five minutes . . . no, not a moment longer . . . I assure you—

YOUNG GENTLEMAN. Well, at least your veil.

YOUNG WIFE. There are two of them.

YOUNG GENTLEMAN. Well, yes, then both veils . . . but at least let me see you.

YOUNG WIFE. Do you really love me, Alfred?

YOUNG GENTLEMAN. *(Deeply hurt.)* Emma— how can you . . .

YOUNG WIFE. It's so warm in here.

YOUNG GENTLEMAN. Well, you still have on your fur coat— you're sure to catch cold.

YOUNG WIFE. *(Finally enters the room and throws herself into the armchair.)* I'm dead tired.

YOUNG GENTLEMAN. May I? *(He takes off her veils; take the pin from her hat, and places, hat, pin, and veils to the side. The Young Wife does not stop him. The Young Gentleman stands in front of her, shakes his head.)*

YOUNG WIFE. What's the matter?

YOUNG GENTLEMAN. You have never been so lovely.

YOUNG WIFE. Why, what do you mean?

YOUNG GENTLEMAN. Alone . . . alone with you–Emma–

(He kneels beside her armchair, takes her hands in his and covers them with kisses.)

YOUNG WIFE. And now . . . now I must go. I've done all you asked of me.

(The Young Gentleman lets his head sink into her lap.)

YOUNG WIFE. You promised me to be good.

YOUNG GENTLEMAN. Yes.

YOUNG WIFE. I'm about to suffocate in this room.

YOUNG GENTLEMAN. *(Rises)* You still have your fur cape on.

YOUNG WIFE. Here, put it beside my hat.

YOUNG GENTLEMAN. *(Takes off her cape and places it beside the other things on the divan.)* There.

YOUNG WIFE. And now—*adieu*—

YOUNG GENTLEMAN. Emma—Emma!

YOUNG WIFE. Those five minutes are long past.

YOUNG GENTLEMAN. Not a single minute has gone by!

YOUNG WIFE. Now, Alfred, for once I want you to tell me exactly what time it is.

YOUNG GENTLEMAN. It's a quarter to seven, exactly.

YOUNG WIFE. I should have been at my sister's long ago.

YOUNG GENTLEMAN. Your sister can see you anytime.

YOUNG WIFE. Of, God, Alfred, why did you ever mislead me into this?

YOUNG GENTLEMAN. Because I . . . worship you, Emma.

YOUNG WIFE. How many others have you told that to?

YOUNG GENTLEMAN. Since I first saw you, no one.

YOUNG WIFE. What a frivolous woman I've become! If anyone had told me of this . . . even just a week ago . . . even yesterday . . .

YOUNG GENTLEMAN. And it was the day before yesterday that you promised me . . .

YOUNG WIFE. You tormented me so. But I didn't want to do it. God is my witness, I didn't want to do it . . . Yesterday I was firmly resolved . . . Do you know that yesterday evening I wrote you a long letter?

YOUNG GENTLEMAN. I didn't receive it.

YOUNG WIFE. I tore it up. Oh, how I wish now I'd sent you the letter!

YOUNG GENTLEMAN. It's better this way.

YOUNG WIFE. Oh, no, it's disgraceful . . of me. I don't even understand myself. *Adieu,* Alfred, you must let me go.

(The Young Gentleman embraces her and covers her face with passionate kisses.)

YOUNG WIFE. Is that how you . . . keep your promise?

YOUNG GENTLEMAN. Just one more kiss . . . just one.

YOUNG WIFE. And the last.

(He kisses her; she returns the kiss; their lips remain locked together for a long while.)

YOUNG GENTLEMAN. Shall I tell you something, Emma? I
know now, for the first time, what happiness is.

(The Young Wife sinks back into the armchair.)

YOUNG GENTLEMAN. *(Sits on the arm of the chair, places his
arm lightly about her neck.)*   . . . Or better still, I know
now what happiness could be.

(The Young Wife sighs deeply. The Young Gentleman kisses her again.)

YOUNG WIFE. Alfred, Alfred, what are you making of me!
YOUNG GENTLEMAN. Tell me now . . . it's not really so
uncomfortable here, is it? And we're so safe here too.
It's a thousand times more wonderful than our meetings in
the open.
YOUNG WIFE. Oh, please, don't remind me of it.
YOUNG GENTLEMAN. I will think of those meetings with a
great deal of joy. Every moment that I've been able to
spend with you will be with me forever.
YOUNG WIFE. Do you still remember the Industrial Ball?
YOUNG GENTLEMAN. Do I remember it . . .? I sat beside
you during supper, quite close beside you. Your husband
ordered champagne . . .
(The Young Wife looks protestingly at him)
YOUNG GENTLEMAN. I was only going to mention the champagne.
Emma, would you like a glass of cognac?
YOUNG WIFE. Just a drop, but I'd like a glass of water first.
YOUNG GENTLEMAN. Yes . . . Well now, where is the–ah,
yes . . .*(He pushes back the doors and enters the bedroom. The Young Wife
watches him. The Young Gentleman re-enters with a decanter of water and
two drinking glasses.)*
YOUNG WIFE. Where were you?
YOUNG GENTLEMAN. In the . . . the next room. *(Pours a glass
of water.)*
YOUNG WIFE. I want to ask you something now, Alfred–and
promise me you will tell me the truth.
YOUNG GENTLEMAN. I promise.
YOUNG WIFE. Has there. ever been another woman in these
rooms?
YOUNG GENTLEMAN. Well, Emma–this house is twenty years old!

YOUNG WIFE. You know what I mean, Alfred . . . with you!

YOUNG GENTLEMAN. With me–here–Emma!–It's not at all nice that you should even think of such a thing.

YOUNG WIFE. Then you . . . how shall I say it . . . But no, I'd rather not ask you. It's better if I don't. I'm the one to blame. Nothing goes unavenged.

YOUNG GENTLEMAN. What is it? I don't understand! What doesn't go unavenged?

YOUNG WIFE. No, no, no, I mustn't come to myself, or I'll sink into the earth in shame.

YOUNG GENTLEMAN. *(With the decanter of water in hand, he shakes his head sadly.)* Emma, if you only knew how you are hurting me.

(The Young Wife pours herself a glass of cognac.)

YOUNG GENTLEMAN. I want to tell you something, Emma. If you are ashamed to be here–if I mean absolutely nothing to you–if you are unable to feel that for me you are all the joy in the world–then I think you had best leave.

YOUNG WIFE. Yes, I shall do exactly that.

YOUNG GENTLEMAN. *(Taking her by the hand.)* But if you are able to realize that I cannot live without you, that to kiss your hand means for me more than the endearments of all the other women of the world . . . Emma, I'm not like these other young people who know how to court a woman –perhaps I'm too naive . . . I . . .

YOUNG WIFE. And what if you were like those other young people?

YOUNG GENTLEMAN. Then you wouldn't be here–because you aren't like other women.

YOUNG WIFE. How do you know?

YOUNG GENTLEMAN. *(Has pulled her to the divan, seated himself close beside her.)* I have thought a great deal about you. I know that you are unhappy.

(The Young Wife is pleased.)

YOUNG GENTLEMAN. Life is so empty, so futile–and then– so short–so terribly short!–There's only one happiness . . . to find another person who will love you.

(The Young Wife has taken a candied pear from the table and puts it into her mouth.)

YOUNG GENTLEMAN. Give me half!

(She proffers it to him with her lips.)

YOUNG WIFE. *(Takes hold of his hands which threaten to go*

astray.)   What are you doing, Alfred . . . is this the way you keep your promise?

YOUNG GENTLEMAN.   *(Swallowing the pear; then more boldly.)* Life is so short.

YOUNG WIFE.   *(Weakly.)*   But that's no reason to—

YOUNG GENTLEMAN.   *(Mechanically.)*   Oh, but it is.

YOUNG WIFE.   *(More weakly.).*   Now you see, Alfred, and you promised to be good . . . And it's so light . . .

YOUNG GENTLEMAN.   Come, come, my only, only . . .*(He lifts her from the divan.)*

YOUNG WIFE.   What are you doing?

YOUNG GENTLEMAN.   It's not at all light in there.

YOUNG WIFE.   You mean there's another room?

YOUNG GENTLEMAN.   *(Takes her with him.)*   A beautiful room . . . and very dark.

YOUNG WIFE.   But I'd rather stay here.

(The Young Gentleman is already through the doorway with her, into the bedroom, and begins to unbutton her blouse.)

YOUNG WIFE.   You're so . . . oh, God, what are you making of me!—Alfred!

YOUNG GENTLEMAN.   I worship you, Emma!

YOUNG WIFE.   Please, wait, can't you at least wait . . . *(Weakly.)*   Go on, I'll call you.

YOUNG GENTLEMAN.   Please, let me—let me—let me help you.

YOUNG WIFE.   You're tearing my clothes.

YOUNG GENTLEMAN.   Don't you wear a corset?

YOUNG WIFE.   I've never worn a corset. And neither does Duse. But you can unbutton my shoes.

(The Young Gentleman unbuttons her shoes, kisses her feet.)

YOUNG WIFE.   *(Has slipped into bed.)* Oh, I'm so cold.

YOUNG GENTLEMAN.   You'll be warm enough soon.

YOUNG WIFE.   *(Laughing softly.)*   Do you think so?

YOUNG GENTLEMAN.   *(Unfavorably moved, to himself.)*   She shouldn't have said that. *(He undresses in the dark.)*

YOUNG WIFE. *(Tenderly.)*   Come, come, come!

YOUNG GENTLEMAN.   *(Suddenly in a better mood.)*   Right away—

YOUNG WIFE.   I smell violets here.

YOUNG GENTLEMAN.   It's you who smell that way . . . Yes— *(To her.)*   it's you.

YOUNG WIFE.   Alfred ... Alfred!!!!

YOUNG GENTLEMAN.   Emma ...

. . . . . .

YOUNG GENTLEMAN. It's obvious that I love you too much
. . . I feel like I've lost my senses.

YOUNG WIFE . . .

YOUNG GENTLEMAN. These past days I've felt as if I were
going mad. I knew this would happen.

YOUNG WIFE. Don't worry about it.

YOUNG GENTLEMAN. Of course not. It's quite natural for a
man to . . .

YOUNG WIFE. No . . . no . . . You're all excited. Calm
yourself now . . .

YOUNG GENTLEMAN. Are you familiar with Stendhal?

YOUNG WIFE. Stendhal?

YOUNG GENTLEMAN. His *Psychology of Love?*

YOUNG WIFE. No, why do you ask?

YOUNG GENTLEMAN. There's a story in it that is very
significant.

YOUNG WIFE. What kind of story is it?
There's a large crowd of cavalry officers
who've gotten together—

YOUNG WIFE. And?

YOUNG GENTLEMAN. And they tell about their love affairs.
And each one reports that with the woman he loves most,
that is, most passionately . . . that he—well, to come to
the point, that the same thing happened to each of them as
happened to me just now.

YOUNG WIFE. I see.

YOUNG GENTLEMAN. I find that very characteristic.

YOUNG WIFE. Yes.

YOUNG GENTLEMAN. Oh, I'm not through yet. One of them
claims that it never happened to him in his entire life.
But, Stendhal adds—he was a notorious braggart.

YOUNG WIFE. I see.

YOUNG GENTLEMAN. Still, it does give one a jolt, that's the
stupid thing about it, even if it doesn't mean anything.

YOUNG WIFE. Of course. And besides, don't forget you
promised me to be good.

YOUNG GENTLEMAN. Don't laugh, it doesn't help matters
any.

YOUNG WIFE. Oh, but I'm not laughing. What you said about
Stendhal is really very interesting. I always thought it only
happened with old men . . . or with very . . . well, you
understand, with men who have lived a great deal . . .

YOUNG GENTLEMAN. What are you talking about! That has
nothing to do with it. Besides, I forgot to tell you the
nicest of all of Stendhal's stories. One of the cavalry
officers even tells how he spent three nights—or was it six,
I don't remember—with a woman he had wanted for weeks
on end—*désirée,* you understand—and all they did during
those nights was cry with happiness . . . both of them . . .

YOUNG WIFE. Both of them?

YOUNG GENTLEMAN. Yes. Isn't that remarkable? I find it so
understandable—especially when you're in love.

YOUNG WIFE. But surely there must be many who don't cry.

YOUNG GENTLEMAN. *(Nervously.)*   Surely . . . that was an ex-
ceptional case, too.

YOUNG WIFE. Oh—I thought Stendhal said that all cavalry
officers cry under the circumstances.

YOUNG GENTLEMAN. There now, you see, you're making fun of me.

YOUNG WIFE. What do you mean! Don't be so childish
Alfred!

YOUNG GENTLEMAN. It makes me nervous, that's all . . . and
I have the feeling that you can think of nothing else.
That's what embarrasses me most.

YOUNG WIFE. I'm not at all thinking about it.

YOUNG GENTLEMAN. Oh, yes you are. If only I were
convinced that you love me.

YOUNG WIFE. What more proof can you want?

YOUNG GENTLEMAN. You see . . .? You're always making
fun of me.

YOUNG WIFE. What do you mean? Come here, give me your
sweet little head.

YOUNG GENTLEMAN. I like that.

YOUNG WIFE. Do you love me?

YOUNG GENTLEMAN. Oh, I'm so happy!

YOUNG WIFE. But you needn't cry too.

YOUNG GENTLEMAN. *(Pulling himself from her, highly
irritated.)*   Again, again! And I begged you so.

YOUNG WIFE. All I said was you shouldn't cry.

YOUNG GENTLEMAN. You said: "You needn't cry, too."

YOUNG WIFE. You're nervous, my sweet.

YOUNG GENTLEMAN. I know that.

YOUNG WIFE. But you shouldn't be. I find it rather nice that
. . . that we . . . well, that we, so to speak, are good . . .
comrades. . .

YOUNG GENTLEMAN. You're at it again!

YOUNG WIFE. Don't you remember! That was one of our first talks together. We wanted to be good comrades, nothing more. Oh, that was a lovely time . . . it was at my sister's, the big ball in January, during the quadrille . . . Oh, for God's sake, I should have been gone long ago . . . my sister's waiting for me—what will she say . . . *Adieu,* Alfred—

YOUNG GENTLEMAN. Emma! Are you going to leave me this way?

YOUNG WIFE. Yes. Just like that!

YOUNG GENTLEMAN. Just five more minutes . . .

YOUNG WIFE. All right. Just five more minutes. But you must promise me . . . not to move. All right?—I'll give you another kiss when I leave. Pst!—Quiet . . . don't move, I said, or I shall get up at once, my sweet . . . sweet . . .

YOUNG GENTLEMAN. Emma . . . my dearest . . .

. . . . .

YOUNG WIFE. My dear Alfred—

YOUNG GENTLEMAN. It's heaven to be with you.

YOUNG WIFE. But now I really must go.

YOUNG GENTLEMAN. Oh, let your sister wait.

YOUNG WIFE. I must get home. It's far too late for my sister. What time is it?

YOUNG GENTLEMAN. Well, how am I to find that out?

YOUNG WIFE. You will have to look at your watch.

YOUNG GENTLEMAN. But my watch is in my waistcoat.

YOUNG WIFE. Then get it.

YOUNG GENTLEMAN. *(Gets up with a mighty push.)* Eight.

YOUNG WIFE. *(Rises quickly.)* Oh, my God! . . . Quick, Alfred, give me my stockings. What am I to tell him? They're sure to be waiting for me at home . . . Eight o'clock . . . !

YOUNG GENTLEMAN. When will I see you again?

YOUNG WIFE. Never.

YOUNG GENTLEMAN. Emma! Don't you love me anymore?

YOUNG WIFE. That's why. Give me my shoes.

YOUNG GENTLEMAN. Never again? Here are your shoes.

YOUNG WIFE. There's a buttonhook in my bag. Please hurry, I beg of you . . .

YOUNG GENTLEMAN. Here's the buttonhook.

YOUNG WIFE. Alfred, this can cost both of us our necks.

YOUNG GENTLEMAN. *(Quite unfavorably moved.)* Why's that?

YOUNG WIFE. Well, what shall I answer him when he asks
    me: "Where have you been?"
YOUNG GENTLEMAN. At your sister's.
YOUNG WIFE. If I could only lie.
YOUNG GENTLEMAN. You'll simply have to.
YOUNG WIFE. All this for a person like you! Oh, come here
    . . . let me kiss you again. *(She embraces him.)*   And now—
    leave me alone, go in the other room. How can I dress
    myself with you here?

*(The Young Gentleman goes into the salon and dresses himself. He eats some of
the pastry and drinks a glass of cognac.)*

YOUNG WIFE. *(Calls after a while.)*   Alfred!
YOUNG GENTLEMAN. My sweet.
YOUNG WIFE. I think it better that we didn't cry.
YOUNG GENTLEMAN.*(Smiling not without pride.)*   How can
    one be so flippant—
YOUNG WIFE. What do you think will happen—if just by
    chance we should meet again one day at a party?
YOUNG GENTLEMAN. By chance?—One day? Surely you'll be
    at Lobheimer's tomorrow, won't you?
YOUNG WIFE. Why, yes. And you?
YOUNG GENTLEMAN. Of course. May I ask you for the
    cotillion?
YOUNG WIFE. Oh, but I can't go! What can you be thinking
    of—Why, I would . . . *(She enters the salon fully dressed,
    takes a chocolate pastry.)* . . . sink into the earth.
YOUNG GENTLEMAN. Well then, tomorrow at Lobheimer's
    that will be lovely.
YOUNG WIFE. No, no . . . I'll excuse myself, absolutely—
YOUNG GENTLEMAN. Then the day after tomorrow . . . here.
YOUNG WIFE. What are you talking about?
YOUNG GENTLEMAN. At six . . .
YOUNG WIFE. Are there any carriages here at the corner?—
YOUNG GENTLEMAN. As many as you like. The day after tomorrow
    then, here, at six. Say yes, my dearest, sweetest. . .
YOUNG WIFE. . . .We'll talk about that tomorrow during the cotillion.
YOUNG GENTLEMAN. *(Embraces her.)*   My angel.
YOUNG WIFE. Don't muss my hair again.
YOUNG GENTLEMAN. Tomorrow at Lobheimer's then, and the
    day after tomorrow, here in my arms.

YOUNG WIFE. Good-bye . . .

YOUNG GENTLEMAN. *(Suddenly troubled again.)* But what will you tell him—today?—

YOUNG WIFE. You mustn't ask . . . you mustn't ask . . . it's too terrible to think about.—Why do I love you so!— *Adieu.*—If I meet anyone on the stairs again, I'll have a stroke.—Ha!—

The Young Gentleman kisses her hand once again. The Young Wife goes off. The Young Gentleman stays behind alone. Then he sits on the divan.

YOUNG GENTLEMAN. *(Smiles and says to himself.)* At last an affair with a respectable woman.

SCENE 5

(The Young Wife and the Husband. A comfortable bedroom. It is 10.30 p.m. The Young Wife is reading in bed. The Husband enters the bedroom in his bathrobe.)

YOUNG WIFE. *(Without looking up.)* Have you stopped working?

HUSBAND. Yes. I'm too tired. And besides . . .

YOUNG WIFE. Well?

HUSBAND. Suddenly at my writing table I felt very lonely. I felt a longing for you.

YOUNG WIFE. *(Looks up.)* Really?

HUSBAND. *(Sits beside her on the bed.)* Don't read any more tonight. You'll ruin your eyes.

YOUNG WIFE. *(Closes the book.)* What is it?

HUSBAND. Nothing, my child. I'm in love with you! But of course you know that!

YOUNG WIFE. One might almost forget it at times.

HUSBAND. At times one has to forget it.

YOUNG WIFE. Why?

HUSBAND. Because marriage would be imperfect otherwise. It would . . . how should I say it . . . it would lose its sanctity.

YOUNG WIFE. Oh . . .

HUSBAND. Believe me— it's true . . . If during these last five years we hadn't forgotten at times that we are in love with one another—well, perhaps we wouldn't be.

YOUNG WIFE. That's beyond me.

HUSBAND. The matter is simply this: we have had perhaps twelve love affairs with one another . . . Wouldn't you say so?

YOUNG WIFE. I haven't kept count!—

HUSBAND. If we had fully experienced our first love affair to its logical end, if from the beginning I had surrendered myself involuntarily to my passion for you, then we would have ended the same as every other pair of lovers. We would have been through with one another.

YOUNG WIFE. Oh . . . is that what you meant.

HUSBAND. Believe me—Emma—in the early days of our marriage. I was afraid it would turn out that way.

YOUNG WIFE. Me, too.

HUSBAND. You see? Wasn't I right? That's why I think it well, for short periods of time, to live together merely as good friends.

YOUNG WIFE. I see.

HUSBAND. That way we can always experience new honeymoons with one another, simply because I never let our honeymoons . . .

YOUNG WIFE. Last for months.

HUSBAND. Right.

YOUNG WIFE. And now . . . would you say another of these periods of friendship has come to an end?

HUSBAND. *(Tenderly pressing her to him.)*   It just might be.

YOUNG WIFE. But just suppose that . . . that it were different with me.

HUSBAND. But it's not different. You are the cleverest, most enchanting creature there is. I'm very fortunate to have found you.

YOUNG WIFE. It's really very nice, this way you . . . court me . . . from time to time.

HUSBAND. *(Has also gone to bed.)*   For a man who has been around a bit in the world—come, lay your head on my shoulder—well, marriage is something far more mysterious than it is for a young girl from a good family. You come to us pure and . . . at least to a certain degree, ignorant, and therefore you have a far clearer conception of the nature of love than we.

YOUNG WIFE. *(Laughing.)*   Oh!

HUSBAND. Of course. Because we're completely confused, made insecure by the various experiences we are forced

into before marriage. You women hear a great deal and
know far too much, in fact you even read too much, but
you have no proper conception of what we men have to
experience. What is commonly called love is made absolutely
repellent to us; for, after all, what are those creatures
on whom we are so dependent!

YOUNG WIFE. Yes, what are they?

HUSBAND. *(Kisses her on the forehead.)* Be glad, my sweet, that
you have never had to become aware of such relationships.
Besides that, they're mostly pitiable creatures—so let us
not cast stones!

YOUNG WIFE. I'm sorry—but this pity—it doesn't seem to me
quite properly placed.

HUSBAND. *(With gentle mildness.)* They deserve it. You young
girls from good families, who enjoyed the protection of
your parents until a bridegroom came along to ask for
your hand—you know nothing of the misery that drives
most of these poor creatures into the arms of sin.

YOUNG WIFE. So they all sell themselves?

HUSBAND. I wouldn't want to say that. And I'm not speaking
only of material misery. There is also such a thing—I might
say—as moral misery; a faulty comprehension of what is
proper, and especially of what is noble.

YOUNG WIFE. But why are they pitiable?—They seem to be
doing rather well.

HUSBAND. You have rather strange notions, my child. You
oughtn't to forget that such creatures as they are destined
by nature to sink deeper and deeper. There's no end to it.

YOUNG WIFE. *(Snuggling close to him.)* It sounds rather nice.

HUSBAND. *(Somewhat pained.)* How can you talk like that,
Emma! I should think that for a respectable woman there
could be nothing more repulsive than a woman who is not
. . . respectable.

YOUNG WIFE. Of course, Karl, of course. I only said it. But
tell me more. I like it when you talk this way. Tell me
more.

HUSBAND. About what?

YOUNG WIFE. Well—about these creatures.

HUSBAND. What are you talking about!

YOUNG WIFE. Don't you remember when we were first
married, I always begged you to tell me something of
your youth?

HUSBAND. Why should that interest you?

YOUNG WIFE. Well, aren't you my husband? And isn't it rather unfair that I know absolutely nothing about your past?

HUSBAND. Surely you can't think me so tactless as to–That will do, Emma . . . it would be an absolute profanation.

YOUNG WIFE. Nevertheless . . . who knows how many other women you've held in your arms, just like you're holding me now.

HUSBAND. Women, perhaps–but not like you.

YOUNG WIFE. But you must answer me one question . . . otherwise . . . otherwise . . . there will be no honeymoon.

HUSBAND. You have a way of speaking that . . . don't forget you're a mother . . . that our little girl is sleeping right in there . . .

YOUNG WIFE. (Snuggling close to him.) But I'd like a boy, too.

HUSBAND. Emma!

YOUNG WIFE. Oh, don't be that way . . . Of course I'm your wife . . . but I'd like sometime to be your mistress too.

HUSBAND. Would you really?

YOUNG WIFE. Well–but first my question.

HUSBAND. (Accommodatingly.) Well?

YOUNG WIFE. Was there . . . was there ever a . . . a married woman among them.

HUSBAND. What's that? How do you mean?

YOUNG WIFE. You know what I mean.

HUSBAND. (Mildly disturbed.) What makes you ask?

YOUNG WIFE. I wondered whether . . . that is– I know there are such women . . . yes. But did you ever . . .

HUSBAND. (Seriously.) Do you know such a woman?

YOUNG WIFE. Well, I'm not really certain.

HUSBAND. Is there such a woman among your friends?

YOUNG WIFE. How can I possibly say yes or no to a thing like that–and be certain?

HUSBAND. Perhaps one of your friends . . . well, people talk a great deal . . . women, when they get together–did one of them confess?

YOUNG WIFE. (Uncertainly.) No.

HUSBAND. Have you ever suspected that any of your friends . . .

YOUNG WIFE. Suspect . . . oh . . . suspect . . .

HUSBAND. Then you have.

YOUNG WIFE. Of course not, Karl, absolutely not. Now that I think about it–I wouldn't suppose them capable of it.

HUSBAND. Not a single one of them?

YOUNG WIFE. Not—not my friends.

HUSBAND. Promise me something, Emma.

YOUNG WIFE. Well?

HUSBAND. That you will have nothing to do with a woman
of whom you have the slightest suspicion that she . . .
well, whose life is not completely above reproach.

YOUNG WIFE. I must promise you a thing like that?

HUSBAND. Of course I know you would never seek out such
acquaintances. But it could just by chance happen that . . .
Well, it's not uncommon that such women whose reputations aren't exactly the best seek out the companionship of
respectable women, partly as a relief for them, and partly
—how shall I say it—partly as a longing for virtue.

YOUNG WIFE. I see.

HUSBAND. Yes, I believe it's quite true, what I've just said.
A longing for virtue. One thing you can believe for certain,
that all of these women are terribly unhappy.

YOUNG WIFE. Why?

HUSBAND. How can you even ask? Emma!—How can you?—
Just imagine the kind of existence these women lead! Full
of lies, viciousness, vulgarity, and full of danger.

YOUNG WIFE. Why, of course. You're quite right.

HUSBAND. Absolutely.—They pay for their bit of happiness
. . . their bit of . . .

YOUNG WIFE. Pleasure.

HUSBAND. Why pleasure? How do you happen to call it
pleasure?

YOUNG WIFE. Well—there must be something to recommend
it—or they wouldn't do it.

HUSBAND. It has nothing to recommend it . . . mere
intoxication.

YOUNG WIFE. *(Reflectively.)* Mere intoxication.

HUSBAND. No, it's not even intoxication. But it is bought at
a high price, that is for certain!

YOUNG WIFE. Then you . . . then you must have known it
at first hand?

HUSBAND. Yes, Emma—It is my saddest recollection.

YOUNG WIFE. Who is it? Tell me! Do I know her?

HUSBAND. How can you think such a thing!

YOUNG WIFE. Is it long past? Was it very long before you
married me?

HUSBAND. Don't ask. Please, don't ask.

YOUNG WIFE. But, Karl!

HUSBAND. She's dead.

YOUNG WIFE. Seriously?

HUSBAND. Yes . . . I know it sounds ridiculous, but I have the feeling that all these women die young.

YOUNG WIFE. Did you love her very much?

HUSBAND. One doesn't love a liar.

YOUNG WIFE. But why . . .

HUSBAND. Intoxication . . .

YOUNG WIFE. Then it does have something to . . .

HUSBAND. Don't talk about it, please. It's all long past. I have only loved one woman—and you are that woman. One can love only purity and truth.

YOUNG WIFE. Karl!

HUSBAND. How beautiful you are! . . . beautiful . . . come here . . . *(He puts out the light.)*

. . . . .

YOUNG WIFE. Do you know what I can't help thinking about tonight?

HUSBAND. About what, my sweet?

YOUNG WIFE. About . . . about . . . about Venice.

HUSBAND. That first night . . .

YOUNG WIFE. Yes . . . it was so . . .

HUSBAND. What–? Tell me!

YOUNG WIFE. Do you love me like that now?

HUSBAND. Just like that.

YOUNG WIFE. Oh . . . if you would always . . .

HUSBAND. *(In her arms.)* What?

YOUNG WIFE. Dear Karl!

HUSBAND. What did you mean to say? If I would always . . . ?

YOUNG WIFE. Yes.

HUSBAND. Well, what would happen if I would always . . . ?

YOUNG WIFE. Then I would always know that you love me.

HUSBAND. Yes. But you must know that already. One can't always be the loving husband; at times one must venture out into the hostile world, he must fight and struggle for an existence! You must never forget that, my child! In marriage everything has its place—that's the beauty of it all. There aren't many couples five years later who can remember their . . . their Venice.

YOUNG WIFE. Of course.

HUSBAND. And now . . good night, my child.

YOUNG WIFE. Good night!

SCENE 6

The Husband and the Sweet Young Thing. A private room in the Riedof Restaurant. Comfortable, modest elegance. The gas stove is burning. On the table are the remains of a meal, meringues with whipped cream, fruit, cheese. The Husband smokes a Havana cigar; he leans into the corner of the divan. The Sweet Young Thing sits beside him on a chair and spoons the whipped cream out of a bowl; she sucks it in with great pleasure.)

HUSBAND. Taste good?

SWEET YOUNG THING. *(Not letting herself be disturbed.)* Oh!

HUSBAND. Would you like another?

SWEET YOUNG THING. No, I've had too much already.

HUSBAND. You're out of wine. *(He pours her some.)*

SWEET YOUNG THING. No . . . I'll just let it sit there, sir.

HUSBAND. You said "sir" again.

SWEET YOUNG THING. Did I?–Well I guess I just always
    forget–don't I, sir?

HUSBAND. Karl!

SWEET YOUNG THING. What?

HUSBAND. "Don't I, Karl?"–not "Don't I, sir?"!–Come, sit
    down over here, by me.

SWEET YOUNG THING. Just a minute . . .I'm not through yet.

(The Husband rises, places himself behind the chair and embraces her, while turning her head toward him.)

SWEET YOUNG THING. What is it?

HUSBAND. I'd like a kiss.

SWEET YOUNG THING. *(Gives him a kiss.)* You're a very forward
    man, sir–I mean, Karl.

HUSBAND. Are you just discovering that?

SWEET YOUNG THING. Oh, no, I knew that before . . . on the
    street.–You certainly must have a nice impression of me,
    sir.

HUSBAND. Karl!

SWEET YOUNG THING. Karl.

HUSBAND. Why?

SWEET YOUNG THING. That I came here so easy with you–to
    a private room and . . .

HUSBAND. Well, I wouldn't say it was that easy.

SWEET YOUNG THING. But you have such a nice way of asking.

HUSBAND. Do you think so?

SWEET YOUNG THING. And after all, what's the difference?

HUSBAND. Of course.

SWEET YOUNG THING. What's the difference if we go for a
 walk or . . .

HUSBAND. Oh, it's much too cold for a walk.

SWEET YOUNG THING. Of course it's too cold.

HUSBAND. And it is nice and warm here, isn't it? *(He has
 seated himself again, puts his arms around the Sweet
 Young Thing and pulls her to his side.)*

SWEET YOUNG THING. *(Weakly.)* Oh–!

HUSBAND. Tell me now . . . you've noticed me before, haven't
 you?

SWEET YOUNG THING. Naturally. In Singer Strasse.

HUSBAND. I don't mean today. But yesterday, and the day
 before yesterday, when I followed you.

SWEET YOUNG THING. A lot of people follow me.

HUSBAND. I can well imagine. But did you notice me?

SWEET YOUNG THING. Do you know what happened to me the
 other day? My cousin's husband followed me in the dark
 without even recognizing me.

HUSBAND. Did he speak to you?

SWEET YOUNG THING. Don't be silly! Do you suppose everyone is as forward as you?

HUSBAND. It happens.

SWEET YOUNG THING. Naturally it happens.

HUSBAND. What did you do?

SWEET YOUNG THING. Why, nothing–I simply didn't answer.

HUSBAND. Hmm . . . but you answered me.

SWEET YOUNG THING. Well, are you sorry I did?

HUSBAND. *(Kissing her violently.)* Your lips taste like whipped
 cream.

SWEET YOUNG THING. Yes, they're always sweet.

HUSBAND. How many other men have told you that?

SWEET YOUNG THING. How many others! The way you talk!

HUSBAND. Be honest for once. How many other men have
 kissed that mouth of yours?

SWEET YOUNG THING. Are you asking me? You'd never believe
 it if I told you!

HUSBAND. And why shouldn't I?

SWEET YOUNG THING. Guess!

HUSBAND. Well, let's say—but you mustn't be angry . . .

SWEET YOUNG THING. Why should I be angry?

HUSBAND. Well then, let's say—twenty.

SWEET YOUNG THING. *(Pulling away from him.)*   Well—why didn't you say a hundred right off?

HUSBAND. I was only guessing.

SWEET YOUNG THING. It wasn't a very good one.

HUSBAND. Well then, ten.

SWEET YOUNG THING. *(Insulted.)*   Sure! A girl that lets herself be approached on the street and goes right into a private room!

HUSBAND. Don't be so childish. What's the difference between running around the streets or sitting in a room . . . Here we are in a restaurant. The waiter could come in any time—there's nothing to it.

SWEET YOUNG THING. That's what I thought too.

HUSBAND. Have you ever been in a private room in a restaurant before?

SWEET YOUNG THING. Well, if you want me to be honest about it: yes.

HUSBAND. There, you see, I like the way you answered that: at least you're honest about it.

SWEET YOUNG THING. But not the way you think. It was with a friend of mine and her husband, during the Fasching Carnival last year.

HUSBAND. It wouldn't exactly be a tragedy if sometime you had been . . . well, with your lover.

SWEET YOUNG THING. Naturally it wouldn't have been a tragedy! But I don't have a lover.

HUSBAND. Now really!

SWEET YOUNG THING. Believe me, I haven't.

HUSBAND. Are you trying to tell me that I'm the . . .

SWEET YOUNG THING. The what?—it's just that I don't have one . . . well, for the last six months, I mean.

HUSBAND. I see—But before that? Who was it?

SWEET YOUNG THING. You're awfully nosy.

HUSBAND. If I am, it's because I love you.

SWEET YOUNG THING. Do you mean that?

HUSBAND. Of course, surely you must have noticed. But tell me about it. *(He presses her close to him.)*

SWEET YOUNG THING. What do you want me to tell you?

HUSBAND. Why must I always beg you? I'd like to know who he was.

SWEET YOUNG THING. *(Laughing.)*   Oh, just a man.

HUSBAND. Well–well–who was he?

SWEET YOUNG THING. He looked a little bit like you.

HUSBAND. Oh?

SWEET YOUNG THING. If you hadn't looked so much like him–

HUSBAND. What then?

SWEET YOUNG THING. Why ask if you already know?

HUSBAND. *(Understands.)*   Then that's why you let me talk to you?

SWEET YOUNG THING. Well, I suppose.

HUSBAND. I really don't know now whether to be happy or angry.

SWEET YOUNG THING. If I were in your place, I'd be happy.

HUSBAND. Well, yes.

SWEET YOUNG THING. And even the way you talk reminds me of him . . . the way you look at a person . . .

HUSBAND. What was he?

SWEET YOUNG THING. And your eyes–

HUSBAND. What was his name?

SWEET YOUNG THING. No, you mustn't look at me that way, please.

(The Husband embraces her. A long passionate kiss.)

HUSBAND. Where are you going?

SWEET YOUNG THING. It's time to go home.

HUSBAND. Not yet.

SWEET YOUNG THING. No, I really must get home. What do you think my mother will say?

HUSBAND. You live with your mother?

SWEET YOUNG THING. Naturally I live with my mother. Where did you think?

HUSBAND. I see–with your mother. Do you live alone with her?

SWEET YOUNG THING. Yes, of course, alone! Five of us! Two brothers and two more sisters.

HUSBAND. Why sit so far away from me? Are you the eldest?

SWEET YOUNG THING. No, I'm the second. Kathi comes first. she works in a flower shop. And then I come next.

HUSBAND. Where do you work?

SWEET YOUNG THING. I stay home.

HUSBAND. All the time?

SWEET YOUNG THING. Somebody has to stay home.

HUSBAND. Of course.–Yes–and what do you tell your
mother when you–come home so late?

SWEET YOUNG THING. It doesn't happen often.

HUSBAND. Then today, for example. Won't your mother ask?

SWEET YOUNG THING. Naturally she'll ask. I can be as quiet
as a mouse when I come home, but she'll hear me every time.

HUSBAND. Then, what will you tell her?

SWEET YOUNG THING. Well, I'll say I went to the theatre.

HUSBAND. And she'll believe you?

SWEET YOUNG THING. Well, why shouldn't she believe me?
I go to the theatre quite often. Just last Sunday I went to
the opera with my girl friend and her husband and my
elder brother.

HUSBAND. Where did you get the tickets?

SWEET YOUNG THING. My brother's a barber!

HUSBAND. Oh, a barber–you mean a theatrical barber.

SWEET YOUNG THING. Why are you questioning me?

HUSBAND. It interests me, that's all. And what is your other
brother?

SWEET YOUNG THING. He's still in school. He wants to be a
teacher. Imagine . . . a teacher!

HUSBAND. And then you have still a younger sister?

SWEET YOUNG THING. Yes, she's a little brat; you really have
to keep an eye on her. You have no idea how a girl can
be ruined at school! Why, just the other day I found her
out with a boy.

HUSBAND. What?

SWEET YOUNG THING. Yes! With a boy from the school just
across from us; she went out walking with him at half-
past seven in Strozzi Gasse. The little brat!

HUSBAND. And what did you do about it?

SWEET YOUNG THING. Well, she got a spanking!

HUSBAND. Are you that strict?

SWEET YOUNG THING. If I'm not, who will be? My elder sister
works, my mother does nothing but nag; and everything
lands on me.

HUSBAND. My God, but you're sweet! (*Kisses her and grows
more tender.*) You remind me of someone, too.

SWEET YOUNG THING. Oh?—Who?

HUSBAND. Of no one in particular . . . perhaps—perhaps of
my youth. Come, my child, have some wine!

SWEET YOUNG THING. How old are you? My goodness . . .
I don't even know your name.

HUSBAND. Karl.

SWEET YOUNG THING. Not really! Your name is Karl?

HUSBAND. Was his name Karl too?

SWEET YOUNG THING. No, I don't believe it, it's a miracle
. . . it's an absolute —why, those eyes . . . that look . . .
(Shakes her head.)

HUSBAND. And still you haven't told me who he was!

SWEET YOUNG THING. He was a terrible man—that's for sure,
or else he wouldn't have walked out on me.

HUSBAND. Did you love him very much?

SWEET YOUNG THING. Of course I loved him very much.

HUSBAND. I know his kind—he was a lieutenant.

SWEET YOUNG THING. No, he wasn't even a soldier. They
wouldn't take him. His father had a house in . . . but
why do you want to know all this?

HUSBAND. (Kisses her.) Do you know your eyes are gray? At
first I thought they were black.

SWEET YOUNG THING. Well, aren't they pretty enough for
you?

(The Husband kisses her eyes.)

SWEET YOUNG THING. No, no—I can't stand that . . . oh,
please—oh, God . . . no, let me up . . . just for a minute
—please.

HUSBAND. (Ever more tenderly.) Oh, no, no.

SWEET YOUNG THING. Please, Karl, please . . .

HUSBAND. How old are you?—Eighteen? Hm?

SWEET YOUNG THING. Nineteen.

HUSBAND. Nineteen . . . and how old am I?

SWEET YOUNG THING. You're . . . thirty . . .

HUSBAND. And a little more.—But let's not talk about that.

SWEET YOUNG THING. He was thirty-two when I first got to
know him.

HUSBAND. How long ago?

SWEET YOUNG THING. I don't remember . . . You know, I
think there was something in that wine.

HUSBAND. What makes you think so?

SWEET YOUNG THING. I'm all . . . well, you know– my head's
turning.

HUSBAND. Just hold tight to me. There . . . *(He presses her
to him and becomes increasingly more tender.)* You know
something, my sweet, I think we might go now.

SWEET YOUNG THING. Yes . . . home.

HUSBAND. Not home exactly . . .

SWEET YOUNG THING. What do you mean? . . .Oh, no, oh,
no . . . I won't go anywhere, what are you thinking of–

HUSBAND. Now just listen to me, child, the next time we meet,
we'll arrange it so that . . . *(He sinks to the floor, his head
in her lap.)* Oh, that's nice, oh, that's so nice.

SWEET YOUNG THING What are you doing? *(She kisses his
hair.)* You know, I think there was something in that wine
–I'm so . . . so . . . sleepy . . . whatever will happen to
me if I can't get up? But, but, look here, but, Karl . . .
what if someone comes in . . . oh, please . . . the waiter . . .

HUSBAND. No waiter . . .'ll come in here . . . if he knows
. . . what's . . .

. . . .

*(The Sweet Young Thing leans with her eyes closed into the corner of the divan.
The Husband walks back and forth in the small room after lighting a cigarette. A
long silence.)*

HUSBAND. *(Looks at the Sweet Young Thing for a long while: to himself.)*
Who knows what kind of person she really is–Damn!
. . . It happened so quickly . . . It wasn't very careful of me . . .
Hm . . .

SWEET YOUNG THING. *(Without opening her eyes.)* There must
have been something in the wine.

HUSBAND. Really? Why?

SWEET YOUNG THING. Otherwise . . .

HUSBAND. Why blame it all on the wine?

SWEET YOUNG THING. Where are you? Why are you way over
there? Come over here by me.

(The Husband goes to her, sits down.)

SWEET YOUNG THING. Tell me now, do you really like me?

HUSBAND. You should know that . . .*(He quickly interrupts
himself.)* Of course.

SWEET YOUNG THING. You know . . . I still . . . Come on
now, tell me the truth, what was in the wine?

HUSBAND. What do you think I am . . . a poison mixer?

SWEET YOUNG THING. I just don't understand it. I'm not that way . . . We've only known each other for . . . I tell you, I'm just not like that . . . I swear to God–and if you believe that of me–

HUSBAND. There now, what are you worrying about! I don't think anything bad of you. I only think that you like me.

SWEET YOUNG THING. Yes. . .

HUSBAND. And besides, when two young people are alone together in a room, having dinner and drinking wine . . . there needn't be anything at all in the wine . . .

SWEET YOUNG THING. I was just talking.

HUSBAND. Yes, but why?

SWEET YOUNG THING. *(Somewhat obstinately.)*   Because I was ashamed of myself.

HUSBAND. That's ridiculous. There's no reason for it. And besides, I reminded you of your first lover.

SWEET YOUNG THING. Yes.

HUSBAND. Your first.

SWEET YOUNG THING. Why yes . . .

HUSBAND. Now I'd be interested in knowing who the others were.

SWEET YOUNG THING. There were no others.

HUSBAND. That's not true, it can't be true.

SWEET YOUNG THING. Come on please, don't pester me.

HUSBAND. Cigarette?

SWEET YOUNG THING. No thank you.

HUSBAND. Do you know what time it is?

SWEET YOUNG THING.   What?

HUSBAND. Half-past eleven.

SWEET YOUNG THING. Really.

HUSBAND. Well, uh . . . what about your mother? She's used to it, is she?

SWEET YOUNG THING. You really want to send me home already?

HUSBAND. But just a while ago you . . .

SWEET YOUNG THING. How you've changed. What have I done to you?

HUSBAND. Child, what's the matter, what are you talking about?

SWEET YOUNG THING. It was the look in your eyes, I swear, otherwise you'd have had to . . . a lot of men have begged me to go to private rooms like this with them.

HUSBAND. Well, would you like to . . . come here again soon
—or somewhere else—

SWEET YOUNG THING. I don't know.

HUSBAND. What does that mean; I don't know?

SWEET YOUNG THING. Well then, why did you ask?

HUSBAND. All right, when? I merely want to explain that I
don't live in Vienna. I only come here now and then, for a
few days.

SWEET YOUNG THING. Go on, you aren't Viennese?

HUSBAND. Oh, I'm from Vienna. But I don't live right in town . . .

SWEET YOUNG THING. Where?

HUSBAND. Why, what difference can that make?

SWEET YOUNG THING. Don't worry, I won't come looking
for you.

HUSBAND. My God, if it will make you happy, come any
time you like. I live in Graz.

SWEET YOUNG THING. Seriously?

HUSBAND. Well, yes, why should that surprise you?

SWEET YOUNG THING. You're married, aren't you?

HUSBAND. *(Greatly surprised.)* Why do you say that?

SWEET YOUNG THING. It just seemed that way to me.

HUSBAND. And it wouldn't bother you?

SWEET YOUNG THING. Well, of course
I'd rather you were
single—But you *are married!*

HUSBAND. Will you tell me what makes you think so?

SWEET YOUNG THING. When a man says he doesn't live in
Vienna and hasn't always got time—

HUSBAND. That's not so improbable.

SWEET YOUNG THING. I don't believe him.

HUSBAND. And it wouldn't give you a bad conscience to
make a married man be unfaithful to his . . .

SWEET YOUNG THING. My God, your wife probably does the
same thing!

HUSBAND. *(Highly indignant.)* I forbid you to say such a thing!
Such remarks are . . .

SWEET YOUNG THING. I thought you said you had no wife.

HUSBAND. Whether I have or not—one doesn't make such
remarks. *(He has risen.)*

SWEET YOUNG THING. Karl, now, Karl, what's the matter?
Are you angry? Look, I really didn't know that you were
married. I only said it. Come on, be nice again.

HUSBAND. *(Comes to her after a few seconds.)*   You're really
  such strange creatures, you . . . women. *(At her side, he
  becomes tender again.)*
SWEET YOUNG THING. No . . . please . . . besides, it's too
  late–
HUSBAND. All right, now listen to me. Let's talk together
  seriously for once. I want to see you again, see you often.
SWEET YOUNG THING. Really?
HUSBAND. But if so, then it will be necessary . . . well, I
  must be able to depend on you. I can't be careful all the
  time.
SWEET YOUNG THING. Oh, I can take care of myself.
HUSBAND. You're . . . well, I can't say inexperienced–but
  you're young–and–men in general are an unscrupulous
  lot.
SWEET YOUNG THING. Oh, Lord!
HUSBAND. I don't necessarily mean that in a moral sense.–
  But you understand what I mean.
SWEET YOUNG THING. Tell me now, what do you really think
  of me?
HUSBAND. Well–if you do want to love me–only me–then I
  think we can arrange something–even if I do usually live in
  Graz. A place like this, where someone could come in at
  any moment, just isn't right.
(The Sweet Young Thing snuggles close to him.)
HUSBAND. The next time, we'll get together somewhere else,
  all right?
SWEET YOUNG THING. Yes.
HUSBAND. *(Embraces her passionately.)*   We'll talk the rest
  over walking home. *(Rises, opens the door.)*   Waiter . . .
  the check!

SCENE 7

*(The Sweet Young Thing and the Poet. A small room furnished in comfortable
good taste. The drapes keep it in semidarkness. Red curtains. A large writing
table upon which paper and books lie about. An upright piano against the wall.
The Sweet Young Thing and the Poet enter together. The Poet locks the door.)*

POET. There, my sweet. *(Kisses her.)*

SWEET YOUNG THING. *(In hat and cape.)* Oh! Isn't this nice! But you can't see anything!

POET. Your eyes have to grow accustomed to this semi-darkness.–These sweet eyes!–*(Kisses her eyes.)*

SWEET YOUNG THING. I'm afraid my sweet little eyes won't have time for that.

POET. Why not?

SWEET YOUNG THING. Because I'm going to stay here for just one minute.

POET. Won't you take off your hat?

SWEET YOUNG THING. For one minute?

POET. *(Removes the pin from her hat and places the hat at a distance.)* And your cape–

SWEET YOUNG THING. What are you doing?–I have to leave right away.

POET. But you must rest first! We've been walking for three hours.

SWEET YOUNG THING. We were in a carriage.

POET. Yes, on the way home–but in Weidling-am-Bach we walked for a full three hours. So why don't you sit down, my child . . . wherever you like–here at the writing table–but, no, it's not comfortable enough. Sit here on the divan.–There. *(He urges her down onto the divan.)* If you're very tired, you can even lie down. *(He makes her lie down on the divan.)* There, your little head on the pillow.

SWEET YOUNG THING. *(Laughing.)* But I'm not tired at all!

POET. You just think not. There–and if you're sleepy, you can sleep a bit. I shall be quite still. Besides, I can play a lullaby for you . . . one of my own . . . *(Goes to the piano.)*

SWEET YOUNG THING. One of your own?

POET. Yes.

SWEET YOUNG THING. Why, Robert, I thought you were a doctor.

POET. How so? I told you I was a writer.

SWEET YOUNG THING. Writers are always doctors.

POET. No, not all. Myself, for example. But why did you think of that?

SWEET YOUNG THING. Well, because you said the piece you were going to play was your own.

POET. Well . . . perhaps it isn't my own. But that's unimportant. Isn't it? It never really matters who does a thing– as long as it's beautiful. Isn't that right?

SWEET YOUNG THING. Of course . . . as long as it's beautiful
—that's the main thing!

POET. Do you know what I meant when I said that?

SWEET YOUNG THING. What you meant?

POET. Yes, what I just said.

SWEET YOUNG THING. *(Sleepily.)*   Oh . . . of course.

POET. *(Rises, goes to her and strokes her hair.)*   You didn't
understand a word of it.

SWEET YOUNG THING. Go on, I'm not that stupid.

POET. Of course you're that stupid. And that's why I love
you. It's a wonderful thing for a woman to be stupid. I
mean, in your way.

SWEET YOUNG THING. Why are you making fun of me?

POET. You angel, you sweet little angel! Do you like lying
on a soft Persian rug?

SWEET YOUNG THING. Oh, yes. Go on, why don't you play the
piano?

POET. No, I'd rather be here with you. *(He strokes her.)*

SWEET YOUNG THING. Say, where do you turn on the light?

POET. Oh, no . . . This twilight is very comforting. We spent
the whole day bathed in sunlight. And now, you might
say, we've just climbed from the bath and are about to
wrap the . . . the twilight about us like a bathrobe– *(He
laughs.)* —or, no—that should be put differently . . .
Wouldn't you say so?

SWEET YOUNG THING. I don't know.

POET. *(Gently moving from her.)*   How divine this stupidity
can be! *(Takes out a notebook and writes a few words.)*

SWEET YOUNG THING. What are you doing? *(Turning toward
him.)*   What are you writing?

POET. *(Softly.)*   Sun, bath, twilight, robe . . . there . . .
(Pockets the notebook. Out loud.)   Nothing . . . Tell me
now, my sweet, would you like something to eat or drink?

SWEET YOUNG THING. I'm not really thirsty. But I am hungry.

POET. Hm . . . I'd rather you were thirsty. I have cognac at
home, but I'll have to go out for the food.

SWEET YOUNG THING. Can't you send out for it?

POET. That will be difficult–the maid's not around any
more–well, all right–I'll go myself . . . what would you
like?

SWEET YOUNG THING. Oh, I don't think it'll be worth it–
I have to be getting home anyway.

POET. Child, you mustn't think such a thing. But I'll tell you what: when we leave, let's go somewhere and have supper.

SWEET YOUNG THING. Oh, no. I don't have time. And besides, where would we go? We might meet friends.

POET. Have you that many friends?

SWEET YOUNG THING. It's bad enough if even one of them sees us.

POET. What do you mean "bad enough"?

SWEET YOUNG THING. Well, what would happen, do you think, if my mother heard about it?

POET. We could go somewhere where no one could see us; there are restaurants with private rooms, you know.

SWEET YOUNG THING. *(Singing.)*   "Oh, take me to a supper in a private room!"

POET. Have you ever been to one of those private rooms?

SWEET YOUNG THING. Well, to tell you the truth–yes.

POET. And who was the fortunate gentleman?

SWEET YOUNG THING. Oh, it's not what you're thinking . . . I was there once with my girl friend and her husband. They took me along.

POET. I see. And you expect me to believe that?

SWEET YOUNG THING I didn't ask you to believe it!

POET. *(Close to her.)*   Are you blushing? Its too dark in here! I can't even make out your features. *(He touches her cheek with his hand.)*   But I recognize you this way, too.

SWEET YOUNG THING. Just be careful you don't confuse me with someone else.

POET. How strange! I can't remember any more what you look like.

SWEET YOUNG THING. Thanks!

POET. *(Seriously.)*   Isn't that uncanny! I can't even picture you. –In a certain sense I've forgotten you.–And if I couldn't recognize you by the tone of your voice either . . . what would you be?–Near and far at the same time . . . uncanny.

SWEET YOUNG THING. Go on, what are you talking about–?

POET. Nothing, my angel, nothing. Where are your lips . . . *(He kisses her.)*

SWEET YOUNG THING. Don't you want to turn on the light?

POET. No . . .*(He grows very tender.)*   Tell me, do you love me?

SWEET YOUNG THING. Very . . . oh, very much!

POET. Have you ever loved anyone else as much as me?

SWEET YOUNG THING. I already told you—no.

POET. *(Sighs.)* But . . . *(He sighs.)*

SWEET YOUNG THING. Well—he was my fiancé.

POET. I'd rather you didn't think about him.

SWEET YOUNG THING. Go on . . . what are you doing . . . look . . .

POET. We can imagine ourselves now in a castle in India.

SWEET YOUNG THING. I'm sure they couldn't be as bad there
as you are.

POET. What a divine thing you are! If only you
could guess what you mean to me.

SWEET YOUNG THING. Well?

POET. Stop pushing me away like that all the time; I'm not
doing anything to you—yet.

SWEET YOUNG THING. You know what?—My corset hurts.

POET. *(Simply.)* Take it off.

SWEET YOUNG THING. Well—but you mustn't be bad if I do.

POET. No.

*(The Sweet Young Think has risen and removes her corset
in the dark.)*

POET. *(In the meanwhile sits on the divan.)* Say, aren't you
at all interested in knowing my last name?

SWEET YOUNG THING. Sure, what is it?

POET. I'd rather not tell you my name, but what I call
myself.

SWEET YOUNG THING. What's the difference?

POET. Well, the name I write under.

SWEET YOUNG THING. Oh, you don't write under your real name?

(The Poet is close to her.)

SWEET YOUNG THING. Oh. . . go on!. . . no.

POET. What a wonderful fragrance rises from you. How sweet
it is. *(He kisses her breasts.)*

SWEET YOUNG THING. You're tearing my blouse.

POET. Here . . . let me . . . let me . . it's so unnecessary.

SWEET YOUNG THING. But, Robert!

POET. And now—enter our Indian castle.

SWEET YOUNG THING. Tell me first if you really love me.

POET. But I worship you *(He kisses her passionately.)* I
worship you, my sweet, my springtime . . . my . . .

SWEET YOUNG THING. Robert . . . Robert . . .

. . . .

POET. That was unearthly bliss . . . I call myself . . .

SWEET YOUNG THING. Robert . . . my Robert!

POET. I call myself Biebitz.

SWEET YOUNG THING. Why do you call yourself Biebitz?

POET. My name isn't Biebitz—I just call myself that . . .
  well, don't you recognize the name?

SWEET YOUNG THING. No.

POET. You don't know the name Biebitz? Oh, how divine
  you are! Really? You're just saying that now, aren't you?

SWEET YOUNG THING. I swear, I never heard of it!

POET. Don't you go to the theatre?

SWEET YOUNG THING. Oh, yes—just recently I went with . . .
  with the uncle of a girl friend of mine, and the girl friend
  —we went to the Opera—*Cavalleria Rusticana*.

POET. Hm, then you don't go to the Burg Theatre.

SWEET YOUNG THING. Nobody gives me tickets for there.

POET. One day soon I'll send you a ticket.

SWEET YOUNG THING. Oh, please! But don't forget! And to
  something funny.

POET. I see . . . to something funny . . . you wouldn't want
  to see anything sad?

SWEET YOUNG THING. Not really.

POET. Not even if it's a play by me?

SWEET YOUNG THING. Oh! . . . a play by you? You write
  for the theatre?

POET. Excuse me, may I light a candle? I haven't seen you
  since you became my love.—Angel! *(He lights a candle.)*

SWEET YOUNG THING. No, don't, I'm ashamed. At least give me a cover.

POET. Later! *(He approaches her with a candle and looks
  at her for a long while.)*

SWEET YOUNG THING. *(Covers her face with her hands.)* Robert,
  you mustn't.

POET. You're beautiful. You are Beauty. Perhaps you are
  even Nature herself. You are Sacred Simplicity.

SWEET YOUNG THING. Oh! You're dripping on me! Look at
  that! Why can't you be careful!

POET. *(Puts the candle aside.)* You are what I have sought
  for a long time. You love only me, you would love me
  even if I worked in a shop as an assistant. That's very comforting. I must confess to you that up to this moment I
  have harbored a certain suspicion. Tell me, honestly, didn't
  you have the slightest idea that I was Biebitz?

SWEET YOUNG THING. Look, I don't know what you want with
me, but I don't know any Biebitz.

POET. Oh, fame, fame! No, forget what I said, even forget
the name I told you. I'm Robert to you, that's all. I was
merely joking. *(Lightly.)*   I'm not even a writer, I'm a shop
assistant, and in the evening I play the piano for some folk
singers.

SWEET YOUNG THING. Now you've really got me mixed up
. . . oh, and the way you look at a person. What is it,
what's the matter?

POET. It's very strange–it's almost never happened to me
before, my sweet, but I could almost cry. You move me
very deeply. We'll stay together for now. We'll love each
other very much.

SWEET YOUNG THING. Did you mean that about the folk
singers?

POET. Yes, but no more questions. If you really love me,
then you will have no questions. Tell me, could you be
free for a couple of weeks?

SWEET YOUNG THING. How do you mean "free"?

POET. Well, away from home.

SWEET YOUNG THING. Oh!! How could I do that! What
would my mother say? And then, well, without me around
the house everything would go wrong.

POET. I thought it might be nice to be alone with you somewhere where there's solitude, in the woods, surrounded by
Nature, for a few weeks. . . to live there with you.
Nature . . . surrounded by Nature . . . And then one
day just to say good-bye–to part from one another without
knowing where to.

SWEET YOUNG THING. You're already talking about saying good-bye!
And I thought you loved me so.

POET. That's why–*(Bends down to kiss her on the forehead.)*
You precious creature!

SWEET YOUNG THING. Yes, hold me tight. I'm so cold.

POET. It's about time you were getting dressed. Wait, I'll
light a few more candles for you.

SWEET YOUNG THING. *(Rises.)*   But don't look.

POET. No. *(At the window.)*   Tell me, child, are you happy?

SWEET YOUNG THING. How do you mean?

POET. I mean, in general, are you happy?

SWEET YOUNG THING. It could be better.

POET. You don't understand. You've told me enough about the conditions at home. I know that you're no princess. I mean, when you set all that aside, do you feel alive? Do you really feel you're living?

SWEET YOUNG THING. Got a comb?

POET. *(Goes to the dressing table, gives her a comb, then looks at her.)* My God, but you're charming!

SWEET YOUNG THING. Now . . . don't

POET. Come on, stay a little longer, I'll get something for supper, and—

SWEET YOUNG THING. But it's much too late.

POET. It's not even nine.

SWEET YOUNG THING. Oh, well then, I've got to hurry.

POET. When will we see each other again?

SWEET YOUNG THING. Well, when do you want to see me again?

POET. Tomorrow.

SWEET YOUNG THING. What day is tomorrow?

POET. Saturday.

SWEET YOUNG THING. Oh, I can't tomorrow, I have to take my little sister to see our guardian.

POET. Sunday then . . . mmm . . . Sunday . . . on Sunday . . . I must explain something to you.—I am not Biebitz, but Biebitz is a friend of mine. I'll introduce you sometime. There's a play of his next Sunday; I'll send you some tickets and come to get you at the theatre. And you must tell me what you think of the play. All right?

SWEET YOUNG THING. And now all this about Biebitz—I really must be stupid!

POET. I'll know you fully only when I know what you thought about the play.

SWEET YOUNG THING. There . . . I'm ready.

POET. Come, my sweet.

(They go out.)

SCENE 8

(The Poet and the Actress. A room in a country inn. It is an evening in spring; the moon shines across the hills and the meadows. The windows are open. Complete silence. The Poet and the Actress enter; as they enter, the candle in the Poet's hand goes out.)

POET. Oh!

ACTRESS. What is it?

POET. The candle.–But we don't need it. Look, it's light enough. Wonderful!

(The Actress suddenly sinks to her knees beside the window, her hands folded.)

POET. What's the matter?

(The Actress is silent.)

POET. *(Goes to her.)* What are you doing?

ACTRESS. *(Indignant.)*   Can't you see I'm praying?–

POET. Do you believe in God?

ACTRESS. Of course–do you think I'm as mean as all that!

POET. I see.

ACTRESS. Come here to me, kneel down beside me. For once in your life you can pray too. You won't lose any jewels out of your precious crown.

(The Poet kneels beside her, puts his arms around her.)

ACTRESS. Libertine!–

POET. *(Rises.)*

ACTRESS. And do you know to whom I was praying?

POET. God, I suppose.

ACTRESS. *(With great scorn.)*   Of course! Of course! I was praying to you.

POET. Then why did you look out of the window?

ACTRESS. Suppose you tell me where you've brought me, you abductor!

POET. But, child, it was all your idea. You wanted to go to the country. You wanted to come here.

ACTRESS. Well, wasn't I right?

POET. Of course, it's charming here. When you think that it's only two hours from Vienna– and all this absolute solitude. What a wonderful country!

ACTRESS. Yes, isn't it. If you had any talent you could write some poetry here.

POET. Have you been here before?

ACTRESS. Been here before? Ha! I lived here for years!

POET. With whom?

ACTRESS. Why, with Fritz, of course.

POET. I see!

ACTRESS. Oh, how I worshiped that man!

POET. Yes, you've told me.

ACTRESS. Well–I'm sorry–I can leave if I bore you!

POET. Bore me? You have no idea what you mean to me.
You're a world in yourself. You're Divinity, you're Spirit.
You are . . . you are Simplicity itself. Yes, you . . . But
you mustn't talk about Fritz now.

ACTRESS. Yes, that was a mistake! Well!–

POET. I'm glad you see that.

ACTRESS. Come here, give me a kiss!

(The Poet kisses her.)

ACTRESS. But now it's time we said good night! Good-bye,
my sweet!

POET. How do you mean that?

ACTRESS. I'm going to bed!

POET. Yes–that's fine, but what's all this good-night
business . . . where am I supposed to sleep?

ACTRESS. Surely there must be other rooms in the house.

POET. But the others have no attraction for me. What do you
say I light a candle?

ACTRESS. Yes.

POET. *(Lights the candle on the night table.)* What a pretty
room . . . and how pious these people are. Nothing but holy
pictures. It might be interesting to spend some time among
them. It's quite another world.

ACTRESS. Don't talk so silly, and hand me my pocketbook
from the table, will you?

POET. Here, my only love!

*(The Actress takes a small, framed picture from her pocketbook and places it on
the night table.)*

POET. What's that?

ACTRESS. A picture of the Madonna.

POET. Do you always have it with you?

ACTRESS. It's my talisman. Go on now, Robert!

POET. You must be joking! Don't you want me to help you?

ACTRESS. No, I want you to go.

POET. And when shall I come back?

ACTRESS. In ten minutes.

POET. *(Kisses her.)*   Good-bye!

ACTRESS. Where will you go?

POET. I'll walk back and forth in front of your window. I'm
    very fond of walking outdoors at night. And especially
    when I'm near you, surrounded with my longing for you
    . . .wafted along by your art.

ACTRESS. You're talking like an idiot . . .

POET. *(Painfully.)*   There are women who might have said
    . . . like a poet.

ACTRESS. Go on now. But don't start anything with the
    waitress.—

*(The Poet goes out. The Actress undresses. She hears the Poet as he goes down the
wooden stairs and as he walks back and forth in front of her window. As soon as
she is undressed she goes to the window, looks down, and sees him standing there;
she calls to him in a whisper.)*

ACTRESS. Come!

*(The Poet hurries up the stairs, rushes to her. She has in the meanwhile gone to
bed and puts out the candle; he locks the door.)*

ACTRESS. There now, you sit down here next to me and tell
    me a story.

POET. *(Sits down beside her on the bed.)*Shall I close the
    window? Aren't you cold?

ACTRESS. Oh, no!

POET. What shall I tell you?

ACTRESS. Well, to whom you are being unfaithful at this
    very moment?

POET. Unfortunately, I'm not being unfaithful . . . yet.

ACTRESS. You mustn't worry about it, because I'm deceiving
    someone, too.

POET. I can imagine.

ACTRESS. Who do you think?

POET. Well, child, I haven't any idea.

ACTRESS. Just guess.

POET. Let me see . . . Well, your producer.

ACTRESS. My dear, I'm not a chorus girl.

POET. It was only a guess.

ACTRESS. Guess again.

POET. One of the actors then . . . Benno—

ACTRESS. Ha! That man never looked at a woman . . . didn't you know? That man is having an affair with his postman!

POET. You must be joking!

ACTRESS. Why don't you kiss me!

(The Poet embraces her.)

ACTRESS. Why, what are you doing?

POET. Why must you torture me this way?

ACTRESS. May I suggest something, Robert? Why don't you come to bed with me?

POET. Accepted!

ACTRESS. Quickly, quickly!

POET. If it had been up to me, I'd long have . . .You hear that?

ACTRESS. What?

POET. The crickets chirping outside.

ACTRESS. You're mad, child, there are no crickets here.

POET. You don't hear them?

ACTRESS. Come here, why are you taking so long?

POET. Here I am. *(He comes to her.)*

ACTRESS. There now, you lie there quietly now . . .now . . . I said quietly.

POET. What do you mean quietly!

ACTRESS. You mean you'd like to have an affair with me?

POET. I thought you'd already have guessed.

ACTRESS. A great many men have wanted to . . .

POET. But at the moment the chances seem to be more in my favor.

ACTRESS. Come, my cricket! I shall call you my cricket from now on.

POET. I like that . . .

ACTRESS. Well—who am I deceiving?

POET. Who? Me, perhaps . . .?

ACTRESS. My dear child, are you certain you're all right?

POET. Or someone . . . you've never even seen . . . someone you don't know, someone—destined for you, but you've never found him . . .

ACTRESS. Why must you talk so silly!

POET. . . . Isn't it strange . . . even you—and one would have thought—But no, it would be depriving you of all that's best about you if one . . . Come, come—come—

. . . .

ACTRESS. This is so much nicer than acting in those idiotic
    plays . . . don't you think so?
POET. Well, I think it's nice that you have the chance to play
    in reasonable plays now and then.
ACTRESS. You arrogant dog, do you mean *your* play?
POET. Of course!
ACTRESS. *(Seriously.)* It's a magnificent play!
POET. There, you see!
ACTRESS. Yes, Robert, you're a great genius!
POET. Now that you have the opportunity, why not tell me
    why you canceled your performance the day before yesterday.
    And don't tell me you were ill.
ACTRESS. No, I wanted to antagonize you.
POET. But why? What did I do to you?
ACTRESS. You were arrogant.
POET. In what way?
ACTRESS. Everyone at the theatre thinks so.
POET. I see.
ACTRESS. But I told them: That man has every right to be
    arrogant.
POET. And what did they say to that?
ACTRESS. What *should* they have said? I never speak to
    them.
POET. Is that right?
ACTRESS. They would all like to poison me. But they'll never
    succeed.
POET. You mustn't think about other people now. Be content
    that we're here together, and tell me that you love me.
ACTRESS. Do you need even more proof?
POET. You don't prove such things.
ACTRESS. How nice! What more do you want?
POET. How many others have you tried to prove it this
    way? Did you love every one of them?
ACTRESS. No. I've loved only one.
POET. *(Embracing her.)* My . . .
ACTRESS. Fritz.
POET. My name is Robert. What can I possibly mean to you
    if you can think of Fritz at a time like this!
ACTRESS. You are a whim.
POET. Thanks for telling me.
ACTRESS. Tell me, aren't you proud?
POET. What's there to make me proud?

ACTRESS. I think you have good reason to be.

POET. Oh, because of that!

ACTRESS. Of course, because of that, my little cricket!–And what about the chirping? Are they still chirping outside?

POET. Certainly. Can't you hear them.

ACTRESS. Of course I hear them. But those are frogs you hear.

POET. You're mistaken: frogs croak.

ACTRESS. That's right, they're croaking.

POET. But not here, my child, they're chirping.

ACTRESS. You are the stubbornest man I have ever come across. Give me a kiss, my little frog!

POET. Please, don't call me that. It makes me nervous.

ACTRESS. Well, what *shall* I call you?

POET. I have a name, don't I? Robert.

ACTRESS. But that's too ridiculous.

POET. But I would rather you call me by my proper name.

ACTRESS. Kiss me, then–Robert.–Oh! (*She kisses him.*) Are you happy now, my little frog? Hahahaha.

POET. Do you mind if I light a cigarette?

ACTRESS. I'll have one too.

(*He takes the cigarette case from the night table, takes out two cigarettes, lights both, and hands her one.*)

ACTRESS. Incidentally, you said nothing about my performance last night.

POET. Performance?

ACTRESS. Really . . .!

POET. That one! I wasn't at the theatre.

ACTRESS. You must be fond of joking.

POET. Why no. After your cancellation the day before yesterday. I assumed you wouldn't be in full possession of your powers, so I thought I'd rather forgo it.

ACTRESS. You missed something.

POET. Oh?

ACTRESS. I was sensational. The audience turned pale.

POET. Could you really see them?

ACTRESS. Benno said: "My child, you were a goddess!"

POET. And so ill the day before.

ACTRESS. That's *right*, and I *was, too*. And do you know why? Out of longing for you.

POET. A little while ago you said you canceled out because you wanted to antagonize me.

ACTRESS. What do you know of my love for you! All this leaves you cold. I had a fever for nights on end. Over a hundred and five!

POET. That's quite a temperature for just a whim.

ACTRESS. You call that a whim? Here I am dying of love for you, and you call it a whim—!

POET. And what about Fritz?   ·

ACTRESS. Fritz? . . Don't even talk to me about that terrible creature!–

SCENE 9

(The Actress and the Count. The bedroom of the Actress. Very sumptuously appointed. It is twelve noon, the blinds are still down, a candle burns on the small night table, the Actress lies in her canopied bed. Numerous newspapers are strewn across the bed cover.

The Count enters in the uniform of a captain of the dragoons. He remains standing at the door.)

ACTRESS. Oh, Herr Count.

COUNT. Your dear mother gave me permission, or I should never have—

ACTRESS. Please, do come in.

COUNT. I kiss your hand. Excuse me—when one enters directly from the street . . . the fact is I still can't see a thing. Ah, yes . . . here we are—*(At the bed.)*   —I kiss your hand.

ACTRESS. Won't you have a seat, Herr Count?

COUNT. Your mother said that you weren't feeling well, Fräulein. I do hope it's nothing serious.

ACTRESS. Nothing serious? I was on the verge of death!

COUNT. Good heavens, is that possible?

ACTRESS. In any case I think it very nice for you to have troubled yourself on my account.

COUNT. On the verge of death! And yesterday evening you played like a goddess.

ACTRESS. Yes, it was rather a triumph, wasn't it?

COUNT. Colossal! The audience was absolutely carried away. And I won't even tell you what I thought.

ACTRESS. Thank you for the lovely flowers.

COUNT. Don't mention it.

ACTRESS. *(Indicates with her eyes a large basket of flowers sitting in a small table at the window.)* They they are.

COUNT. Yesterday you were absolutely overwhelmed with flowers and garlands.

ACTRESS. They are all still in my dressing room. I brought only your basket with me.

COUNT. *(Kisses her hand.)* That was very sweet of you. *(The Actress suddenly takes his hand and kisses it.)*

COUNT. But, my dear!

ACTRESS. Don't be afraid, Herr Count, that doesn't obligate you in any way.

COUNT. What an extraordinary creature you are . . . one might almost say an enigma.—*(Pause.)*

ACTRESS. Fräulein Birken might be easier to . . . solve.

COUNT. Oh, little Birken is no problem, although . . . but of course I know her only superficially.

ACTRESS. Ha!

COUNT. Believe me. But you are a problem. A kind that I have always longed for. I never realized until last night, when I saw you act for the first time, what an extraordinary pleasure I had let slip from me.

ACTRESS. Is that possible?

COUNT. I'm accustomed to dining late . . . so that when I do arrive the best part of the play has already gone by.

ACTRESS. From now on you must eat earlier.

COUNT. Yes, I've considered that. Or perhaps not dining at all. Actually dining is no pleasure for me any more.

ACTRESS. What *does* a young old man like you take pleasure in?

COUNT. I often ask myself the same question! But I am not an old man. There must be another reason.

ACTRESS. Do you think so?

COUNT. Yes. For example, Louie says I'm a philosopher. What he means, Fräulein, is that I think too much.

ACTRESS. Think . . . yes, well that is a misfortune.

COUNT. I have too much time on my hands, and so I think. But then, you see, I thought that if they were to transfer me to Vienna things might be different. There's amusement and stimulation here. But the fact is that it's not much different here than it was there.

ACTRESS. Where is "there"?

COUNT. Why, in Hungary . . . the small towns where I was generally stationed.

ACTRESS. Whatever did you do in Hungary?

COUNT. But I just told you, Fräulein, the Army.

ACTRESS. Well then why did you stay *so long* in Hungary?

COUNT. That's the way it happens.

ACTRESS. It must be sufficient to drive one mad.

COUNT. Why do you say that? Of course there's more to do there than
here. Such things as training recruits, breaking in the horses . . .
and then, too, the region isn't all as bad as they say. It's really quite
lovely, the low-lying plains–and the sunsets . . . It's a pity I'm not a
painter; I've often thought that if I were, I would paint it. There
was one young man in the regiment, his name was Splany, he could
have done it.–But why am I telling you all these dull stories,
Fräulein.?

ACTRESS. Oh, please, I'm terribly amused.

COUNT. You know, Fräulein, it's quite easy talking to you.
Louie told me it would be. And that's something you don't
often find.

ACTRESS. Well, in Hungary, I suppose so.

COUNT. And definitely in Vienna! People are the same everywhere. The only difference is that where there are more
people, the crowds are larger. Tell me, Fräulein, are you
fond of people?

ACTRESS. Fond? I hate them! I can't *look* at a human being!
I *never* see them! I am always alone, no one ever enters
this house.

COUNT. You see, I was right when I believed you a misanthrope!
It happens often where artists are concerned. When one exists in
those higher regions . . . well, it's all right for you, at least you know
why you're living!

ACTRESS. Who ever told you that? I have no idea why I'm
living!

COUNT. But I beg to differ–you're famous–celebrated–

ACTRESS. Is that what you call happiness?

COUNT. Happiness? I'm sorry, but there is no such thing as
happiness. Most of the things that people talk about so freely don't
really exist . . . love, for example. It's the same there too.

ACTRESS. You are quite right.

COUNT. Pleasure . . . intoxication . . . fine, there's nothing to say against
them . . . they are something positive. If I take pleasure in something, fine, at least I know I take pleasure in it. Or else I feel myself
intoxicated, excellent. That's positive too. And when it's past, well
then, it's past.

ACTRESS. *(Grandly.)* It's past!

COUNT. But as soon as one fails to, how shall I say it, as soon as one fails to live for the moment, and starts thinking about the future or the past . . . well, then it's all over with. The future . . . is sad . . . the past uncertain. In short, it only confuses one. Am I right?

ACTRESS. *(Nods, her eyes large.)* You have gone directly to the heart of the matter.

COUNT. So you see, my dear madam, once you have perceived the truth of this, it really makes little difference whether you live in Vienna or in Pussta or even in Steinamanger. For example . . . excuse me, where may I put my cap? . . . Oh, thank you . . . now what were we talking about?

ACTRESS. Steinamanger.

COUNT. Ah, yes. It's just as I said, the difference is very slight. It's all the same to me whether I spend my evenings at the Casino or at the Club.

ACTRESS. And how does all this relate to love?

COUNT. If one believes in it, he'll always find someone to love him.

ACTRESS. Fräulein Birken, for example.

COUNT. Really, my dear, I don't know why you always seem to return to poor little Birken.

ACTRESS. She's your mistress, isn't she?

COUNT. Who ever said that?

ACTRESS. Everyone knows.

COUNT. Except me. Isn't that remarkable!

ACTRESS. You even fought a duel for her sake!

COUNT. Perhaps I was even killed and didn't notice it.

ACTRESS. Yes, Count, you are a man of honor. Won't you sit closer?

COUNT. May I?

ACTRESS. Here. *(She draws him to her and runs her fingers through his hair.)* I knew you would come today!

COUNT. How?

ACTRESS. I knew yesterday at the theatre.

COUNT. Could you see me from the stage?

ACTRESS. My dear man, couldn't you tell that I was playing for no one but you?

COUNT. How can that be?

ACTRESS. I felt like I was walking on air when I saw you in the first row!

COUNT. Walking on air? On my account? I had no idea you even saw me!

ACTRESS. You know, you can drive a woman to desperation with your dignity.

COUNT. Fräulein!

ACTRESS. "Fräulein"!–At least take off your saber!

COUNT. If I may. (*He unbuckles the belt and leans the saber against the bed.*)

ACTRESS. And now kiss me.

(*The Count kisses her; she does not let loose of him.*)

ACTRESS. Oh, how I wish I had never seen you!

COUNT. It's much better like this!–

ACTRESS. Count, you are a poseur!

COUNT. How so?

ACTRESS. How happy do you think many a man might be to find himself in your place at this moment!

COUNT. But I am happy. Very.

ACTRESS. I thought there was no happiness. Why are you looking at me that way? I do believe you are afraid of me, Herr Count!

COUNT. As I said, madam, you are a problem.

ACTRESS. Oh, don't bother me with your philosophizing . . . come here. And now, ask me for something. You may have anything you like. You're far too handsome.

COUNT. If I have your permission then–(*Kissing her hand.*) —I will return tonight.

ACTRESS. Tonight? . . . But I'll be playing.

COUNT. After the theatre.

ACTRESS. Is that all you're asking for?

COUNT. I shall ask for everything *after* the theatre.

ACTRESS. (*Offended.*) And you'll have to ask for a long time, you miserable poseur.

COUNT. Well, you see, you see, we've been so open with one another up till now. I would really find all that so much nicer after the theatre . . . more comfortable than now. Well, I have the feeling that a door could open on us at any moment . . .

ACTRESS. The door doesn't open from the outside.

COUNT. Don't you feel that it would be careless to spoil something at the start, something that might quite possibly turn out to be beautiful?

ACTRESS. "Quite possibly"?

COUNT. To be quite honest, I find love in the morning really rather ghastly.

ACTRESS. Well–you are easily the most insane man I have ever met!

COUNT. I'm not talking about just *any* woman . . . after all, in general it scarcely matters. But women like you . . . no, call me a fool a hundred times over if you like . . . women like you . . . aren't to be had before breakfast. And so . . . you see . . .

ACTRESS. My God, but you're sweet!

COUNT. You do see what I mean, don't you. The way I see it . . .

ACTRESS. *Tell* me how you see it!

COUNT. I thought that . . . I would wait for you after the theatre in a carriage, and then we could drive somewhere together and have supper–

ACTRESS. I am not Fräulein Birken.

COUNT. I didn't say that you were. It's simply that one must be in the mood. And I always find myself in the mood after supper. It's always nicer that way, when after supper you drive home together, and then . . .

ACTRESS. And then what?

COUNT. Well, then . . . then it simply depends on how things develop.

ACTRESS. Sit closer to me. Closer.

COUNT. *(Sitting on the bed.)* I must say there's a lovely aroma coming from your pillows–mignonette, isn't it? *(The Count bends down and kisses her throat.)*

ACTRESS. Oh, but, my dear Count, that's not on your program.

COUNT. Who says so? I have no program.

(The Actress draws him to her.)

COUNT. It certainly is warm.

ACTRESS. Isn't it? And so dark, as though it were evening . . . *(Pulls him to her.)* It is evening . . . it's night.– Close your eyes if it's too light for you. Come! Come!

(The Count no longer defends himself.)

. . . .

ACTRESS. What was that about being in the mood, you poseur?

COUNT. You are a little devil.

ACTRESS. What a thing to say!

COUNT. Well then, an angel.

ACTRESS. You should have been an actor! Really! You understand women! Do you know what I shall do now?

COUNT. Well?

ACTRESS. I shall tell you that I will never see you again.

COUNT. But why?

ACTRESS. No, no. You're too dangerous for me! You'd drive
a woman mad. There you are, standing in front of me now,
as though nothing had happened.

COUNT. But . . .

ACTRESS. I beg you to remember, Herr Count, that I have
just been your mistress.

COUNT. I shall never forget it!

ACTRESS. And what of tonight?

COUNT. How do you mean that?

ACTRESS. Well—you were going to wait for me after the theatre?

COUNT. Yes, fine . . . what about tomorrow?

ACTRESS. What do you mean "tomorrow"? We were talking
about tonight.

COUNT. But that wouldn't make sense.

ACTRESS. You old fool!

COUNT. Don't misunderstand. I mean it more, how shall I
say, from the spiritual standpoint.

ACTRESS. What's your soul got to do with it?

COUNT. Believe me, that's part of it too. I find it completely
false that the two can be kept apart.

ACTRESS. Don't bother me with your philosophizing. When
I want that, I'll read books.

COUNT. One doesn't learn from books.

ACTRESS. I agree! That's why you should wait for me this
evening. We'll come to some agreement about the soul,
you scoundrel!

COUNT. Well then, with your permission, I shall have my
carriage waiting–

ACTRESS. . . . . After the theatre.

COUNT. Of course. *(He buckles on his saber.)*

ACTRESS. What are you doing?

COUNT. I think it's time I was going. For a formal call I
believe I have overstayed my time a bit.

ACTRESS. But tonight it won't be a formal call.

COUNT. Really?

ACTRESS. You let me take care of that. And now give me another kiss,
my sweet philosopher. Here, you seducer, you . . . sweet child, you
slave dealer, you polecat . . . you . . . *(After having kissed him resound-
ingly several times, she pushes him vigorously from her.)* Count it was a
great honour!

COUNT. I kiss your hand, Fräulein! *(At the door.)* Au revoir!

ACTRESS. *Adieu,* Steinamanger!

SCENE 10

(The Count and the Prostitute. Morning, around six o'clock. A miserable little room with one window; the dirty yellow blinds are down; worn green curtains on the window. A chest of drawers with a few photographs on it and a conspicuously tasteless cheap woman's hat. A number of cheap Japanese fans behind the mirror. On the table, covered over with a reddish cloth, stands a kerosene lamp, still feebly alight and emitting its odor; over it is a yellow paper lampshade. Beside it is a jug with leftover beer and a half-empty glass. On the floor beside the bed there is a disarray of woman's clothing, as though they had rapidly been taken off and thrown down. The prostitute is asleep in the bed; she breathes quietly. Fully dressed on the divan lies the Count in his overcoat, his hat on the floor at the head of the divan.)

COUNT. *(Moves, rubs his eyes, rises quickly, remains sitting, looks around.)* How did I get . . . oh yes . . . then I did go home with that female. . . *(He rises quickly, sees her bed.)* And here she is . . . The things that happen to a man my age! I can't remember . . . did they carry me up here? No . . . I saw–I came into the room . . . yes, I was still awake . . . or . . . or is it that this room reminds me of somewhere else?– My God, yes, yes . . . I saw it yesterday all right . . . *(Looks at his watch.)* Hm! Yesterday! A couple of hours ago, that's when I saw it–But I knew that something had to happen . . . I felt it . . . yesterday when I began drinking, I felt that something . . . And what did happen?–Nothing . . . Or did I . . .? My God . . . not for . . . not for ten years has anything happened to me that I haven't remembered. Well, in any case I was drunk. If only I could remember when I got that way.–At least I remember when I went into that whores' café with Louie and . . . no, no . . . it was after we left Sacher's . . . and then on the way . . . Yes, that's right, I was driving along with Louie ... But what am I racking my brains for! It doesn't matter. Just see that you get our of here. *(Gets up. The lamp shakes.)* Oh! *(He looks at the sleeping girl.)* At least she's sleeping soundly I don't remember a thing, but I'll put the money on the night table ... and good-bye ... *(He stands looking at her for a long while.)* If only one didn't know what she is! *(He looks at her thoughtfully for a long while.)* I've known a lot of her kind that didn't look so virtuous even in their sleep. My God ... Louie would say I'm

philosophizing . . . but it's true, it seems to me sleep
washes away all differences—like his brother Death.—
Hm, I wish I knew whether . . . No. I'd remember that.
No, no, I came straight in and fell onto the divan . . .
and nothing happened . . . Isn't it remarkable how sometimes all women look alike.—Well, time to go. *(He is
about to leave.)*   Oh, I forgot. *(He takes out his wallet and
is about to remove a bill.)*

PROSTITUTE. *(Wakes up.)*   What! . . . who's here so early?
(Recognizing him.)   Hello!

COUNT. Good morning. Sleep well?

PROSTITUTE. *(Stretches herself.)* Oh! Come here. Give me a
little kiss.

COUNT. *(Bends down to her, considers, pulls up.)*   I was just going . . .

PROSTITUTE. Going?

COUNT. It's about time.

PROSTITUTE. You want to go, like this?

COUNT. *(Almost embarrassed.)*   Well . . .

PROSTITUTE. All right, so long; come back some other time.

COUNT. Yes. Good-bye. Won't you give me your hand?

(The Prostitute extends her hand from under the cover.)

COUNT. *(Takes the hand and kisses it mechanically, becomes
aware of himself, laughs.)*   Like a princess. After all, if one
saw only . . .

PROSTITUTE. What are you looking at me like that for?

COUNT. If one saw only that little head, like now . . . when
they wake one looks as innocent as the next . . . my God,
one could imagine all sorts of things, if only it didn't
smell so of kerosene . . .

PROSTITUTE. Yes, that lamp's always a bother.

COUNT. How old are you?

PROSTITUTE. Guess.

COUNT. Twenty-four.

PROSTITUTE. Sure, sure.

COUNT. You mean you're older?

PROSTITUTE. I'm going on twenty.

COUNT. And how long have you . . .

PROSTITUTE. How long have I been in the business? A year.

COUNT. You started early.

PROSTITUTE. Better early than too late.

COUNT. *(Sits down on the bed.)* Tell me something, are you
really happy?

PROSTITUTE. What?

COUNT. Well, what I mean is, how are you getting on?

PROSTITUTE. Oh, right now I'm getting on all right.

COUNT. I see.—Tell me, didn't it ever occur to you that you become something else?

PROSTITUTE. Like what?

COUNT. Well ... you're really quite a lovely girl. You could have a lover, for example.

PROSTITUTE. What makes you think I ain't got one?

COUNT. Yes, of course—what I meant was one who, you know, one who would support you, so you wouldn't have to go around with just anyone who came along.

PROSTITUTE. I don't go around with just anyone. Thank God I ain't that hard up. I pick and choose.

(The Count looks around the room.)

PROSTITUTE. *(Noticing this.)* Next month we're moving into town. Spiegel Gasse.

COUNT. We? Who do you mean?

PROSTITUTE. Why, the madam and the couple other girls who still live here.

COUNT. There are others living here?

PROSTITUTE. Next door ... can't you hear? ... that's Milli, she was in the café too.

COUNT. Someone's snoring.

PROSTITUTE. That's Milli all right! She'll snore like that all day long till ten at night. Then she gets up and goes to the café.

COUNT. That must be a terrible life.

PROSTITUTE. Sure. The madam gets fed up enough too. I'm out on the street every day by noon.

COUNT. What do you do on the street at noon?

PROSTITUTE. What do you think I do? I walk my beat.

COUNT. Oh, I see ... of course ... *(He rises, takes out his wallet, and places a bill on the night table.)* Good-bye.

PROSTITUTE. Going so soon?—So long—Come back again soon. *(She turns onto her side.)*

COUNT. *(Stops again)* Say, tell me something; does it really mean anthing to you any more?

PROSTITUTE. What?

COUNT. I mean, it holds no enjoyment for you any more ...

PROSTITUTE. *(Yawns.)* I'm sleepy.

COUNT. It makes no difference whether a man is young or old. . .

PROSTITUTE. What do you want to know all this for?

COUNT. Well—*(Suddenly struck by an idea.)* My God, now I remember who you remind me of, it's . . .

PROSTITUTE. I remind you of someone?

COUNT. It's unbelievable? Please now, don't say anything, just for a moment . . . *(He looks at her)* The same face, exactly. *(He suddenly kisses her on the eyes.)*

PROSTITUTE. Say . . .

COUNT. My God, what a pity that you . . . that you aren't something else . . . you could really be a success.

PROSTITUTE. You're just like Franz.

COUNT. Who is Franz?

PROSTITUTE. A waiter at the café

COUNT. How am I like Franz?

PROSTITUTE. He's always saying that I could be a success, and that I should get married.

COUNT. Why don't you?

PROSTITUTE. No, thanks . . . no, I don't want to get married, not for all the money in the world. Later, maybe.

COUNT. Your eyes . . . it's your eyes that . . . Louie would say I'm a fool—but I do want to kiss your eyes, just once more . . . there . . . and now, good-bye, now I really must go.

PROSTITUTE. So long . . .

COUNT. *(At the door.)* Say . . . tell me . . . doesn't it surprise you that . . .

PROSTITUTE. That what?

COUNT. That I want nothing of you?

PROSTITUTE. A lot of men aren't in the mood for it in the morning.

COUNT. Yes, I suppose . . . *(To himself.)* How silly of me to want her to be surprised . . . Well, Good-bye . . . *(He is at the door.)* Still, it does annoy me. I know that girls like her do it only for the money . . . but why did I say: "Girls like her?" . . . it's nice at least that . . . that she doesn't pretend, that should be some satisfaction . . . *(To her.)* Say— I'll tell you. I'll come back again soon.

PROSTITUTE. *(With her eyes closed.)* Good.

COUNT. When are you at home?

PROSTITUTE. I'm always in. Just ask for Leocadia.

COUNT. Leocadia . . . Good.–Well then, good-bye *(At the door.)* I can still feel that wine. Isn't it remarkable . . . here I am with one of her kind, and I did nothing more than kiss her eyes, just because she reminded me of someone . . . *(Turns to her again.)* Say, Leocadia, does it happen often that a man leaves you . . . like this?

PROSTITUTE. Like what?

COUNT. Like me.

PROSTITUTE. In the morning?

COUNT. No . . . I wondered whether it happened often that a man comes to you . . . and doesn't ask for anything.

PROSTITUTE. No, that never happened to me.

COUNT. What do you mean? Do you think I don't like you?

PROSTITUTE. Why shouldn't you like me? You liked me okay last night.

COUNT. Why do you say that?

PROSTITUTE. Why all the silly questions?

COUNT. Last night . . . yes, well, didn't I fall onto the divan right away?

PROSTITUTE. Sure . . . with me.

COUNT. With you?

PROSTITUTE. Sure, don't you remember?

COUNT. You mean I . . . that we . . . yes . . .

PROSTITUTE. But you went right off to sleep.

COUNT. Right off to sleep . . . I see . . . So that's the way it was . . .

PROSTITUTE. Sure, lovey. You must have had a real load on, not to remember.

COUNT. I see . . . Still . . . There is a faint resemblance . . .

COUNT. Of course. *(In the entrance hall.)* Well . . . it would have been beautiful even if I had only kissed you on the eyes. That would almost have been an adventure in itself . . . Well, I suppose it wasn't meant to be.

(The Parlor Maid stands at the door, holding it open for him.)

COUNT. Oh–*(He hands her some money.)* –here you are . . . Good night.

PARLOR MAID. Good morning.

COUNT. Yes, of course . . . good morning . . . good morning . . .

(Curtain.)

Hugo von Hofmannsthal (1874-1929)

Electra

The plays of Schnitzler, like those of his fellow physician-playwright Chekhov, develop primarily within the conventions of the realistic theater, even though the structure is never that of the well-made play. But with the work of Hugo von Hofmannsthal, a great friend and admirer of Schnitzler, there is a violent reaction against the materialist philosophy of naturalism in art and a strong drive to revive the poetic, imaginative, inward values of the drama. Hofmannsthal wanted to return to the heart of the Austrian theatrical tradition of color, music, spectacle, and fantasy, and to turn away from the external aspects of society. Through the use of symbols, legend, and myth projected through rich verse dialogue, Hofmannsthal was the leading symbolist playwright in Austria at the close of the nineteenth century. Since his talents, as was the case with most symbolists like Yeats, Maeterlinck, Verlaine, and Mallarmé, were lyric rather than dramatic, he made great use of existing plays from the past and ranged over the entire rich literary heritage of Western Europe for his sources of inspiration. Throughout a distinguished career his work was a continuous effort to achieve a theatrical form that could combine the rich language and imagery of the symbolists with action that was dramatically not lyrically conceived.

Hofmannsthal was born in 1874, the son of a well-to-do Viennese banker, and his mixed inheritance was South-German, Italian, and Jewish—a cultural heritage that mirrored the crosscurrents of Austrian culture. By the age of seventeen Hofmannsthal was already famous throughout Austria for the poetic maturity of his work and as the spokesman for a generation committed to poetic beauty and sensitive refinement rather than the harsh realities of naturalism. His cosmopolitan outlook made him at home in all past ages, especially ancient Greece, the Italian Renaissance, Baroque France and Spain, and the great eras of Austria's own cultural past; and his ability to reinterpret the spirit of the past was tremendously influential in his dramatic work.

His first plays and poems seem to be saturated with the *fin de siècle* mood of aesthetic decadence. *Gestern (Yesterday;* 1891) is the ironic portrait of a young man who asserts the impossibility of living for more than the day, and yet finds that the past cannot be ignored. Others, like *Der Tod des Tizian (The Death of Titian;* 1892), *Das Kleine Welttheater (The*

Little Theatre of the World; 1897), and *Die Frau im Fenster (The Woman at the Window;* 1897), are really dramatized lyrical poems, "full of precocious wisdom, early doubt, and yet with a deep, questioning longing." These lines from a prologue to one of the playlets sum up the quality of all these early dramatic pieces. All stress the transitory life and the closeness of death. The theme is most poignantly realized in his best-known play from this period, *Der Tor und der Tod (Death and the Fool;* 1893). In it the young nobleman, Claudio, faces Death seen in the guise of a fiddler, who summons from the shadows of the past all the mistakes of Claudio's misspent life. In the hour of death the selfish aesthete is condemned by the fiddler as one who has not truly lived.

Other plays in the same general pattern include: *Der weisse Fächer (The White Fan;* 1897), *Der Kaiser und die Hexe (The Emperor and the Witch;* 1897), and *Das Bergwerk zu Falun (The Mine at Falun;* 1899.) All are steeped in poetic and mystical intuitions—critiques of aestheticism by a melancholy, poetic aesthete. Then, in his late twenties, Hofmannsthal underwent a spiritual crisis from which he emerged a more mature person and playwright. Life, from which he had hidden, he now recognized as a challenge to be faced. He abandoned the lyric poem and the short verse play for the full-length drama and the dramatic and theatrical effects of the living stage. His plays at the turn of the century all involve in one way or another the theme of man's failure or success in facing the challenges of life.

In *Der Abenteurer und die Sängerin (The Adventurer and the Singer;* 1898), he portrays that favorite of Viennese writers, the Casanova figure, meeting in Venice a former mistress who had become a great singer. The aging adventurer realizes with ironic understanding that what had been a trivial incident to him had shaped the woman's entire rise to success. In *Die Hochzeit der Sobeide (Zobeida's Wedding;* 1899) a poor girl, forced into a wedding with an elderly merchant, asks to be released on her wedding night to join the poor boy who loves her. She is allowed to go, only to find the boy in the arms of a prostitute, and so throws herself in despair from a tower.

But these plays were merely a prelude to a group of dramas based on earlier classics. In *Das gerettete Venedig (Venice Preserved;* 1905) Hofmannsthal deepened the psychological motivations and poetic force of Otway's seventeenth-century tragedy, while in *Elektra (Electra;* 1903) and *Oedipus und die Sphinx (Oedipus and the Sphinx;* 1905) classic restraint is transformed into Freudian repression and violence. He had already, as early as 1893, recast Euripides' *Alkestis (Alcestis;* 1893) into more modern terms but in a purely lyrical vein. He now turned to the archaic Greek period for his setting, ignoring the religious significance of the myths in favor of Freudian psychological, pathological patterns of development. It is particularly in *Elektra,* reprinted here, that the terseness and violence of the action is carried to an extreme that reminds the reader of Oscar Wilde's *Salomé.* Agamemnon's daughter, Electra, renounces her womanhood for the sworn purpose of avenging her father's murder. She pursues this quest with the violent determination of one possessed.

When she finally persuades the returning Orestes to murder Clytemnestra and Aegisthus, and he has commited the bloody deed, she breaks into a frenzied, Maenad-like dance whose repressed violence leaves her dead at the close of the play. The play is an excellent reflection of the inner hysteria, fears and repressions that plagued Viennese society during the old empire's final decade of decay. It was this play, produced by Max Reinhardt in Berlin, which gave Hofmannsthal his first great theatrical success and led to his first collaboration with Richard Strauss on the operatic version of 1909.

Soon after these violent plays, Hofmannsthal moved in new directions—into comedy and opera. His comedies are in prose and sometimes in Viennese dialect as with Raimund and Nestroy, yet they never stoop to mere entertainment, and they come from the same poetic source as his serious work. Though he adapted several Molière plays *(Le Medicin Malgré lui, Les Facheux, Le Bourgeois Gentilhomme),* his first completed prose comedy is *Christinas Heimreise (Christina's Journey Home;* 1909), based on an incident in Casanova's *Memoirs.* He contrasts the lighthearted philanderer and the man of constancy and shows that life's real value lies beyond the reach of the young rake. The same idea is at the base of his second prose comedy, *Der Schwierige (The Difficult Man;* 1918). Laid in postwar Vienna, it still embodies prewar ideals and shows a cultivated Austrian aristocrat, Count Bühl, learning that constancy and marriage are a necessity for personal fulfillment even in the rarified world in which he has lived. The play is undoubtedly Hofmannsthal's subtlest and best comedy.

It was followed by a more conventional comedy, *Der Unbestechliche (The Incorruptible Man;* 1923), which deals with the officious butler who controls his master's love affairs and saves his shaky marriage. But the best known of Hofmannsthal's comedies are two opera librettos, *Der Rosenkavalier (The Cavalier of the Rose;* 1911) and *Arabella* (1933). The first beautifully captures the combined moods of Maria Theresa's and early-twentieth-century aristocratic Vienna; the latter, rather less successfully, portrays the mood of Vienna in the 1860s. His other opera librettos for Richard Strauss—*Ariadne auf Naxos* (1912 and 1916), *Die Frau ohne Schatten (The Woman Without a Shadow;* 1919), and *Die ägyp-*

tische Helen (Egyptian Helen; 1928)–indicate Hofmannsthal's instinctive awareness that his particular poetic gifts would find their fullest realization in music, and that his festive concept of theater could find one of its best expressions in opera.

The dissolution of the Austrian Empire in 1918 deprived Hofmannsthal of a cultural base, but he refused to dwell on the past, and in the last decade of life he showed renewed creativity. A year after the war he founded with Max Reinhardt the famous Salzburg Festival, which had for its central presentation his re-creation of the famous morality play, *Jedermann (Everyman;* 1911). Here he attempted a religious drama of universal as well as Roman Catholic appeal, and he followed it with an adaptation from Calderón, *Das Salzburger grosse Welttheater (The Great World Theatre of Salzburg;* 1922) whose theme, that the world is the stage for a play enacted for the glory of God, is in the full tradition of the Austrian Baroque. Hofmannsthal, in the face of postwar problems, directly puts forward the ideal of a hierarchical society based on Christian principles. It is this theme that lies at the core of his last, most comprehensive work, *Der Turm (The Tower;* 1925). This work, inspired by the Calderón play *La Vida es Sueño,* is laid in seventeenth-century Poland, but it is legendary and symbolic rather than historical. *Der Turm* is a political drama that sums up the conflicts of several centuries of European history in the theme of conflict between material power and spiritual integrity. His first version of the play ended with a vision of a new future, but the final version of 1927 ended in unrelieved tragedy.

As a playwright, Hofmannsthal, despite his fascination with the theater, lacked the power of the true dramatist. He remained a poet to the end, and today is seen as an opera librettist and one of the leaders of that neoromantic, symbolist movement that swept European letters at the turn of the century.

None of Hofmannsthal's dramas have had major Broadway professional productions in the United States, though his librettos for the Richard Strauss operas are continuously before the public; and *Jederman* was included in the Max Reinhardt Company tour to New York in 1927. It was also frequently reviewed in the *New York Times* as a major event at the Salzburg Festival in the 1920s. *Electra* was presented at the New Yorker Theatre in 1930 under the auspices of Carl Reed with Marika Cotopouli as Electra and Katina Paxinou as Clytemnestra. Brooks Atkinson in the *New York Times* for December 27 commented on the fury, power, and tension of the play, but said that he preferred the Sophocles version of the story. *Electra* is also occasionally produced by colleges and universities as was the case at Stanford University in

1974 in a production directed by Ellen Mease. Robert Burmister of the *San Mateo Times* (November 28, 1974) commented on the performance as follows: "Hofmannsthal's sordid little bedtime tale came from a period of Viennese intellectual life which was preoccupied with neurotic sexual motivations. It was the Vienna of Sigmund Freud. While Freud claimed he gave up sex at the age of forty-one, apparently Hofmannsthal entertained no such folly. *Electra* is concerned with family sex run amuck." C. E. Maves in *The Palo Alto Times* (November 27, 1974) observed that the characters were not people, "they are simply grotesque, and can't even be thought of as diseased because one can't imagine them ever being healthy." As in all Hofmannsthal plays, there is more concern with ideas and moods than with events, and it is not surprising that his international reputation today is that of a superb opera librettist rather than a playwright.

Electra

by

HUGO VON HOFMANNSTHAL

Translated by Carl Richard Mueller

Characters

CLYTEMNESTRA
ELECTRA
CHRYSOTHEMIS $\Big\}$ her daughters
AEGISTHUS
ORESTES
THE GUARDIAN OF ORESTES
CLYTEMNESTRA'S WOMAN
THE TRAIN BEARER
A YOUNG SERVING MAN
AN OLD SERVING MAN
THE COOK
THE WOMAN OVERSEER
THE WOMEN SERVANTS

(The inner court, bounded by the back of the Palace and the low buildings in which the servants live. Women servants at the draw-well, downstage left. Women overseers among them.)

FIRST WOMAN SERVANT. *(Lifting her water jug.)*
Where is Electra?
SECOND WOMAN SERVANT. Time has come again,
the hour when she howls out for her father,
till all the walls resound.
(Electra enters running from the already darkened hallway. They all turn toward her. Electra recoils like an animal into its lair, one arm covering her face.)

FIRST WOMAN SERVANT. Did you see the look she gave us?
SECOND WOMAN SERVANT. Furious
    as any wildcat.
THIRD WOMAN SERVANT. A moment past I saw her
    lie and moan—
FIRST WOMAN SERVANT. She always lies and moans
    when the sun is low.
THIRD WOMAN SERVANT. The two of us went towards her,
    but came too close—
FIRST WOMAN SERVANT. One thing she'll not endure
    is to be looked at.
THIRD WOMAN SERVANT. Yes, we came too close.
    And then she screeched out at us like a cat:
    "Away with you, you flies!" she cried, "away!"
FOURTH WOMAN SERVANT. "Blow-flies, away!"

THIRD WOMAN SERVANT. "Must you eat at my wounds!"
    And struck out at us with a straw.
FOURTH WOMAN SERVANT. "Away,
    blow-flies, away!"
THIRD WOMAN SERVANT. "You shall not feed upon
    the sweetness of my agony nor smack
    your lips to lick the foam from off my madness."
FOURTH WOMAN SERVANT. "Go on, crawl to your beds," she
    screamed at us.
    "Eat sweets and fats and sneak to bed with your men,"
    she screamed and you—
THIRD WOMAN SERVANT. I was not idle—
FOURTH WOMAN SERVANT. —answered her!
THIRD WOMAN SERVANT. Yes: "If you are hungry," I
    answered her
    "then you eat, too." She sprang up then and shot
    horrible glances at me, stretched her fingers
    claw-like towards me and cried out: "I am feeding
    a vulture here within my body," she cried.
SECOND WOMAN SERVANT. And you?
THIRD WOMAN SERVANT. I said to her: "And that is why
    you're always crouching where there's smell of carrion,
    and scratching the ground for a body long since dead!"
SECOND WOMAN SERVANT. What did she say to that?

THIRD WOMAN SERVANT. She howled and cast herself
    back to her corner.
(They have finished drawing the water.)
FIRST WOMAN SERVANT. I can't but be amazed
    that the queen should let this demon run about
    freely in house and court to do her mischief.
THIRD WOMAN SERVANT. Her own child, too!
SECOND WOMAN SERVANT. If she were mine, by God,
    I'd keep her under lock and key.
FOURTH WOMAN SERVANT. Don't you feel
    they're hard enough on her now? Don't they place
    her bowl so she eats with the dogs?
    (Softly.)   Haven't you seen
    the master strike her?
FIFTH WOMAN SERVANT. *(Young, with a tremulous, excited
    voice.)*   I will throw myself
    down before her feet and kiss those feet.
    Is she not the daughter of a king, and
    made to endure such outrage! I will annoint
    her feet with oil and wipe them with my hair.
WOMAN OVERSEER. Get on with you! *(Pushes her.)*
FIFTH WOMAN SERVANT. There's nothing to be found
    in all the world more royal than she. She lies
    in rags upon the threshold, but not one, *(crying out)*
    not one in all this house can look in her eyes!
WOMAN OVERSEER. Get on! *(Pushes her through the low
    open doorway downstage left.)*
FIFTH WOMAN SERVANT. *(Jammed in the doorway.)*
    Not any one of you is worthy to.breathe the air that she breathes!
    O if only I could see all of you, all hanged by the neck
    see you strung up in some dark granary,
    for all that you have done against Electra!
WOMAN OVERSEER. *(Shuts the door, stands with her back
    against it.)*
    Did you hear that? What we've done against Electra!
    When told to eat with us, she knocked her bowl
    clear off the table and spat at us and called us
    dirty female dogs.
FIRST WOMAN SERVANT. What? What she said was,
    there's no dog can be humiliated,
    and that's why they broke us in like animals
    to wash away with water, with fresh water,

the everlasting blood of murder from the floor—
THIRD WOMAN SERVANT. –and to sweep, said she, the outrage
    into the corner,
    the outrage that renews itself day and night—
FIRST WOMAN SERVANT. —and our bodies, she cried out
    are stiffening
    with the dirt that we are bound in bondage to!
(They carry their jugs into the house left.)
WOMAN OVERSEER. *(Who has opened the door for them.)*
    And screams out when she sees us with our children,
    that there is nothing, nothing, so accursed
    as children that we've littered in this house,
    slipping upon the stairs in blood like dogs.
    Did she say that or not?
THE WOMEN SERVANTS. *(Already inside.)*
    Yes! Yes!
FIFTH WOMAN SERVANT. They're beating me!

(The Woman Overseer goes in. The door falls shut. Electra steps from the house. She is alone with splashes of red light which fall obliquely from the branches of the fig trees upon the ground and upon the walls like splashes of blood.)

ELECTRA. Alone! All, all alone. My father gone,
    held prisoner in the coldness of the grave.

(Toward the ground.)

    Father, where are you? Have you not the strength
    to make your way to earth again and me?
    The hour is come, the hour that is our own!
    The same cold hour in which they slaughtered you,
    your wife and the thing that shares her bed with her,
    who sleeps with her in your once royal bed.
    They slew you in your bath, your blood ran red
    down across your eyes, and all the bath
    streamed with your blood; this coward took you then
    and lugged you by the shoulders from the chamber,
    head first, your legs trailing on behind you;
    your eyes, staring, open, saw into the house.
    And so you'll come again, and set one foot
    in front of the other, and suddenly appear, ·
    your eyes wide open, and a royal round

of purple placed upon your brows that eats
upon the open wound it finds there.
Father!
I must see you, don't leave me here alone!
Show me yourself, if only as a shadow,
there, in the wall's niche, like yesterday!
Father! Your time will come! The stars decree
our times, and so a time will come when blood
from a hundred throats will gush upon your grave,
will flow as from a hundred upset jugs,
stream from the throats of shackled murderers,
and round the naked bodies of their helpers,
like marble jugs, from men and women both,
and in a single flood, one swollen stream,
shall all of their life's life gush out of them;
and we shall slaughter the horses of your house,
and drive them to your grave, and they shall snuff
death, and neigh in the air laden with death,
and die; and we shall slaughter for you the hounds
because they are the litter of the litter
of that same pack you hunted with, and who
would lick your feet, to whom you threw the morsels,
their blood must flow to serve you, and we, we,
your blood, your son Orestes and your daughters,
we three, when all is done and purple canopies
are raised high by the steam of your royal blood,
which the sun sucks to itself, then shall we dance,
then shall your blood dance round about your grave;
and over every corpse my knee·shall rise
higher with every step, and they who see me,
dancing thus, yea, they who see from afar
only my shadow dancing, they shall say:
How great must be this king whose flesh and blood
would celebrate so grand a feast for him;
happy that king with children who would dance
so royal a dance of victory round his tomb!
*(Chrysothemis, the younger sister, stands in the doorway of the house. She
looks anxiously at Electra, then calls softly.)*
CHRYSOTHEMIS. Electra!

*Electra starts like a sleepwalker who hears his name called out. She staggers. She
looks about as though not quite able to find her way. Her face becomes distorted as*

she sees the anxious features of her sister. Chrysothemis stands depressed in the doorway.)

ELECTRA. Ah, that face!

CHRYSOTHEMIS. Is it so hateful?

ELECTRA. What is it? Tell me, speak, what do you want?
    Then go away and leave me!

(Chrysothemis raises her hands as though warding off a blow.)

ELECTRA. You raise your hands?
    Our father once raised both his hands that way
    and then the axe struck down cleaving his flesh.
    What is it you want, daughter of my mother?

CHRYSOTHEMIS. They're planning something terrible, I
    know it.

ELECTRA. Both the women?

CHRYSOTHEMIS. Who?

ELECTRA. Why, my mother, of course,
    and then that other woman, the cowardly one,
    Aegisthus, yes, Aegisthus, the brave assassin,
    whose only hero's deeds are done in bed.
    What have they in mind?

CHRYSOTHEMIS. They mean to throw you
    in a dark tower where neither sun nor moon
    will visit you again.

(Electra laughs.)

CHRYSOTHEMIS. They will, I know,
    I've heard them.

ELECTRA. Yes, I think I've heard it, too.
    At table, wasn't it? Just before finishing?
    He loves to raise his voice then and brag about,
    I think it helps his digestion.

CHRYSOTHEMIS. No, not at table,
    nor was he boasting. He and she together
    discussed it secretly.

ELECTRA. Oh, secretly?
    How did you hear them then?

CHRUSOTHEMIS. I heard at the door.

ELECTRA. Let no doors ever be opened in this house!
    There's nothing in these rooms but gasping for air
    and the death-rattle of strangulation. Never
    open a door that stifles a groan behind it:
    for surely they cannot always be in there killing,

at times they are alone in there together!
Open no doors! Do not prowl about.
Sit on the ground like me and wish for death
and for judgment upon her and him.
CHRYSOTHEMIS. I cannot sit and stare into the dark
   like you. O there's a burning in my heart
   that makes me rove the house incessantly.
   There's not a room to comfort me, and so
   I wander up the stairs and down the stairs,
   from one place to another; O it seems a
   room will call to me, and once I'm there,
   there's nothing but an empty, staring room.
   I'm so afraid, my knees tremble beneath me
   day and night; it seems as if two hands
   are here at my throat; I can't even cry;
   I've turned to stone! Sister, pity, pity!
ELECTRA. Pity whom?
CHRYSOTHEMIS. It's you who have bound me here
   with hoops of iron. Were it not for you,
   they would not keep us here. Were it not for your hate,
   for your unsleeping and excessive temper,
   which makes me tremble, they would not keep us
   locked and chained here in this prison, sister!
   I will get out! I will not sleep each night
   here until my death! Before I die
   I want to know what life is! I want children
   before my body withers, and even though
   they marry me with a peasant, I will bear him
   children and will warm them with my body
   through cold nights when storms beat at our hut!
   But there is one thing I'll endure no longer,
   this living here like animals with servants
   who are not our kind, locked in here day and night
   with mortal fear! Are you listening to me?
   Speak to me, sister!
ELECTRA. Pitiable creature!
CHRYSOTHEMIS. Have pity on yourself, have pity on me.
   Who profits from this anguish? Father perhaps?
   Our father is dead. Our brother does not come home.
   Day after day time graves his token
   in your face and in mine, and there, outside,
   the sun rises and sets, and women I knew

when they were slender are heavy now with blessing;
they make their way to the well, scarcely able
to lift the pail; then suddenly they're loosed
of their burden and they come again to the well,
and out of them there flows a draught of sweetness,
and new life clings sucking to their bodies,
and their children grow—and we sit here on our perch
like captive birds, turning our heads to left
and right, and no one comes, no brother comes,
no news of our brother, no news of any news,
nothing! I were better dead than live without life.
No! I'm a woman, I will bear a woman's lot.

ELECTRA. Shame on the thought! Shame on the thinker of it!
To be the hollow where the murdered
is safe after the murder; play the beast
for the pleasure of a beast—that's even worse!
Ah, she slept with one and pressed her breasts
on both his eyes, and nodded to another
who crept from behind the bed with net and axe.

CHRYSOTHEMIS. How terrible you are!

ELECTRA. Why terrible?
Are you such a woman? You will become one.

CHRYSOTHEMIS. Why is it you cannot forget, Electra?
My mind is a wasteland. I cannot remember
from one day to the next. Sometimes I lie here
like this, and then I am what once I was,
and do not know why I am young no longer.
Where has it gone, Electra, where has it gone?
This is not water flowing on its way,
this is not yarn flying back and forth
on a spool, it is no one but myself!
I want to pray some god will kindle a flame
here in my breast that I may find myself
again. Were I not here, how soon I would
forget these evil dreams—

ELECTRA. Forget? Forget?
Am I a beast then that I should forget?
The beast will sleep with its half-eaten prey
hanging from its jaws; the beast forgets itself
and starts to chew, the while death sits on him,
strangling out life; the beast forgets what crept
from its own body, and with its own young

allays its hunger—I am no beast, I cannot
forget!

CHRYSOTHEMIS. O must my soul forever feed
upon this food it loathes, that it so loathes!
The smell of which makes me shudder, which I would never
have touched, never have known that there existed
anything so horrible as that,
never to have known that, never to have seen,
never heard! So terrible a thing is
not for the hearts of men! And when it comes
and when it shows itself, then we must flee
our houses, flee to the vineyards, to the mountains!
And then when it stands astride the mountain tops
we creep down to hide again in our houses;
we must never be with it, never live
together in one house! I must get out!
I must conceive children, I must bear them,
who will know nothing of this. I'll wash my body
in every stream, dive deep, deep in the water,
wash every part of me, wash clean the sockets
of my eyes—they must never be afraid
when they look up into their mother's eyes!

ELECTRA. When **they look up into their mother's eyes!**
And how will you look into our father's eyes?

CHRYSOTHEMIS. O stop!

ELECTRA. May your children, when you have them,
do unto you as you do to our father!
(Chrysothemis cries out.)

ELECTRA. Why must you howl so? Get in! That's your place.
There's a noise broken out. Are they preparing
your wedding? I hear running. Everyone's up.
Either they are in birthpangs or at murder.
Should there be corpses lacking, they must make some,
or else they'll not sleep soundly in their beds!

CHRYSOTHEMIS. Stop, O stop! That's past and done, it's
done.

ELECTRA. Past and done? They're up to some new crime
now!
Do you think I don't know the sound of bodies
as they drag them down the stairs, whispering
and wringing out cloths sopped in blood!

CHRYSOTHEMIS. Sister!
    You must not stay.
ELECTRA. This time I will be here!
    Not as before. This time I will be strong.
    I'll throw myself upon her, I'll tear the axe
    out of her hands and swing it over her head—
CHRYSOTHEMIS. You must not stay here, hide before she
    sees you.
    Don't cross her path today, she scatters death
    Wherever she looks. She's had terrible dreams.

(The noise of people approaching draws nearer.)
    You must not stay. They're coming through the passage
    They'll come by here. She's had terrible dreams;
    I don't know what, I heard it from her women,
    I don't know if it's true, sister, but they say
    she has had terrible dreams of Orestes,
    and that she cried out in the middle of night
    like one about to be strangled.
ELECTRA. I! I!
    I sent it to her. I sent her this dream
    from my own breast! I lie in bed and hear
    the footsteps of the specter haunting her.
    I hear him make his way from room to room
    and lift the curtain from her bed: screaming
    she leaps from the bed, but he is always there,
    close behind her on the stairs; the chase continues
    from one vault to another and another.
    It is far darker now than any night,
    far quieter and darker than the grave,
    she gasps and staggers in darkness, but he is there:
    he swings the torch to right and left of the axe
    And I like a hunting-hound am at her heels:
    should she hide in a hollow, I spring after,
    sideways, upon her trail, and drive her on
    till a wall end her flight, and there in darkness,
    there is deepest darkness—I see him still,
    his shadow, and his limbs, the light of his eyes—
    there sits our father, who neither sees nor hears,
    and yet, it must happen: we drive her to his feet,
    and the axe falls!
(Torches and figures fill the passage, left of the door.)

CHRYSOTHEMIS. They're coming now. She's driving her
    women on
    with torches. Look, they're dragging animals
    and sacrificial knives. O sister, Electra,
    she is most dreadful when she is afraid;
    you must not cross her path today, not now!
ELECTRA. I have a mind to speak with my mother now
    as I have never spoken!

*(A noisy and shuffling procession hurries past the glaringly lighted windows.
Thee is a tugging and hauling of animals, a subdued chiding, a quickly stifled
cray, the swish of a whip, a pulling back and a staggering forward again.)*

CHRYSOTHEMIS. I will not hear it. *(She rushes off through the door of the
court.)*
*(The figure of Clytemnestra appears in the wide window. Her sallow, bloated
face, in the light thrown from the glaring torches, appears even more pale above
her scarlet dress. She supports herself upon one of her women, dressed in dark
violet, and upon an ivory staff embellished with precious jewels. Her train is
carried by a yellow figure, whose black hair is combed back like an Egyptian, and
whose sleek face resembles a poised snake. The Queen is almost completely
covered with precious stones and talismans. Her arms are full of bracelets, her
fingers almost rigid with rings. The lids of her eyes seem excessively large, and it
appears to be a great effort for her to hold them open. Electra stands rigid, her
face toward the window. Clytemnestra suddenly opens her eyes and trembling
with anger goes toward the window and points at Electra with her staff.)*

CLYTEMNESTRA. *(At the window.)*
    What do you want? Look there! Look at it there!
    See how it rears its swollen neck at me
    and hisses! And this thing I let run free
    in my own house!
    O how she'd like to kill me with those eyes!
    Gods, why must you weigh so heavy on me?
    Why must you send destruction on me? Why
    do you cripple all the strength within me, why am
    I, a living being, like a wasteland.
    covered with weeds and nettles that grow on me,
    and I have not the strength to root them out!
    Why must I suffer this, immortal gods?
ELECTRA. Gods? The gods? But you are a goddess yourself!
    The same as they.

CLYTEMNESTRA. What? What was that she said?
    Did you understand what she said?
THE WOMAN. That you, too
    stem from the gods.
TRAIN BEARER. *(Hissingly.)* But she means it only in spite.
CLYTEMNESTRA. *(As her heavy eyelids fall shut.)*
    How familiar it sounds, like a thing forgotten
    long, long ago. How well she knows me.
    Yet no one ever knows what she will do.
(The Woman and the Train Bearer whisper together.)
ELECTRA. You are yourself no longer. Reptiles hang
    from your body. What they hiss into your ear
    severs your thoughts forever; you go about
    in a frenzy, as though living in a dream.
CLYTEMNESTRA. I will go down to her. I will speak to her.
    She is no beast today—talks like a doctor.
    The hours hold our fate firm in their hands.
    Nothing is so unbearable but once
    must show a pleasant aspect in its nature.
*(She walks from the window and appears at the doorway, her Woman at her side,
the Train Bearer behind her, and torches bringing up the rear.)*
CLYTEMNESTRA. *(From the threshold.)*
    You call me a goddess. Why? Did you say it
    in malice? Then take care. For this may be
    the last time you will see the light of day
    and breathe the free air.
ELECTRA. If you are not
    a goddess, tell me, then, where are the gods!
    There's nothing in this world makes me tremble so
    than to think your body was the dark door
    through which I crept into the light of the world.
    Have I lain here naked upon this lap?
    Have you lifted me up to reach these breasts?
    Well, then, I must have crept from my father's grave
    and played about in swaddling-clothes upon
    the place where my father was murdered. Then you must be
    a colossus whose brazen hand I never escaped.
    You have me by the bridle and can tie me
    to what you will. You have cast up like the sea
    a living being, a father, and a sister.
    I do not know how I should ever die—
    unless you die before me.

CLYTEMNESTRA. Is this how you honor me? Is there so little
 respect in you?
ELECTRA. I lack not of respect!
   What troubles me troubles you as well.
   I grow ill to see Aegisthus, your husband,
   wear the robes of my father, who's dead, as you know;
   he was the former king. It makes me ill,
   believe me, for they do not fit him well.
   I think they are too broad across the chest.
THE WOMAN. What she says is not what she means.
TRAIN BEARER. Every word a lie.
CLYTEMNESTRA. *(Angrily.)* I will not listen. Whatever comes from you
   is only Aegisthus' breath. I do not want
   to find fault everywhere. But say to me
   what I would gladly hear, then I will listen
   to what you say. Truth is not so easily
   discovered by mortal man. No man on earth
   can know the truth of any hidden thing.
   Are there not certain men in prison here
   who dare to call me murderess, and Aegisthus
   assassin? When I wake you in the night,
   does not each of you give different answer?
   Do you not cry out that my eyes are swollen
   and that I am sick; and do you not
   whimper in my other ear that you've seen demons
   with long pointed beaks sucking my blood,
   and show me the marks on my body? Do I not
   believe you then and slay, and slay, and slay one
   sacrifice after another? Am I not torn
   to death between your words and your replies?
   I will no longer listen when you tell me:
   this is truth and this is not truth.
   Should anyone speak pleasantly to me,
   were it even my daughter, were it that one,
   I would remove the veils around my soul
   and let soft breezes, come from where they may,
   envelop me, as they do those sick people
   who in the evening sit beside a pool
   and bare to the cool air their boiled and reeking
   bodies, and think only of relief.
   And so I must begin to serve myself.
   Leave me alone with her.

(With her stick, she impatiently motions the Woman and the Train Bearer into the house. They hesitantly disappear through the doorway. The torches disappear, too, and now only a faint light emerges from the inside of the house across the paved corridor and into the courtyard, so that the figures of the two women are lightly touched by the light.)

CLYTEMNESTRA. *(After a pause.)*   I do not sleep at night
Do you know
some remedy for dreams?

ELECTRA. *(Moving closer.)* For dreams, Mother?

CLYTEMNESTRA. Have you no other words to comfort me?
Tell me what you know. Yes, yes, I dream.
When one grows old, he dreams. But that can be
dispelled. Why are you standing there in darkness?
We must learn to make use of our own powers
that lie scattered. There are customs. Yes,
there must be customs, usages for all things.
How one articulates a word or sentence
can make much difference. Even the hour it's spoken.
And whether one's fed or fasting. Many a man
has perished for entering too soon into his bath.

ELECTRA. Are you thinking of my father?

CLYTEMNESTRA. That is why
I am so behung with jewels. In everyone
exists a certain power. One must but know
how to use them. If it were your pleasure,
I know that you could tell me how to use them.

ELECTRA. I, Mother, I?

CLYTEMNESTRA. Yes, you! For you are wise.
Your mind is sound. You talk of old things
as if they happened yesterday. But I
decay. I think, but all things are confused.
And when I start to speak, Aegisthus cries,
and what he cries out is hateful to me,
and then I would rise up and would be stronger
than all his words, but I find nothing, nothing!
I do not even know if what he said
which makes me tremble with rage, was said today,
or long ago; I grow dizzy then
and no longer know who I am; it's a terrible thing
to sink, alive and breathing, into chaos!
And then Aegisthus! then Aegisthus scorns me!

But I can find nothing, find no terrible thing
to silence him and turn him pale as myself,
staring into the fire. But you have words.
You could tell me much to help me now.
And even if a word is but a word?
What is a breath? And yet between night and day,
as I lie with eyes open, a something creeps
across my body, it is not a word,
it is not a grief, it does not press upon me,
it does not choke me, but leaves me lying there
just as I am, and there, there at my side
Aegisthus lies, and beyond him, there, is the curtain:
and all things look at me as though it were
from eternity unto eternity:
and it is nothing, no, not even a nightmare,
and yet it is so dreadful that my soul
longs to be hanged, and every part of me
thirsts after death; and yet I am alive,
and am not even sick. You see me here:
do I look sick? Is it then possible
to perish like a foul carcass while still alive?
to decompose and still not even be sick?
to have a waking mind decay, like a garment
eaten by moths? And then I sleep and dream,
dream till the marrow runs liquid in my bones!
I stagger from my bed again and not
the tenth part of an hour has passed by,
and what I see grinning beneath the curtain
is still not the ash-gray dawn, no, but only
the torch outside the door that starts and quivers
horribly like some living thing, spying
upon my sleep.
I do not know them who play this game with me,
whether they are at home above or below,
but when I see you standing there before me
as now you are, I cannot but believe
but you are in léague with them. Who are you really?
Why can't you speak, now, when I would hear you?
Who is it could be so much helped or hurt
by whether you live or die? Why do you look
so hard at me? I will not have you look
that way. I say these dreams must have an end.

Whoever sent me them, whatever the demon,
we will be left in peace to sleep our nights
when the right blood is spilt.

ELECTRA. Are you so certain!

CLYTEMNESTRA. And must I let bleed each beast that
creeps and flies,
and rise each day and sleep each night in the stream
of their blood, like the race that lives in farthest Thule
in bloodred mist: I will not dream again.

ELECTRA. Your dreams will end when the right blood-
sacrifice
falls beneath the axe.

CLYTEMNESTRA. *(Steps closer.)*   Then you must know
what sacred beast must fall–

ELECTRA. A most profane beast!

CLYTEMNESTRA. That lies within there?

ELECTRA. No! It still runs free.

CLYTEMNESTRA. *(Eagerly.)*   What rites must we use?

ELECTRA. Wonderful rites, that must
be strictly observed.

CLYTEMNESTRA. Why do you keep silent?

ELECTRA. Can't you divine my meaning.?

CLYTEMNESTRA. Why would I ask?
Tell me the name of the victim.

ELECTRA. It is a woman.

CLYTEMNESTRA. *(Eagerly.)*   One of my women-servants? Is it?
Tell me!
A child? A young virgin? Has this woman
known a man yet?

ELECTRA. Known a man? Yes! Yes
that's it!

CLYTEMNESTRA. And for the sacrifice? What hour?
And where?

ELECTRA. Anywhere, at any hour,
day or night.

CLYTEMNESTRA. And tell me what rites to use!
How must I do it? I myself will–

ELECTRA. No.
This time you will not hunt the victim down.

CLYTEMNESTRA. Then who? Who'll bring it here?

ELECTRA. A man.

CLYTEMNESTRA. Aegisthus?

ELECTRA. I said a man!

CLYTEMNESTRA. Who? Tell me! Tell me who!
Someone of the house? Or must a stranger come
and—

ELECTRA. Yes, yes, a stranger. But of course
he is of our house.

CLYTEMNESTRA. Why must you speak in riddles?
Electra, you listen to me. How pleased I am
to find you not so headstrong for a change.
When parents must act harshly towards their child,
the child forces them to it. There's no word
so stern it can't be revoked; and when a mother
sleeps ill, how rather would she know her child
sleeps in a marriage-bed and not in chains.

ELECTRA. *(To herself.)* It's different with the child: the child
would rather
the mother were dead than in her marriage-bed.

CLYTEMNESTRA. What are you murmuring there? I say that
nothing
is irrevocable. Do not all things pass
before our eyes, changing like the mist?
And we ourselves, we, we and our deeds!
Our deeds! We and our deeds! Those are mere words
Am I still she who did it? And if so!
Did is done, is done! What's done is done!
Don't throw these words at me! There, there he stood,
that one you can't forget, he stood there,
and there I stood and over there Aegisthus,
then all our glances met: and nothing done:
all still to do! How your father's look
changed in death, so slowly, horribly,
but always looking at me—then it was done:
nothing between the doing and the deed!
First it was undone, and then it was done—
and in that moment between, I did nothing.

ELECTRA. Of course, the axe that slew him lifted itself.

CLYTEMNESTRA. You cut me with your words.

ELECTRA. But not so nimbly
and well as your axe cut him.

CLYTEMNESTRA. I'll hear no more
of this. Be silent. If your father came
to meet me here today— I would speak with him

the same as I speak with you. It may well be
I shudder here before him, yet it may be
I could be tender with him and could weep,
like two old friends meeting together again.

ELECTRA. *(To herself.)*   Horrible! She talks about the murder
like a quarrel before supper.

CLYTEMNESTRA. Tell your sister
she need not run from me like a frightened dog
into darkness. Bid her speak more friendly with me,
as becomes her station, and give me civil greeting.
And then I do not know what should hinder me
from giving you both in marriage before winter.

ELECTRA. And our brother? May our brother not come
home?

CLYTEMNESTRA. I have forbidden you to speak of him.

ELECTRA. Then you're afraid of him?

CLYTEMNESTRA. Who says that?

ELECTRA. Mother,
you're trembling!

CLYTEMNESTRA. Do you think I'd be afraid
of an imbecile?

ELECTRA. An imbecile?

CLYTEMNESTRA. They say
he stammers, lies in the courtyard with the dogs
and knows no difference between man and beast.

ELECTRA. He was sound as a child.

CLYTEMNESTRA. They say they gave him
a wretched hole to live in and the animals
of the courtyard for companions.

ELECTRA. Ah!

CLYTEMNESTRA. *(With lowered eyelids.)*   I sent
gold on top of gold for them to keep him
as befits a king's child.

ELECTRA. You're lying, Mother!
You sent gold for them to strangle him.

CLYTEMNESTRA. Who told you that?

ELECTRA. I see it in your eyes.
And by your trembling I know that he lives.
I know that day and night you think of nothing
but him. And that your heart dries up with dread
because you know he's coming.

CLYTEMNESTRA. Don't lie to me.

Who lives without this house is not my concern.
I live here and I am mistress here.
I have enough servants to guard the gates,
and when I will, I shall have three armed servants
stand guard, day and night, before my chamber.
I quite ignore these things that you have told me.
Nor do I know this one, you're speaking of.
I'll never see him; so what concern is it
of mine, whether he be live or dead.
But I have dreamt of him enough. These dreams
are signs of illness, they fatten on our strength,
and I would live and be the mistress here.
I will not have another such attack,
to bring me here like any hawker-woman,
and pour out to you the secrets of my nights.
I am as good as sick, and the sick, they say,
prattle of their ills, and nothing more.
But I will no longer be sick. I will have from you
(She raises her stick threateningly against Electra.)
one way or another the word I must have.
You have already betrayed yourself once
that you know the proper sacrifice and rites
that I have need of. If you will not tell me
in freedom, then you'll tell me so in chains;
if not well fed, then you shall tell me fasting.
One can be rid of dreams. Who suffers from them
and does not find the means to cure himself,
he is a fool. I will learn some way
who must be let blood, that I may sleep.

ELECTRA. *(Leaps out at her from the darkness approaching her closer and closer, growing increasingly more frightening.)*

Who must be let blood? You! Your own
neck,
when the hunter has hunted you down! And he will hunt
you:
but only in the chase! Who slaughters a beast
of sacrifice in its sleep! He'll hunt you down,
he'll chase you through the house! And if you turn right,
there is the bed; and left, your bath, foaming
like blood! The darkness and the torches cast
black-red nets of death across your body—

(Clytemnestra, shuddering with speechless fear, wants to enter the house. Electra pulls her back by the robe. Clytemnestra shrinks back to the wall. Her eyes are wide open; the stick falls from her trembling hands.)

ELECTRA. You want to cry out, but the air strangles
　　　the unborn cry in you and lets it fall
　　　silent upon the ground; your neck stretches out,
　　　as brooding on the deed, and you feel the sharp blade
　　　to the very marrow of you, though he holds back:
　　　the rites are not yet fulfilled. He takes you by
　　　the tresses of your hair, and all is silence,
　　　you hear your heart beat against your ribs;
　　　this time—yes, this time spreads out before you
　　　like a dark gulf of years—this time is given you
　　　to know the fear that shipwrecked men must know
　　　when their vain cry gnaws at the dark clouds
　　　and the blackness of death; this time is given you
　　　to envy those chained to prison walls,
　　　those who cry out from the bottom of a well
　　　for death as though for deliverance; for you,
　　　you lie so prisoned up within yourself
　　　as though in the glowing belly of a beast
　　　of bronze and, just as now, you cannot cry out!
　　　And I stand there beside you, and your eyes
　　　can never leave me, for you hope in vain
　　　to read that word upon my silent face;
　　　you roll your eyes, you'd grasp at any thought,
　　　you'd have the gods smile down at you from the clouds:
　　　but the gods, the gods are at supper, just as when
　　　you slew our father, they're sitting there at supper
　　　and are just as deaf now to any death-rattle!
　　　Only a half-mad dog, the god of laughter,
　　　staggers in: he thinks its all a game,
　　　a love-game that you're playing with Aegisthus,
　　　but when he sees his error, he laughs at once,
　　　loud and shrill, and vanishes like that.
　　　And you have had enough. The bile drops bitter
　　　upon your heart, and dying you would recall
　　　one word, would speak one single word more,
　　　no matter which, instead of weeping tears
　　　of blood, which are denied no dying beast.
　　　I stand before you there, and now you read

with staring eyes the monstrous word that's written
upon my face, for my face is composed
of the features of my father and of you;
and I with my silent presence here
have brought to nothing your last word, your soul
is caught up in your self-turned noose, the axe
falls with a rush, and here I stand and see you
die at last! You will dream no longer then,
and I will dream no more, and who lives after,
let him rejoice and be happy in his life!

(They stand eye to eye, Electra in wildest intoxication, Clytemnestra breathing horribly with fear. At this moment the passageway grows light and the Woman comes running from the house. She whispers something in Clytemnestra's ear. She appears not to understand at first. She gradually comes to herself. Beckons for lights! Serving Women enter with torches and stand behind Clytemnestra. She beckons for more lights! More are brought in, station themselves behind her, so that the entire court is full of light and a reddish-yellow blaze floods the walls. Clytemnestra's features slowly change now, and the tension of her fear gives way to an evil triumph. She lets the message be whispered to her again, at the same time never permitting Electra out of her sight. Satisfied to the full, with a wild joy she extends both her hands threateningly toward Electra. Then her Woman lifts her stick from the ground, and leaning on them both, hurriedly, eagerly, snatching up her robe from the stairs, runs into the house. The Serving Women, as though chased, follow her in.)

ELECTRA. *(Meanwhile.)* What are they saying to her? Why is
she happy?
Why, why can't I think? Why is this woman
so happy?

(Chrysothemis enters, running, through the door of the court, howling loudly like a wounded animal.)

ELECTRA. Chrysothemis! Quickly! Quickly!
I must have help. Tell me what in this world
could make a person happy!
CHRYSOTHEMIS. *(Crying out.)* Orestes! Orestes
is dead!
ELECTRA. *(Motions her to keep away, as though demented)*
Be silent!
CHRYSOTHEMIS. *(Close to her.)* Orestes is dead!
(Electra moves her lips.)

CHRYSOTHEMIS. I came
> from the house, and they knew of it already.
> They all stood about and knew already,
> only not we.

ELECTRA. No one knows it.

CHRYSOTHEMIS. Every one knows!

ELECTRA. No one knows: because it isn't true.

(Chrysothemis throws herself to the ground.)

ELECTRA. *(Pulls her up.)* It isn't true, I tell you! No! I tell
> you, it isn't true!

CHRYSOTHEMIS. The strangers stood against the wall, the
> strangers
> sent here to tell us of it: there were two,
> an old man and a young man. They had told
> everyone already, they made a circle
> around them and they all knew already.

ELECTRA. It isn't true.

CHRYSOTHEMIS. Only they didn't tell us!
> No one thinks of us. Dead! Dead, Electra!

YOUNG SERVING MAN. *(Hurries from the house, stumbling over
> the figure lying at the threshold.)*
> Make way here! What's this loitering at the door?
> Ah, I should have known! Bring a groom here!

COOK. *(Enters through the door, right.)*
> What is it?

YOUNG SERVING MAN. I call out for a stableboy
> and what creeps from the hold but the old cook.

OLD SERVING MAN. *(With a gloomy face, appears at the door
to the courtyard.)*
> What's needed from the stable?

YOUNG SERVING MAN. Saddle something up,
> as quick as you can, you hear? A carthorse, an ass,
> a cow, for all I care, but do it quickly!

OLD SERVING MAN. Who for?

YOUNG SERVING MAN. For him who orders you to do it!
> Don't gape at me! Be about it! Quickly!
> For me! Hurry! Don't stand there! I must ride out
> to find and bring our master from the field,
> for I have news for him, news great enough
> to ride one of your mares to death for it.

(The Old Serving Man disappears.)

COOK. What news is it? Just one word!

YOUNG SERVING MAN. Just one word,
    my good cook, really wouldn't serve you well.
    And then to sum up everything I know
    and must tell my master, and all this in a word,
    and so offhandedly, is no small task:
    be satisfied with knowing that a message
    of highest import has arrived just now,
    a message that—how long it takes an old man
    to saddle up a horse—that ought to please you
    as a faithful servant; whether you know or not
    what it's about, it ought to please you still.

(Shouting into the court.)

    A whip too, you fool! How can I ride
    without a whip? It's you and not the nag
    who's keeping me here!

(To the cook, ready to rush out.)

    Well then, in a word:
    the young lad Orestes, the son of the house
    who never was at home and for that reason
    as good as dead: in short then let me say
    this son who, so to speak, has always been dead,
    this son, so to speak, is really dead now! *(Rushes off.)*

COOK. *(Turns toward Electra and Chrysothemis, who lie pressed so closely to
    one another that they seem one body shaken by Chrysothemis' sobbing, and
    from which the death pale, silent face of Electra raises itself.)*
    Yes, yes, I have it now. They say dogs howl
    when the moon is at its full, but you howl now
    because your moon will always be a new one.
    Dogs are run out when they disturb the house.
    Take care, they may treat you the same.

(He goes in again.)

CHRYSOTHEMIS. *(Half raised up.)*
    To die among strangers! Dead, buried, there,
    in a strange land. Killed and cut to pieces
    by his own horses! His face, they say, was torn,
    unrecognizable. We never saw his face!
    We think of him, but always as a child.
    But he was a man. I wonder if his mind
    thought of us when he died. I could not ask them:
    they were crowded out with people. O Electra,

We must find the men and speak with them.

ELECTRA. *(To herself.)* Then we must do the deed.

CHRYSOTHEMIS.   Electra, listen,
we must go in. There are two of them,
an old man and a young one. When they learn
that we are his sisters, his poor sisters,
they will tell us everything.

ELECTRA.   What more should we know?
We know that he's dead.

CHRYSOTHEMIS.   That they should bring us nothing,
no lock, no single lock from his dear head!
As though we no longer exist, his two sisters.

ELECTRA.   Therefore we must prove we are his sisters.

CHRYSOTHEMIS.   Electra?

ELECTRA.   We! We must do the deed.

CHRYSOTHEMIS.   Electra, what?

ELECTRA.   It must be done today,
tonight.

CHRYSOTHEMIS.   But, sister, what?

ELECTRA.   What? The work
that's fallen to us now that he will not
return, the work that cannot be left undone.

CHRYSOTHEMIS.   What work?

ELECTRA.   You and I together
must go inside to that woman and her husband,
and kill them.

CHRYSOTHEMIS.   Sister—not our mother. No.

ELECTRA.   Our mother. And her husband. We must do it
unafraid.

(Chrysothemis is speechless.)

ELECTRA.   Be still. Our words are nothing.
There's nothing to consider, only: how,
how we will do it.

CHRYSOTHEMIS.   I?

ELECTRA.   Yes. You and I.
Who else? Has our father other children
hidden in this house to help us now?
No. I know that much.

CHRYSOTHEMIS.   Must we both go?
We? The two of us? With both our hands?

ELECTRA.   That will be mine to do.

CHRYSOTHEMIS.   If you had a knife—

ELECTRA. *(Contemptuously.)*   A knife!

CHRYSOTHEMIS. Or else an axe—

ELECTRA. *An* axe! *The* axe!

The same axe they used when they killed our—

CHRYSOTHEMIS. You?

You have the axe? You horror!

ELECTRA. For our brother,

that's why I kept it. Now it's ours to use.

CHRYSOTHEMIS. You mean you'd kill Aegisthus with these
arms?

ELECTRA. First him, then her; first her, then him; no matter.

CHRYSOTHEMIS. You frighten me. You're not in your right
senses.

ELECTRA. They have no one guarding at their door now.

CHRYSOTHEMIS. You'd murder them in their sleep, and then
live on?

ELECTRA. The question is of him, and not of us.

CHRYSOTHEMIS. If only you could see how mad you are!

ELECTRA. A man asleep is an offering already bound.

If they do not sleep together, I can do it
alone. But you must come with me.

CHRYSOTHEMIS. Electra!

ELECTRA. You!

You must! For you are strong!
(Close to her.)   How strong you are!

How strong your virginal nights have made you grow.
Your loins, your loins are slender here and lithe!
You can slip through any crevice, raise yourself
to the window! Let me, let me feel your arms:
how cool they are and strong! I feel their strength
by the way you push me from you. You could crush
what you embrace in them. You could press
me or any man to these cool, firm breasts
till we suffocate in them! O every part
of you is powerful! It streams like cool
dammed water from a rock. It floods with your hair
down your strong shoulders!

CHRYSOTHEMIS. Let me go!

ELECTRA. No! No!

I'll hold you! With my wretched withered arms
I'll wind about your body, and if you resist
the knot is pulled tighter; I'll twist myself

like tendrils round your body, sink my roots
deep inside you and engraft my will
into your blood!

CHRYSOTHEMIS. Let me go! *(She escapes a few steps.)*

ELECTRA. *(Goes after her wildly, grasps her by her garment.)*
No! No!

CHRYSOTHEMIS. Electra!
Let me go!

ELECTRA. I will not let you go.
We two must grow like one, so that the knife
that severs both our bodies will bring death
at once, for we are alone now in this world.

CHRYSOTHEMIS. Electra, listen. I know how shrewd you are,
help us escape from here, help us get free.

ELECTRA. *(Without hearing her.)*
You are full of strength, your sinews here
are like a colt's, and how slender your feet are,
how easily I can catch them in my arms
as though they were a rope. And here beneath
the coolness of your skin I feel your warm blood
flowing, with my cheek I feel the down
on your young arms: you are like a fruit
on the day that it grows ripe. From this time on
I will be your sister as I have never
been your sister yet! I'll sit in your chamber
with you and wait for the bridegroom, and for him
I will annoint your body; you shall plunge
like a young swan into the fragrant bath
and hide your precious head upon my breast
until he draws you–you, glowing like a torch
beneath your veils–draws you with his arms,
his strong arms, into the marriage-bed.

CHRYSOTHEMIS. *(Closes her eyes)*
No, sister, no, you must never utter
such words inside this house.

ELECTRA. O I shall be more
than ever a sister was from this day on.
I'll serve you, be a slave. When you are in labor
I'll stand there day and night beside your bed,
protect you from the flies, draw cool water,
and then when suddenly some living thing
lies there between your legs, almost afraid,

I'll lift it up, this high, so that its smile
shall fall into the deepest and most secret
fissures of your soul, and like the sun,
melt in you that last icy horror
and let you weep bright tears.

CHRYSOTHEMIS. O take me from this!
I shall die if I stay here!

ELECTRA. *(On her knees.)*   Your mouth is beautiful:
but when will it open wide and cry in rage!
Out of your chaste strong mouth a terrible cry
must come, a cry as terrible as that
of the Death goddess, when someone should awaken
suddenly and see you standing there
above his head like the Death goddess; when someone
should lie bound at your feet and look up at you,
as I do now, look up at your slender body
with fixed eyes like shipwrecked men look up
at the rocky crag above them as they die.

CHRYSOTHEMIS. What are you saying?

ELECTRA. *(Rising.)*   Before you can escape
this house and me, you must help me.

(Chrysothemis tries to speak. Electra puts her hand across her mouth.)

ELECTRA. There is
no way for you but this. I'll hold you here
till you have sworn to me, mouth upon mouth,
that you will help me.

CHRYSOTHEMIS. *(Wrenches herself loose.)* Let me go!

ELECTRA. *(Grabbing her again.)*   Swear to me
that you will come to the foot of the stairs tonight
when all is silent.

CHRYSOTHEMIS. Let me go!

ELECTRA. *(Holding her by her garment.)*   Stay still!
No drop of blood will light on your body;
you will slip quietly from your bloody garment
and clothe your clean body in your bridal dress.

CHRYSOTHEMIS. Let me go!

ELECTRA. You must not be a coward!
The fear you conquer now will be repaid
night after night with raptures of joy–

CHRYSOTHEMIS. I cannot!

ELECTRA. Say that you will come!

CHRYSOTHEMIS. I cannot!

ELECTRA. Look at me,
    lying here at your feet– I'll kiss your feet!
CHRYSOTHEMIS. *(Escapes through the house gate.)*
    I cannot!
ELECTRA. *(After her.)*   Then be damned! *(To herself with wild*
    determination.)
    Well then–alone!

(She begins to dig passionately at the wall of the house, beside the threshold, noiselessly, like an animal. She leaves off for a moment, looks around, then digs again. Orestes stands in the door to the court, black against the last rays of light. He enters. Electra looks up at him. He turns around slowly until he looks at her. Electra starts violently, trembling.)

ELECTRA. Who are you? What do you want?
    Why do you prowl
    about here in the dark spying upon what
    others do? It may be that you, too
    intend what you would not have others know.
    So leave me here in peace. I have some business
    to do. It's none of your concern! Get out,
    and let me grub about upon the ground.
    Didn't you hear? Or has your curiosity
    too strong a will? I am not burying,
    I'm digging up. And not the dead bones
    of a little child I buried some days ago.
    No, my friend, I have given no one life,
    and so I have no need to take a life,
    nor to bury it. If the body of earth
    should ever receive anything from my hands,
    then it must be what I came forth from, not
    any being that ever came forth from me.
    What I dig up–O you will have scarcely gone
    and I will have it and hold it to my heart
    and kiss it as it were both brother and son.
ORESTES. Have you nothing on earth that you can love,
    that you must dig this something from the ground
    to kiss? Are you really so much alone?
ELECTRA. I am no mother, nor have I any mother.
    I am no sister, nor have I brother or sister.
    I lie at the door, and yet I am no watchdog.
    I speak and yet I do not speak. I live

and do not live. I have long hair and feel
nothing they say a woman must feel:
in short, then, please go! Leave me! Leave me!
ORESTES. I must wait here.
ELECTRA. Wait?

(Pause.)

ORESTES. Are you of this house?
   Are you a maid of this house?
ELECTRA. Yes, I serve them.
   But you have no deed to do here. Let that please you
   and go.
ORESTES. I told you once that I must wait
   until they call me.
ELECTRA. They inside? You're lying.
   I know myself the master isn't home.
   And she, what would she want with you?
ORESTES. I
   and another who came with me have a message
   for the lady of the house.

(Electra is silent.)

ORESTES. We were sent to her
   to testify the death of her son Orestes
   which we ourselves saw. For his own horses
   dragged him to his death. I was the same age
   as he and his companion day and night;
   the other who came with me is an old man,
   he was guardian and servant to us both.
ELECTRA. Why must I see you here? Why did you have to
   make your way here to my sad corner,
      O herald of misfortune! Why can't you trumpet
   your news there where it will make them rejoice!
   You live–and he who was better than you
   and nobler a thousand times, a thousand times
   more needed now to be alive–is dead!
   Your eyes stare at me now, and his are clouded.
   Your mouth speaks to me now, but his is stopped
   with earth. O could I stop your mouth with curses!
   Get out of my sight.

ORESTES. What do you want of me?
    The others here received the news with joy.
    Let the dead be. Forget Orestes.
    Orestes is dead now, what's come is come,
    and had to be. He took too much pleasure
    in living, and the gods cannot endure
    the far too bright and ringing sound of joy:
    the far too heavy rush of wings at evening
    repulses them; they grasp the nearest arrow
    and nail the creature to the dismal tree
    of his dark fate that somewhere has grown in silence
    a long while. And so he had to die.
ELECTRA. How knowingly he speaks of death, this—creature!
    As if he'd tasted it and spat it out.
    But I! But I! I must lie here and know
    that the child will never again come home,
    that those inside the house rejoice and live,
    that this vile brood lives on inside its hole
    and eats and drinks and sleeps and multiplies,
    while down below the child lingers in the chasm
    of horror, and dare not approach its father.
    And here am I, alone upon the earth,
    living as no beast ever lived, alone
    and monstrously!
ORESTES. Who are you?
ELECTRA. Why should you care
    who I am? Did I ask you who you were?
ORESTES. I can think nothing else but that you are
    closely related in blood to them who died,
    Agamemnon and Orestes.
ELECTRA. Related? I?
    I am that blood! That blood spilt so brutishly!
    King Agamemnon's blood! I'm called Electra.
ORESTES. No!
ELECTRA. He doesn't believe me. He scorns me first
    and then takes from me my name. Even the children
    ridicule me because my father and brother
    are dead! And everyone who comes this way
    kicks at me, and now they want even my name!
ORESTES. Electra must be ten years younger than you,
    Electra is tall; her eyes are sad, but gentle,
    while yours are filled with blood and hate. Electra—

Electra lives apart from the common people,
she spends her days guarding at a tomb.
She has always two or three women about her,
who serve her silently, and animals
steal timidly about the house she lives in,
and nestle to her when she walks.

ELECTRA. *(Clapping her hands.)*   True! True!
What other pretty stories can you tell me!
I'll tell it to her when I—*(With choked voice.)*
-see her again.

ORESTES. Is it true then? Is it really true?
You? *(Quickly.)*
And have they left you here to starve or—
have they beaten you?

ELECTRA. You with your questions—
who are you?

ORESTES. Have they? Have they? Tell me! Please!

ELECTRA. Both! Both! Both! Queens do not flourish
fed with the refuse from the garbage-heap,
and a priestess is not made to spring about
when she's been whipped, nor go about in rage
in place of flowing robes. Leave go my dress,
why must you muss it so to wipe your eyes!

ORESTES. Electra!
Where have they made you sleep your terrible nights!
Your eyes are dreadful.

ELECTRA. *(Sullenly.)* Go into the house there,
inside you'll find my sister always ready
for festivities!

ORESTES. Electra, listen to me.

ELECTRA. Don't come near me, I don't want to know
who you are. I will not see anyone!

(She cowers, her face against the wall.)

ORESTES. Listen, I haven't time. Listen. I dare not
speak too loud. Listen: Orestes lives.

(Electra turns sharply.)

ORESTES. Don't make a sound. One movement from you
now
and you betray him.

ELECTRA. Then he's free? Where is he?
You know where he is? Is he hidden? He is
a prisoner, cowering in some corner,

waiting for his death! And I must see him die!
They sent you here to torture me, to tie
my soul with a rope, and draw it high, and then
dash it to earth again.

ORESTES. He's as unharmed
    as I.

ELECTRA. Then rescue him! Before they kill him.
    Why can't you warn him? O I kiss your feet
    that you may warn him. By your father's body
    I beg you, run as quickly as you can,
    run and bring him away! The child must die
    if he should spend one night inside that house.

ORESTES. And by my father's body that is why
    the child entered the house, so that this night
    those who must die will die—

ELECTRA. (Struck by his tone.)Who are you?

(The gloomy Old Servant rushes in silently from the court, throws himself down
at Orestes' feet, kisses them, collects himself, looking about fearfully, and rushes
out again silently.)

ELECTRA. (Almost without control.)
    Who are you then? Tell me! You frighten me.

ORESTES. (Softly.)   The dogs that lie in the yard remember me
    but not my own sister.

ELECTRA. (Cries out.)   No! Orestes!

ORESTES. (Feverishly.) If anyone inside the house there heard
    you,
    he holds my life in his hands.

ELECTRA. (Very softly, trembling.)   O Orestes!
    No one's moving. Look at me, Orestes!
    Look at me! No, no, you mustn't touch me!
    Step back, I'm so ashamed that you should see me.
    I do not know how you can look at me.
    I am but the dead body of your sister,
    my poor child. I know it makes you shudder
    to see me. Still. I was a King's daughter!
    I believe I was beaautiful once: When I'd blow
    the lamp out at my mirror, I would feel
    a virgin thrill run through me as my naked
    body's chastity glowed through the sultry night
    like a thing divine. I would feel the moon's thin rays

bathe me in her snowwhite nakedness
as in a pond; my hair, O my hair then
was such as made men tremble, this same hair,
straggled, dirtied now, humiliated!
These, my brother, are the sweet delights
I had to sacrifice to my father.
Do you think if I enjoyed my body
that his sighs and groans would not throng so
about my bed? For the dead are jealous:
and he has sent me hatred, hollow-eyed hatred,
as a bridegroom. And so to my sleepless bed
I took this horror that breathed like a viper,
and let him crawl on top of me and force me
to know all that happens between man and woman.
The nights, O, O the nights that taught me this!
My body was cold as ice, though hot as coals,
charred in its depths. And then when I knew all
then I knew what wisdom was, and the murderers—
my mother, I mean, and that one with her—
they could no longer look into my eyes!
Why do you look about so anxiously?
Speak to me, speak! Why are you trembling so?
ORESTES. Let my body tremble. Do you think
it would not tremble otherwise if it knew
the way that it must go, the way I'll lead it?
ELECTRA. You'll do it? You? Alone? O my poor child!
And you have brought no friends along with you?
ORESTES. You must not speak of it. My old servant
is with me here. But I will do the deed.
ELECTRA. I've never seen the gods, and yet I'm certain
that they will be here with you, they will help you.
ORESTES. I do not know the gods, but I know this:
they have laid this deed upon my conscience,
and they will scorn me if I tremble at it.
ELECTRA. You will do it!
ORESTES. Yes, yes, I only wish
I need not look my mother in the eyes.
ELECTRA. Then look and see what she has made of me.
(Orestes looks sadly at her.)
ELECTRA. O child, O child! How stealthily you've come here,
speaking of yourself as though dead,
and yet you are alive!

ORESTES. *(Softly.)* Be careful!

ELECTRA. Who
am I, that you should cast such loving looks
at me? See, I am nothing. All I was
I had to sacrifice: even that modesty,
that sweetest thing of all, which, like the silvery,
milky haze of the moon, hovers about
a woman and protects her and her soul
from all things horrible! My modesty
was sacrificed as though I'd fallen among thieves
who stripped my last garment from me! I have
known the wedding-night, as no other virgins
have known the pangs of women who bear children,
but have brought nothing into the world, nothing;
I have become a perpetual prophetess,
and have brought nothing forth from my body
except eternal curses and despair.
At night I never slept, but made my bed
high on the tower and cried down to the court
and whimpered with the dogs. I have been hated.
I have seen everything, have had to see everything
just like the watchman on the tower,
and day is night and night becomes day again,
and I have found no joy in sun or stars,
for all things, for his sake, were nothing to me,
all things were but signs, and every day
a marker on the road.

ORESTES. O my sister.

ELECTRA. What is it?

ORESTES. Does our mother look like you
in any way?

ELECTRA. *(Wildly.)*   Like me? No, I will not
have you look her in the face. When she is dead
then we together will look her in the face.
O my brother, she threw a white shirt
upon our father, and then she struck away
at that which stood before her, helpless, sightless,
which could not turn its face to hers, whose arms
could not work free—are you listening to me?—
she struck down at this with her axe raised high
above him.

ORESTES. Electra! No!

ELECTRA. O now her face
  is mirror to the deeds that she has done.
ORESTES. I will do it! I must do it quickly!
ELECTRA. Happy the man who does! Who dares to do!
  A deed is like a bed on which the soul
  can rest, a bed of balsam where the soul
  that is a wound, a blight, a running sore,
  a sore that flames like fire!

(Orestes' Guardian stands in the door to the court, a strong old man with flashing eyes.)

ELECTRA. Who is this man?
GUARDIAN. *(Quickly to them.)*
  Are you both mad? Can't you hold your tongues
  when a breath, a sound, when nothing might undo
  both us and our work together—
ELECTRA. Who is this man?
ORESTES. Don't you know him? If you love me, thank him.
  You must thank him I am here. This is Electra.
ELECTRA. You! You! O everything is true now!
  Everything comes to me now! Here, let me kiss
  your hands! I know nothing of the gods,
  I do not know them, therefore I would rather
  kiss your hands.
GUARDIAN. Be still, Electra, be still!
ELECTRA. No, I will rejoice over you, for you
  have brought him here. When I was steeped in hatred
  I kept nothing but silence. Hatred is nothing,
  it consumes itself, and love is still less
  than hatred, it grasps out at everything,
  but fastens onto nothing, its hands are like flames
  that cannot grasp; and thought, too, is nothing,
  and all that comes from our mouths is feeble air:
  that man alone is happy who comes to *do!*
  And happy who dares to touch him and who digs
  his axe from the earth, who holds the torch for him,
  who opens the door, who listens there.
GUARDIAN. *(Takes hold of her roughly and presses his hand to her mouth.)*
  Be silent!
(To Orestes in great haste.)
  She's waiting inside. Her maids are looking for you.
  There's not a man in all the house. Orestes!

(Orestes collects himself, controls his terror. The doorway of the house grows bright and a Woman Servant appears with a torch, behind her Clytemnestra's Woman. Electra has sprung back; she stands in darkness. The Woman does obeisance to the two men and nods for them to follow her inside. The Woman Servant secures the torch in an iron ring at the doorpost. Orestes and the Guardian go inside. Orestes closes his eyes momentarily as though dizzy; the Guardian is close behind him; they exchange a quick glance. The door closes behind them.

Electra is left alone in dreadful suspense. She runs back and forth in front of the door, her head bent forward, like a captive animal in its cage. Suddenly she stands still.)

ELECTRA. I didn't give him the axe! They've gone inside,
and I didn't give him the axe. There are no gods
in heaven!

(Another fearful waiting. From inside there comes the shrill cry of Clytemnestra.)

ELECTRA. *(Cries out as though possessed.)*   Again! Again!
(A second cry from inside. From the servants' quarters, left, enter Chrysothemis and a crowd of Women Servants. Electra stands at the door, her back pressed against it.)
CHRYSOTHEMIS. Something has happened.
FIRST WOMAN SERVANT. She cried like that in her sleep.
SECOND WOMAN SERVANT. There must be men inside, I heard
men's footsteps.
THIRD WOMAN SERVANT. All the doors are locked.
FOURTH WOMAN SERVANT. They're murderers!
There are murderers in the house!
FIRST WOMAN SERVANT. *(Cries out.)*
O!
ALL. What is it?
FIRST WOMAN SERVANT. Don't you see? There's someone at
the door!
CHRYSOTHEMIS. That's Electra! That must be Electra!
SECOND WOMAN SERVANT. Why is she standing there so
quiet?
CHRYSOTHEMIS. Electra,
why do you stand there so quiet?
FIRST WOMAN SERVANT. I must get out.
I must get the men. *(Runs off left.)*
CHRYSOTHEMIS. Open the door, Electra!

SEVERAL WOMEN SERVANTS. Electra, let us in the house!
FIRST WOMAN SERVANT. *(Comes running back through the courtyard gate crying out.)*
    Get Back!
(They all grow startled.)
FIRST WOMAN SERVANT. Aegisthus! Aegisthus! Quick! Get
    back to our rooms!
    Aegisthus is crossing the court! If he finds us,
    and something's happened inside, he'll have us killed!
ALL. Quick! Get back! Get back!
(They disappear into the house, left)
AEGISTHUS. *(At the entrance on the right.)* Is there no one
    here
    to light my way? Will none of these scoundrels help me?
    Impossible to teach these people manners!

(Electra takes the torch from the ring, runs down toward him, and bows.)

AEGISTHUS. *(Startled at the wild-looking figure in the flickering light, steps backward.)*
    What ghastly thing is this? I have forbidden
    that an unknown face approach me!
(Recognizes her, angrily.) What? Is it you?
    Who bade you to come near me?
ELECTRA. May I not
    light your way?
AEGISTHUS. Well, I suppose the news
    concerns you most. Where will I find these strangers
    who tell us of Orestes?
ELECTRA. Why–inside.
    They found a gracious hostess there to greet them.
    They're amusing themselves with her.
AEGISTHUS. And their news?
    That he is dead? Is it true beyond a doubt?
ELECTRA. My lord, their proof is not in words alone,
    O no, they have bodily signs with them,
    which cannot be denied.
AEGISTHUS.· What's that in your voice?
    What's happened to you that you even speak to me?
    Why do you stagger back and forth this way
    with this light you hold!
ELECTRA. I am become wise at last

and hold myself with them that are the stronger.
May I light your way?
AEGISTHUS. As far as the door.
Why are you dancing? Be careful!
ELECTRA. *(While circling about him, as though doing a sinister dance, suddenly bows deeply.)* Have care! The
steps! You mustn't fall.
AEGISTHUS. *(At the door to the house.)*   Why is there no light
here?
Who are those people.
ELECTRA. They are the very ones
who'd pay you their respects in person, my lord.
And I who've often disturbed you with the arrogant
impudence of my presence have learned at last
to withdraw myself at the proper moment.

(Aegisthus enters the house. A short silence. Then noise inside. Aegisthus appears at once at a small window at the right, tears back the curtain and cries out.)

AEGISTHUS. Help! Murder! Help your master! Murder,
murder!
They're murdering me! *(He is dragged away.)*
Will no one listen to me?
No one listen? *(Once again his face appears at the window.)*
ELECTRA. Agamemnon listens!
AEGISTHUS. *(Torn from the window.)* Ah!

(Electra stands breathing fearfully, turned toward the house. The Women run out wildly, Chrysothemis among them. As though unconscious they run toward the door of the court. They suddenly stop there and turn around.)

CHRYSOTHEMIS. Electra! Sister! Come, O come with us!
It's our brother there inside! It's Orestes
who did it.

(A confusion of voices, tumult outside.)

CHRYSOTHEMIS.   Come! He's in the entrance hall,
they're round about him in circles, kissing his feet;
all who hated Aegisthus in their hearts
have thrown themselves on the others, everywhere,
in all the courts, the dead are lying about;

those who are still alive are spattered with blood
and bear wounds themselves, but their faces are radiant,
all embrace one another—

(The noise outside increases, the Women have run out, Chrysothemis is alone. Light spills in from outside.)

CHRYSOTHEMIS. —and rejoice;
　　a thousand torches are lighted. Don't you hear it?
　　Don't you?
ELECTRA. *(Crouching on the threshold.)* Don't I hear it? Hear
　　the music?
　　That music comes from me. Those thousands and thousands
　　with torches, they whose boundless myriad footsteps
　　make hollow rumbling round the earth, all these,
　　these, wait upon me: I know that they all,
　　all, wait upon me to lead the dance,
　　and yet I cannot; the ocean, the monstrous ocean
　　the manifold ocean weighs me down with its burden
　　in every limb; I cannot lift myself!

CHRYSOTHEMIS. *(Almost screaming with excitement.)*
　　Don't you hear them? Listen! They're carrying him,
　　they're carrying him upon their hands, their faces
　　are all changed, their eyes and the cheeks of the old
　　glisten with tears! They're crying. Don't you hear?
　　Ah! *(She runs out.)*

(Electra has raised herself. She strides down from the stairs, her head thrown back like a Maenad. She thrusts forward her knees, she stretches out her arms: it is an indescribable dance in which she strides forward. Chrysothemis appears again at the door, behind her are torches, a throng, faces of men and women.)

CHRYSOTHEMIS. Electra!
ELECTRA. *(Stops short, stands staring at them.)*
　　Be silent and dance. All must come!
　　All must join with me! I bear the burden
　　of joy, and I dance here before you all.
　　One thing alone remains for him who is happy:
　　to be silent and dance!

(She does a few more steps of her most tense dance of triumph and collapses. Chrysothemis rushes to her. Electra lies motionless. Chrysothemis runs to the door of the house and knocks.)

CHRYSOTHEMIS. Orestes! Orestes!

(Silence.)

Franz Werfel (1890-1945)

Goat Song

The major dramatic work of Franz Werfel is an excellent example of the influence of mysticism and expressionism on the theater in the years before and after World War 1. Born in Prague like Kafka and Rilke, Werfel absorbed the mystical traditions of his Jewish faith and combined the abilities of a poet and dramatist. He projected that special blend of Austrian temperament and outlook that characterized the work of Raimund, Grillparzer, and Hofmannsthal. His work was a combination of richness, symbolism, sensuous details, theatricality, and a gnawing sense of melancholic sadness. Though equally famous for his novels and his poetry, many critics feel that he made his major contribution in the area of symbolist-expressionist drama. His play, *Bocksgesang (Goat Song;* 1921), reprinted here, is an outstanding example of one aspect of the expressionist style and, after its premiere in Vienna, was widely produced in central Europe and in an outstanding Theatre Guild production in the United States in the years between the two World Wars.

Prague was a major city in the Austrian Empire during Werfel's early years, and this young son of a wealthy Jewish merchant was given an excellent education that included a complete background in the Jewish folklore of the city.He had a strongly antagonistic attitude toward his rather overbearing father and left home in 1910 to take a position as a shipping clerk in Hamburg. Throughout his work there runs a strong theme of difficult father-son relationships, and even God is always depicted as the fatherly lawgiver and an agent of repression against his earthly children.

In 1911-12 Werfel served his year of compulsory military service and then accepted a postion in the young publishing firm of Kurt Wolff in Leipzig. During this time his first volume of poems, *Der Weltfreund (Friend to the World;* 1911), was published, and he was immediately hailed as one of the best of the new Austro-German poets. He continued to write during his years spent on the Italian front during World War I and his first play, *Der Troerinnen,* a re-creation of Euripides' *The Trojan Women,* was published in 1915. In it he stressed the need for a new dedication in Europe to a religious outlook and a sense of moral responsibility in the face of an entire world at war. His third book of poetry, *Einander (To One Another;* 1915), made him famous as a leader among German expressionist poets, but his pacifism led to his arrest for high treason toward the end of the war, and he was only released with the fall of the empire.

He settled in Vienna after the war and fell in love with the widow of Gustav Mahler, Alma Maria Schindler. The story of their courtship and marriage has been fully told in her book, *And the Bridge of Love*. They lived the life of the Viennese intellectual elite with frequent journeys abroad, and Werfel came to love Vienna and identify with its temperament and character. In 1920 he published *Der Spiegelmensch* (*The Mirror Man*), A so-called "magic trilogy" in verse that was a major contribution to the development of expressionist drama. The setting is vaguely oriental, and the central character, a kind of Faust figure, proceeds on a spiritual journey through life accompanied by his mirror image or Mephistophelian alter ego which embodies his baser instincts (a concept made popular by Raimund in *Der Alpenkönig under der Mensch-enfeind*). He wins a redemption in death, and the mirror image joins the mirror to become a window that looks out on a vision of a perfect future life. It was a kind of summary of the leading expressionist motifs and was considered important enough to win a performance at the Vienna Burgtheater.

In 1921 he adapted his novel *Bocksgesang* into play form, and many have considered it his most original contribution to the theater. Based on a brief newspaper clipping about a monster and a slavic rebellion in the late eighteenth century, Werfel transformed the incident into a symbolist-expressionist allegory of the brutality of man in rebellion. The action turns on an uprising among Slavonic peasants on the Danube, and Werfel uses this rebellion to symbolize the release of man's primeval instincts against the established order. In a kind of religious ecstasy the mob worships a monster, half-man and half-goat, that has emerged from the woods. The rebellion is crushed, and the monster perishes in flame, but not before impregnating the daughter of a wealthy peasant. Thus a heritage of violence and bestiality is passed on to the child born from this union. The play's title alludes to the origin of tragedy in the song and the primitive scapegoat ritual of the goat-footed god Dionysus. This type of complicated symbolism infuses the entire drama. Yet despite its seemingly remote and mystical content, it did speak to the violence and emotional upheaval of postwar society.

In the United States the play, in an elaborate production by the Theatre Guild, opened on January 25, 1926, with an all-star cast that included Edward G. Robinson, Albert Bruning, Blanche Yurka, George Gaul, Lynne Fontanne, Helen Westley, Alfred Lunt, and Herbert Yost. The moodily ominous setting with its great cyclorama was by Lee Simonson. The *New Yorker* for February 6, 1926, commented on its powerful symbolism: " . . . every hen and loiterer, housewife or gypsy stands for a whole class, a nation at large, some force or foolishness in the human race." The critic summarized the message by suggesting that we create what we dread—that the greatest evils are those fears that become the realities that we eventually have to face. In "Second Thoughts on First Nights" in *The New York World* for February 11, 1926, Alexander Woollcot said that *Goat Song* is "a timeless, untethered play, of the stature, say of *Peer Gynt.*"

Schweiger (The Silent One; 1922). which followed *Bocksgesang,* once again takes up the idea of the schizoid personality, portraying a man who remembers a terrible crime while under psychoanalysis. He tries to atone for the deed, becomes involved in contemporary political struggles, realizes that only love can save him, and finally commits suicide when his wife leave him and her love is removed. After this rather turgid piece, Werfel turned to historical drama to make his points about good and evil, and in *Juarez und Maximilian* (1924) he achieved his greatest theatrical success. He underlined the ideal-pacifist nature of the Austrian archduke, who was crowned emperor of Mexico, and stressed the powerlessness of the good man caught in the web of complex historical events. Like *Goat Song, Juarez and Maximilian* was produced in the United States by the Theatre Guild in 1926 with Alfred Lunt as the Emperor Maximilian. The play also won the famous Grillparzer Prize from the Vienna Academy of Science.

Paulus unter den Juden (Paul Among the Jews; 1926), another historical drama, dealt with the conflict between inspired prophecy and organized religion among the early Christians, while *Das Reich Gottes in Böhmen (The Kingdom of God in Bohemia;* 1930) portrayed the Hussite movement during the fifteenth century and how its bestial methods destroyed the ideals and humane outlook of its leader. Also during the mid-twenties, Werfel wrote a long novel based on the life of Giuseppe Verdi accompanied by three adaptations of his librettos for the German stage. The most successful of these was *La Forza del Destino.* Then true international fame came, not from one of his plays, but from his novel, *Die Vierzig Tage Musa Dagh (The Forty Days of Musa Dagh;* 1933), which detailed the cruel treatment of certain Armenian villages by the Turks.

It was the rise of Nazi persecution in Germany that brought Werfel back to the theater with a verse play, *Der Weg der Verheissung (The Road of Destiny;* 1936), which glorified the unconquerable spirit of the Jews in their persecuted march through history. As *The Eternal Road,* it was spectacularly produced in New York in 1937 by Max Reinhardt, but it turned out to be more a sweeping visual pageant than an important work about the Jews. At this time he also wrote *In Einer Nacht (One Night;* 1937), an unsuccessful attempt to dramatize a soul's return to earth to communicate with the living. During this period his health was not too robust, he was deeply upset by events in Germany, and he traveled more and more in an attempt to find relief from his growing melancholy.

When the Germans overran Austria in 1938, he was away from his homeland and was never to return. He lived with his wife for almost two years in an old mill in the south of France, and here he wrote the novel *Der veruntreute Himmel (Embezzled Heaven;* 1939). This was later made into a play and presented on Broadway in 1944 with Ethel Barrymore and Albert Basserman. When France fell, the Werfels, realizing the precariousness of their position, escaped over the Pyrenees on foot and for a time found refuge at the shrine of Lourdes. At the time he vowed that if he reached America he would sing the *Song of Bernadette* to the world. He finally did reach the United States on a Greek ship and settled in California amid a colony of artistic and intellectual expatriates. He completed *Das Lied von Bernadette (The Song of Bernadette;* 1941), which became a Book-of-the-Month selection and as a film won five academy awards. He also wrote *Jacobowsky und der Oberst (Jacobowsky and the Colonel;* 1944), a comedy based on material gathered during his escape from France. It portrays how a Jewish refugee by his intelligence and ingenuity manages to get an anti-Semitic Polish officer and his mistress through the German lines to the coast. It was presented on Broadway in 1944 with Louis Calhern and Oscar Karlweis in the leading roles. It was later made into a film with Danny Kaye and Kurt Jurgens.

By this time Werfel was a sick man. He declined most speaking engagements, though he did accept an honorary doctorate from the University of California in 1943. His last novel, *Stern der Ungeborenen (Star of the Unborn;* 1946) was a mystical fantasy of the future. This and revisions of his collected poems from 1908 to 1945 were carried out at a secluded cottage in Santa Barbara that afforded him the quiet of a monastery for his work. It was here that he died at the early age of fifty-five in 1945.

The plays of Werfel represent what might be called the mystical or religious side of expressionism in the drama, for they deal less with the social events of the time than with the timeless problems of human existence. As he expressed his philosophy in his first play, the adaptation of *The Trojan Women:* "There is an essential tragedy in the world, a break, an original sin, wherein all participate, and from which the understanding soul suffers most." In this melancholic assessment he is distinctly Austrian and closely reflects the philosophical outlook of the great Franz Grillparzer.

Goat Song

by

FRANZ WERFEL

Translated by Ruth Langner

Characters

GOSPODAR (SQUIRE) STEVAN MILIC
MIRKO, his son
MIRKO'S MOTHER
GOSPODAR JEVREM VESILIC
STANJA, his daughter
STANJA'S MOTHER
STARSINA
THE OLD MAN OF KRASNOKRAJ
THE OLD MAN OF MODRYGOR
THE OLD MAN OF MEDEGYA
THE OTHER OLD MEN
THE CLERK
BABKA
A SERVANT
A POPE (Greek Orthodox Priest)
THE PHYSICIAN
A MESSENGER
BOGOBOJ WITH THE WHITE BEARD
JUVAN, the student
TEITERLIK, an acrobat
THE AMERICAN
FEIWEL
KRUNA
THE OTHER RETURNED WANDERERS, UNLANDED MEN, AND VAGABONDS
AN INNKEEPER
A BASHI BAZOOK
SOLDIERS IN THE REGIMENT OF JANISSARIES
THE DRUNKEN BUTCHER

The action of the play takes place in a Slavic countryside, beyond the Danube at the close of the eighteenth century.

312

ACT 1

(The big farm kitchen of Gospodar Stevan Milic's house. Left, near the door, the oven with a bench running around it. . . . Right, many little windows lighted by a later March afternoon. In the darkening background a stair leads left, and in an alcove is the shrine of the holy pictures. A deserted table.)

SCENE 1

(Gospodar Stevan Milic, Mirko, Mirko's Mother, Gospodar Jevrem Vesilic, Stanja, Stanja's Mother, Babka, A Maid. The two families stand in a stiff and solemn row before the oven. Babka and the Maid hand them little wooden cups of prune brandy under the watchful housewife's eye of Mirko's Mother.)

STEVAN. One more little swallow before you go! Your health, my dear guests. *(They drink.)*

JEVREM. *(Wiping his mouth.)*   You make a stiff drink here.

MIRKO'S MOTHER. I hope it brings you good health.

STANJA'S MOTHER. We thank you. *(Babka and the Maid exit.)*

STEVAN. Now we've talked it over to our heart's content and everything is signed and sealed. We are happy to see your little Stanja as the betrothed of our son, our son Mirko. Why is your daughter so silent? She hasn't said a word all day—the pretty one.

STANJA'S MOTHER. *(Nudges her daughter.)* Go on, talk, say something.

STANJA. *(Stands motionless. Only her bridal wreath of flowers and ribbon trembles lightly.)*

JEVREM. A silent one she is. Silent at home, as well. Don't think her stupid. I tell you brother, she's cleverer than we old ones.

STEVAN. Other days, other ways. When our father gave me and Mother to each other no one asked us anything and no one would have listened to us anyway. Other days, other ways. Therefore I ask you, Stanjoschka, is there anything on your mind against Mirko here for a husband?

STANJA. Nothing!

JEVREM. Nothing, you hear?

STANJA'S MOTHER. Nothing, you hear?

MIRKO. *(Angrily.)*   Why these questions, Father? It's not for you to ask her that.

Goat Song by Franz Werfel, translated by Ruth Langner, is reprinted from *The Theatre Guild Anthology* (New York: Random House, Inc., 1936). By permission of the publisher and the heirs of Franz Werfel.

STEVAN. Son, you know nothing of the ways of Women. *(To Stanja.)* Well, then you are invited, dear Stanja, to stay here in the house until the fourth Sunday, as is the custom, and learn to know your new home. Look about the household, make the servants trust you. Mother will tell you whatever you want to know. But no work for you during these happy days. Enjoy your life with us to the full. Are you content?

STANJA. I am, and I thank you.

JEVREM AND HIS WIFE. We, too, thank you.

STEVAN. This is solemn talk for young folks. Run along, children, no need to stand there before us old people shifting from one foot to the other. Go, and God be with you.

MIRKO. Come, Stanja! *(They exit.)*

SCENE 2

JEVREM. *(Shakes hands cordially with Stevan.)* Ah! Today I'm truly happy.

STANJA'S MOTHER. A young couple such as God smiles on.

MIRKO'S MOTHER. —And folks will envy.

JEVREM. We are both rich, dear kinsman and neighbor,
and masters of many souls. Each of us
gives as good as he gets. We need not hate
each other like some fathers-in-law, for neither
your child nor mine gets the worst of it. God grant
you're as happy as I am.

STEVAN. I am, I am.

JEVREM. What a future for us both!

STEVAN. Yes, our paths go upward.

JEVREM. Our fathers were still tenant farmers and vassals to
the Turk. But the Spahi has grown old and sits
puffing his nargileh in the stone house of the
Vilajet, or looking wearily down from his battle
towers into the rippling stream.

STEVAN. We have taken what was ours.

JEVREM. And the Moslem; God protect him. His soldiers will
defend us, for there is murmuring aplenty
among the peasants against us, their masters and
the owners of the land.

STEVAN. Let him fear who has evil on his mind.
Once our farmers, servants, tenants, barnyards,
dairies, and vinyards are united, they will
truly make a lord's estate.

JEVREM. You know, that has been my thought for
    a long while. If a man gathers and multiplies his wealth
    and bows to the authorities, he's sure of their help to guard his land.
    Are there many vagrants in your part of
    the country?
STEVAN. All too many. And especially this year
    when such a lot of people have come home
    from beyond the Danube. It means trouble enough
    for me and the council of elders.
    (He sighs.)
JEVREM. It might be wise to be neighborly and allow
    them a bit of land for farming. Unused woods eat up the
    fruitlands and cry for tilling . . .
    (Stevan nods.)   And better still– your son,
    our son, the future master, will raise him
    a regiment of followers out of these landless men.
    Such things have happened.
STEVAN. That would please his vanity.
    (Jevrem ostentatiously takes out a fat watch;
    Stevan opens his eyes wide.)
JEVREM. This comes from Vienna.
STEVAN. Yes. We are beginning to live in the world again.
JEVREM. God of my fathers! It's high time we went.
    We've long outstayed our welcome.
STEVAN. Don't say that! Stay a little longer.
JEVREM. Impossible! We'd get home late at night.
STEVAN. I will have your horses hitched, then.
    (Goes to the door.)
JEVREM. I'll go with you.
STEVAN. The women can wait here for us till then.
    (Both exit.)

SCENE 3

STANJA'S MOTHER. I envy your house, my dear. Everything
    shining–dishes, silver, ornaments. And even the food
    you put before us. They can't bake or stew more
    tastily at the Emperor's in Vienna.
    I will tremble when you come to us.
    We poor people! And I envy my daughter Stanja, too,
    with the chance to copy your receipes; although the bad girl
    has no mind for those things.

MIRKO'S MOTHER. I'll find everything at your house just the
same as mine. *(Politely.)* They say that you
weave better than we can here.
(Pause.)

STANJA'S MOTHER. Parden me, my dear. You won't take offence
if I say something? You look sad—not happy . . . . I say this
only because I'm so fond of you.

MIRKO'S MOTHER. Forgive me! I am happy. God didn't bless
me. I cannot show my happiness.

STANJA'S MOTHER. God *has* blessed you! Aren't you proud of
your boy?

STANJA'S MOTHER. A son is always different from a daughter.
The men are never satisfied with daughters. My
old man . . . he's not near so good tempered as
he seems . . . Many's the beating I've had because I
bore a girl. That you've been spared. When the
only child is a son there's joy in the house, and the
fault findings are silenced. But (forgive me my
love talks,) perhaps some old, old sorrow
clouds your joy . . . I remember . . . *(She
shifts inquisitively on her chair.)*Two years
before our fine boy came along . . . didn't
you go the full nine months?

(Mirko's Mother is silent.)

STANJA'S MOTHER. *(Sympathetically watchful.)* The baby
died quite young, eh? Even women who have
ten or twelve and mix the children's
names never forget little ones like that.
My love talks . . .

MIRKO'S MOTHER. The baby died at birth.

STANJA'S MOTHER. A boy?

MIRKO'S MOTHER. No.

STANJA'S MOTHER. Oh, a girl?

MIRKO'S MOTHER. No.

STANJA'S MOTHER. What? How so?

MIRKO'S MOTHER. *(Quickly.)* How stupid! Forgive me! It
was a boy. Of course, a boy.

THE MEN'S VOICES. *(Through the window.)*
Hey! You women!

MIRKO'S MOTHER. *(Rising swiftly.)* Let us not keep our old
men waiting. *(Both off.)*

SCENE 4

(Enter Babka with dishes, the Young Serving Man following.)

MAN. Babka! It is hollering for you.

BABKA. What's hollering?

MAN. Or was it singing? Maybe it's singing! Hahaha! haha ....

BABKA. Fool, what are you talking about, and laughing at?

MAN. Oh, I'm a fool, am I? But just the same ...

BABKA. *(Interrupting.)* What?

MAN. That!

BABKA. It won't be long before you've eaten your last spoonful of rice soup here.

MAN. *(Sings.)* "If you have eyes to see
A wanderer you will be."

BABKA. You have a mouth, too–to shut.

MAN. I know another song;
"And the little house of stone
Has a fire of its own."

BABKA. You go sing your songs to the sheep.

MAN. You can't make me stop. *(Sings.)*
*"Iron hinges on the door
Seven locks and seven more—
Who carries all those keys?"*

BABKA. Rascal! Get out of the master's room
They're coming. *(Man withdraws mockingly.)*

SCENE 5

(Mirko and Stanja enter, Babka exits.)

MIRKO. Your parents are gone now. Are you sad?

STANJA. No, I am not sad.

MIRKO. Then you don't love your parents?

STANJA. I love them.

MIRKO. Then you must be sad. Doesn't it hurt you
when something is over? The axle creaks,
the horses draw up, the whip . . . And
then, something is ended.

SCENE 6

(Stevan enters.)

STEVAN. Still in the house, children? Away with you.
    They are finishing the dancing on the village green.
    The folks want to see you. It's only right
    the master's son and daughter should lead
    the dancers. *(To Mirko.)*   What's the matter?
MIRKO. *(Urgently.)*   Father!
STEVAN. You are your own master now. Here is
    some money. Make merry with your betrothed
    and treat your friends. *(Mirko hesitates.)*   Off with you.
    (Impatiently.)   Go! *(Mirko and
    Stanja go to the door.)*   And call Babka
    for me. *(Mirko and Stanja exit. Stevan quickly takes
    a long gun with a jointed butt down from the
    wall and loads it. Then he stands rigid for
    a few moments and hangs the weapon up
    again as hastily as he took it down.)*

SCENE 7

(Babka enters.)
BABKA. Peace to you, master, peace at last.
STEVAN. *(Rousing from his abstraction, suddenly
    hoarsely.)*   His sickness?
BABKA. Master, he's getting better. The poor thing ate,
    drank and slept for the first time in many
    days.
STEVAN. *(Clenching his fists.)* Christ, why do you not help?
BABKA. His eyes roll again . . . round the walls . . .
    without stopping.
STEVAN. *(Almost screaming.)*   On two feet or four
    Babka?
BABKA. *(Quietly.)*   On two and four—both.
STEVAN. Do you see to him daily?
BABKA. Daily at twilight, at the hour of the evening
    meal.
STEVAN. *(Looks at her in horror.)*   You . . .
BABKA. Can I shun what I have suckled, shun him,
    the wild big thing that once was tiny with
    a greedy mouth?

STEVAN. He screamed today, the second time in his
  cursed life.
BABKA. He screamed for the joy of health with his
  ever silent voice.
STEVAN. Does he never greet you?
BABKA. No, but he knows his old Babka.
STEVAN. Did anybody hear the cry?
BABKA. Oh yes, they heard him.
STEVAN. Heard? Satan . . .
BABKA. *(Interrupting him.)*   That's what many say.
STEVAN. The people . . . get them all out of the house
  you hear? To play games or to dance on the green–not a man or
  woman home before midnight. You hear?
BABKA. I knew your will, master. They are gone
  Do nothing evil. *(Stevan motions her to go. Babka at the door.)* Do
  nothing evil. *(Turns to go.)*
STEVAN. Babka, has he a human face?
BABKA. The face of a man, of an old man, a hundred
  years old, a face shrewd and knowing.
STEVAN. Give me the key.
BABKA. Why master? Turn from such thoughts
  Your life is happy now.
STEVAN. The key. *(Babka takes out a key and hands
  it to him.)* You do not let it rust.
BABKA. You have the key now, master. *(Exits
  slowly.)*
STEVAN. *(Slowly, to himself.)*   Shame, shame! Pain,
  shame! *(Groans. Collapses over the table.)*

SCENE 8

(Mirko's Mother enters.)
MOTHER. The people are gone. We are alone now. It
  is terrible.
STEVAN. *(Turns to her wildly.)*Tell me, tell me at
  last, tell me your awful secret. What you hid from me and
  then bore to our shame.
MOTHER. I had no secret from you but my pain at
  knowing that while I was heavy with child
  you lay with all the wrenches.
STEVAN. Twisting my words again, with your
  woman's tongue!

MOTHER. You're brave enough to handle wild steers
with your naked fists, but you'll lie to me
till death, you coward.

STEVAN. You twister of words, you sly one. Who
begot him in you? He cannot be my child.
Sound stock, sound to the tenth generation,
my seed.

MOTHER. Don't lie about yourself, you waster. How
you must have filthied your seed that it
could so lower me. Sound as I was, and
clean when you took me.

STEVAN. There is much of you I do not know.

MOTHER. There is much of you I do not know.

STEVAN. But this I know. My first born was not
baptised.

MOTHER. Who was it mocked the sacrament? Not I
—not I.

STEVAN. Would you have had the courage to be a
thing of loathing to the world?

MOTHER. Now the poor thing, unbaptised, will drag
us with him down to hell.

STEVAN. Not us. You, you! This shame to me grew
in your body.

MOTHER. *(On a scream.)* Oh, stop, stop . . .

STEVAN. *(Pleading.)* Don't cry, don't cry . . . Mother
. . . don't cry.

MOTHER. A child after the night of pain, seven
hours old, when the dawn came . . . rosy, sweet, as
milk, lying there in its own basket with the little
cap already on its downy head . . . No!
That morning you did not look at him . . .
nor I.

STEVAN. It is my fault?

MOTHER. *(Even more wearily than he.)* Is it mine?

STEVAN. *(Bitter.)* Well-formed babies who have
smiled up at their fathers die. Many, many.
He is alive, has lived for three and twenty
years. What does God mean?

MOTHER. Can't you ever stop thinking of it?

STEVAN. No. Everywhere I go I drag the secret, drag
the secret with me.

MOTHER. Why do you never go in to him?

STEVAN. You ask that, you, his mother, his loving
  mother? Why have you never dared to look
  at that which you so love?
MOTHER. *(Trembling.)*   Because I love so . . .
  (A knock, the Physician enters.)

SCENE 9

PHYSICIAN. A good evening to you, Stevan Milic, a
  good evening to you, dear mistress of the
  house. I hear there has been a betrothal in
  this house. I give you my best wishes. Yes,
  money flows to money as water does to
  water. And I in my little wagon have
  grown to be sixty with no second nag to
  make up my team. How long is it, Gospodar,
  since I last visited you?
STEVAN. I can tell you to the day, Master Physician.
  It's twelve years.
PHYSICIAN. Gracious heavens. I used to come this way
  more often. Everything gone well with
  you?
STEVAN. As well as God wills.
PHYSICIAN. God, God!! Are you still harping upon
  Him? I, for my part carry Voltaire with
  me. And your . . . what is his name:–
  Marko,–Mirko? The little fellow's grown
  I wager into a strapping bridegroom.
MOTHER. So he has, with the help of God.
PHYSICIAN. And then . . . the other? The bio-
  anatomical-morphophysiological wonder? Pardon
  the heartless phrases of science!
STEVAN. Still living.
PHYSICIAN. On this farm? Still hidden in the little
  stall? *(An acquiescent silence. Physician
  paces up and down with huge strides, then
  remains standing close in front of Stevan.)*
  Stevan Milic, you are the head of a family and a big
  farm, a councillor of the town, one of the
  gentry, and even if this blueblood talk is all
  nonsense, you still owe it to your position
  to be a little broadminded. I know, yes, yes, I know, you

believe that the Evil One in person became the
fruit of your loins, and that you must
forever hide the shame of your
fatherhood. Why do you make a
deformed creature more unhappy than need be? Puny man, you
who measure all creation in your image, what is there that
you do not consider monstrous and deformed?
(Emphatically.)   Nature, the
gambling dreamer, rules everywhere,
and fulfills her own divine intention with
joy more holy than all your scribbled revelations.
Listen to me: *(In the tone of a*
teacher.)   In the womb on our way from seed
to sense we pass through all the stages
of plant and animal life. We are one by
one and all in one the pollen and the lily,
the gnat and the reptile, fish, fowl, and man. Many and many an
obstacle must the child outgrow to become a child. Is that not
natural? Well, in your wife's body the child was
not able to overcome these obstacles
which the lower forms imposed on him.
For each form wants to be supreme and
undying. It is like the ravening ambition
of a king. And these earlier forms
have left their mark upon this creature
which could not fit itself for human life.
But neither is it fit for death. Is that not
natural?

STEVAN. It may be natural.

PHYSICIAN. *(Gruffly.)*   It is very natural. Three out of
every hundred children born are warped
like yours, though to my recollection this
case somewhat exceeds the common. But who
can curb the pranks of nature? The
universe itself, eternally a child, plays, plays, plays.
God and Satan have no hand in the game.

MOTHER. How can you know that?

PHYSICIAN. You fools, fools, fools. You cherish the
horror here in your house. You are all black
with lies, excuses, slyness and reserves. And
so little's needed to release you. In the big
city, there on the other side of the river,

are homes for crippled humans, for monsters
of this sort, homes where the unhappy
creatures are kept clean and guarded, and
allowed to savor their poor twilit lives. The
spider has its pleasure, the otter and the eel,
why not a half-man? But seriously . . . give me
this sport of nature. I will take him to the
city, to that home. The journey will not
cost you dear. For when science stands to
gain I gladly trim my bills.

STEVAN. That will not do. People would hear of it.

MOTHER. He would be seen. No night would be
black enough to hide such a journey.

PHYSICIAN. Right! I would be at no pains to hide him.

MOTHER. *(Quickly.)* I'll never, never let him go.

STEVAN. Tell me! When he's entered in this house
will his name, which is mine as well, be
written down?

PHYSICIAN. Yes, indeed, Stevan Milic.

STEVAN. Never! No! Never!

PHYSICIAN. Oh, you . . . *(Swallows the insult.)* Why
not?

STEVAN. Sir—we are ashamed.

PHYSICIAN. Did you make the world?

STEVAN. You are a bachelor and a bookworm. You cannot
understand us.

PHYSICIAN. You cannot be helped. Never again will I say
another word. But be warned! Your neighbors have
noses.

STEVAN. My secret is well guarded.

PHYSICIAN. Very well. Then give me the key to his stall.
I'm more than a little eager to see how the wonder
has grown up. *(Stevan hesitates.)* Have
no fear. I would be no scientist if I could pass by
such a wonder. It is years ago but I
remember the place well.

STEVAN. *(Gives him the key.)* Take care of yourself
when you're with him.

PHYSICIAN. A doctor is a soldier. Many's the giant madman
these old bones have tamed. Wait for
me. *(Exit.)*

STEVAN. Mother, bring a light. *(Mother goes.)*

PHYSICIAN. *(Sticks his head in at the door.)*   Did you
    give me that key before?
STEVAN. You just took it.
PHYSICIAN. *(Searching his pockets.)*   Did I? My taper
    . . . my flint . . . Ah, here it is. Oh, I am
    getting old. I'm getting old.
STEVAN. Take care of yourself, Master. It's getting
    dark. *(Physician disappears.)*

SCENE 10

(The Mother brings the light, then silence.)
STEVAN. As soon as the wedding's over, I shall go on a
    pilgrimage to Mount Athos.
MOTHER. And leave me?
STEVAN. I will keep nothing. Mirko is old enough
    When I return he shall take over the whole
    place and my position, as my heir.
MOTHER. And we?
STEVAN. Will flee . . .
MOTHER. *(Laughs maliciously.)* With him?
STEVAN. Perhaps I'll gather strength enough upon
    the pilgrimage to talk to Mirko. I must find
    the strength to tell him everything.
MOTHER. You will leave your son an evil house with
    pious speeches.
STEVAN. That is true. But sooner or later he must
    know. I'd rather journey to the monks of
    Temesvar.
MOTHER. Oh, husband! Cowardly as ever. Must your son,
    who still lives happily, carry the burden
    you've thrown down?
STEVAN. You are right. I will be silent.
MOTHER. *(Quickly.)*   And what's to happen when
    we die?
STEVAN. We daren't die.
MOTHER. Death might come to me this very hour.
STEVAN. *(Clinging tightly to her.)* No, my companion.
    I need you–to share my secret.
MOTHER. And I need you for the sake of the child
    that is your child too. If you were to die
    and leave me I'd go mad.

STEVAN. We are no longer human.

MOTHER. Because we no longer need each other for
each other's sake.

STEVAN. There's no way out.

MOTHER. No. Not even if we both should kill ourselves
this hour. Mirko, the unsuspecting would
have to find out everything tomorrow.

STEVAN. *(Agonized.)*   I will speak to him tonight.

MOTHER. Speak . . . keep silent . . . speak . . . To
what end? I can see Mirko's face. And she? She's a
smart one. I hate her already.

STEVAN. Not even death my refuge. *(Softly, to the
mother.)*   Accursed!

SCENE 11

(A Messenger enters.)

MESSENGER. The old men are assembled in the big
house in council. They ask the Gospodar if they
are still to wait.

STEVAN. Let them wait a little longer. But if I take
too long, let them begin the meeting. Say
that to the Starsina. *(Messenger exits.)*

MOTHER. The joy in your eyes, the joy at not having
to be in the house tonight near him, with
me . . .

STEVAN. Yes, joy, joy indeed. I breathe, I breathe
relief because I do not have to be here all this
evening.

MOTHER. *(Whimpering.)* Don't leave me alone, Father,
take me with you, don't leave me alone
here in the house. *(Stevan stands rigid for a moment
intensely thinking.)* . . . Ah you are not
listening to me.

STEVAN. *(Very curtly.)*   Go now. The doctor, I
want to be alone with him.
(Mother goes off slowly rear. Physician enters.)

SCENE 12

PHYSICIAN. *(Shaken.)* It almost makes you turn to
God again. Cool-headed as I am, I dripped with sweat.

(Has to sit down.) Nature is boundless and
imagination nothing. Milic,
I do not envy you.

STEVAN. The braggart's trembling now.

PHYSICIAN. You have not seen him since birth?

STEVAN. A servant brought him up.

PHYSICIAN. Well! Formerly I still could comprehend it.
But now! The ancients.believed that at high
noon something could spring from
quivering nature, formless but visible horrible
and full of majesty, blasting all that
crossed it, like the vision of the Whole
compressed into a second . . . Understand
me or not—I saw something like that just
now.

STEVAN. Have you ever spoken of my misfortune to
anyone, Master?

PHYSICIAN. Never. That goes without saying. I am a
physician.

STEVAN. *(Painfully.)* I must speak to you, Master.

PHYSICIAN. That I can well imagine.

STEVAN. *(Struggling for breath.)* Master! He . . .
he . . . must go away.

PHYSICIAN. Of course. And you can thank me for it.
Listen. Give me a big wagon with a team of your
best horses. It's a troublesome business,
but I'll bring the creature to the place where
it belongs. *(Scratches himself under his
wig.)* Wonder if they'll accept it? Well
that's my affair.

STEVAN. That's . . . not what I want.

PHYSICIAN. What do you want?

STEVAN. He must go differently.

PHYSICIAN. Differently?

STEVAN. You must have something in your pocket,
something . . . that you can't give much of to
sick people . . .

PHYSICIAN. Poison?

STEVAN. *(Relieved.)* Poison.

PHYSICIAN. And you want me, just like that, to make
away with a creature I did not create; something
which breathes, eager for life? Such an

extraordinary, if you will allow
me, master prank of nature, into the bargain?

STEVAN. *(Suddenly the humbly stupid peasant.)*
Yes, yes, do that!

PHYSICIAN. Sir, I am a physician. I am here to lengthen
life.

STEVAN. Poison . . . in . . . his . . . food!

PHYSICIAN. I understand you. So that's what you want.
But we doctors have our superstitions too, and hold
with many of Mohammed's maxims. I think,
you see, that we are reborn in all the patients
we help from life to death. Salaam
Aleikum! *(Exit.)*

STEVAN. Mother! Mother!

SCENE 13

(Mother enters swiftly.)

STEVAN. The Bible! The Bible! *(Mother moves the
desk with the church calendar to the light. Stevan
leafs it through with mad fingers.)* Abraham,
Isaac, Abraham, Isaac . . .

MOTHER. *(Totters to him, screaming.)* No! Mother
Mary! Not that! Not that!

STEVAN. Yes! That! That! *(Savoring the
words.)* And you will hold the light.

MOTHER. Agh . . . I carried him without knowing
and now . . . woe, woe. . . .

STEVAN. My house must be made over. I must do it
for Mirko, for his future and his children.
Way for Mirko!

MOTHER. Mirko . . . no! *(Beaming.)* It's him . . .
him . . . him I love.

STEVAN. Quiet.

MOTHER. Never seen . . .

STEVAN. You'll see him now.

MOTHER. *(Rigid, slowly.)* Unloved . . .

STEVAN. *(Grabs the gun from the wall.)* Take the
lamp.

MOTHER. *(Looks into the distance.)* His little heart
. . . a human heart.

STEVAN. *(Stamps.)* Keep still!

MOTHER. His blood . . . my blood . . .

STEVAN. Mine. I gave it. I take it.

MOTHER. *(Tenderly—tenderly.)*   Mine . . . Mine!
And so . . .

STEVAN. Come! *(Suddenly Babka appears in the
shadows.)* Not you! Babka, take the light!

BABKA. *(Quietly.)* I suckled him, but I obey the
master. *(Holds the lamp high.)*

STEVAN. *(At the door.)*   Lord of life! I do not know
what your plan is, but I am of it. *(Off Babka off.
Mother alone in the dark.)*

MOTHER. Nothing . . . No remembrance . . . Never
seen . . . Nothing . . . Nothing left. Was
in me. Now, now . . . his heart . . . beats in
mine. *(She listens, listens. Awaking.)* The shot! Why
is there no shot? Mother of God!. . . *(She
falls in a faint.*

SCENE 14

*(Quick steps outside. Stevan holds to the doorpost, swaying. Babka, with the
lamp, behind him.)*

STEVAN. The key, the key! The old man left the door
unlocked. He's gone, broken loose,
escaped! Ah, ah! *(Shakes the unconscious
mother.)*   Mother, do you hear? He's free!
Free!

(Curtain.)

ACT 2

*(Scene: Council Room. A low ceiling. In the background a long table stretching
all the way across the stage with a corresponding bench behind it. Right, a little
table for the presiding officer and the clerk. Left, an oven with an oven bench.
The ten elders have already gathered. Some sit on the long bench with their jugs,
some walk back and forth talking, or change their seats. The Starsina sits at the
little table and watches the Clerk cutting a pen. Krasnokraj and Modrygor as
"Elders" sit on the oven bench talking. The little oil lamp hanging above the
presiding officer's table is the only light.)*

SCENE 1

STARSINA. *(Raps on the table.)* Are we going to wait
    any longer?
SEVERAL VOICES. *(From the long table.)* The bell in the linden
    has not rung yet. *(The conversations continue.)*
ELDER OF KRASNOKRAJ. Can you remember a meeting when
    he hasn't kept us waiting?
ELDER OF MODRYGOR. It is usually unhappiness that
    keeps us men at home.
KRASNOKRAJ. He? He hasn't a wish in the world.
    Today he betrothed his son to the daughter
    of the rich man of Kouxelnivrh.
MODRYGOR. But they say the bride is a trouble-maker.
KRASNOKRAJ. He was given cattle from the land
    of the Magyars for breeding. His stock is
    better than ours.
MODRYGOR. But it is always suffering from worms and
    sore feet.
KRASNOKRAJ. He has cut timber and floated his long logs
    down our stream to the Danube.
MODRYGOR. But the merchant from the north still owes
    him for them.
KRASNOKRAJ. Yes, that is true. There's always a "but"
    for him. What his right hand wins his left hand
    loses. Always a curse on the play.
MODRYGOR. Not master enough to my mind. He might be
    a real master. He has the brains.
KRASNOKRAJ. It is his eyes, I tell you. That's where the
    trouble lies. He is forever hiding something.
    A dog hides the stolen bone. He has an evil
    treasure hidden somewhere.
MODRYGOR. Eyes that roam—trouble at home.
KRASNOKRAJ. Things are not going too well for us, either.
    All this trouble these last years with the
    landless and the returning emigrants. The flies
    settle thickly on the carcass.
MODRYGOR. We will take council upon that today.
KRASNOKRAJ. You can't go peacefully cross-country any
    more. Out of the grainfield, out from behind
    tree shadows, out of the ditches, suddenly you
    see an unknown face with its eager,

hungry eyes. Eh! An honest man shudders
at all the shadowy dancers.

MODRYGOR. The Turk has grown sleepy. We who were once
weak, miserable, and oppressed by him are
grown great. But the children of the men
who had to fear his vengeance, the exiles
and the refugees, have also smelt the green
tang of our air. They have a claim on it.

KRASNOKRAJ. If they turn against Mahomet, they will turn
against us. We are too well off. Stevan Milic's
fists are much too soft.

MODRYGOR. He has troubles enough in his own
precinct. His own people, so they say, won't stand behind him.

ELDER OF MEDEGYA. *(Coming over to the others.)* Have you
heard the strange things our brother of Pozar
has been telling us? In their town a dead man
goes about sucking the blood of the living in the
night. Next morning there is a little
mark no larger than a mole on the breasts of
those he attacks. (The Emperor has sent out
a commission.) They pricked the corpse with a flowering thorn.
Fresh red blood burst from the heart, the eyes
glowed and there was no stench to the
flesh.

KRASNOKRAJ. Yes, witches and vampires are breeding. A
werewolf from the mountains of Woljo
. . . has . . . *(Distant bell rings.)*

STARSINA. *(Raps three times.)* The meeting will begin.
(All take their places.) Clerk, read the
order of the day.

CLERK. The business of this evening's meeting,
ad punctum, primum, et ultimum is as
follows: The cases of the landless, the
returned natives and vagabonds, the question
being whether they shall be ordered on or
allowed to settle, or what legal measures
shall be taken. Further, audience is to be
given to three of their members, men whom
they have chosen as spokesmen, to
wit: the American who does not know his
father's name, Teiterlik, a tumbler and acrobat,
and finally the Jew, Red Feiwel,

born here. The said three persons are outside
the door. Finally a vote and decision on the
above-mentioned case. *(Sits.)*

STARSINA. Has anyone an objection to this procedure?
(Silence.) To the procedure? *(Silence.)*
You elders know that it has been unsafe for
a year and a day to travel on the streets
paths, and by-roads leading from village to
village. When the herdsman goes his
rounds of a morning it is not uncommon
for him to come on a cold corpse by the
hedgerow. It is not the fox that steals all
the fowl, nor the hawk that lifts all the
lambs from the fold. We know the guilty persons well. The
Turkish Bassa in his mercy and
wisdom has appointed honorable and
well born men of our race for our
governors, and the peasants no longer pay tribute
to the turban, but to a Christian landowner. Well we know the
men who sneak in to poison their
minds. Let us decide wisely so as not to lose the
good will of the peasants. And now I propose that we let in the
men who wait outside the door. *(All the elders
raise their hands in approval.)*
Let them in. *(Clerk off.)*

SCENE 2

*(The American, Teiterlik, and Feiwel enter; the Clerk comes back to his former
place. The American is pockmarked, dressed in ragged farm clothes with long
leather boots and a sombrero. Teiterlik has one upstanding clown's curl on his
otherwise bald head, his nose is snub, eaten away, his body is emaciated in his
stage tights, with one red, one yellow leg. Feiwel has a full head, red cheeks,
kaftan, and fur cap. All three bow before the Starsina and the Elders, the
American slightly, the Rope-walker and the Jew to the ground.)*

STARSINA. The fool speaks first.
TEITERLIK. *(Makes a few forced, stiff pirouetting steps).*
Highly honored, excellent and
landed sirs! The world is big, the heart little; a
little mill of flesh that grinds and grinds yet never grinds out the
last grain of our hope.

FEIWEL. *(Maliciously.)* He he! He he!

TEITERLIK. There are many cities. There is London,
and the Thames flows through it, the
stream from which the fogs come and
where the state drowns criminals and heretics.
Then there is Vienna with its Prater. There
the Emperor rides in a golden wagon and ten
thousand riders follow him. And Naples,
too, known awhile back as Babylon, which is another city
than Lisbon. In this here Naples is the mountain
called Vesuvius, the chimney of hell. . .

FEIWEL. Oi, the stupid. In the newspapers I read of
that mountain.

AMERICAN. Pah, you never swallowed salt water, that's
why your tongue wags so fast.

STARSINA. Let the tumbler talk.

TEITERLIK. Worshipful landowners. You landed
gentlemen! I have been in all these cities and
a thousand cities, markets, and towns more,
good and bad. We always halted,
whether I was master or apprenticed to the
troupe, at the edge of the town where the
commons are gray and shaggy like the pelt
of an old dog. On Sunday, at sunset, the
silver would rain on our plates, but on
weekdays we often went to sleep without a
bite. Of course later on I was not alone, for
I found my woman—but in my trade you
can't enjoy the women much. It weakens supple
joints and makes the eyes see the
tight-rope double and triple. Many's the
comrades I lost that couldn't say no to
them.

AMERICAN. Make it shorter, man.

TEITERLIK. How fine it all is when you're young. You
get up early from under the leaves—
a-cracking your joints, and sling a stone at
the sun. But suddenly, worshipful landowners,
this feeling, this awful feeling, comes over you. When your joints
are too
stiff for the job, you feel the shame of
smirking and bowing, and—not being able to

sit at a Christian table. At night the
cough gnaws at your back like a wolf and you
can knock your heart out at the hospital
and there's no welcome for you. Yes, the
pain was there and would not let go.
And I thought of my old folks and how they tilled their fields in
this place, and I called to mind the doorstep of their
home here, where as a little boy I used to sit. A
piece of land–for the love of God! It is
like sleep to the weary. Weary am I, and
those with me are weary. You worshipful
landowners, you are rich, with many unused
acres, hills and bottomlands that you
leave fallow. Give us, the children who
have come back–give us of your plenty.
(Softly.) We are weary.
FEIWEL. *(Very loudly, to the Starsina.)* I am the
Jew Feiwel. I should think you know that.
Who does not know me?
AMERICAN. *(Pushes him away.)*   No one asked you to
speak.
FEIWEL. And who asked you to speak?
STARSINA. The Jew comes last.
FEIWEL. *(With deliberate, ironical gesture of
mouth and hand.)* Don't I know it.
AMERICAN. Mesch'schurs and Señores. America is a
wonderful country. It is called the new
world and the men there talk little. Therefore,
I will talk briefly but to the point.
Across the great water, there was a war between
the new men and the old English. The
new men,–(I fought on their side),–won.
And that is well. Their land is
monstrous, huge. The Indians, brave fighters,
were conquered by the firewater. The
new men were not born there but came
from the whole world, to settle inland and
on the coast. They are free and obey no
one. The stranger knocks at the blockhouse
at night and the head of the house asks
him no questions about who, whither, or
whence, but pushes him up a chair to

the fire and they smoke great cigars, these
self-reliant souls. No man thinks himself
better than the rest, and the son of the
hanged and the daughter of the whore
have nothing to fear there. They know
nothing of high and low, landowners and
landless men. The government gives away
land with both hands to all men, and they
grow grain, cut timber, pasture flocks, become
rich, and no one is downtrodden.

    I was one of them, and I did well. Then
this cursed sneaking homesickness came
over me, and now I have come back here
and am ashamed to name my father's
name. I who was rich lie with the beggars,
a beggar myself, with hate in my heart. I tell
you this so you may act like the Americans, and
put aside your greed and give each of
your countrymen some of the waste land.
Then a new race may grow here, rich in
experience and goods, and no one live in
misery. We that have nothing to eat and no
place to sleep have a claim on you, you
farmers! Beware of our hatred!

MURMUR OF THE ELDERS. Who dares threaten us?

AMERICAN. I—I who have travelled far and know the
world much better than you left-behinds.
If you knew anything of business, you would
not let new sources of revenue escape
you.

TEITERLIK. See our weariness! Only a patch of ground
and place for the beggar's hut.

FEIWEL. *(Stepping before the table, fumbles the
question.)* I?

STARSINA. *(Contemptuously.)* Jew!

FEIWEL. *(Waving his hands about for silence.)* Ssh
now!—Am I or am I not the important person
that I am? Do I belong with these
beggars here, with whom do I belong? Who
brings the women needles, thread, yarn, wool, buttons, cotton,
handkerchiefs, kerchief silks? Who buys the toys for the
children, the tools you need for house and kitchen,

wick lamps, and oiled paper? Who brings
your mousetraps, bracelets, pipes?
Who travels into the world for you
Who runs the life out of his body for love of you?
Who brings you the latest news and
gossip? But for me who would know that
in France they have kicked out their king and
that the Messiah will arise there? The *Turks* are a good people.
The Jews may live among them.
They can come home *Erev Shabbos* and light their
candles without fear. But you? I was born here, as
without fear. But you, I was born here, as
my father, *Olav Hosholom,* was born here. But my
grandchildren yet will have to live with the
gallows-birds. That's you! You! You!

SCENE 3

(Stevan enters quickly. He carries the gun in his hand. Three of the Elders rise and the Starsina leaves his place.)

FEIWEL. *(Resigned.)*   May a Jew only say two words?

STEVAN. *(Taking the Starsina's place.)*   Clerk, send a rider after
the Physician, to catch up with his wagon
outside the city. Tell him I want him to
come back. *(Clerk off. Stevan stares into
the air, long. The Elders shake their heads
and mutter.)*

ELDERS. What is the matter with him?

STEVAN. *(To the three delegates.)*   You?

TEITERLIK. *(Bows low, his arms crossed.)*   Land, Excellency,
a bit of land from your overflow, for us, the
miserable, who have come home.
It's time to settle down and be human.

AMERICAN. *(Gruffly.)*   Rich man! Give of your waste
land to the beggars. Give them their share.
They're sturdy people. It's not a charity, but an investment.

STEVAN. How many are you?

FEIWEL. Excellence, I have the count. In round
numbers, four hundred: men, women, children,
Jew, Gipsy, and Christian.

STEVAN. What do the Elders say?

KRASNOKRAJ. Never ground and land to the worthless.

MODRYGOR. We must weigh the matter.

STEVAN. *(In an uncontrollable outburst of rage.)*
Nothing's to be weighed. *(He presses toward
the three. Trembling, they retreat.)*
Damn you! Have you human faces? No,
not human faces. Ha, pockmarks, nose, missing teeth, popeyes,
foxbeard. The face of the ageless, shrewd,
goatlike ape; his face, the face that
must stay hidden. There, there's where it broke loose. Our ances-
tors covered up there secret sin, but now, no cloth is thick
enough to smother it and it walks abroad. Oh,
you sons of the blood sin, would you settle among us to whom
the land belongs, who have bettered and built it? Among us
sons of light, us? By day and by night shall these scarecrows surround us in church and inn? Do you want to walk
upright or on all fours among us? Away, away! Go, go!

KRASNOKRAJ. I don't understand all the Gospodar is saying
there, but one thing is true. You are not
peasants and never will be, for none of you
is fit to till, lazy as you arc, and practised
in nothing but thieving. You're neither
clean nor decent, just a vain and worthless
lot who want to hurt your betters, and
that's us.

MODRYGOR. Do not be too hasty.

TEITERLIK. I have worked much, in danger of my life,
to satisfy your love of wonders. None of
you graybeards has dared as much as I, no,
not if there's a king among you.

AMERICAN. Sir, Over there I was one of you! And over
there a man who throws insults at decent men
is dead a long time. *(Clerk enters again.)*

FEIWEL. *(Persuading the Elders, vehemently.)*
Can't you see it? Milic is drunk!

STEVAN. *(In a mighty voice.)* Away. Out of our country
by to-morrow. Let no landless man show
himself here after three days' time.
Ten pair of bloodhounds will track on you.
And those who resist will be tied to a tree
and flogged.

A FEW VOICES. We're here too. This is not decided on.

STEVAN. It has been ordered. Clerk, write the order.

AMERICAN. Man! Such an order befits no one but the
   Pasha of the Kaimakamluks. Where shall
   we poor devils go?
STEVAN. To the mines, to the harbors, to foreign
   lands. Only let me be free again. *(Slowly.)*
   Oh, you outcasts who call nothing your own,
   if you knew how happy you are. *(Beside himself, swings the gun to hit the*
   three.) Away with you. *(Elders near the madman in great*
   excitement.)

SCENE 4

(Enter Babka with a lantern. She stands at the door.)
STEVAN. *(Screams to her.)*   Where?
BABKKA. Nowhere.
STEVAN. No trace?
BABKA. None!
STEVAN. Speak!
BABKA. Looked . . . nothing.
STEVAN. Screams?
BABKA. None! Vanished!
STEVAN. With whose aid?
BABKA. The devil's!
STEVAN. Elders! The meeting is over. I must go
   hunting. *(Stevan tears the lantern out of*
   Babka'a hand and runs off.)
ELDERS. *(Scared, huddled, confusedly.)* He is mad.

(Curtain.)

ACT 3

SCENE 1

(Garden of a decayed inn. Left a shed which serves as a residence and inn. Right
front a table surrounded by benches, further to the back a second, wholly
worm-eaten table without a bench. In the distance, rear, screened by trees and
shubbery, the glare of campfires and many shadows moving here and there.
Distant, thin music and the stamping of feet on the dance-floor. A full moon. In
the foreground, surrounded by a crowd of children and listeners among them
fifteen year old Kruna, stands white-bearded Bogoboj. At the table front, alone,
sits Juvan, the student.)

BOGOBOJ. *(His eyes closed, as if in a trance.)* On these clear
    moonlit nights they ride over the backs
    of the hills and lie on the ledges, the
    summits, the plateaus. Their sheep-boys
    shepherds, and milk-maids, and herdsmen roam with them and
    guard the flocks. But the serving folk are not
        immortal like them. They only live a thousand years. The animals
        they herd are mostly roe and goats; no matter how high they climb
        and how wildly they frolic they never stray off to the haunts of men.
KRUNA. Why do they have only goats, father?
BOGOBOJ. They live on goatmilk. But what they prepare in their
    big cauldrons when the mountain fires
    burn, that no one knows.
KRUNA. Will they ever come back again?
BOGOBOJ. Oh, their hearts are trembling now with
    the joy of return. They hug the trees in
    monstrous glee and they listen to the pulsing
    sap of the pine. They kiss the hardy blossoms of
    the mountain-tops and feel bittersweet
    on their lips the taste of their own
    immortality. With loving hands they fondle the fur
    of the sacred untamed herds. The goats bleat and they answer the
    song from the depths of their souls   *(Weaving his head rhythmically.)*   I
    hear in the wind the song of the goats.
KRUNA. And mortals?
BOGOBOJ. Some of them have come down from the
    hills and loved a mortal. So they have children,
    outposts, in many places. And in
    their eyes a diamond burns. *(To Juvan.)*
    Hear, son of the sorceress.
KRUNA. And have they messengers?
BOGOBOJ. The devils who serve them. *(To Juvan.)*
    Hear, son of the sorceress.
JUVAN. *(Beating his fist wildly on the table.)*   Don't
    call me that, old idiot. The midwife was
    my mother. Not even the money for her
    coffin could her magic win her.
BOGOBOJ. And your father, unbeliever?
JUVAN. I do not know my father. You know that.
BOGOBOJ. Indeed you do not know your father, son of
    the sorceress.
JUVAN. Be still! General of the billygoats. You're crazy.

KRUNA. Don't cross the old man. He is a prophet.

JUVAN. A gabbler, that's what he is.

BOGOBOJ. You cannot cross me, student. I alone know
your mission.

JUVAN. *(Carried away, to himself.)* Mission? I, of all
men in that monstrous, strange city the
lowest? Bed on the benches. Winter. Women
gliding by. They and their rustling,
God rot them. Sitting at the oven in the classroom, jealous of those
seated closer, hearing nothing in my hunger and exhaustion.
Cheekbones jutting. Hammering Greek into flabby rich children
for one gulden a month ... No! That was not all. They learned to
know me ... And now I am here. Among you. Among you.

BOGOBOJ. It was ordained that you should come.

KRUNA. Once they chose a man like you.

A VERY OLD WOMAN. "And purple the slippers of our Prince."

AN OLD MAN. Strong youth, you, a writer and a reader,
are the man to help us.

KRUNA. *(Comes closer to the table.)* Why do you
stay with us?

JUVAN. *(After a pause.)* Because I hate the others
and you mean nothing to me. I hate them.
Perhaps I hate you too.

KRUNA. You always sit apart.

JUVAN. Lucky for you. I'd spoil your fun.

KRUNA. You haven't had much fun, have you?

JUVAN. *(Slowly, simply.)* True. Perhaps I've only
had one joy in all my life, the time I saw a
forest burn ...

BOGOBOJ. *(Softly.)* Rulers of our people. He is your son.

JUVAN. *(To himself.)* And that's no lie. *(Aloud.)*
And why should I not sit apart? The biggest
fools among you are gone to the potato
diggers to beg them for a bit of land. Soon
you will all be farmers and farmers' women,
stingy eaters of prune mash and lovers
of stuffy rooms. Soon you will have forgotten
how to steal. *(Spits.)*

A MAN. Spit at us, do you? What do you want?

JUVAN. I want nothing. Nothing of you, nothing
of myself. Only to lie on a cliff, smoking, staring at the
treetops, drinking.

BOGOBOJ. *(Softly.)* Empty must be the jar into which
    they pour their milk. *(Juvan laughs.)*
KRUNA. Why do you laugh, student?
JUVAN. That is my greatest talent. I can laugh because
    I'm bored. You bore me. Perhaps
    that's why I stay with you.
BOBOOBOJ. That is a lie you crafty one. Know that you wait.
JUVAN. *(Struck.)* I wait! Yes! Since childhood! I
    wait.
BOGOBOJ. And they have ordained . . .
JUVAN. Innkeeper! Ljuben!
BOGOBOJ. . . . They are agreed.
JUVAN. *(Loudly.)* Innkeeper! Ljuben!
BOGOBOJ. And it shall come to pass . . .
JUVAN. *(Bellows.)* Innkeeper!
BOGOBOJ. And it must come . . .
JUVAN. *(Sharply, excited.)* What?
BOGOBOJ. You know.
JUVAN. *(Jumping up.)* Then woe . . . *(Inkeeper enters,
    Juvan laughs.)* Woc to the innkeeper
INNKEEPER. Hey?
JUVAN. A bottle.
INNKEEPER. Money first . . . you know that.
JUVAN. *(Throws down three silver gulden.)* Dog!
    (Innkeeper whistles through his teeth.)
    Just for that you'll have to crawl for it.
    *(Innkeeper off hastily. Juvan declaims
    gravely.)*
        If I've not a farthing
        I'll ride in a coach
        And if I've a million
        I'll starve with the pack.
(Innkeeper brings the bottle.)

SCENE 2

*(Teiterlik, the American, Feiwel. Behind them a crowd of motley vagabonds.
Bogoboj and his audience go to meet them.)*

AMERICAN. All's lost, you people.
CHORUS. Curse them. Curse them!
AMERICAN. Your packs and beggar's traps up on the
    wagons quickly.

YOUNG MAN. Why do we yield?

OLD MAN. The powder horn hangs by their hearthstones.

AMERICAN. To-morrow they will drive us from our home land with their dogs.

JUVAN. Good! That's right!

CHORUS. Where can we go?

TEITERLIK. Who's playing still and dancing? *(Distant bass rhythms stop.)* You poor things! We poor things! Whither to-morrow?

CHORUS. Whither to-morrow? No one to lead us— no one to help us.

FEIWEL. What's that? No one leads? No one helps? I made a speech for you before the council. You should have heard me. They ought to write my speech down and put it in the papers. Hey, Mr. Ropedancer? Hey, Mr. American? How was my speech? What kind of lawyer am I? *(To the many who now come from the dance floor.)* All honor, says I, to the needy and they shook their fists in my face and their knives, and still I spoke on for your rights.

AMERICAN. That's a lie, man.

FEIWEL. *(Softly.)* Ssh, Mr. American, that's politics! *(Loudly.)* And now I speak to you! I have connections in the highest circles. The king of Sweden is my friend. I'll write him a petition. Sure! I'm a Jew, and brave. Why are you frightened? You are so many? Why do you let yourselves be chased? Is man an animal? *(He has grown moody.)*

JUVAN. *(Very loudly.)* Light on the table, Ljuben!

FEIWEL. *(Suddenly breaks off, afraid.)* Always at your service. *(Dives into the crowd.)*

TEITERLIK. *(To Juvan.)* You in the laced coat and scholar's cap, help us now

AMERICAN. You didn't get your learning in a Sunday school.

TEITERLIK. You are learned. They will fear you.

JUVAN. *(Turns brusquely.)* What do you want?

AMERICAN. You have to talk to them.

JUVAN.   I? With them? With them? It bores me.

TEITERLIK. Beg him, the Gospodar, in our behalf.

JUVAN.   *(Slowly, sharply.)* It bores me. *(Innkeeper lights a lamp.*

AMERICAN.   Ask them to give us more time.

JUVAN.   You were born upon this land but there's no land left for you.

TEITERLIK. Think of the children wandering forever; no church, no teaching!

JUVAN.   You teach them to dance on the tightrope and stand on their heads.

AMERICAN. Comrade! Why talk like that? Something must be done. You can help. I'll help too.

JUVAN.   I will help you if the devil helps you. *(Bogoboj murmers strange words.)*

AMERICAN. Well at least give us some advice, man, if you're so brainy.

JUVAN.   *(Almost phlegmatic.)* Advice enough.
Steal. Steal ducks, pigs, calves, but don't
forget the iron things you kill with. And
do you want some fine advice? Disguise
yourselves as medicant monks; steal in,
ruin the women, pervert the children. Pretend
you're doctors, give out tinctures, sell
henbane juice as a love philtre; or pour
brandy on their open wounds. *(Suddenly in
earnest.)* And here's the best advise of all.
Rip the big limbs from off the trees,
strip them, and dip them in pitch.

AMERICAN. I'll follow that last advice, man!

FEIWEL. *(Close to Juvan's ear.)* I know a good
place. Mehmet Muchlis in the town. He
rents weapons. *(Juvan brusquely turns his
back on them all.)*

BOGOBOJ. *(Rising.)* Will you be awake when the
hour comes, son of the unknown father?

JUVAN. *(Over his shoulder.)* You know I sleep
only by day. *(The crowd withdraws to the
rear.)*

(Stanja and Mirko enter.)

MIRKO. This is damned unreasonable, Stanjoschka!
    What are these vagabonds to us? They
    own nothing, they are dirty, they do not
    go to communion. Our fathers are fighting
    them. Let's go back.
STANJA. But I don't like your friends on the dancing
    green tinkling their silver chains.
MIRKO. How can you talk so? Duko Petkovic is
    there: he was one of the Emperor's Hussars
    at Temesvar for a whole year, and his old
    man has put by a good ten thousand. And
    your Trifunovic who inherited the bakery
    and knows the great Pasha. *(Stanja's
    expression stops him in midsentence.)* You
    cat! You woman! I know you want to take
    my friends from me; comrades I've known
    since I was a child, who understand me if
    I so much as blink at them.
    Woe to me that I am in love with you,
    sniffing the odor of your body like a hound.
    I love, so I must bend to you, you cold one.
STANJA. Go to your friends.
MIRKO. I can't because you tell me to. But if I weren't
    such a coward . . . Jesus–Jesus. I would
    leave you standing here.
STANJA. But I am tired. I want to sit down.
MIRKO. That table with the candle! No . . . there's
    a man sitting there.
STANJA. The table's all right. Come.
MIRKO. A man is sitting there, I told you.
STANJA. What does it matter? Aren't you my
    betrothed? Can't you protect me?
MIRKO. *(Whimpering.)* Oh . . . I don't want to . . .
    oh!
STANJA. Don't stand there looking stupid. Come.
    (Both go to Juvan's table.)
MIRKO. *(Very stiffly.)* We came along the road
    very late. Hm . . . hm . . . *(Juvan stares at*

him in silent calm.) You will allow us . . .
*(Juvan stares, without answering, at
Mirko. Mirko confused.)* We don't disturb you?

JUVAN. *(After a pause.)* This is an inn for all comers.
And you are noble guests such as do
not come every day.

MIRKO. *(Vaguely oppressed, to Stanja.)* Come
away! *(Juvan moves to one side, Mirko
and Stanja sit so that Stanja is behind the
light, with a man on either side of her and
almost in darkness. Mirko whispers.)* His
scholar's cap and laced coat! Is it the student?

STANJA. He? I never saw him before.

MIRKO. *(To himself.)* Suppose she's lying!

MIRKO. *(To Juvan.)* We're here because we lost
our way, brother. You can't help roaming
about, festival time.

JUVAN. Now none of your silly tricks, Mirko Milic.

MIRKO. He knows me! Damn it! *(In flattered
tones to Stanja.)* I'm not Gospodar's son for
nothing. *(To Juvan.)* And now! We'll have a drink
together! *(Takes coins from his pocket.)*
I'll treat.

JUVAN. One minute, friend! Who sat here first? I!
Therefore I am the host, the land owner,
the king, and you are guests. You are my
guests! He! Ho! Ljuben!

MIRKO. Allow me— *(Innkeeper comes.)*

JUVAN. Two of the same! *(Innkeeper off.)*

MIRKO. Allow me, and forgive me. You are respectable,
a follower of the arts, with your laced coat,
but . . .

JUVAN. But . . .

MIRKO. Poor! Anyone can see that. You belong to
the crowd over there by the fires. *(Enter
Innkeeper with two bottles. Mirko counts
the coins into his own hand ringingly.)*
You'd just as soon have me pay, wouldn't
you?

JUVAN. *(Takes Mirko's hand as it lies on the table
and closes it.)* Don't worry. Even if it's
stolen my money's good. *(To the Innkeeper.)*

The ruby glasses, you ass, for guests
like these.

INNKEEPER. Knew that.

MIRKO. I meant no offence.

JUVAN. No matter. *(Innkeeper places Bohemian
glasses on the table.)* These glasses are
stolen too.

STANJA. You're an awkward boor. You'll never do
anything but shame me. You can learn
from him what manners are.

MIRKO. *(In hurt tones.)* Stanjoschka, you! *(Juvan pours.)*

STANJA. *(Slightly exaggerated.)* I like this place.
Air that tastes like honey floats down from
the hills. The new mown hay has a different
smell than the dry grass heaped in
your meadows. *(She laughs up the scale.)*

JUVAN. *(Gravely.)* Why are you cooing, daughter
of the rich?

STANJA. I laugh at the burning moths. At the bats
up there I laugh . . .

MIRKO. *(Between his teeth.)* You've found your
tongue, silent one!

STANJA. If I was silent with you, I speak now,
grumbler, and laugh.

JUVAN. I know well how to laugh. But I am never
merry.

STANJA. I drink to the man who is never merry, to
make him so.

JUVAN. *(Quietly.)* Do not touch my glass, rich woman.

MIRKO. Shameless . . . you see? Shameless . . .

STANJA. Do what you like! *(Drains her glass, laughing.)*
It pleases me to sit between two men,
one a well brought up son who sees only
the things he's meant to see, and the other
you, you poacher laced in the laced coat.
(Pointing to the background.) And all
these motley ragged men; they please me,
too.

JUVAN. The same men, daughter of the rich, that
you are going to chase out with your dogs
tomorrow.

STANJA. That shall not be. I say so.

JUVAN. *(Emphatically.)* It shall be—I say so. It
shall be your chase until they turn on you.
Then let it turn again.

MIRKO. *(Rises.)* Stanja, come now. We're going.

STANJA. Go if you like. You can't order me. I'm still
free.

MIRKO. *(Sits.)* You don't know what you're doing.
You're playing with fire.

JUVAN. Mirko Milic, drink. Drink, my guest!

MIRKO. That I will do, student, I am not afraid.
*(Drinks two glasses full, one after the
other.)*

STANJA. Don't drink so much. You know you cannot
stand it, mother's boy! *(Mirko groans.)*

JUVAN. Laugh at her, Milic, she's nothing but a
woman!

MIRKO. *(Speaking thickly.)* Can't . . . think . . .
any more . . .

JUVAN. Why do you look at me so, bride?

STANJA. Did I look at you? Well, I didn't see you then.

JUVAN. What are you thinking?

STANJA. I was just thinking I hate blondes and like
the swarthy lads. *(Mirko shatters his glass.)*
Fool!

JUVAN. *(Gravely.)* A guest's privilege. *(To Stanja.)* You are
mistaken, girl, I am your enemy.

STANJA. If you only were.

JUVAN. You are right. I used too big a word. I do
not love possession, but I love to steal possessions.
I do not love the booty, but I love
to fling it from me.

STANJA. Those who know the merchant's fingers
bless the robber's hand.

JUVAN. *(Leans toward her.)* You're beautiful
enough.

STANJA. Enemy!

JUVAN. With your glistening hair.

STANJA. *(In quiet triumph.)* Enemy!

JUVAN. I am no bed-robber.

MIRKO. *(Starting up in mad rage.)* Ah! Ah! Ah!
You insulted my betrothed. Draw your knife. *(Stands with
his knife raised.)*

JUVAN. *(Leisurely.)* I have not even touched your
    betrothed, Mirko Milic.
MIRKO. Whether you have or haven't, come on!
JUVAN. Go your way! Too early yet for bloodshed.

SCENE 4

(Teiterlik, American, Feiwel, Kruna, the crowd, group about the three.)

VOICES. The son of the Gospodar. The little fellow.
    They're going to fight . . .
MIRKO. Ah! Everything is over now. If you live, I
    must take her like a beggar at your hands.
    So you must die, because I love her.
    Come on!
JUVAN. Is it your will, daughter of the rich? Shall
    we spill blood?
STANJA. It is my will. And may you fall.
JUVAN. Come on, then, Mirko Milic! The moon is
    shining for us. *(Opens his knife. Brilliant growing moon-*
    light. Confusion of voices dies down. Mirko and
    Juvan stand in position with blades
    bared.)

SCENE 5

(Lightening, then quick darkening of the stage. Total darkness for the space of
three pulse-beats. Equally quick lighting of the stage. It seems as though a giant
shadow has passed above them. Endless pause of panic-stricken numbness. Every
one— each petrified in a different attitude, looks in a different direction. Only
the knife falls from Juvan's hand as he stands in a listening attitude as if some
one had called him. At the sound the paralysis breaks into a nameless, hysterical
confession.)

MIRKO. *(In the foreground, his knife still raised.)*
    Come! Or I'll kill you. *(Tears Stanja away with him.*
    Fluttering laugh of fear from the crowd. It is repeated
    on all hands.)
FEIWEL. *Shma Ysroel!*
TEITERLIK. Did you . . . oh, oh, oh, . . . did you see the
    shadow?
CRIES. We saw! . . . We didn't see.
AMERICAN. Quiet, children. The shadow won't eat you.

FIRST VOICE. I saw him. It was a man.
SECOND VOICE. It was no man.
THIRD VOICE. A goat . . . a giant goat.
FOURTH VOICE. No, a man!
FIFTH VOICE. Where did he go? The goat, the goat!
SIXTH VOICE. Turning handsprings down the road.
TEITERLIK. No, no . . . into the house!

SCENE 6

(The Innkeeper rushes out of the house howling, his eyes wild, sinks on his knees.)

INNKEEPER. Holy Mary, pray for us! Holy Anna, pray
    for us! Holy Joseph, pray for us!
AMERICAN. *(Shakes him.)* Speak Ljuben! Calm yourself!
    What did you see?
INNKEEPER. Holy Chrysostome, pray for us! Holy Athanasius,
    pray for us! Cyril and Methodius,
    intercede for us!
AMERICAN. *(Shakes him wildly.)* Man alive–what's
    the matter?
INNKEEPER *(Stumbling over his words.)*   Beneficent
    hermits, pray for us! Oh, he . . . oh, it . . .
    (Falls unconscious.)

SCENE 7

(Whitebearded Bogoboj in white, fantastically mysterious robe, hair and beard decorated with flowers, enters. He carries panpipes in his hand.)

BOGOBOJ. The terror has been sent to us. They send
    the terror before them. I slept, but now I
    am awake. The terror has been
    sent to us. Where is their son, where is he?
    *(Blows on the pipes. Juvan rouses with a
    fearful start and runs through the avenue
    of frightened people to the house.)*
TEITERLIK. He is a dead man now.
AMERICAN. Great God! What courage!
KRUNA. *(Enchanted.)* Juvan, our leader! Now he
    begins to live. *(Long pause of listening
    suspense. A shrill penetrating laugh in the crowd.)*

FEIWEL. Stop that laughing, God of my Fathers!
BOGOBOJ. Gather, children, gather and prepare! They
   will command you. The son is with the messenger. Gather!
   (*He blows on the pipes.*)

SCENE 8

(*Juvan, deadly pale, steps out of the door. Closes it with widespread arms.*)

JUVAN. The hour has struck. Seize whatever weapons
   you can find; pitchforks, axes, knives,
   and fire.
   Juvan the man of many conspiracies, the
   son of this mountain soil, commands you.
   The doom of the rich is at hand. For he has
   come to us—the one who has been denied.
   He has escaped. Now has the secret given
   itself into my hands.

(*Curtain.*)

ACT 4

(*Scene: Interior of a wooden village church: Greek Orthodox. The room is dominated by the Ikonostas, the gay wall of gold, silver, and colored pictures which guards the holy of holies. The Ikonostas is broken by two small side doors, and the big central door, called "royal gate." These three doors, used during the sacred performance for the exits and entrances of the priests and diakons, are now shut. A few scattered tapers are burning.*)

SCENE 1

(*Front stage before the Ikonostas, Juvan and the Priest. Two armed Revolutionaries stand guard at the church door.*)

PRIEST. (*His teeth chattering.*) The last day! The
   high altar no longer protects, nor the gracious
   place of communion. Let me go.
   Let me die outside.
JUVAN. (*Points to the royal gate.*) Did you see him in there?
PRIEST. See? Him? Did I dare to look at him? Eh,
   eh! He laughs at his bonds, the shaggy one.

JUVAN. And do you know who is is?

PRIEST. Do not say his name! Do not name him!
you ... you! Let met out! Let me out!

JUVAN. So you do not doubt? You believe he is
what he is?

PRIEST. I believe in the death of the world. Leave
me.

JUVAN. *(Takes him by the throat.)* If you believe.

PRIEST. *(Groaningly.)* His given name's uprising,
murder, arson, and heresy . . .

PRIEST. *(Quickly takes the big Bible and a silver
paten out of hiding.)* I want to save the
holy vessels.

JUVAN. *(Knocks the two things out of the Priest's
hand with his weapon.)* Jewels, gold and
silver, those are what you want to save, my
shrewd priest.

(Running off.) I believe it is he. I believe!

SCENE 2

*(Teiterlik comes in drunk, clad half in a remarkable uniform, half in his clown's
costume.)*

TEITERLIK. Captain! . . . A clean sweep! . . . Captain!
We're in clover! We wallow in brandy in
the barrooms. Beg to announce army growing.
Serfs, tenants, yeomen, farmhands, all
with us. The charcoal burners from the
wood, the smugglers, and many bearded
strangers forming gangs. Beg to announce
sky is red. You're to be king, so they say.
And I get promotion, too, if doing and dying's
deserving. Captain, I'll make a good
lieutenant. I'll walk before them on my
hands. Think I'm not young enough?
Look. *(Tries to turn a Catherine wheel.)*

JUVAN. You shall be lieutenant as long as you are
drunk. But as soon as I see you sober,
you're going to be shot.

TEITERLIK. Orders're orders.

JUVAN. How big is the army, lieutenant?

TEITERLIK. A thousand of us, they say. And all those
weapons! Swords, guns, and one little cannon
that won't shoot. *(He falls on his
knees and crosses himself.)* The one in
there has brought the weapons here by
magic.

SCENE 3

(Feiwel enters stormily.)

FEIWEL. Well, Mr. General, now look here! *(To
himself.)* . . . Me in a church! *(To Juvan.)*
Why are you looking at me so?
JUVAN. Insolence! You are not my equal to speak
to me so!
FEIWEL. Ts, ts. Christian stays Christian. Fine revolutionaries,
the *Goyim.* Give them a sabre
and they strut around and play soldiers.
JUVAN. Your news!
FEIWEL. Well, Mr. General, I thought this was to be
the hour of justice and freedom. But what
must I see? Murder, Mr. General! Everywhere
the drunkards, the fanatics, are murdering.
Nobody resisting, yet they murder.
Blood of men, Mr. General, human blood,
flowing under the doors, over the threshold,
down the steps . . . "Oh, woe, woe to
us!" everywhere in my ears. You must
stop it, you must order them back. I cannot
see blood. And he is there–if he really is
in there–what would he want that for?
JUVAN. Jew! Do you know why you are the lowest
of all men?
FEIWEL. Everyone has a different reason.
JUVAN. Because you cannot understand bloodlust.
FEIWEL. Look at that. I thought that was what
made us the chosen people!

SCENE 4

(American enters.)

AMERICAN. Man, I put order in that crowd. Divided
and drilled them in squads, like I learnt to
in war, and each has its orders. The farms
to the southward are all blazing, and now
the people have broken out against the
Gospodar. But there's no holding them any
longer, especially the women. They want to
see him.

JUVAN. They will see him.

AMERICAN. Congratulations, student. You know people.
You did a good job not to show the
hidden one, but to bring him here tight in
a covered cage.

JUVAN. Fear death, if you cannot believe.

AMERICAN. Don't let's fool ourselves, sir. I see straight.
I wasn't born yesterday. I learned a lot
across the water. There are great settlements
there, and suddenly the spirit comes over
these sons of Adam; they pray wildly,
journey over the land, murdering and
burning in religious frenzy, tearing the
clothes from their bodies, and practicing
vice in the name of the Lord. But there's
something to be learned by a man with
brains, from both God and madness.

JUVAN. I lived a prisoner in my body. Then came the vision,
fever broke loose in me, and seized
you all. I will do my work beause
I believe. And you, American, must believe
too!

AMERICAN. Like you I will believe in revenge. My
father ended very high. Five feet above
ground.

TEITERLIK. The crowd's outside!

SCENE 5

(Enter Bogoboj, dressed as at the end of Act 3.)

BOGOBOJ. Prince of the people! Son of the unknown!
You are to prophesy and show him to us.

JUVAN. How strong is your madness, how high
your faith?

BOGOBOJ. Of blood we have drunken that was wine.
And of wine that was blood.

JUVAN. Are you ready, then, for the service?

BOGOBOJ. We are thirsty unto death for the mass, we
are ravening for the liturgy.

SCENE 6

(The crowd flows into the room, drunk and lusting for miracles. Men and women carry all sorts of weapons, scythes and threshing flails, and a few tar torches.)

CHORUS. Let us see him . . . see him . . . see him!

KRUNA. *(At Juvan's feet.)* You our lord, exalt us!

JUVAN. You are not yet fit to worship his presence.

KRUNA. Teach us!

JUVAN. If you can grasp his meaning you may
redeem the world.

KRUNA. And you our ruler.

BOGOBOJ. Many centuries have you slept. Now you
are awake.

JUVAN. What are you all?

KRUNA. Men!

JUVAN. That is just it. He says unto you, "Be men
no more."

KRUNA. What are we to be?

JUVAN. Look into your soul and find the answer.
(Kruna looks at Juvan with a curious expression,
then slowly loosens her long hair,
and shakes her head so that it floats about
her.) Have you seen and understood?

KRUNA. Release!

CHORUS. *(On a scream.)* Release—!

JUVAN. Yes, release! For man is knotted, man is
   cramped–

CHORUS. Break through our torment—*(Juvan breaks
   a great cross over his knee
   and throws it into the crowd.)*

FEIWEL. Oi, my poor brother!

JUVAN. Man is the animal crucified.

BOGOBOJ. Did you hear the word?

KRUNA. Lord, take us from the cross!

JUVAN. I will give you back to the fields, you doe
   with dancing eyes! All of you! In your
   eyes I see the struggle of animals in death. I
   am wide awake. I see the beasts. There!
   Look of the murdered stallion! There!
   Look of the strangled wild cat. There! Last
   glint from the eyes of a dying wolf. *(The vision of the
   faces is too strong. He closes his
   eyes for a moment.)*

KRUNA. Free the poor animal!

CHORUS. Free the beast!

JUVAN. *(Gesturing toward the royal door of the
   Ikonostas.)* The sight of him will free you!

CHORUS. Show us the holy god! *(The people start
   a wild milling. The women
   shake out their unbound hair and
   begin to tear their clothes. The men have
   hard work to keep on their faces the
   expression of sullen brooding embarrassment
   which is the lightning that precedes a
   frightful mass outbreak.)*

JUVAN. He is the way back, the way home. We
   broke out of the ancient forests of night,
   blinking in the sunlight. Let us return to
   the forest. Our eyes will become big and
   quiet again. He will lead us home to the
   night when our task is done, when nothing
   built by man is left standing; when the
   hereditary lie is wiped out and vengeance
   wreaked on man; when the last plow lies
   rotting in a bloody ditch.

BOGOBOJ. *(Holds an embroidered vestment before
   him.)* So, with three fingers, I grasp the

narrow stola of the Diakon and hurry down
through the temple, flying with the drunken
flight of the heavenly spirits. . . *(Moves
tottering through the church.)* To the services,
you believers! Come, rouse your
sense to the surge of the mass, to the flow
of the ritual. *(Turns back to the Ikonostas.
Chorus turns, as one, to the altar.)*

JUVAN. Begin your service, Diakon.

BOGOBOJ. So be it.

JUVAN. What light is fitting to receive him?

BOGOBOJ. Darkness.

JUVAN. What color for his greeting?

BOGOBOJ. Color of flesh slain in lust.

JUVAN. What music to acclaim him?

BOGOBOJ. Swelling and deafening.

JUVAN. Where are the musicians?

BOGOBOJ. You grimy ones. Begin! *(Charcoal
burners group at one side of the altar.
They wear fur clothing and horn
ornaments on their heads. Their instruments are
drums, bag-pipes, tambourine, and two-sided
guzla. Candles go out.)*

AMERICAN. *(To Juvan.)* Enough of this madness! Are
you bent on destruction? *(The charcoal burners start, softly,
at first, to play their monotonous music
which repeats one rhythmic figure again and again.
Juvan steps into the shadow.)*

BOGOBOJ. *(Enchanted.)* Beloved, sing the litany with
me! *(Psalm-wise.)*

> Tragos Lyaios Oikoloi
> Venga Venga Chaire moi
> Pomiluj Nas Pomiluj!

(Music becomes louder and quicker.)

CHORUS. *(On their knees.)*

> Tragos Lyaios Oikoloi
> Venga Venga Chaire moi
> Pomiluj Nas Pomiluj!

*(The women start screaming, the men cry
out graspingly.)*

FEIWEL. *(In the grip of his eternal difference,
prays.)* Shma ysroel, adonoi, elohenu adonoi echod.

AMERICAN.   *(Fighting the hypnosis in vain.)* I have a
   clear head, but it's got me. *(Throws himself
   down howling.)* Pomiluj Nas Pomiluj!
ALL.   *(In a rhythmic daze.)* Pomiluj Nas Pomiluj!
   (Juvan steps forth.)

SCENE 7

*(Stevan, the Mother, Mirko, Stanja, Babka, the Elders, Modrygor and Kras-
nokrai, a few farm-hands with lanterns, make a path for themselves through the
throng, which gives way before them, suddenly dumb. Music breaks off.)*

STEVAN.   *(His foot on the altar step, to Juvan.)* Rioters!
   Blasphemers, murderers! I come unarmed,
   with the women of my household,
   bringing you the message of the Elders.
CHORUS.   Beat them to death!
JUVAN.   Not a sound from you! *(To Stevan.)* And
   what do you wish?
STEVAN.   You have burned down our villages, more
   ruthless than the Turkish hordes. You have
   murdered and maimed men, women and
   children, dazed and defenceless. If I wished
   to act according to the word of men and
   God I would not be standing here.
JUVAN.   What do you want?
STEVAN.   My heart was always too soft. Do you
   think I sent riders to the city to the Turkish
   governor, for soldiers to trample down your
   madmen? No, I did not send, you
   bloodsuckers. Understand that!
AMERICAN.   We're not crazy enough to swallow that!
JUVAN.   And what do you wish?
STEVAN.   I wish to bargain with you. You destroyer
   in a scholar's coat!
JUVAN.   What do you want us to do?
STEVAN.   Drop your weapons, your plunder, your
   torches and disband.
JUVAN.   What do you offer in return?
STEVAN.   Is it not enough that you go free and unpunished?
JUVAN.   That is not the sort of bargain you
   bargainers are in the habit of making.

STEVAN. Kneel before me, all of you and hear the
    merciful decision of the council of Elders.
    If you submit immediately, all the bloodshed
    will be forgotten, and . . . kneel, weep,
    you murderers . . . and every landless,
    wandering immigrant will receive some of our
    waste land and seed for its sowing. *(Chorus silent
    and sullen.)*
TEITERLIK. *(Whimpering.)* Though I'm a lieutenant
    . . . land . . . my land . . .
JUVAN. You have not told us all your demands.
STEVAN. *(Softly.)* You must surrender him—
    instantly.
JUVAN. Whom?
STEVAN. *(Shamefaced, between his teeth.)* The
    unbaptised!
JUVAN. His name!
STEVAN. *(Writhing with shame.)* Don't pretend,
    you fiend! There—in the holy of holies . . .
JUVAN. Name him!
STEVAN. *(Loudly, tonelessly.)* His name? I
    do not know his name. He is my son.
MIRKO. Father! You!
BOGOBOJ. A God was born to the poor in a stable.
MAN'S VOICE. But this one was born to the rich.
WOMAN'S VOICE. Hehehahaha! The rich people's secret!
BOGOBOJ. Who dares say: "He is my son?"
JUVAN. Gospodar! Your demand is refused.
    He, who is our victory remains.
STEVAN. Who stands in a father's way?
    *(Tries to advance, but armed men who
    have gathered about Juvan hold their
    weapons towards him.)*
MOTHER. *(Stepping forward.)* This father hates his
    son. But no man knows what my life has
    been since that day. Let me go to him . . .
BABKA. Back, woman. *(Pushes Mother aside.)* His
    parents denied him. But I suckled him, I
    nursed him, his only servant till this day. I
    alone have power over him. He went to
    sleep to my songs. *(To Juvan.)* Devil! I
    warn you. Let me coax him.

JUVAN. There is another woman with you!

MIRKO. *(Seizes Stanja in an iron grip.)* Hide!

JUVAN. Gospodar! See, I'll show you what Juvan is.
Suddenly he changes his mind. He spits
now on what was precious and holy to
him. Your terms are accepted and I will
close with you.

CHORUS. Traitor.

AMERICAN. I never understood him . . .

BOGOBOJ. Bow to the will. It does not come from
him.

JUVAN. *(Very emphatically.)* I close with you. You
shall have him. He returns if she, the pretty
one, there– Mirko's bride, if . . . if she goes
in and leads him to you.

STEVAN. The face that its father did not dare to look
on, year after year . . . she, a maiden?

JUVAN. She can save you.

STEVAN. *(Softly, horrified.)* Away from here, my
daughter!

MIRKO. *(Slackly, with infinite sadness.)* For the
second time we must flee from him, Stanja.
The student is stronger that we. And . . .
we bring no happiness for each other . . .
I shall die without you . . . I release you.

ELDERS OF KRASNOKRAJ AND MODRYGOR. *(Whispering
to Stanja.)* Do not be afraid.
We'll arm ourselves and take you back
secretly to your parents.

STEVAN'S FAMILY AND THE ELDERS. *(Speaking
all together to Stanja, softly.)*
Away! Softly! Unnoticed! Escape!

JUVAN. What answer?

STANJA. *(Slowly ascending the altar steps.)* This!
*(Stanja and Juvan look long into each
other's eyes.)*

BOGOBOJ. *(Seized by a fit of trembling.)* Children!
The secret of the mass is at hand!

CHORUS. *(Moved, melodious.)*
　　　　The fair one is fair,
　　　　A wreath of ribbon in her hair,
　　　　And bridal clothes, and bridal clothes.

KRUNA. *(Wraps herself in her hair.)* Weep!
   *(Russian music, softly, in a different
   rhythm.)*
MOTHER. Never has he seen a young woman. She
   goes to her death.
MIRKO. To my brother.
JUVAN. Stanja. Am I your enemy now?
STANJA. Not as much as I am yours.
JUVAN. Are you doing this to save your people?
STANJA. Mine? They are not mine.
JUVAN. Why are you doing it then, Stanja?
STANJA. Robber! I fling away your booty.
JUVAN. *(Haughtily concealing his
   defeat.)* Step down. You shall
   not be my sacrifice.
STANJA. Your sacrifice? Who are you? Did I ever
   know you? I do not know. *(She bends before
   the Ikonostas.)* Here I have already
   stood to receive God. *(Rising above her
   triumph.)* Go, servant! Open!
JUVAN. Here is a knife for you. You understand?
   A knife.
STANJA. *(Takes the knife.)* I will cut through his
   bonds. But for myself I will not use it.
   Open! *(Juvan raises his hand, but cannot move.
   Stanja without looking back, disappears through
   the royal gate. Music ceases.)*

SCENE 8

*(Mirko has taken the half of the broken cross with the two silver-set arms and
throws himself on Juvan.)*

MIRKO. For the second time I meet you! *(He falls
   upon the outstretched steel of one of the
   guards.)* Oh ... oh ... oh ... Father ...
   oh ... oh ... oh ... *(Dies.)*
STEVAN. *(Kneeling by the dead man, after a long
   pause.)* He is not breathing *(With a hoarse
   cry.)* But he ...
MOTHER. *(Who cannot hide the crazy light of sinful
   joy in her eyes.)* Justice! O Justice!

(Throws herself upon the corpse.)

BABKA. *(Coldly, seeing the mother's conflicting
emotions.)* Woman! Stand up!

STEVAN. *(Rises. In a hard voice, to a farmhand.)*
Take hold of the dead man and lift him.)

MODRYGOR. Brother! Are you going to desert the girl?

STEVAN. Her betrothed is dead. She is no longer
ours. Pass.

(Men with the corpse move toward the door, Stevan, Mother, Babka following.)

KRASNOKRAJ. *(To Modrygor.)* Kinsman! Let us hide and
wait for the daughter of Kauzelnivrh.

STEVAN. *(Calling into the room from the
church door.)* If you want to destroy us, hurry. I
deceived you. The Janissaries have been on
the march for hours. *(He and his family off.)*

SCENE 9

BOGOBOJ. I feel the holy approach. Prepare! Pray! A
moment more, and you will see him.

CHORUS. *(Drowning their rising fear in song.)*
Pomiluj Nas Pomiluj. *(Juvan suddenly,
starting up, in haggard triumph.)*

JUVAN. Jew, out to the green. To the linden bell!
Ring, Jew, ring the bells, the wedding bells.

FEIWEL. Hei! Hei! The Jew is going to ring the
Christian bells, the Jew, the Jew! *(Runs off.)*

AMERICAN. It seemed to me just now that I heard
distant trumpets.

TEITERLIK. Damn! I'd rather be on a rope stretched
between two roofs. The chill of dawn is in
my bones. Who wants my job?

JUVAN. What have I done? *(A monstrous cry of joy sings on,
descending chromatically, not human, inhumanly
superhuman, sounding from the holy of
holies. The bells chime in wildly.)*

BOGOBOJ. Lo, the miracle!

KRUNA. Why did you not sacrifice me?

CHORUS. She is dead. *(Juvan with a hollow
cry, throws himself against the royal
gate. Bogoboj bars his way with
outstretched arms.)*

JUVAN. Save her . . .

BOGOBOJ. Stay not the sacrifice.

JUVAN. Back, old man.

BOGOBOJ. Endure the holy moment. *(He clings to Juvan with monstrous strength.)*

JUVAN. I suffer. *(The struggle. The bells cease. The two Elders appear by the altar rail.)*

KRASNOKRAJ. Hold me! My knees are trembling.

MODRYGOR. There! Ah, I saw something! Now! There! Behind that last window. A girl's shadow. Quick! Through the little door. *(They disappear through a secret door.)*

FEIWEL. *(Appears at the rail, his teeth chattering, softly.)* Horns! Horns sound from all the hills—*(Makes off.)*

JUVAN. *(Has overcome the giant old man, who totters aside.)* Stanja! *(Scarcely has he taken the first wild step toward the holy of holies when he becomes rigid.)*

CHORUS. He is coming! *(Everyone on the stage retreats, a dark mass. The great royal gate of the Ikonostas slowly opens of its own accord. Behind it the great high altar becomes visible, blindingly radiant with a thousand candles.)*

BOGOBOJ. *(On his face.)* I see.

CHORUS. *(Prostrate.)* We see him. *(The high altar is tremulous with flame. Before the audience can see anything else clearly the curtain falls.)*

(Curtain.)

ACT 5

(The ruins of Stevan's farm, the courtyard. In the background the walls of the outbuildings. The big courtyard door alone stands open and unharmed, and behind it the devastated fields are visible. Left, the blackened but not crumbled farmhouse, with the door, to which three steps lead. At either side of the door a rough bench. In the middle a spring. Right foreground a small grassy rise in the ground, rising off into the wings, indicates that a street leads through the courtyard. Late morning.)

SCENE 1

(Stevan and the Physician step out of the door.)

PHYSICIAN. *(Playing with the key.)* Your secret, this
    key to it, and my absent-mindedness, have
    sufficed, and a whole little world has been
    destroyed. Oh, marvelously complete chain
    of causation which needs no superhuman agency to fulfill its inevit-
    able wonders. God himself, as Voltaire says, would have
    to convert himself to atheism.

STEVAN. What's all that you're saying?

PHYSICIAN. Ah, yes, I know. The secret was the primal
    cause that started it. But what, at bottom,
    is your secret? Nothing but leftover fears,
    the dregs, the undigested food in the belly
    of evolution. Ah , you ought to learn to
    read French.

STEVAN. Sir!

PHYSICIAN. Superstition, Stevan Milic, that's all it was
    —yours and theirs. You cannot blame me.
    I always warned you. I offered over and
    over again to take the fearful changeling
    to a home. But vanity with its serpent eye
    froze all of you in terror. A day had to
    come when the stench would be discovered,
    even in the house of the mighty . . . Now
    it has been hideously brought to light.

STEVAN. Yes, and in all my misery I thank God for
    it.

PHYSICIAN. The superstition of those poor people is
    more justifiable than yours. For need and
    suffering crave redemption, and they easily
    see God or His opposite in a human
    monster.

STEVAN. Now I, too, am as poor as the poorest.

PHYSICIAN. *(Claps him on the shoulder, heartily.)*
    You won't be for long. For a man is born to
    poverty or riches just as he is to prophecy.
    It is simply a certain arrangement of the
    human tissues. The rabble have shed much
    blood, but the soldiers have shed even more
    blood of theirs. The poor pay double. Did
    you lose your son?

STEVAN. Both sons, Master.

PHYSICIAN. The other, they say, ran off into the
burning woods and died there.

STEVAN. Stifled or burned to death, who knows?

PHYSICIAN. Did they find him?

STEVAN. I have asked no one.

PHYSICIAN. Well, life still lies before you.

STEVAN. I feel as if I had lived many lives.

PHYSICIAN. You are only fifty.

STEVAN. And now for the first time I feel as
though that age were really youth.

PHYSICIAN. I wish I were made of your mettle. *(Looks
at the house-walls.)* Traces of the
Janissaries' bullets here, too. After all, the best
of them was the student. What do you
know of him?

STEVAN. Not a lad of us but knew his pretty mother
once.

PHYSICIAN. He was a great man. He was well known
to the authorities, an arch-schemer, slippery
as an eel. My diagnosis is a plain case of
religious mania. They will never let him
off with a flogging.

STEVAN. I hate no one any more.

PHYSICIAN. And that crazy graybeard, the prophet,
nothing could be done for him, either.
They buried him yesterday.

STEVAN. Tell me, Doctor, how could all these things
happen in so short a time?

PHYSICIAN. The world of men, my friend, no less than
that of nature, has, I regret to say, its unplumbed
seasons, eclipses, northern lights, and
magnetic storms; convulsions of the
established order. Original chaos surges to
the surface. The animal hidden in us takes
possession.

STEVAN. I do not understand what you are saying.
But it may well be. For all my sorrow my
heart feels so light, so light!

PHYSICIAN. That is a noble sentiment, Stevan Milic!
Haha! See how catastrophes, like everything
else, are only there to be gabbled about.

And over there in the shed lies a poor
patient shot through the lung. A poor ropedancer, who cannot live out the day. I must
steal a march on that damned priest.
(Raises his tricorn.) You can always find
me if you want me. Excuse me now. *(Off.)*

SCENE 2

(Mother appears in the doorway.)

STEVAN. Mother! *(Takes her by the hand.)* Have
you come out of that black room at last,
and dressed in this lovely old dress I like
so well?
MOTHER. Yes, Father. This morning dawned so blue
... I ... I ... I ... Come sit down with me,
Father. *(They sit on the bench by the door.)*
STEVAN. What are you hiding from me?
MOTHER. I am lost. I must tell you something
terrible, something mortally sinful.
STEVAN. I know. Say it!
MOTHER. Mortal sin, Father.
STEVAN. Say the word, Mother.
MOTHER. *(Softly.)* I am happy.
STEVEN. I understand. I, too ... I too ... *(Buries
his head in his hands.)* ... am happy.
MOTHER. Our children are dead.
STEVAN. The well formed and the other.
MOTHER. Our pride and our shame.
STEVAN. One could not live without the other. That
was fate.
MOTHER. Eternal bliss is barred to me ... for, Father
... as Mirko lay bleeding ... happiness
welled up in my heart, happiness for the
other one.
STEVAN. He was the one you really loved.
MOTHER. I never looked upon his face. So he was my
pain day in and day out. And yet I worshipped
him, the poor accursed one. Now he
has gone in flaming death ... I suffer
... and yet I am released.

STEVAN. Released! Children do not make men
    happy.

MOTHER. Only women, as long as the milk is in their
    breasts.

STEVAN. But children and rooftree grow and crowd
    out man's heaven.

MOTHER. And his love.

STEVAN. Do you know, Mother, there is something
    else that makes me happy and young.

MOTHER. Tell me.

STEVAN. *(With a gesture toward the ruins.)* This
    destruction.

MOTHER. Yes, we are poor. The barns and dairies are
    burned down, the pens empty, the storehouses
    stripped . . .

STEVAN. But our hidden shame is gone. This I have
    discovered. Possession is concealment and
    in all order grins the hidden thing. And as
    our secrets wax, so wanes our youth. But
    to shoulder each day, boldly carefree, singing,
    that . . . that is youth. *(Stretches our
    his arms.)* And I have it again.

MOTHER. Father!

STEVAN. Mother!

MOTHER. What are you saying? We are no longer
    father and mother.

STEVAN. True, father and mother no longer. But
    what are we?

MOTHER. Don't you know the word?

STEVAN. *(Looks at her long.)* Wife!

MOTHER. *(Her voice trembling.)* Husband!

STEVAN. So long since I used that word—

MOTHER. *(Tears streaming.)* So long . . . and where was I?

STEVAN. By my side. But awakening from all this
    fever I see you now, you . . . for the first time
    I see you again.

MOTHER. But this is no longer I —

STEVAN. I had to lose everything to find you.

MOTHER. I am no longer I.

STEVAN. Lovelier, lovelier, than ever I find you. The
    sun, this golden sun on your face–what
    matter if it is the light of your sunset?

MOTHER. You never looked at me when I was
      beautiful.
STEVAN. The ripened years are best. This gray in
      your hair moves me, moves me so, so deeply.
      (Hovering over her.) Holy–sweet–
      mysterious.
MOTHER. *(Her voice fails.)* You . . .
STEVAN. No silver wedding will I seal with you but
      our second betrothal . . . *(Mother sinks
      into his arms.)* . . .with this kiss! *(They
      kiss long and deeply. He rises, stamps his
      feet wide apart, loudly.)* Ah! He! Ho! Haha!
      Wife! You! Mine! I am new, all new.
      Do you hear? Bold, unthinking, whistling,
      to meet the day. *(After a little pause.)* An
      old lame horse is all that's left, but we can
      harness him and start again singing . . .
      hahaha . . . singing!
      *(Goes off to the fields through the courtyard door. Mother looks after him,
      her arms timidly stretched toward him.)*

SCENE 3

*(Stanja enters slowly, sits on the edge of the well and remains rigid, impene-
trable.)*

MOTHER. Still here!
STANJA. Always here. Why do you distrust me,
      Mother?
MOTHER. Our son is dead. Nothing more binds you
      to us.
STANJA. I stay true to your son, Mother.
MOTHER. Your people have sent for you.
STANJA. My people! Always my people. Who are
      my people! Let me stay with you.
MOTHER. You see there is no longer any home here.
      Your place is where wealth and happiness
      are, at home where the new suitors are already
      standing at the door. Here there is
      room for nothing but hard hands that want to
      work.

STANJA. My hands want to work, Mother.

MOTHER. Why should you wear out your days with
us old folk that have worn out our own?

STANJA. Because I am true to your son.

MOTHER. You never loved him, you strange girl, and
now he is dead.

STANJA. Why do you distrust me?

MOTHER. I don't distrust you any more. When you
came to us, young, pretty, silent, my
haughty daughter-in-law, with your youthful
breasts, a stranger, then I did hate you.
I do not know what happened to you that
night. Let me see your face. *(Stanja turns her face
away.)* Child! I no longer hate you. No, I trust you now.

STANJA. Then let me stay here.

MOTHER. Why do you not tell—

STANJA. *(From a distance.)* Tell—

MOTHER. No, don't tell me. Ah, when I look at you
I cannot believe you are so much younger
than I, daughter. Now I begin to love you.

STANJA. I know you are not my enemy any longer.

MOTHER. That is just why it is that, with a heavy
heart, I tell you . . . go, go. What do you
want here? Everything is soon over for a
woman. She has only one day, one hour, on
which to build her power. You will find a
new man, you are so pretty; perhaps a better
man.

STANJA. I am true to your son. Let me stay. I am
not afraid to work. Let me help you,
Mother.

SCENE 4

(Feiwel, his peddler's pack on his back, comes along the road.)

FEIWEL. *(From a distance, in great excitement.)*
God, how much has happened! God, what
I have had to see! Almighty, what I am
still living through! This lovely courtyard,
this princely courtyard, this royal courtyard.
Eijajajei! Such a fortune. Gone!
(Clenching his fists.) The blood hounds.

MOTHER. You cannot have lost much, Feiwel. You
    carry your wealth on your back.

FEIWEL. Is sympathy nothing, and sleepless nights?
    It is true my fortune is all moveable, but that's just why I mix with so
    many people. With my soft heart . . . how can I–help
    myself? . . . I have to live everyone's sorrows,
    his bankruptcies, his misfortunes. God, what don't I have to bear?
    The Christians
    are wonderful beings, but they don't
    know what sympathy is.

MOTHER. And yet you egged them on and spoke for
    them.

FEIWEL. *(Answers with an exaggerated start.)* God
    of Justice, who put that lie on me? My
    enemies, the godless in Mizraim. I am an
    educated man. I can read the German
    newspapers, and I know what politics is.
    And because I'm a born speaker I made a speech to the Elders.
    What good did it do
    me? I spoke up for the starving out of sympathy. The greatest
    statesmen make
    speeches pro and con. And that is why,
    God of Justice, they call me a man who egged them
    on? But of course, when the hail
    falls, the Jew is stoned.

MOTHER. Weren't you one of the wildest, Feiwel?

FEIWEL. I? Woe! I must sit down *(Sits on the
    bench)* That is my fate, I am in it but not
    in it and not in it but in it. I was coming
    along the road just like now. Feiwel is
    weak–Feiwel is timid. Feiwel would
    never make trouble, but they swept me
    along. Why did I go? Why? To calm the
    wild *Goyim.* I was only a Kibbitzer. Out
    of sympathy for you. But I know, you want
    to accuse me, ruin me . . .

MOTHER. No, not that, Jew. I accuse no one.

FEIWEL. That is a speech that God will write down
    in His golden book. All those whom He
    would smite–He has smitten. The American
    is dead. The rope-dancer–he's dying,
    and the leader of the rabble—

STANJA. *(Nonchalantly.)* The leader?

FEIWEL. *(Shades his eyes, peering into the distance.)* Wait, perhaps we can see it from here.

STANJA. What?

FEIWEL. *(Grinning.)* Ah, miss, nothing for you. Still, I must say, with all respects for the young miss . . .

STANJA. What are you looking at?

FEIWEL. You can't see it from here.

STANJA. What can't be seen?

FEIWEL. What they've fixed on the hill for the student.

STANJA. *(Quietly.)* Then it is all over?

FEIWEL. No! It takes place at noon. But the crowd is gathering now. Something else only Christians can stand. *(Takes his pack off.)* But I'm forgetting business. I'll show you what kind of man I am. I am only one who fitted himself to what has happened. In the midst of the fighting, (oh, my cramps), I got hold of all the things that are needed for building homes again. *(Peddler's whine.)* Nails of all sizes, practical tools for sale, lime, real gold cheap collar-buttons Christian holy pictures, guaranteed durable, sweet-tasting laxative . . .

MOTHER. Go, Feiwel.

FEIWEL. I stay where I'm not wanted? Your servant, ladies. *(Zigzags off.)*

STANJA. *(Takes Mother's hand.)* Mother?

MOTHER. I do not understand you, but . . . *(Kisses her.)* . . . live with us from now on, bride of my son. I will tell my husband. *(Stanja sinks her head on her breast, Mother goes into the house. Stanja sits on the edge of the well again.)*

SCENE 5

(Enter Gospodar Jevrem Vesilic and Stanja's Mother.)

JEVREM. We have come ourselves. You paid no

attention to all our messengers and
the wagon that was to have fetched you came
back empty.

STANJA'S MOTHER. So we toiled along the hard road
ourselves, child, and we have come to take you home.

STANJA. *(As if she had not heard.)* How are you,
Father and Mother?

JEVREM. Heaven destroys only Sodom.

STANJA'S MOTHER. But he spares the righteous.

JEVREM. We have no evil secret.

STANJA'S MOTHER. And we hide no sin in our house.

JEVREM. Pride goes before a fall.

STANJA'S MOTHER. A pitcher at the edge of a table
is ready to be smashed.

JEVREM. It is well that they are not here so we need
speak no false words.

STANJA'S MOTHER. The souls of the righteous shun
the godless . . .

JEVREM. And we are glad nothing came of it.

STANJA'S MOTHER. The dream man was a rag in the wind.
Sorrow and shame has been all our portion.

JEVREM. Such a match. We are highly respected, but
it is almost a stain on us.

STANJA'S MOTHER. We will burn candles.

JEVREM. And we have just the man for you.

STANJA'S MOTHER. A better man.

JEVREM. With a family such as you don't get
every day.

STANJA'S MOTHER. And they are richer than these here were.

JEVREM. Be happy, then you wicked girl, and
say a word to us.

STANJA. I am Milic's betrothed, Father.

JEVREM. *(Overcome by excitement against
his daughter.)* Don't cross me, girl. I came
But I am full of wrath.

STANJA'S MOTHER. You are not the same to us after all this business.

STANJA. What harm did I do you?

JEVREM. Everybody is to blame for his own
misfortunes.

STANJA'S MOTHER. You always were one for not
wanting to obey, you sly cat. That
brings misfortune.

JEVREM. All your friends bring their parents
    happiness. All of them well married. Misfortune
    is a disgrace.

STANJA. I obeyed you, my parents.

JEVREM. Yes, but unwillingly, and with the bit
    between your teeth. We do not understand
    you. I beat you too little.

STANJA. Why do you abuse me now?

JEVREM. Bad results deserve the stick.

STANJA. You brought me to this house yourselves.

JEVREM. Don't contradict your father. The gall is
    rising in me. Come now.

STANJA. I stay here, my parents, in my widowhood.

STANJA'S MOTHER. Widowhood, you crazy thing?
    You are a virgin, and that is the only thing left
    to you that pays.

JEVREM. For the last time I tell you, come.

STANJA. Go back home, Father and Mother.

JEVREM. *(Furious, raises his stick at her.)* Ah! Woe!
    You belong to me. Get up, you bitch. The
    devil knows what you've been up to.

STANJA'S MOTHER. Jesus! Can't you see what you're
    doing to your father? Don't anger him
    any more. He is old.

JEVREM. *(Gasping.)* My heart, my heart . . .

STANJA'S MOTHER. *(Shrieks.)* If anything happens to him,
    you killed him.

STANJA. Father and Mother, go away from here, go.

JEVREM. I go, go. I won't drag you away, I won't
    see you again, you are no longer my daughter.
    But one last word. If by **tomorrow**
    sundown you have not crept home hugging
    the cross, you will die of my curse.
    (Bellowing.) My curse! *(Quickly off.)*

STANJA'S MOTHER. *(Hurrying after him.)* Vesilic, don't!
    Don't Jevrem Vesilic. *(She calls back menacingly.)* You! You—

STANJA. *(Alone.)* Not of this curse will I die.
    (Choked.) Where? . . . Where? Where?
    (Looks in the same direction as Feiwel did,
    then suddenly turns to find Juvan, in
    chains, before her. Behind him is an escort
    consisting of the Bashi Bazook and two soldiers.)

SCENE 6

JUVAN. Bashi Bazook! Did I take advantage of the privilege of the condemned?

BASHI. You waved aside the food and left the wine standing.

JUVAN. Then you still owe me the fulfillment of a wish.

BASHI. That is not written in my orders.

JUVAN. Nor is it written in your orders that if you deny me I can still escape. It would not be the first time.

BASHI. I will have your feet shackled.

JUVAN. There is no need. See the truth in my eyes. You have my word. Let me talk to this woman, only for a moment. I will give you no trouble.

BASHI. Will you keep your word?

JUVAN. See the truth in my eyes!

BASHII. Then for your sake I will overstep my orders, even though you do eat unclean meat. *(Commanding the two Janissaries.)* About face. Ten paces forward. March! Halt. Turn. *(Soldiers posted outside audience's line of vision. Bashi commands them.)* Shoulder arms. Hup, hup, hup. *(To Juvan.)* Make one move and you will both be shot. I shall stand over there and count several times to a hundred. *(Off to the soldiers.)*

SCENE 7

JUVAN. You know where I am going. *(Stanja silent.)* I knew that I would meet you on this road. So I went with my eyes closed.

STANJA. I waited.

JUVAN. You know the fearful question burning in me Stanja.

STANJA. *(Very tenderly.)* I know it. Go in peace, in peace, Juvan.

JUVAN. But he screamed, a scream of love!

STANJA. Clean I am and yours, until death. Go in peace, Juvan.

JUVAN. How is it, beloved? This is the first time I have spoken to you. And yet how many paths we have walked together hand in hand.

STANJA. This is not the first time I speak to you. I have heard this new voice of yours in many dreams.

JUVAN. Speak, speak, speak! Back there a man is counting.

STANJA. One rainy night you came into the house for shelter. You sat on the bench and I passed through the room, once, twice . . .

JUVAN. I have . . . forgotten.

STANJA. I have not forgotten.

JUVAN. Wait! I have not forgotten. In my darkness, searching–a gleam of light beneath the door.

STANJA. And though you did not recognize me when I sat at the table with my betrothed, I know you knew me.

JUVAN. Yes. That is so. Why else should I have had to wound you? And then the secret leaped between us.

STANJA. *(Very softly.)* The animal.

JUVAN. See! Now I feel as if the secret had broken loose from us. *(Grasping her hand.)* No, no. Not from you . . . me!

STANJA. *(Low, as if comforted.)* Was it you?

JUVAN. But I threw you before him.

STANJA. *(A flash of bitterness in her pride.)* That is not true. I conquered you. I went in myself, of my free will.

JUVAN. You conquered me. As I gave you the knife, trembling, I was lost, my cause was lost, and that of my people, and the Turkish crescent threatened from the hill.

STANJA. *(Mothering.)* You . . . now you have come to me.

JUVAN. Madness! Who was I! Who! Lying on my back I stared at the dead sky without thoughts, full only of a passion for

vengeance on something I had never known,
perhaps my unknown father. Hate for the
secure, the righteous, the smug, and pious.
Longing to return to animal eyes and
breath. Only one lust in me, the lust for
ruin. Only one happiness, to bellow into
the storm, only one light, the light of a
great fire. Forever joined to my companions
in my thirst for the ecstasy of
destruction. But then . . .

STANJA. Then, my love?

JUVAN. ᐧ Then came day after all those burning
nights, and I woke under this spring sky.
It is my last day. Because I hated, a woman
had to shatter and wake me. Oh, the miracle
of the morning came to me. For the
first time I heard the lark, a burning song,
against the sun, and a shout broke from
me because of the wonder of the world.
Then I knew you, you, everywhere.

STANJA. Speak, speak, speak. A man is counting
over there.

JUVAN. Loving you, I loved. My chained hand was
softly hollowed to gather, to caress. Oh,
woman, with your clear strong limbs! Love
. . . first love . . . is so strong . . . so
strong . . . (*Tears run down his cheeks.*)

STANJA. Then, tell me, mouth that is still alive,
why, if we were made for one another, it
was not to be?

JUVAN. Because everything eternal fears
fulfillment.

STANJA. (*Screaming.*) I want you, forever, forever.
Do not go from me, now. I must tell you.

JUVAN. (*Tearing at his chains.*) Stanja! Speak!
He . . .

STANJA. (*In a shining voice.*) No, my beloved. No!
This life is yours.

JUVAN. Are you saying that just to make my dying
easier?

STANJA. (*Clings to him.*) How can I live when you
no longer live?

JUVAN. *(Suddenly.)* I feel he has stopped counting.

STANJA. Listen and act quickly, while there is time.
If you love me, let us die together. One
step and they will kill us both.

JUVAN. Tell me again that you escaped unharmed.

STANJA. You know the truth. And now, my life,
just a few steps. They will shoot and all will be well.

JUVAN. *(After a pause.)* No!

STANJA. *(Trembling.)* There is yet time.

JUVAN. No, you must live. I must know that you,
my wife, are still in the world like light
and like warmth and that I leave a hearth
behind me.

STANJA. *(Sliding down to his feet.)* Again you deny
me. Again!

SCENE 8

(Bashi Bazook and soldiers appear.)

BASHI. I have graciously counted. Now come,
student! *(Lays his hand on him.)*

JUVAN. *(Shakes off the hand.)* You are only the
last link in the chain of my destiny. Death
is the climax of my life's fulfillment.
(Quickly off, followed by the escort.)

STANJA. *(Alone.)* A mere moment longer for him.
But I must bear out my life–all my life–
accursed.

MOTHER. *(Stepping out of the house.)* I have cooked
a meal. We must call your father. Who is
coming?

NINTH AND LAST SCENE

(Drunken Hangman-trapper comes in his rude wagon drawn by a miserable donkey.)

HANGMAN. Huah! Prr! Prr!
Hey! You women of the house! Have you
a little brandy left? *(Women silent in
horror.)* What, no one here? The inn gone?
Well! I have enough for now. Do you know me?

MOTHER. Go away . . . Hangman!

HANGMAN. Ow, what, what a name. I'm a state . . .
state . . . offizhiel. But if you knew what I
have today!
(Singing a folksong.)
> *The hero walks unharmed*
> *Through fire and war before us*
> *And lead us on to victory.*

(Snaps his whip.)
> *Business is good!*

MOTHER. *(Swaying.)* Into the house!

STANJA. *(Holds her back.)* No, stay!

HANGMAN. Ah, I knew, cu . . . curious, like all the
women. But I'm always nice to pretty
ladies. Today I have three spiked dogs,
three drowned cats, all very good skins, in
the wagon here . . . and then . . . cur . . . curious women are.

MOTHER. Let me go!

STANJA. *(Holds her in an iron grip.)* Stay!

HANGMAN. And then something very, *very* curious. It
was lying there in the charred wood, lying
lying there without a hair singed. A wonder.
The priest must bless it for me. Here
I have the fiend himself to whom my soul
would soon belong . . . *(Mother screams
softly. Distant whirl of drums.)* Go on drumming. No more gallows
goods for the furrier. *(Stanja advances a little
step.)* No! Can't do it! Got to pay to see it.
And not even a sip of brandy for me.
Huah, aho! *(Off with his wagon.)*

MOTHER. *(Rousing after a long rigidity.)* He was in
me, growing in my body. I bore and loved
him. Even if I did not dare look at him,
yet I listened for ten thousand anguished
nights toward the place where his heart
was beating, and was happy that he lived.
. . . And now he will be thrown to the carrion,
he, who sprang from me, and not a
name, not even a trace, of the secret of my
womb will be left in the world.

STANJA. You are wrong, Mother. He is still in the
world. *(Coldly controlling a twitching.)* I am carrying his child.

(Quick curtain.)

Fritz Hochwälder (1911-)

The Raspberry Picker

A leading dramatist of our time, Fritz Hochwälder was born in Vienna in 1911, but since 1938 has lived in Switzerland. He started life as a cabinetmaker and upholsterer, as did young Molière, then moved into labor-union work. Caught in the crosscurrents of politics and violence that preceded the Austrian *anschluss* of 1938, his sensitive and observant nature was shocked by the hysteria and enthusiasm that was engendered in much of his homeland by the Nazi occupation. When he had to leave Austria in 1938, he settled in Zurich and has returned to his native land only for intermittent visits relating to honors or productions of his plays since that time. Even though he was quite free to return after the war, the memories of the crowds welcoming Hitler to Vienna have been too strong for him. His passionate moral beliefs, so fully embodied in most of his plays, have kept him in Zurich, still asking those questions that any moral, intelligent man might ask: how could his people have turned against the Jews who had been a major force in the art, culture, and intellectual life of Austria, and yet today act as if those wild and hysterical emotions of 1938 had never existed? Thus he has returned to accept official signs of recognition, to supervise productions of his plays, but not as a native son or Austrian citizen.

Hochwälder's playwriting method, though undertaken in a variety of modes from realism to expressionism and from farce to tragedy, has always been marked by a strong sense of craftsmanship. He is a master of stagecraft and playwriting technique even when he is acting as a passionate moralist.

In his first period of exile in Zurich he was closely associated with the aging expressionist playwright Georg Kaiser, who was instrumental in leading him to writing and to the drama as a means of personal expression. His first play, *Das Heilige Experiment* (1943), presented in English as *The Strong are Lonely,* made him famous overnight. It was first presented in Bienne, Switzerland, in March 1943, then in Paris in 1952, in London in 1955, and on Broadway in 1953. The New York adaptation (made from the French version of the play) was by Eva Le Gallienne and the direction was by Margaret Webster. Brooks Atkinson in the *New York Times* for September 30, 1953, commented on the moral power that lay in the central dilemma of the play, but he noted that "after the spiritual leader of the state has accepted the awful decision against him, *The Strong are Lonely* is a good deal less interesting." It is a brilliant look at power politics and ethics in the attempt by the Jesuits to establish a utopian community in Paraguay in the eighteenth century, and at the destruction and personal disillusionment that followed.

His second play, *Der Flüchtling (The Fugitive;* 1945), directly based on a story outline developed by his friend Georg Kaiser, presents the ethical and philosophical dilemma of a border guard and his wife who are plunged into a situation demanding immediate moral decisions by a fugitive who seeks refuge in their house. After a period of dramatic discussion, the guard finds in himself the strength to remain behind and die for his newfound sense of personal freedom, while the fugitive flees with the wife.

Der Öffentliche Anklager (The Public Prosecutor; 1947) is a play ostensibly dealing with the problems of the French Revolution, though they are essentially the problems of persecution found in any closed political system. As the public prosecutor pursues a case against an unknown enemy of the people, he eventually, as did Oedipus, finds that he himself is that man. In *Donadieu* (1953), which takes place in the sixteenth century during the Huguenot Wars, a strong religious and moral theme is again presented. A Huguenot aristocrat, recognizing in a stranger who seeks asylum in his castle the murderer of his wife, determines to carry out a plan of vengeance. But in the resultant ethical struggle that takes place in his own conscience, he realizes that he cannot succeed in winning true justice in the sight of heaven, and so gives punishment into the hand of God. In *Die Herberge (The Lodging;* 1956), which is set in a remote country inn the drama centers around the theft of a sizable bag of gold. As the investigations into the past histories of the characters involved proceed, it is gradually made clear that much greater crimes lie in each individual's background than that of mere complicity in the stealing of the gold. In 1958 he wrote a comedy, *Der Unschuldige (The Innocent One),* about a respected citizen in a community who has an unexplained skeleton dug up in his garden. Gradually, as all evidence appears to indicate that he has murdered someone, the leading character begins to believe that he *may* actually have committed a crime, even though it is eventually proved that the skeleton was that of a Napoleonic soldier. In 1959, for the Salzburg Festival, Hochwälder diverged from his previous playwriting method to write *Donnerstag (Thursday),* which he subtitled *A Modern Mystery Play.* In it he presents an Austrian version of the Faust legend transferred to the present, and both in spirit and form it is in the time-honored tradition of the Viennese *zauberstück,* reminding one of certain plays by Raimund. The play *1003,* written in 1963, is in many ways a sequel to *Donnerstag* though presented in a very different form. It substitutes modern staging techniques, double characterization, and tape recordings in place of magic and fantasy. There are actually only two characters, the author and a character in his imagination, and, as in Pirandellow's famous work, the imaginary character proves more alive than his creator.

The play reprinted here, *Die Himbeere Pflücker*, translated into English as *The Raspberry Picker*, was originally developed for television, but was later expanded into a three-act stage play that was first presented in Zurich on September 23, 1965. It is a strong satire on one of the themes that has nagged Hochwälder most persistently about post war Austria and Germany—namely, the nostalgic backward look at the "camaraderie" and "exciting deeds" performed under the Nazi regime. Since Hochwälder was a refugee from Nazi repression, he has strong personal feelings on the subject, and like anyone who suffered through the Nazi period, he is nagged by the feeling that the human drives that caused that black period in his country's history are not dead, but merely hidden.

Like Brecht, Eliot, and Joyce, Hochwälder is a highly sophisticated craftsman who enjoys using literary analogies and allusions in his dramatic work; in *The Raspberry Picker*, for instance, he makes excellent use of the theme and character situation found in Gogol's *Inspector General*. In Gogol, the ruling clique in a remote provincial village mistakes an adventurer for a government inspector sent to report on the quality of municipal administration, while in Hochwälder the ruling group in an Austrian town mistakes a minor criminal for a major Nazi whom all feel bound to help and assist to safety "for old times' sake." The fact that they also want to move him along because they fear he may lay claim to their ill-gotten war treasure, compounded of gold from the teeth of concentration-camp victims, adds unpleasant but irresistible black humor to the proceedings. It is also interesting to note, along the lines of black humor, that it is not awe for the virtue of the intruder, as in Gogol, that arouses the leaders in the community to action, but admiration for the horror and immensity of the man's wartime record. Though the play begins with a sharp and deft picture of provincial dullness and complacency in a typical western-European, bourgeois community, a man, who appears to be a great exterminator from the former Nazi regime, is shown as able to immediately awaken all manner of nostalgic admiration for the horrific and bloody past. Even though Hochwälder, following the lead of Gogol, exaggerates for satiric effect, the problem of nostalgia for the days of excitement and power is brilliantly presented. Just as in the 1840s the aging members of the Imperial Guard used to turn the great blood baths under

Napoleon into heroic times of grandeur and personal glory, so Hoch-wälder sees the aging participants in World War II turning the epic crimes perpetrated by the Nazis into Wagnerian-style legends. Nostalgia and memory thus cover a gigantic evil with the rosy glow of "past times" and "long ago" and turn war criminals into epic heroes.

The play is thus not just a play about postwar Austria, but about all postwar periods, while it also exemplifies the best attributes found in satiric comedy. Certainly the characters and events of the play are not presented from a neutral or objective point of view. Just as Gogol presents his characters and actions in a heightened, slightly hysterical manner to press home the moral lesson he wishes to project, so the characters and situations in this comedy are exaggerated to give bite and edge to the satiric points that Hochwälder wishes to make. He wishes the audience to laugh at the exaggeration, yet say to themselves at each exposé of character and deed: "How true that is," or "How right he is."

Certainly this is a difficult form of comedy to write since it depends on the right balance between reality and exaggeration. Carry it too far and it will seem superficial and ridiculous; be too subtle and the audience will miss the author's essential outrage at the characters and events presented. Like Molière before him, Hochwälder appears to have the essential moral outrage coupled with the comic writer's sense of the ridiculous and the absurd that can make this kind of play deadly serious and truly comic at the same time.

The Raspberry Picker

A Comedy in Three Acts

by

FRITZ HOCHWÄLDER

Translated from the German by Michael Bullock

Characters (in order of appearance)

SIEGLINDE

ZAGL

BURGERL

HUETT, headmaster

SCHNOPF, doctor

YBBSGRUBER, builder

ZIEREIS, police inspector

ALEXANDER KERZ

GRAPPINA

KONRAD STEISSHÄUPTL

SUPPINGER, lawyer

STANDLMEIER, factory owner

PLACE: Bad Brauning.

TIME: The present.

SCENE: The White Lamb Inn–a picturesque small-town inn with a wrought-iron sign. At ground level, stepped back, several acting areas: on the left a private room, next to it the public bar, on the right a family room with a table and chairs, next to it the entrance to the kitchen. In the center background part of the entrance hall, reception desk and

This play is reprinted from *The New Theatre of Europe*, vol. 4, edited by Martin Esslin (New York: Delta Publishing Company Inc., 1970). Copyright 1965 by Fritz Hochwälder. All inquiries concerning productions should be addressed to the author's representative, Kurt Hellmer, 52 Vanderbilt Avenue, New York, N.Y. 10017.

381

stairs leading up to the bedrooms, of which only one–disproportion-
ately wide and immediately under the eaves–is seen in the course of the
play.

The Raspberry Picker was first performed at the Schauspielhouse,
Zurich, Switzerland, on September 23, 1965.

ACT 1

*(An Autumn morning. The retired medical officer of the town, Dr. Schnopf, and
the headmaster of the local school, Huett, are sitting at the table in the private
room. Schnopf is reading the morning paper. In the family room on the other
side, twenty-one-year-old Sieglinde is standing in front of the fat cook, Burgerl,
and the thin, ageless factotum, Zagl.)*

SIEGLINDE. What are you staring at me like that for? Do you think
    I've murdered someone?

ZAGL. Your hair.

BURGERL. It's a disgrace.

SIEGLINDE. What's it got to do with you? Mind your own business.

BURGERL The color–bright red . . .Herr Steisshäuptl will go nuts when
    he gets back from the Town Hall.

ZAGL. You just can't do that to him, Fräulein Sieglinde.

SIEGLINDE. Times have changed, it's time Father realised that.

ZAGL. Him! Where morality's concerned he's a man of iron, widower
    and mayor that he is. And in the end I'm the one who has to carry
    the load; I don't care for that.

BURGERL. He's quite capable of smashing up the whole
    place; don't forget he used to be a draymen.

ZAGL. Maybe he was, but now he's a respected citizen.
    (To Sieglinde.) Don't be childish, have your hair changed
    before there's a disaster. He won't be home till twelve today,
    there's still time.

BURGERL. Zagl's right, go back to the hairdresser and tell him
    it's burning.

SIEGLINDE. *(Angrily.)* Get lost, all of you! *(Goes out into the hall.)*

ZAGL. Now she's running to the hairdresser.

BURGERL. Let's hope so. *(Goes out into the kitchen.)*

HUETT. *(Shouts from the other side.)* Zagl!

ZAGL. *(Hurries across.)* You called, sir?

HUETT. A beer, and make it snappy.

ZAGL. Something for you, Doctor?

SCHNOPF. I'll have a beer too.

ZAGL. At once, gentlemen. *(Closes the door; goes to the bar; taps a fresh barrel.)*

(Schnopf hangs up the newspaper on the hook again.)

HUETT. Anything new?

SCHNOPF. A jeweler's shop was broken into at Ganselstadt, fellow called Rosenberg.

HUETT. A Jew.

SCHNOPF. No, a Balt, originally. *(Confidentially.)* Like our Rosenberg.

HUETT. *(Dreamily.)* Ah, our Rosenberg . . .

SCHNOPF. You haven't been long in Bad Brauning, Headmaster, comparatively speaking.

HUETT. I had a tough time.

SCHNOPF. So I heard.

HUETT. The man who is loyal to his country pays, whether it's in small coin or large.

SCHNOPF. Loyalty, yes . . .

HUETT. Did the thieves take much?

SCHNOPF. When?

HUETT. The robbers.

SCHNOPF. Where?

HUETT. *(Surprised.)* In Ganselstadt, from the jeweler's

SCHNOPF. Oh, I see. *(Takes the paper.)* An international gang, apparently . . . Highly organized . . . Two shopbreakers arrested at the scene of the crime, an Italian and a Frenchman, the others vanished without trace with the swag—mainly gold articles, watches, earrings, and so on . . .

HUETT. In the last analysis it all comes from the senseless elimination of the outstanding men who serve a healthy nation as examples. In our day we knew how to deal with riffraff, we cut their heads off or put them in concentration camps; stern measures are required—don't you agree, Doctor?

SCHNOPF. What do you expect? Those days are over.

HUETT. Everything comes back again.

SCHNOPF. That's an illusion.

HUETT. Deafeatism is out of place. We remain what we always were.

SCHNOPF. *(Pacifically.)* If you say so.

HUETT. *(Points to the newspaper.)* Look at China, look at Africa—it's still all a question of race.

(Zagl brings the beer.)

ZAGL. Sorry I was so long, gentlemen. I had to tap a new barrel.

HUETT. Your health, Doctor.

SCHNOPF. Your health, Headmaster. Cheers. *(Drinks; then bitterly.)* Lukewarm.

HUETT. *(Contemptuously.)* What a dump.

(Zagl fetches a broom and sweeps the floor.)

SCHNOPF. Do you have to do that now?

ZAGL. How do you mean?

SCHNOPF. We swallow enough dust anyhow; don't ruin our lungs even more–take that broom away!

ZAGL. *(Puts the broom away.)* Sorry, but the place has to be kept clean.

(Ybbsgruber, the builder, enters through the back door that links the private room with the street. He is a coarse fellow who is also addressed as "Colonel".)

SCHNOPF. Ah, Herr Ybbsgruber.

HUETT. Good morning, Colonel.

YBBSGRUBER. *(Full of go.) Heil,* gentlemen. No one else there? How about Steisshäuptl? Oh, of course, still at the Town Hall. Doesn't matter. *(To Zagl.)* A double schnapps! *(Sits down.))* Have you heard the latest– have you read the news?

HUETT. About the robbery, yes.

YBBSGRUBER. What robbery?

SCHNOPF. In Ganselstadt, from Rosenberg the jeweler.

YBBSGRUBER. Who the hell cares about that? Let the police get on with it, instead of forever making difficulties over building permits. I'm no cop. *(Takes a large newspaper out of his pocker.)* Here! In our Old Comrades paper–I thought you gentlemen were all subscribers–the latest edition, came last night . . .

(Zagl comes with the schnapps.)

YBBSGRUBER. You've given me short measure again, Zagl. Like master, like man. That's supposed to be a double; where's the line and where's the schnapps? You think I'm going to let you get away with that? What do you take me for? Go back and fill it up properly. The schnapps must have a real head, one I have to lick off before I raise the glass. Get going!

(Zagl, who understands perfectly what Ybbsgruber means, hurries off.)

YBBSGRUBER. As I was saying, gentlemen . . . *(Opens the newspaper.)* Here, in heavy type, deeply moving and inspiring . . . *(Reads.)* "A manhunt, exclamation mark." *(Looks up.)* That hits home, doesn't it? *(Reads.)* "Subtitle: Our honor is loyalty." And now listen to this! "Once again in these wonderful autumn days, honest men, who fought shoulder to shoulder with us until after the eleventh hour, are being forced to flee from the land of their fathers—

ZAGL. *(Brings the schnapps.)* Is that right now, Colonel?

YBBSGRUBER. Why are you interrupting me? Can't you see I'm making an important announcement? Stay here and listen! You're in the picture too; we must stand together as one man in the new situation.

ZAGL. Very good, sir. I'm listening.

YBBSGRUBER. Silence! *(Searches through the paper.)* "We do not hesitate to state . . ." No, that's later . . . "On the basis of underhand accusations and lying statements by witnesses . . . threatened with heavy terms of imprisonment, even though the supposed misdemeanors took place decades ago . . ." *(Looks up.)* Misdemeanors in inverted quotation marks–that's biting irony. *(Searches further.)* " many of those now being persecuted have built up a civilian existence for themselved by dogged hard work; they are doing no harm to anyone . . . honest men who fought shoulder to shoulder with us . . ." Oh, I've read that already! *(Throws the newspaper on the table.)* The situation as I see it, gentlemen, is as follows. We in Bad Brauning must also do our bit. Word will spread like a prairie fire in our small but closed circle–It's a pity Steisshäuptl isn't here; Zagl, you will inform him of the position.

ZAGL. What position, please?

YBBSGRUBER. Idiot. *(To the others.)* In a word, how shall we react if a fugitive comes to us seeking help, begging for refuge–one of those now forced to flee from this Old Testament vengeance? *(Silence.)*

SCHNOPF. *(Clears his throat.)* Well . . . who is going to come to us?

YBBSCRUBER. Who knows? Perhaps he is already on his way . . . *(Leans forward.)* When I read this poignant article yesterday evening after supper, I immediately got in touch with the proper quarters by telephone, as president of the local Old Comrades Association . . . *(Bangs the table.)* Yes, I took action on my own account and I accept complete responsibility! *(Folds up the *paper and puts it in his pocket.)* It was assured that our offer was much appreciated; they will probably send us a high-ranking refugee; their only request is that the incognito of any possible arrival shall be rigorously respected until, by our united efforts, he has been got across the nearby frontier–to Egypt, South America, or somewhere–gentlemen, that is all. *(Pause.)*

HUETT. Colonel you did the only possible thing!

SCHNOPF. Undoubtedly, but *(Cautiously.)* do you think that everyone will be in agreement?

YBBSGRUBER. Who will not, for example?

SCHNOPF. It depends who they send us. An incognito like that is a tricky business. Twenty years ago there were people from a wide area round here who disappeared; I won't say people who don't matter– because in principle everyone matters– but people who . . . well, I mean . . .

YBBSGRUBER. *(With a grin.)* Cunning fox.

SCHNOPF. What do you mean?

YBBSGRUBER. You're thinking of the Raspberry Picker, of course; admit it.

SCHNOPF. You've guessed it.

YBBSGRUBER. No, I'm afraid we can't hope for that. In the end he was sent to fight the partisans, and no one came back from there.

SCHNOPF. A lot of people have popped up who were thought to be dead.

YBBSGRUBER. *(With a thoughtful smile.)* The Raspberry Picker . . .

HUETT. Excuse me, who is–or was–the Raspberry Picker?

YBBSGRUBER. Of course, you weren't here then . . . *(Straightens up.)* The Raspberry Picker was a troop leader in the camp over at Wüstenhofen . . . It's a sort of museum now, but at that time . . .*(After a pause.)* He used to order the prisoners into the quarry, in summer, to pick raspberries to supplement their diet; then he used to knock them off one by one with a telescopic rifle. *(Makes the appropriate gesture.)* Pft! *(Apologetically.)* He was a passionate sharpshooter . . .*(Leans back.)* He is supposed to have been here in Brauning just before the Yanks arrived, for the first and last time, with a lorry and a driver. But no one saw him, no one knows his name or what he looks like; none of us would recognize him—

ZAGL. Excuse me, I would.

YBBSGRUBER. You?

ZAGL. At a glance.

YBBSGRUBER. *(Contemptuously.)* Go on . . .

ZAGL. *(Eagerly.)* I was the only one who saw him over by the edge of the forest, when I was given orders by the local Group Leader to—*(Breaks off.)*

YBBSGRUBER. Orders *(With interest.)* to do what?

ZAGL. *(With embarrassment.)* My God, it's so long ago . . .

(The Police Inspector, Ziereis, has appeared in the entrance hall and is approaching the private room.)

ZIEREIS. *(Opens the door. In a not particularly friendly tone.)* Sorry to disturb you, good morning. *(To Zagl.)* Come outside, I have something to say to you, officially.

ZAGL. *(To Ybbsgruber.)* I'll be back in a minute. *(Goes out to the Inspector.)*

YBBSGRUBER. *(Shouts after him.)* I'll buy a round, for you too, Zagl, and of course for the inspector. *(In an undertone to Huett and Schnopf.)* We'll talk about something else–I don't trust that fellow.

ZIEREIS. Show me the registration book.

ZAGL. The registration book–why? We've got no visitors–this is the off season, October, nothing doing at all.

ZIEREIS. Nevertheless I want to see it. *(Goes with Zagl to the reception desk; inspects the registration book.)* In the future every guest is to sign the register immediately they arrive. Foreigners are to produce their passports—

ZAGL. We've never been so fussy—

ZIEREIS. Never mind what you used to do, Zagl. From now on you will carry out the regulations, I shan't let you get away with anything in the future, bear that in mind.

ZAGL. *(Offended.)* The Chief isn't going to like that—

ZEIREIS. *(Sharply.)* I know what my duty is–without respect of persons!

ZAGL. What's come over you all of a sudden?

ZIEREIS. *(Puts the registration book back on the desk.)* That's an official secret.

(Sieglinde enters with her hair unchanged.)

ZIEREIS. *(Transformed.)* How you've grown up, Fräulein Sieglinde, . . .

SIEGLINDE. *(Coolly.)* Good morning, Herr Ziereis. *(To Zagl.)* Is he back yet?

ZAGL. *(Horrified.)* It's just the same!

SIEGLINDE. I didn't ask you about my hair, I asked you whether he's back yet.

ZIEREIS. *(Looking at her hungrily.)* My God, I'd like to have
a daughter like you; it wouldn't necessarily have to be a
daughter . . .

(Sieglinde turns towards the entrance hall.)

ZIEREIS. *(By her side; in a low voice.)* Shall we go for a walk and
have a bit of a chat?

SIEGLINDE. *(In a loud voice.)* So you can pinch my bottom again, I
suppose? *(Hurries out.)*

ZAGL. The way young people talk nowadays!

ZIEREIS. *(Gruffly.)* You know what to do—see that you do it!

ZAGL. There's a schnapps waiting for you.

ZIEREIS. I'm on duty. *(Goes.)*

YBBSGRUBER. *(In the door of the private room.)* How about that
round of drinks? How long are you going to be? *(Speaking over
his shoulder.)* All clear.

ZAGL. *(In a low voice.)* A disaster . . .

YBBSGRUBER. What?

ZAGL. Sieglinde's hair . . . The boss will go nuts . . . *(At the
bar, fills the glasses.)* The schnapps is coming at once.

(Ybbsgruber returns to the table in the private bar.)

HUETT. Psychopath, butcher, sadist—what else, Doctor? *(Straightens
up.)* And what would have happened if they could have done
as they liked with us? I mean, if Roosevelt hadn't been unmasked
as a Communist just in time?

SCHNOPF. I beg your pardon—

HUETT. *(Carried away by a vision.)* They would have dragged us off
to distant, inhospitable regions, to Russia and America; no one
would have been spared, the earth of our homeland would have
been laid waste, and those sinister figures whom the Raspberry
Picker left alive would today be sadistically wielding the whip
over us. Before my mind's eye I see the triumphant faces of those
sub-men, contorted with glee as they gloat over our systematic
destruction; our fields and meadows would have become deserted,
our German forests gone to rack and ruin, there would have been
no economic miracle. Reduced to skin and bone, a shadow of
our forner selves, deprived of all human dignity, we should have
provided slave labor for our enemies, who would then have
achieved their Satanic aim: the final extermination of the
patriotic element!

SCHNOPF. Meaning who?

HUETT. Us!

YBBSGRUBER. *(Who has been listening reverently.)* It's true, that is beyond the power of the imagination; therefore I say: right or wrong, it was pure self-defense. *(Zagl comes with the schnapps.)* Consequently every fugitive who comes to us for help is welcome, without exception. *(Raises his glass.)* Gentlemen—in the name of solidarity!

(All drink, including Zagl.)

YBBSGRUBER. *(Stands up.)* I've got to go and see Stadlmeier at his factory now, on private business. If anything happens, I shall be there till three. *(To Zagl.)* Put it all on my account.

ZAGL. Thank you very much, Colonel.

HUETT. *(Also rising.)* I'll walk with you part of the way. *(To Schnopf.)* Are you staying here?

SCHNOPF. I shall have a bite to eat. It's too dreary at home—a housekeeper, life on a pension . . . Goodby, gentlemen.

(Ybbsgruber and Huett leave through the back door. Sieglinde hurries from the hall, runs upstairs and off. Immediately afterward a curious couple appear in the hall: Alexander Kerz, middle fifties, a Levantine type, slim, smartly dressed; and Grappina, late thirties, blonde, rather the worse for wear but still attractive. He is carrying a suitcase, she merely a beauty case.)

GRAPPINA. *(In an undertone.)* You're crazy.

KERZ. Why, we've got to put up somewhere—

GRAPPINA. Who're you kidding, Sasha, you're simply after that girl—

KERZ. *(Admonishingly.)* Grappina!

GRAPPINA. *(Drags him back into the entrance hall.)* We're getting out of here!

(Zagl is putting the used glasses on a tray.)

SCHNOPF. He's very eloquent, the headmaster, there's no denying that.

ZAGL. Yes, that's education.

SCHNOPF. A small goulash with a gherkin—and another beer.

ZAGL. Certainly, just a moment. *(Goes out with the tray, puts it down, goes across to the kitchen.)* A small goulash, for Dr. Schnopf! *(Goes to the bar, fills a glass, serves it in the private room.)*

(Kerz comes back alone, looks round.)
(Zagl in the private room.)
(Kerz beckons with his right forefinger.)

ZAGL. *(Closer.)* Can I help you, sir?

KERZ. *(In a low voice, hurriedly.)* A double room with a bath–got anything available?

ZAGL. As many as you want; they're all empty as it happens.

KERZ. Just a moment! *(Turns round, hurries out into the hall, comes back with Grappina; in an undertone.)* What did I tell you? It's all right! *(Takes the beauty case from her, puts it on the reception desk; to Zagl.)* Lead on!

ZAGL. Coming, sir. *(Takes a key from the rack behind the reception desk.)* Number 7, with a bath as you wished–every convenience; the toilet is in the corridor; we're going to rebuild next year. *(Pushes the registration book towards Kerz.)* If you will be so good– a mere formality. *(Kerz pretends to enter his name in the book, but slips a hundred-mark note between the pages instead.)*

ZAGL. You'll like Bad Brauning, it can be beautiful in October, splendid walks, the mountain path, the ruins on the Fuchsenberg, a cinema, a swimming pool, paved since the spring, and if there is anything special the lady would like, just let me know–my name is Zagl. *(Takes the registration book.)* Thank you, sir . . . *(Dumbfounded.)* but . . . there's nothing there—

KERZ. *(In a low voice and sharply.)* Are you blind?

(Zagl spots the hundred-mark note, looks up, studies Kerz carefully for the first time, suddenly starts.)

KERZ. *(In a low voice.)* Put it in your pocket.

(Zagl does not take his eyes off him; feels for the hundred-mark note, puts it in his pocket.)

KERZ. Carry on.

ZAGL. *(Involuntarily military.)* Very good, sir! *(Pauses. Kerz nods to him, takes the key, signs to Grappina with a nod to walk ahead of him; both go up the stairs and off.)*

(Zagl stands as though turned to stone.)

(Burgerl comes out from the kitchen with the goulash.)

BURGERL. One small goulash for the doctor.

(Zagl as above.)

BURGERL. *(Closer.)* What are you standing there like a stuffed
   dummy for?

ZAGL. *(After a pause, in a muffled voice.)* Speak of the devil . . .

BURGERL. What devil?

*(Zagl's eye lights on the beauty case; he grabs it and runs
   upstairs and out.)*

BURGERL. *(Shaking her head.)* I've known him for twenty years
   and he gets more and more stupid . . .*(Goes into the private
   bar; serves the goulash.)* I'm sorry, Doctor, Zagl has just gone
   running upstairs like a madman; someone special must have
   arrived; he said something about the devil.

SCHNOPF. *(Looks up.)* No roll, no bread?

BURGERL. Sorry, he'll bring it in a minute. *(Crosses to next room,
   meets Zagl as he comes down the stairs, absolutely
   flabbergasted.)* You've got a memory like a sieve! Take the doctor a
   roll.

(Zagl takes no notice of her, walks past her into the private room.)

BURGERL. *(Gazes after him; mutters to herself.)* Of course his father
   was already in the loony bin at that age . . . *(Goes out into the
   kitchen. Zagl approaches the table in the private room, stands in
   front of the doctor.)*

SCHNOPF. What's the matter? You're as white as the wall.

ZAGL. *(As though in a trance.)* He's . . . here . . .

SCHNOPF. Who?

ZAGL. The . . . Raspberry Picker. . . .

SCHNOPF. The Raspberry . . . *(Lowers his knife and fork.)* Is that
   meant to be a joke, or—

ZAGL. *(Wakes up, hurriedly.)* With a woman in Number 7, with
   bath. His manner is the same as it was then on the edge of the
   forest: "Are you blind?" "Carry on!" The manner, the tone of
   voice, the hooked nose–unmistakable. In those days his hair
   was black, now it's streaked with gray, but he still looks very
   smart–without a uniform, of course, that takes something away
   from him.

SCHNOPF. What are you talking about!

ZAGL. *(Leans over the table.)* It's no surprise. The colonel said he
   was coming . . . and then . . . I checked up: the gold! *(Breaks
   off.)*

(Pause.)

SCHNOPF. Well then . . . I wouldn't like to be in your chief's
   shoes . . . People said all sorts of things at the time: first a
   drayman, then a local Group Leader . . . after forty-five

suddenly made of money . . . innkeeper, cinema owner . . .
mayor.

(Pause.)

SCHNOPF. I believe in thought transference. As a matter of fact
the moment Ybbsgruber started talking about it the thought
flashed through my mind: the Raspberry Picker . . .

ZAGL. *(In a low voice.)* Who'd have thought it . . .

SCHNOPF. *(With an undertone of malicious pleasure.)* You can
always expect the unexpected. *(Stands up, takes his coat and
hat.)* I'll pay this evening or tomorrow morning, as the case may
be. *(Turns toward the back door.)*

ZAGL. *(Plaintively.)* Doctor.

SCHNOPF. *(The door knob in his hand.)* Yes?

ZAGL. If you wouldn't mind keeping it to yourself for the moment
—perhaps I'm wrong after all.

SCHNOPF. *(Ironically.)* Perhaps. *(Goes.)*

(Pause.)

ZAGL. The cunning dog . . . *(As he clears the table; lost in
thought.)* the boxes . . . the gold . . .

(Burgerl comes out of the kitchen and lays the family table standing nearby.)

(At the same time Sieglinde races downstairs.)

SIEGLINDE. He's here!

BURGERL. *(Turns round, claps her hands together above her head.)*
Heavens above, you haven't had it changed!

SIEGLINDE. I wouldn't dream of it, I've just made a conquest with
it . . . *(Closer.)* the gentleman who has taken a room here, with
an old tart.

BURGERL. Don't talk like that! Your father will break your
neck if he hears you.

SIEGLINDE. *(Rapturously.)* What a man!

(Zagl comes out of the private room.)

SIEGLINDE. Hey, Zagl—who is the man in Number 7?

*(Zagl busies himself with the plates and glasses, pretends to be
deaf.)*

SIEGLINDE. Have you gone deaf, or . . . *(After a pause.)* All right,
I like secrets, and all of a sudden I'm hungry. I'm going to the
kitchen for a quick bite. *(In the kitchen doorway.)* A fine-looking
man, no youngster, but a real gentleman. It's about time a man
like that came our way for a change! *(Goes.)*

BURGERL. *(Indignantly.)* Shameless hussy! *(Follows her off.)*

ZAGL. *(Goes to the stairs and looks up.)* He looks just as demonic
as ever, even without a uniform—that's another proof. *(Turns*

round.) The red hair–and now the Raspberry Picker . . . One
disaster after the other for the chief. I really don't envy him!
(Goes out into the hall and off.)

(Darkness on stage level; at the same time the double room under the eaves comes into sight.)
(All sorts of goldware on the table and beside it the open suitcase and the beauty case.)
(Grappina is tanding by the window, Alexander Kerz by the table.)

KERZ. Don't worry! The idiot didn't even see the gold–on the
contrary. He stood to attention in front of me, and even if he
did, I'll talk my way out of it–that's my specialty *(Taps his
forehead.)* It's working away in there like the inside of a clock,
but I'll find an answer to everything. Don't imagine I'm going to
let people like that get the better of me; I've been in far tighter
spots than this . . . *(Offended.)* but of course, instead of backing
me up you keep complaining all the time, while I'm trying
to think how we can slip across the frontier unmolested and
(Irritably.) what did you say?

(Grappina says nothing.)

KERZ. *(Points to the gold articles.)* Just tell me, who snapped that
lot up with the speed of a monkey; who got clear with you at the
last moment? You know where you would be without me?
Where the other two are stewing at the moment! Can I help the
unfortunate incident with the cretin just now? Why did you
have to leave your beauty case standing downstairs; was that
my fault? Yes, I admit I should have locked the door, but who'd
have expected anyone to come in without knocking; I suppose
they've never heard of manners around here. But it's no use
crying over spilled milk! Is there anything else?
(Grappina says nothing.)
KERZ. One way or the other we need money; we can't dispose of
the stuff at the moment–patience! I'll think of something in the
twinkling of an eye. I suppose you don't believe me, do you?
(Grappina says nothing.)
KERZ. *(In a different tone.)* The robbery yesterday was only half
successful, therefore *(Emphatically.)* be sensible–what's done is
done, why worry about whose fault it was? The fact is—
GRAPPINA. *(Scathingly.)* That you should have given the night
watchman a crack on the head!

KERZ. *(Squirming.)* Don't go on about that now—

GRAPPINA. The arrangement was that you and I were to keep a
lookout, Vito and Frédéric were to clear the shop, and if the
night watchman or anyone else came along, you were to give
him one with the brass knuckles—

KERZ. Stop it!

GRAPPINA. Was that the arrangement?

KERZ. Yes, yes, but—

GRAPPINA. Why didn't you do it?

(Kerz stares at the floor, tugs at his mustache.)

GRAPPINA. Why didn't you give him one? *(Closer.)* Why not?

KERZ. *(Embarrassed.)* Because–you haven't known me long, what
are two months? You won't understand, Grappina ... I have
my peculiarities; everything has to be the way I
picture it, and if anything goes wrong, then ...*(After a pause.)* In
short, I'm no thug!

GRAPPINA. *(Perplexed.)* With your reputation?

KERZ. Yes, yes, I know–but that's misleading. I can't bear the sight
of blood, it simply turns my stomach . . . I'm game for
anything, but murder *(In a low voice.)* No!

(Pause.)

GRAPPINA. *(Sarcastically.)* A fine hero

KERZ. *(Looks up.)* Here? What makes you say that? I've never
been a hero and never shall be one. I'm international: eighteen
previous convictions in five countries, but I can't lay into a
human being with a chunk of iron . . . *(Sits down.)* I can't . . .
I can't . . .

(Pause.)

GRAPPINA. And that's what I've ended up with, who would have
believed it . . . The fellows I had before you–none of them
gave a damn for doing someone in, I used to feel safe with them,
it was like being at home . . . Michel *(She pronounces the
name the French way.)* the man of iron with the flick-knife in
his bag, if someone so much as looked at me askance, and that
used to happen often, he would whip it out and wham! Right
between the ribs. *Un mauvais garçon,* sure, but what a man! And
the others, during the war . . . and before, and after . . . in
Perpignan, Lyons, Le Havre . . . wherever I popped up . . .
no coward had any chance with me, and now *(Kerz rises and goes
to the door.)*

GRAPPINA. Sasha!

KERZ. *(The doorknob in his hand.)* Find yourself a hero, I'm off.

GRAPPINA. You beast, you pig. *(Hurries after him, clings to him.)* Do you think you're going to dump me here on account of that young tart downstairs—

KERZ. Let go of me!

GRAPPINA. You belong to me!

KERZ. Let go!

GRAPPINA. *(Lets go of him; in a low voice.)* Are you going to stay?

KERZ. And who's going to rustle up some money—you maybe?

GRAPPINA. *(Anxiously.)* Are you coming back?

KERZ. Of course.

GRAPPINA. *(Relieved.)* Sasha . . .

KERZ. There's an old saying, where there are people they can be robbed. Do you bet me I come back this evening empty-handed? *(Severely.)* Stay in the room; order what you like, we'll pay later, if at all . . . Do something to pass the time, play solitaire, take a bath—

GRAPPINA. A bath, yes . . .

KERZ. In a few hours we'll scram, *d'accord?*

GRAPPINA. *D'accord. (Goes to the table, takes the beauty case, stops in front of the bathroom door.)* But . . . don't get into mischief downstairs.

KERZ. Who with?

GRAPPINA. *(Describes Sieglinde with an appropriate gesture.)* With the redhead.

KERZ. As though I had no other worries just now.

GRAPPINA. I know you, when a girl with a backside like that comes along . . . You watch out! *(Off.)*

KERZ. Stupid, just too stupid! . . . *(Goes to the table, puts the jewelry in the case, locks it, puts the key in his waistcoat pocket, takes a battery shaver from his overcoat, goes to the wall mirror, feels his chin.)* The redhead? *(In a low voice.)* Not bad . . . not bad at all . . . *(He begins to shave.)*

(Darkness, at the same time the scene at stage level is lit up. From the entrance hall comes Zagl with Steisshäuptl, a powerfully built man.)

STEISSHÄUPTL. *(Furious.)* Bright red dyed hair—the very thought makes me see red! *(Yells.)* Dinner, I've got to get to Ganselstadt for the meeting; bring it here before I starve to death!

ZAGL. Can't it be postponed?

STEISSHÄUPTL. Out of the question—it's a meeting of the local fire brigade, as fire chief I'm indispensable. Burgerl!

(Burgerl in the kitchen door.)

STEISSHÄUPTL.   What have you got for me?

BURGERL.   *(Respectfully.)* Liver dumpling soup, roast pork with warm cabbage salad, and fried—

STEISSHÄUPTL.   Haven't you got anything nourishing?

BURGERL.   —and cheese strudel, left over from yesterday.

STEISSHÄUPTL.   *(Bitterly.)* That's the way you get served in your own inn, it's scandalous. The liver dumpling soup, but be snappy!

(Burgerl goes.)

STEISSHÄUPTL.   She'd better keep out of my way, or I shall give her a piece of my mind. What does the bitch thing she's up to? Whose daughter does she think she is, a village shopkeeper's, proletarian's? Doesn't she know what she owes her father, morally speaking? A bright-red beehive, like a strip-tease girl probably. Just wait till I get hold of her!

ZAGL.   And then there's another thing.

STEISSHÄUPTL.   Stop it, I've had enough!

ZAGL.   *(Jerking his head in the direction of the private room; in a low voice.)* In there where no one can overhear . . .

STEISSHÄUPTL.   Are you drunk?

ZAGL.   I'll lock the front, you lock the back. *(Crosses over; locks the door to the street.)*

STEISSHÄUPTL.   *(Follows him.)* What nonsense is this?

ZAGL.   Lock up, Chief.

(Steisshäuptl does so, shaking his head, then sits down at the table in the private room.)

(Zagl approaches and whispers in his ear.)

STEISSHÄUPTL.   *(Jumps up.)* What, Ybbsgruber—

ZAGL.   *(Pulls him back onto the chair.)* Listen to the rest of it . . . *(Whispers to him.)*

(In the family room Burgerl has laid the table and brought in the soup.)

BURGERL.   Fräulein Sieglinde!

(Sieglinde in the kitchen door,)

BURGERL.   I've changed my mind. Give him the roast pork right away and the strudel with it; he's at his most peaceful at dinner time and I want peace in the house. In you go, get moving! *(Both into the kitchen and off.)*

STEISSHÄUPTL.   *(Slowly.)* Are you sure it's really him?

ZAGL.   I give you my word.

STEISSHÄUPTL.   *(Shattered.)* The Raspberry Picker in Brauning—

that had to happen, just when we were expecting crowds of
visitors next year, people from the Old Reich, English people,
maybe even Americans . . . The slightest scandal and we can
go swimming in our own newly paved swimming pool, because
no one else will. *(Jumps up.)* It's a disaster; am I to stand by and
do nothing while I'm being ruined? *(Up and off.)* I'm the
mayor, the welfare of the town is at stake, every empty room
loss to me during the season, I can just see on the front page
of the newspaper: "The Raspberry Picker arrested in the White
Lamb, proprietor Steisshäuptl." The scandal, the press poking
their noses in, the loss of turnover ! . . *(Stands still.)* What is
he thinking of? Does he imagine I'm in league with him?

(Zagl looks at him.)

STEISSHÄUPTL. What are you looking at me like that for?
ZAGL. I'm not looking at you. *(Pause.)*
STEISSHÄUPTL. Everything was so peaceful here, a heavenly peace,
all we thought about was making money, and now all of a sudden
this fellow comes along with his eight thousand dead—
ZAGL. Six thousand at the most.
STEISSHÄUPTL. Six thousand, eight thousand, I don't give a damn.
. . . Perhaps he even imagines I'm going to stick my neck out
for him. If so, he's making a big mistake, those days are over;
I don't even know what he looks like; he never let himself be
photographed the cunning fox . . .*(Resolutely.)* I know what
I shall do: I'll go straight up and tell him to get the hell out of
here, and right away! *(Goes to the door; unlocks it.)*
ZAGL. *(In a weak voice.)* Suppose he asks for his gold back?
STEISSHÄUPTL. *(Turning round.)* *(His gold—?*
ZAGL. *(Stands up.)* The boxes I took over from his driver in 1945
—on your orders! *(Comes up to him; in a low voice.)* Dental gold
mainly, from the camp. Secret affair of state. *(Steisshäuptl stares
at him.)*
ZAGL. He stood at the edge of the forest and watched, I can see
him today . . . The driver was killed later during the retreat,
and we drew a sigh of relief and thought the other would get his
too, fighting the partisans.

(Steisshäuptl as above.)

ZAGL. When I went into his room just now without knocking, I
saw a pile of gold on the table. Then it dawned on me. He is

collecting it all together again, for the Odessa Organization . . . Ybbsgruber specially told us to maintain the strictest incognito; we mustn't tell the Raspberry Picker who he is. So in your place I would begin by finding out what he wants from you, or rather how much . . .

(Steisshäuptl as above.)

ZAGL. Besides, times change . . . How will you look if one day he comes back as a hero . . . You haven't only got friends here, you know, Chief . . .

(Pause.)

STEISSHÄUPTL. *(Comes slowly back to the table in the private room, sits down; in a different tone.)* If you think about it seriously, it's an injustice. After all, it's twenty years ago, and they're still hunting men as though they were beasts; I don't care for that. The others murdered too; what about the bombs? Was that nothing? I'm not defending him, but there comes a time when you have to call a halt. These people are too full of hate to see that. The man has paid dearly, he's like a wounded beast, we can't turn him away from the door; here the feelings must speak and reason stay silent.

ZAGL. That's silent anyway, just ask your daughter. You know, he radiates something, there's no getting away from it.

STEISSHÄUPTL. *(Thoughtfully.)* My daughter, just a minute . . .

ZAGL. Although he's got a woman with him, for camouflage, a poor creature on the wrong side of forty.

(Pause.)

STEISSHÄUPTL. *(Looks up.)* Tell me Zagl.

ZAGL. Yes.

STEISSHÄUPTL. What did we do with the boxes in 1945?

ZAGL. *(Uncomprehending.)* We–?

STEISSHÄUPTL. Listen. We immediately sank the two boxes in the Katzlsee–in the deepest part, beyond all hope of salvage.

ZAGL. *(Perplexed.)* In the Katzlsee–?

STEISSHÄUPTL. You were a witness . . . *(Rises threateningly.)* or weren't you?

(Pause.)

ZAGL. *(Intimidated.)* Sure, Chief.

STEISSHÄUPTL. Up to now the only one who knows is the old doctor, and I guarantee he'll keep his trap shut . . . And tell

the inspector to keep his nose out of it. I'm the boss here!
And in general, you're responsible for seeing that no one comes
into contact with the Raspberry Picker, got it?

ZAGL. Okay, Chief.

STEISSHÄUPTL. In a few hours the whole situation will be clear.
Either I'm going to be treated as a comrade, or . . . Providence
has never let me down! *(Turns round; goes across to the family table.)*

ZAGL. *(Gazes after him; in a low voice.)* No one can get the better
of him. A born leader. *(Unlocks the back door; off.)*

STEISSHÄUPTL. *(Sits down, tries the soup, throws down the spoon.)*
Ice-cold, of course. *(Shouts.)* The roast pork!

(Sieglinde with a tray from the kitchen.)
(Sieglinde serves her father in silence.)
(Steisshäuptl looks up.)

SIEGLINDE. The pork. The cheese strudel.

(Steisshäuptl leans back and looks at her.)

SIEGLINDE. *(Strikes a pose; defiantly.)* Well?

(Pause.)

STEISSHÄUPTL. *(Appreciatively.)* Very smart.

SIEGLINDE. *(Surprised.)* Really?

STEISSHÄUPTL. It's not my taste, but then I'm an old square.
(Begins to eat.) Relax. Come and sit with your father, what have
I got a pretty daughter for? . . .

(Sieglinde sits down.)

STEISSHÄUPTL. *(Pushes the strudel across to her.)* Here, eat this!
That stuff will lie on my stomach all the way through the meeting;
I'll buy myself some pig's feet in Ganselstadt.

SIEGLINDE. *(In a low voice.)* This is not like you at all.

STEISSHÄUPTL. People don't always behave as they should. We're
only human. At bottom I'm a sensitive plant. A beer!

(Sieglinde goes to the bar; fills a tankard.)
*(Steisshäuptl rises, goes to the kitchen door, shuts it, comes back to the table.
Sieglinde brings the beer.)*

STEISSHÄUPTL. *(Takes it; drinks standing, puts the tankard down,
sits down.)* I hear you're interested in the gentleman in Number
7–

SIEGLINDE. *(Disparagingly.)* Oh, him!

STEISSHÄUPTL. Why shouldn't you be? We're only flesh and blood.

Why shouldn't you take a liking to someone–especially when
he is such a personality—

SIEGLINDE. *(Astonished.)* Do you know him then?

STEISSHÄUPTL. Eat!

(Sieglinde sits down.)

STEISSHÄUPTL. *(In a low voice.)* He knows me . . . *(Emphatically.)*
Just so you know–that man can ruin me. Everyone has
his duty in life, especially with a hairdo like that. I need you now
like a hungry man needs bread; I want you to get into a personal
conversation with him, that's all I'm interested in.

SIEGLINDE. You want me to–?

STEISSHÄUPTL. Eat, I said!

SIEGLINDE. *(Reaches for the strudel.)* But he has a lady with
him—

STEISSHÄUPTL. Don't make me laugh, that old hag. Just take a look
at yourself! It's a matter of life and death; I must know tonight
what he wants from me or how much. Don't let me down!

SIEGLINDE. I must say, I'm surprised—

STEISSHÄUPTL. Get your teeth into it!

(Sieglinde takes a bite; eats.)
(Pause.)

STEISSHÄUPTL. *(Elegiacally.)* We are helpless against earthly
beauty, I remember that from your dear mother, a captivating
woman, even the old photographs show that. We didn't call you
Sieglinde for nothing; we hoped then with all our hearts–and
then it was all over, a dream of blood and loyalty . . . *(In a
reverie.)* Is it surprising if one had a moment of weakness? Who
wouldn't think of his family? The Americans had enough anyway,
so one simply used it . . .

SIEGLINDE. *(Puts down the strudel.)* Used what?

STEISSHÄUPTL. Once in a while one can do something for one's
father. You can get to know each other, go for walks in the forest
up to the höhenweg, show the stranger the sights, the
Fuchsenberg ruins, very romantic, the raspberry canes in among
them—

SIEGLINDE. The raspberry canes–?

STEISSHÄUPTL. –and how the river down below winds its silvery
way around the little town as it lies there as though in an old

painting; you will sit on a bench provided by the Society for the
Improvement of Local Amenities—that's my work, you can slip
in—not a soul in sight to disturb the perfect peace . . . the
crickets . . . one word leads to the next, and suddenly it all
comes out! *(Stands up; in a different tone.)* Fetch my loden coat,
I don't want to catch cold in Ganselstadt.

*(Sieglinde goes to the stairs, Kerz comes down, steps aside; Sieglinde goes up and
off.)*
(Kerz stares after her.)
(Steisshäuptl clears his throat.)
(Kerz turns to him.)

STEISSHÄUPTL. *(Standing to attention.)* Steisshäuptl—mayor, innkeeper,
and owner of the cinema next door.
KERZ. *(Shakes hands with him.)* How d'you do.
STEISSHÄUPTL. May I heartily welcome you. I haven't had the
honor to meet you personally, but one hears all sorts of things.
KERZ. *(Impudently.)* What?
STEISSHÄUPTL. *(Intimidated.)* Nothing.
(Kerz steps back, eyes him from head to foot.)
STEISSHÄUPTL. *(With a shudder.)* That look . . .
KERZ. What?
(Pause.)
STEISSHÄUPTL. *(Uncertainly.)* You haven't been here for a long
time . . .
KERZ. I?
STEISSHÄUPTL. That's to say . . . please don't think that I would
do anything to . . . I am the soul of discretion . . . I would
just like to point out, if I may, that not everything people say is
true—
KERZ. What do people say?
STEISSHÄUPTL. A man works hard and earns money, he gets some-
where in life, and then—it's sad, very sad. *(In a different tone.)*
The latest films . . . a wide screen, you've no idea what that
costs . . . Every Sunday two programs, afternoon and evening,
generally poorly attended and altogether . . . *(Close; in a low
voice.)* But I'm a man one can come to terms with.
KERZ. *(Interested.)* Can one—
STEISSHÄUPTL. *(Confidentially.)* Like you, I have remained just
what I was. If you were to cut me open you would see.
KERZ. Cut you open?

STEISSHÄUPTL.   Metaphorically, as they say. *(Again in a low voice.)* It is still too early to go into details. What I want to know is whether I can count on your understanding.

KERZ. *(After brief reflection.)* You may. *(Leans forward; in a low voice.)* I too am a man one can come to terms with.

STEISSHÄUPTL. *(Radiant.)* That's fine!

(Sieglinde comes in with his loden coat.)

STEISSHÄUPTL.   Thanks, girl. *(Takes the coat to Kerz.)* I am afraid I have to go out, to a meeting, otherwise I would myself . . . May I introduce my daughter, Sieglinde. She will have the honor of showing you round a bit; she can do it better than I can, can't you, angel?

SIEGLINDE.   Only if the gentleman has no other plans.

KERZ.   I was going to ask the young lady to do just that.

SIEGLINDE.   Really?

KERZ. Word of honor.

SIEGLINDE.   Shall we go straight away, or—

KERZ. Straight away, if that suits you. *(Holds out his arm for her; to Steisshäuptl.* Goodby, my dear fellow.

STEISSHÄUPTL. Goodby and enjoy yourself, Herr–!

(Kerz goes off with Sieglinde; in the entrance hall they meet Zagl, who stands still and gazes after them.)

STEISSHSÄUPTL.   We talk the same language.

ZAGL.   *(Approaches; admiringly.)* So you've done it again, Chief.

STEISSHÄUPTL.   His appearance, his bearing, his tone, his eyes–a leader of men!

ZAGL.   That's exactly what I felt.

STEISSHÄUPTL.   And a man like that is hunted through every continent– incomprehensible . . . *(After a pause.)* None of what is talked and written about it gets to the heart of the matter; the grandeur, the heroic spirit. A few dark patches, eight thousand victims and so on, are of no significance by comparison . . . *(Straightens up.)* Think of what we were then and what we are now. Rich, but from the point of view of ideals, scum! *(With growing enthusiasm.)* Local Group Leader! When I think about it the present seems to me like a bad dream. In those days hope ruled our lives and we were ready to sacrifice ourselves for the future. In those days we forgot commonplace existence–no, it

forgot us; there was no commonplace existence, there were
trumpets and flags and standards, the streets resounded under our
marching feet, black leather, the breath of history . . . And
suddenly it all comes back, all of a sudden I am the old, young
militant again, and why? *(Without giving Zagl a chance to answer.)*
Because once again there is "Blood and Honor" around
me; he has brought it back—yes, I am proud that a hero has
come to stay in my inn; I shan't hide my thoughts: I should like
to march on, even if everything falls in ruins!

(Goes quickly out into the hall.)

ZAGL. *(Stands where he is; dreamily.)* And tomorrow the whole
world . . . *(Looks up.)* Listening to him, it's as if we were back
in the old days . . .

(Curtain.)

ACT 2

(Afternoon. Zagl and Burgerl are sitting at the family table drinking coffee.)

BURGERL. Another cup of coffee?
ZAGL. *(Lost in thought.)* No.
(Pause.)
BURGERL. It's three-thirty already and she still isn't back.
ZAGL. So much the better.
BURGERL. Why?
(Zagl does not answer.)
BURGERL. I'm only surprised that the chief allows it. He isn't
usually like that. A pretty young thing all alone in the forest with
an absolute stranger, no one knows who or what he is; how easily
something can happen; only the day before yesterday there was
a rape in the paper, and half a year ago a pervert over in Breitenau
murdered two women in one night and bathed in their blood.
ZAGL. *(Superciliously.)* He doesn't bother with little things like
that.
BURGERL. There's no knowing.
ZAGL. *(Vigorously.)* I know.
BURGERL. Go away, don't put on such airs.

ZAGL. Shut your mouth, you silly cow!

BURGERL. *(Disconcerted.)* What a way to talk to me!

ZAGL. Your slanders irritate me. What do you know in your steamy kitchen about leaders of men, do you think the soul of honor means nothing? *(Not giving her a chance to speak.)* You stick to your dumplings and don't poke your nose into the breath of history, you can think what you like about me, but don't make any unseemly remarks—you don't know me.

BURGERL. *(Indignantly.)* That's what comes of being nice to a creature like you—it'll be a long time before I make you a coffee with a double rum again! *(Off into the kitchen carrying the coffeepot, slams the door behind her. Meanwhile the lawyer has appeared in the entrance hall and is approaching the family table.)*

SUPPINGER. Trouble in the family?

ZAGL. *(Turns round; in surprise.)* Herr Suppinger . . . *(Stands up; coolly.)* You wanted something?

SUPPINGER. For the moment *(Sits down.)* a glass of mineral water.

ZAGL. That's a lot, but I must point out to you, Herr Dr. Suppinger, that you are sitting at the family table—

SUPPINGER. Listen, Herr Zagl, you must do me an urgent favor, you won't regret it. *(Takes hold of his lapel.)* Speak to the Raspberry Picker for me!

ZAGL. *(Pulling away.)* Where am I to find a raspberry picker? The season was over long ago.

SUPPINGER. Watch out! Your life is at stake. *(Pulls Zagl toward him; confidentially.)* You know, these present trials . . . First they'll pick on the prominent figures, and after that . . . *(Whispers in Zagl's ear. Zagl starts.)*

SUPPINGER. Is it bound to come to that? By no means! But if it does, then I, as a lawyer, shall stand by you . . . *(Smiling.)* free of charge, please note. *(Emphatically.)* The man is as important to me as I am to him; he has been seen walking around with Steisshäuptl's daughter, he will be back soon; I must get hold of him; I guarantee you an agent's fee—I'm not going to let this case get away from me! *(Zagl stares at him wide-eyed.)*

SUPPINGER. *(Rises.)* I'll wait for you in the private room, okay?

ZAGL. No, I'll take you up to Number 2, but *(Anxiously.)* it won't go any further?

SUPPINGER. Of course not.

ZAGL. *(Takes him to the bar.)* Strictly incognito—that's an order.

SUPPINGER. Do you take me for an idiot?

ZAGL. *(Takes a key from the wall-rack.)* I'm only a small man; it's not for me to pass judgment. *(Stands aside to let Suppinger go first; both go upstairs and off.)*

(Kerz and Sieglinde enter from the hall.)

SIEGLINDE. I've never had a man like you before–it was like nirvana–

(Burgerl in the kitchen door.)

KERZ. *(To Sieglinde, in a low voice.)* Behave yourself!

SIEGLINDE. What are you staring at?

BURGERL. *(After a pause.)* I was only looking . . . *(Clears the cups from the table; off into the kitchen.)*

SIEGLINDE. Father was quite right: You're a personality.

KERZ. Sure, but how does he know me?

SIEGLINDE. I don't know, he just said that you knew him–you do know him, don't you?

KERZ. Of course, but—

SIEGLINDE. What does he matter to us? *(Close, in a low voice.)* Come to me, in my room!

KERZ. Again–?

SIEGLINDE. Oh, you . . .

KERZ. What else did he say?

SIEGLINDE. Don't ask, you know already.

KERZ. All right, either you spill the beans or . . . *(Turns away.)*

SIEGLINDE. *(Holds him back.)* No, no . . . *(Whispering.)* He also said that you could ruin him—

KERZ. I could ruin him?

SIEGLINDE. –and that his life was at stake, he was once weak, that's all I know. Are you coming now?

KERZ. Just a moment! *(Embraces her.)* When was he weak, what is he offering, and how much? *(Zagl comes downstairs.)*

KERZ. *(Lets go of her, steps back; in a formal tone.)* The view is overwhelming . . . the raspberry canes among the Fuchsenberg ruins . . . an unforgettable experience . . .

(Zagl whispers in his ear in passing.)

KERZ. What, who–?

ZAGL. *(Aloud.)* Then I'll serve coffee in the private room! *(Off into the kitchen.)*

SIEGLINDE. First floor, in the corridor at the back, on the right. *(To the stairs turns round.)* Come now! Come soon! *(Upstairs off.)*

KERZ. *(Takes the handkerchief from his breast pocket, wipes his brow.)* Now it's getting strenuous . . .

(Zagl comes with the coffee tray.)

KERZ. *(Goes up to him.)* What sort of lawyer?

ZAGL. *(Standing in front of him, in a whisper.)* A very sharp one, you listen to what he says. *(Hands him the tray.)* I'll send him right over. *(Upstairs and off.)*

KERZ. *(Stands for a while irresolute; then.)* Oh well, the main thing is it looks as though there might be money in it . . . *(Walks across with the tray, sits down, pours coffee; drinks.)*

(Zagl comes in with Suppinger.)

ZAGL. You must be as quick as lightening. I'll stand guard outside. Afterward I'll walk along with you. I must be kept informed, otherwise it will call come to nothing. *(Holds him back.)* Don't forget my agent's commission!

SUPPINGER. *(Pulling away.)* My word is as good as my bond.

(Zagl goes out through the entrance hall.)

(Suppinger enters the private room.)

(Kerz looks up.)

SUPPINGER. *(Standing to attention.)* Eduard Suppinger, lawyer.

KERZ. How do you do.

SUPPINGER. Time presses, you won't mind if I come straight to the point. *(Sits down.)* First of all: regarding the boxes—

KERZ. *(Astonished.)* The boxes?

SUPPINGER. *(Smiling.)* You remember . . .

KERZ. I see . . . *(Impudently.)* of course, yes, the boxes!

SUPPINGER. *(Leaning forward.)* It would be madness to let the matter rest; up to now it was impossible to prove anything against Steisshsäuptl; things are different now, there can be no doubt about it, he pocketed a million—

KERZ. A million?

SUPPINGER. At a conservative estimate.

KERZ. A million. . . .

SUPPINGER. Up to now you couldn't follow the matter up, you had other worries, but *(Whispering.)* if we only get half of it out of him, it will be well worth-while.

KERZ. How . . .

SUPPINGER. May I make a suggestion?

KERZ. *(Sits down.)* Please do.

SUPPINGER. *(Moves closer.)* To judge by human standards, you are unassailable—

KERZ. Am I?

SUPPINGER. Absolutely. Ideologically speaking there is complete unanimity here. All the same, just in case anything should happen I should like to ask you to empower me to act for you. This applies equally to the material aspect, please note–payment by results! The important thing is not to take any steps without consulting me. I prophesy that Herr Stadlmeier will try to get in on the act—

KERZ. Who?

SUPPINGER. Leopold Stadlmeier, managing director of the famous mineral water factory, rolling in money . . . How he got it is another story. Ybbsgruber, the builder, will also start pestering you, a scoundrel if ever I saw one. A man who talks about ideals and runs after lost valuables. *(Shows his teeth.)* We know his sort, don't we? Make no promises for the time being; refer the petitioners straight to me, your legal representative; here is my card. *(Hands it to him.)* You can get in touch with me at any time, in the office or at home. May I ask you for a definite decision?

KERZ. *(Glances at the card; then in a low voice.)* Some things are not clear to me—

SUPPINGER. They will be. To see you is to tremble.

KERZ. You mean–?

SUPPINGER. A shudder runs down everyone's spine . . . *(In a low voice.)* even mine–that means something.

KERZ. Very well then. *(Puts the card in his pocket; rises.)* Agreed.

SUPPINGER. *(Jumps up.)* I guarantee final victory. *(Hurries out through the back door.)*

KERZ. *(Gazes after him; in a low voice.)* Payment by results? You'll be lucky! . . . *(Straightens up.)* To see me is to tremble . . . it seems I'm something military . . . *(Resolutely.)* What the hell, five hundred thousand–I'll make you a general too for that! *(Hurries into the next room, upstairs and off.)*

(For a few seconds the stage remains empty, then Dr. Schnopf enters through the back door and Headmaster Huett from the hall. At first they make sure that they are alone, then Huett creeps quietly forward, while Schnopf approaches the door of the private room and silently opens it. The two men catch sight of each other simultaneously and stand rigid.)

SCHNOPF. *(Gets possession of himself; jovially.)* Headmaster–what a surprise.

HUETT. I could say the same of you, Doctor.

SCHNOPF. Why, it's not surprising that I should be here, I've got nothing to do all day, but you—

HUETT. I'm not answerable to anyone.

SCHNOPF. No, of course not, but *(Closer.)* prevention is better than cure.

HUETT. I've no idea what you're talking about.

SCHNOPF. Admit it, you're out to make a certain contact.

HUETT. Contact—who with?

SCHNOPF. Yes, yes, the unrest of the heart . . . No sooner does word get round than plenty of people are trembling—

HUETT. *(Anxiously.)* Who is trembling?

SCHNOPF. You never can tell . . . I thought right away, you wouldn't be altogether pleased—

HUETT. I forbid you to make remarks like that!

SCHNOPF. Well, one man is persecuted because of eight thousand, and the other—

HUETT. Put your own house in order before you start slandering decent people. I shall just say: Old Age Home.

SCHNOPF. And I say: manhunt.

HUETT. Be quiet!

SCHNOPF. You be quiet! *(Burgerl appears in the kitchen door.)*

BURGERL. Gentlemen, gentlemen, what has hapened to make you two go for one another like savages, two educated men. You should be ashamed to behave like that in front of the foreigner. . .

SCHNOPF. *(Grimly.)* You'll hear more of this.

HUETT. *(Likewise.)* So will you.

(Huett goes into the hall, Schnopf out through the private room.)

BURGERL. *(Gazes after them.)* It must be the weather. . .

(The inspector enters from the hall.)

ZIEREIS. Isn't the chief back yet?

BURGERL. Why?

ZIEREIS. Are you deaf? I asked you whether he is back yet.

BURGERL. He will probably come back on the six o'clock train. He's in Ganselstadt at a meeting.

ZIEREIS. You don't need to tell me that. I know everything! Where is Zagl.?

BURGERL. How should I know? I'm not married to him. *(Calls.)* Zagl! *(Silence.)*

BURGERL. *(Shrugging her shoulders.)* He's not there . . .

ZIEREIS. With the six o'clock train . . . *(Vigorously.)* Right, I'll wait for him at the station!

BURGERL. Has something happened, Inspector?

ZIEREIS. *(Threateningly.)* Watch out—you! *(Into the hall and off.)*

BURGERL. *(Shaking her head.)* Now he's starting too . . . *(Into the kitchen and off.)*

(Meanwhile Stadlmeier, the factory owner, has appeared in the private room accompanied by Ybbsgruber.)
(Stadlmeier, a soigné city gentleman, generally chooses his words carefully and speaks quietly.)

YBBSGRUBER. My dear Herr Stadlmeier, if I may say so, you're on the wrong track there. I know Steisshäuptl, brute force is the only thing that will work with him. What do you expect from an exdrayman?

STADLMEIER. Nothing, for the moment . . . It is most convenient that our rival is not here. Do you think that otherwise I should have come to this place?

YBBSGRUBER. Yes but—

STADLMEIER. Let us consider the situation quite calmly—

YBBSGRUBER. One moment, first I should like to *(Goes to the communicating door, opens it.)* Zagl! *(Goes out, looks round.)*

(Stadlmeier sits down.)

YBBSGRUBER. *(Comes back.)* The place is deserted . . . it's odd; ordinarily Zagl is always here . . . *(Sits down with Stadlmeier.)* I'm sorry, I interrupted you.

STADLMEIER. Don't mention it. No let us consider the situation as it appears at the moment. No doubt those comrades who sent the man here know nothing about the things that disappeared at that time—

YBBSGRUBER. *(Briskly.)* That's just what I have been asking myself ever since Dr. Schnopf told me about it. I think it would be best for me to make a long-distance phone call right away. *(Rises.)*

STADLMEIER. Are you mad?

YBBSGRUBER. Why, I only want—

STADLMEIER. Sit down.

(Ybbsgruber sits down.)

STADLMEIER. It is a positive blessing for us that the higher-ups know nothing about the whole affair. Do you think that if they did Steisshäuptl would still be running around free?

YBBSGRUBER. Ah, that's true . . .

STADLMEIER. Therefore our most urgent task is to ascertain the approximate value of the misappropriated boxes, and before our dear Steisshäuptl comes to some agreement with the Raspberry Picker. Is that clear?

YBBSGRUBER. Yes, but how are you going to do that so quickly?

STADLMEIER. I believe I am fairly experienced in this sort of thing. First and foremost we must have those with firsthand knowledge on our side–the stick and the carrot! First the moronic Zagl, then the Raspberry Picker. Let us wait until the factotum appears.

YBBSGRUBER. He ought to have been here long ago, the idiot.

STADLMEIER. With regard to subsequent events, I imagine I can take it for granted that the profit we expect to make on the . . . on the things . . . will go to the mineral water factory established by myself. We are doing a great deal for certain comrades, consequently we are entitled to this recompense.

YBBSGRUBER. No one doubts that; nevertheless I should appreciate it if you would let me have a share in the money; after all, I did act as go-between, so to speak; moreover I have been working like a Trojan day and night for the same end–

STADLMEIER. *(Friendly.)* Don't worry, we will discuss that at the proper time.

YBBSGRUBER. Couldn't we set it down in writing now. *(Takes a sheet of paper and a fountain pen from his pocket.)* One of us might die—

STADLMEIER. Later, my dear Ybbsgruber, later .. . .

(Zagl enters through the back door.)

ZAGL. Herr Stadl–! *(The rest sticks in his throat.)*

STADLMEIER. At last . . . *(Rises, goes to meet him, shakes his hand.)* Come my dear fellow, sit down with us.

ZAGL. No, the chief doesn't allow that–no hobnobbing with customers.

YBBSGRUBER. We don't give a damn for what Steisshäuptl allows or doesn't allow. Sit down!

ZAGL. *(Intimidated.)* If it's an order.

(The two take him in between them.)

STADLMEIER. We were just talking about you, Herr Zagl. You see, we both agree that a man of your abilities is entitled to get on in life. In short, at the present moment there is a vacant post for a caretaker at my factory: a two-roomed flat with a kitchen and bath, telephone, refrigerator, washing machine, television of course, forty-hour week, and so on; and as to salary–suppose we started at, say, three thousand?

ZAGL. *(His eyes popping out.)* Three–?

STADLMEIER. *(Friendly.)* –thousand.

ZAGL. It would be fine, but *(Worried.)* he won't let me go from here.

STADLMEIER. Are you a free man or a slave?

ZAGL. Oh well, free, of course, more or less, but *(With a sigh.)* it's mainly a question of loyalty.

YBBSGRUBER. Listen, I'll tell you something. From today on Steisshäuptl is done for, finished. I'll give it to you in writing that we are the stronger, understand?

STADLMEIER. *(Gently.)* Your life is at stake.

YBBSGRUBER. You could get married!

ZAGL. Oh heavens, no one will take me.

YBBSGRUBER. And what about Burgerl?

ZAGL. Burgerl?

YBBSGRUBER. You'll see–she's crazy about you!

STADLMEIER. Marriage is really a wonderful institution.

YBBSGRUBER. Three thousand for a start and more later.

ZAGL. *(Wrestling with himself.)* Refrigerator . . . television . . . washing machine . . . Burgerl crazy about me . . . *(Looks up; decided.)* Herr Stadlmeier, I won't say no!

STADLMEIER. Bravo! And now fetch the Raspberry Picker and watch like a hawk that no one disturbs us.

ZAGL. *(Jumps up; servile.)* Very good, sir– Raspberry Picker, hawk– *(Impudently.)* Do I also get a Christmas bonus as caretaker?

(Ybbsgruber gestures peremptorily to him to go out and up. Zagl runs upstairs.)

STADLMEIER. Brilliant, the marriage idea clinched it.

YBBSGRUBER. Yes, I'm good at that sort of thing . . . Tell me, are you serious about the three thousand?

STADLMEIER. *(Smiling.)* For a time–why not?

YBBSGRUBER. I see. But it won't be so simple with the Raspberry Picker. Don't forget–strictly incognito.

STADLMEIER. Don't worry, my dear Ybbsgruber.

(Kerz comes down with Zagl.)

ZAGL. Forgive me—I thought you were with your lady—

KERZ. Did you say Stadlmeier and Ybbsgruber?

ZAGL. That's right. The gentlemen are already on tenterhooks—
I shall stand guard outside to see that nothing happens. *(Into
the hall and off.)*

KERZ. *(Stops outside the private room; in a low voice.)* Ybbsgruber,
Stadlmeier . . . Well, here goes! *(Enters the private room.)*

YBBSGRUBER. *(Militarily.)* Ybbsgruber, from the Old Comrades
Association!

STADLMEIER. My name is Stadlmeier, I run the local mineral water
factory.

KERZ. *(Impertinently.)* I'm not a fool—I know everything!

YBBSGRUBER. You know—?

KERZ. I'm not in thehabit of bluffing, Herr Ybbsgruber. Why
are you standing, gentlemen? Sit down.

(They sit down.)

KERZ. My time is precious. I have all sorts of things to do. *(Crosses
one leg over the other.)* Well then, what can I do for you?

STADLMEIER. May I . . . *(Clears his throat.)* Might I ask whether
you have already talked to Herr Steisshäuptl?

KERZ. Just a few words, nothing binding.

STADLMEIER.   Ah, excellent.

YBBSGRUBER. You've taken a load off our minds.

STADLMEIER. I don't suppose I should be wrong in thinking that
you will negotiate with us first.

YBBSGRUBER. You'd be a fool if you didn't—Oh, I beg your pardon!

STADLMEIER. You can speak quite frankly, we're game for anything.

YBBSGRUBER. Have no illusions; we're the stronger, any child here
can tell you that.

STADLMEIER. One might express it differently, but it's true.

(Pause.)

KERZ. Is that all?

STADLMEIER. We should like to hear the rest from you.

YBBSGRUBER. Go ahead, we're dying to hear.

KERZ. Gentlemen *(He rises; indignantly.)* who do you take me for?

(Ybbsgruber and Stadlmeier look at each other in dismay.)

STADLMEIER. *(In a low voice.)* We know who you are.

KERZ. You know who I am. Interesting. But when I listen to you,
I can't help thinking that you mistake me for someone of no
special account—

YBBSGRUBER. What an idea!

STADLMEIER. We wouldn't do such a thing!

KERZ. You wouldn't? Then please note that my time is not
  unlimited. Either you put your cards on the table, or else—

STADLMEIER. Oh, come–as comrades surely we can talk the matter
  over quietly—

KERZ. Herr Stadlmeier, if you think you can make a fool of me
  you're mistaken. I value clarity and frankness. *(Identifying himself
  more and more enthusiastically with his imaginary identity.)*
  There was a time when a word from me was enough–what am
  I saying? A word? a movement of the hand, so! And that meant
  finished, done for! I repeat, you don't know who you are dealing
  with; people stood to attention when they talked to me—

(The two jump up and spring to attention.)

KERZ. Yes, like that, more or less. I give short shrift–there are
  people who could tell you a tale about that, I'll say no more!
  In here *(Taps his forehead.)* Its like clockwork. I remember
  everything for years, for decades; if you knew how many
  thousands have passed through my hands, you would rate me
  higher;
  I weigh my words *(His voice rising.)* thousands, thousands!

YBBSGRUBER. *(Respectfully.)* Actually eight—

KERZ. Eight? What are you talking about, Herr Ybbsgruber? Do
  I look as though I bother with trifles? Or do you think you can
  beat me down! If I say thousands, I mean tens of thousands, I
  haven't got the figures in my head–they're all dust and ashes
  now!

(Ybbsgrubber and Stadlmeier stand as though paralyzed.)

KERZ. Your offer, or I shall turn to someone who knows the value
  of a millon—

STADLMEIER.⎫ *(Simultaneously.)* A million?
YBBSGRUBER.⎭

KERZ. I know what I know. *(Sits down.)* Make up your minds.

STADLMEIER. Just a moment ... a few seconds ... *Whispers
  urgently with Ybbsgruber; then to Kerz.)* I should like to propose
  an interim solution that will be to the advantage of both parties.
  You think the matter over carefully–after all, one can make
  mistakes–and call on me tomorrow morning at my villa, where
  I shall introduce you to my closest collaborators–all of them
  men of your stamp, even if not of the same caliber. We shall

make you a suitable offer–don't forget, we are the stronger,
morally and materially. One moment! As a token of our good
will, we ask you to accept an immediate advance–let us say,
five thousand.

KERZ. *(Raising his eyebrows.)* Five–?

STADLMEIER. All right then, eight–No, you won't be satisfied
with that. Very well, we'll round it off–ten thousand, will that
do?

KERZ. *(After a pause.)* Hand it over *(Stretched out his right hand.)*
out of pure comradeship.

STADLMEIER. *(To Ybbsgruber.)* **Pay up!**

YBBSGRUBER. *(Horrified.)* **But I'm broke–!**

STADLMEIER. *(Ironically.)* With a wallet full of thousand-mark
notes?

YBBSGRUBER. Yes, because I've got more payments to make—

STADLMEIER. *(Emphatically.)* Ten thousand, at once!

YBBSGRUBER. *(Takes out his wallet with a sigh.)* That would
happen to me . . . *(To Kerz, as he counts out the notes.)* I'm
really sorry about the eight thousand. . .

KERZ. *(Counts them after him, puts the notes in his pocket.)*
That's over and done with.

STADLMEIER. One more request. Avoid any discussion with Herr
Steisshäuptl. We'll deal with him later.

YBBSGRUBER. Yes, properly!

KERZ. *(Rises.)* Agreed.

STADLMEIER. Tomorrow at ten sharp in my villa. Zagl will take
you there inconspicuously.

KERZ. Right, gentlemen. Till tomorrow then! *(Strolls over to the
bar; off.)*

(Dusk falls.)

STADLMEIER. *(Reproachfully.)* And you nearly showed me up in
front of that man.

YBBSGRUBER. *(Embarrassed.)* Why, I really have payments to
make, and apart from that —

STADLMEIER. *(Sharply.)* You did all right out of building my factory!

YBBSGRUBER. But Herr Stadlmeier—

STADLMEIER. *(Crossly.)* All right. *(Through the back door and off.)*

YBBSGRUBER. *(Stunned.)* Now he's offended . . . *(Calls after him.)*
Herr Stadlmeier– *(After a pause; bitterly.)* A postwar
phenomenon! *(Off.)*

(Huett appears in the entrance hall.)

HUETT. Huett . . . Arnold Huett . . .

KERZ. *(Startled.)* Who?

HUETT. *(Closer.)* One of your men . . .

KERZ. Pleased to meet you. Is there anything I can do for you?

HUETT. *(Hurriedly.)* Beward of the doctor!

KERZ. The doctor? Am I ill?

HUETT. *(Hurriedly.)* Schnopf didn't suffer like us, he was
   everything, even a Socialist. *(Looks anxiously towards the
   communicating door.)* Take care! I'll tell you more tomorrow! *(Off.)*

KERZ. Yes, but–

*(Schnopf, who has entered the private room from the street, is standing in the
communicating doorway.)*

SCHNOPF. Don't believe a word that Huett says! He's an utter
   opportunist–recently he has become an ardent Catholic.
   (Hurriedly.) My name is Schnopf, Friedrich Schnopf; we almost
   met—

KERZ. Where, when?

(Zagl comes in from the hall.)

SCHNOPF. *(In a whisper.)* Reich Medical Association! *(Draws
   back.)* Don't do anything before tomorrow morning! *(Through
   private room and off.)*

KERZ. What an odd lot . . . *(Turns to Zagl.)* Tell
   me, what did my . . . what did the lady say just now?

ZAGL. She wanted to know when you were coming back.

KERZ. Nothing else?

ZAGL. No, I took her a meal in the middle of the day, at her
   request, and two bottles of Zierfandler.

KERZ. Two–?

ZAGL. *(Confidentially.)* It seems to me the lady likes drinking.

KERZ. *(Dropping his usual tone.)* You're telling me!

ZAGL. I beg your pardon? *(Pause.)*

KERZ. *(Takes a thousand-mark note out of his pocket.)* Can you
   change that?

ZAGL. Sorry, I've no change–this is the off season.

KERZ. *(Pushing the note into his hand.)* Keep the change.

ZAGL. *(His hands on the seams of his trousers; in a whisper.)* We
   shall march on till everything falls in ruins!

KERZ. *(Laughing.)* Of course—do you think I'm a fool? *(Hurries upstairs and off.)*

ZAGL. *(Gazes after him; in a low voice.)* They were the elite . . . The chief should have thought it over before. Charity begins at home, three thousand a month . . . a comfortable home . . . *(Thoughtfully.)* Burgerl . . . well, why not? I like good solid women. *(To the kitchen door.)* Burgerl! Burgerl!

(Burgerl in the doorway.)

ZAGL. *(Waving the thousand-mark note.)* What do you say to that?

BURGERL. Where did you get hold of that thousand-mark note?

ZAGL. Don't ask; it's still a secret. There's going to be a marriage. Yes, I'm going to marry you, if you want to know. We're moving to Stadlmeier's, two rooms, refrigerator, television, washing machine—Don't talk about it for the time being, keep out of the chief's way until victory is ours. Do as I've told you! *(Into the hall and off.)*

BURGERL. *(Is so taken aback that she only gradually finds words.)* Marriage . . . the rat, the traitor—and a fellow like that talks about the soul of honor! *(Off into kitchen. The stage grows dark. The room above comes into view, lit by a lamp burning over the table. Kerz is standing by the window, Grappina sitting in an armchair near the table, a full wineglass in her hand.)*

KERZ. *(Triumphantly.)* Well, who was right? Ten thousand in hand, the rest to follow; I won't take less than half a million, even if the gentlemen explode! *(Closer.)* What do you bet we aren't out of our difficulties by tomorrow?

(Grappina drinks.)

KERZ. Your everlasting drinking is getting on my nerves; stop it —two bottles are enough. I work as I did in my best days, and you . . . put that glass away!

GRAPPINA. *(Puts the glass on the table.)* Who do they think you are?

KERZ. Who do they think I am? You should worry! A hell of a fellow, top brass! What does it matter, so long as the idiots keep on coughing up the money—

GRAPPINA. A hell of a fellow—oh, oh, my little Sasha—

KERZ. Shut your trap! Instead of giving me a boost, you put me down. Listen to me: I really am a hell of a fellow. I can slip

into any skin I like. Just think of all the things I've been—a
film magnate, a managing director, an officer, a Spanish grandee,
Barone di Treviso, and all the rest. Why not the man they all
tremble before here?

GRAPPINA. That's okay with me, but . . . how did you hit on the
idea?

KERZ. How? Why through the landlord in the first place, a fellow
I shouldn't like to meet alone in a wood, and then of course
through his daughter—

GRAPPINA. *(Attentively.)* Who?

KERZ. His daughter—are you deaf?

GRAPPINA. Aha.

KERZ. What do you mean, aha?

GRAPPINA. That's why you're shaking like a leaf.

KERZ. *(Despairingly.)* So now I'm shaking like a leaf again!

GRAPPINA. Come here.

KERZ. Why?

GRAPPINA. Come, come.

KERZ. *(Beside her.)* What's up now?

GRAPPINA. *(Pulls the hanging lamp across, looks at his face.)*
Rings under your eyes, like a —

KERZ. Blind drunk! *(Tears the lamp out of her hand and lets it
swing back.)* It's always the same; that's the only thing you ever
think about. Apparently you think I'm a goat—

GRAPPINA. I've no reason to. *(Ironically.)* A hell of a fellow, maybe,
but not with me.

KERZ. Of course, to you I'm nothing but a petty crook. You're
always dreaming of your past heroes. Did any of them ever dig
up a fortune out of nothing *(Taps his forehead.)* just with that?

GRAPPINA. Wait and see.

KERZ. Of course, what else? A good night's sleep, lights out
shuteye! We must be fit for tomorrow—

GRAPPINA. Tired?

KERZ. Who says so? What rubbish—

GRAPPINA. *(Stands up, smiling.)* It suits me if you're full of beans.
(Off into bathroom.)

KERZ. *(Sighing.)* Now that . . . *(Resigned.)* Well, if it has to be.
. . .*(Takes off his jacket, hangs it over the back of the chair,
undoes his tie, slips out of his shoes, goes to the double bed,
throws back the blanket, sits down on the edge of the bed and
waits.)*

(The sound of the shower from the bathroom.)

KERZ. *(Sleepily.)* Redheads, yes . . . one isn't twenty any
  more . . . *(Yawns.)* Oh well, tomorrow . . . it'll all . . . be
  over . . .
(Sinks onto the bed, falls asleep.)
(After a while Grappina appears, in her underclothes.)
GRAPPINA. Sasha . . .
(Silence.)
GRAPPINA. I'm sorry, I wasn't nice to you just now . . . I'll keep
  my fingers crossed for you tomorrow. . .
(Silence.)
GRAPPINA. Can you hear me?
(Silence.)
GRAPPINA. *(By the bed.)* Sasha!
(Kerz snores.)
GRAPPINA. *(After a pause, between her teeth.)* Crapule! *(Darkness;
  at the same time the lights go on below, Steisshäuptl enters
  with Ziereis from the hall.)*
STEISSHÄUPTL. No need to apologize. I like to be met at the
  station. By the way, would you like a drink?
ZIEREIS. *(Reserved.)* I'm afraid I must refuse.
STEISSHÄUPTL. As you wish, Herr Ziereis. Well then, what's on
  your mind?
ZIEREIS. I have to inform you that you are harboring a man **whom**
  the authorities have been seeking for twenty years. *(Takes the
  wanted notice out of his briefcase.)* Ernst Meiche, known as
  "The Raspberry Picker," born March 19, 1910 in Klausenburg.
STEISSHÄUPTL. Show me that.

(Ziereis hands him the list.)
(Steisshäupatl sits down at the family table, studies it.)

ZIEREIS. I was here in the morning already following another clue
  that came to nothing, and I specially told Zagl to enter every
  guest the moment he arrived and that I wouldn't turn a blind
  eye any more *(Bitterly.)* and this is the result.
STEISSHÄUPTL. *(Looks up; calmly.)* Now at least we know his
  civilian name. Wait a minute, I'll make a note of it. *(Takes out
  his notebook.)* I simply can't remember names nowadays.
  (Writes.) Ernst Meiche . . . born March 19, 1910 . . .
  Klausenburg . . .

ZIEREIS. *(Disconcerted.)* You knew?

STEISSHÄUPTL. *(Puts away the notebook, hands back the list.)* Everything is orderly here.

ZIEREIS. Just a minute, Herr Steisshäuptl–!

(Burgerl in the kitchen doorway.)

BURGERL. You're back at last! There's something I must tell you.

STEISSHÄUPTL. *(Gruffly.)* Later!

(Burgerl goes back into the kitchen and shuts the door.)

STEISSHSÄUPTL. *(Friendly.)* Inspector.

ZIEREIS. Apparently you don't know *(Goes up to him.)* that your daughter was seen with him up in the forest, in the old hunting lodge. They were in there for two hours. I know everything. I have my informants–things look different now, don't they?

(Pause.)

STEISSHÄUPTL. *(Shouts.)* Burgerl!

(Burgerl in the kitchen doorway.)

STEISSHÄUPTL. Tell Sieglinde to come down, this instant!

BURGERL. *(Closer; urgently.)* Chief–

STEISSHÄUPTL. This moment, I said!

(Burgerl goes to the stairs; mounts groaning.)

ZIEREIS. The man is on the list of wanted persons. I'm not interested in politics; I shall arrest him at once!

STEISSHÄUPTL. *(Calmly.)* Don't let me stop you.

(Ziereis turns towards the stairs.)

STEISSHÄUPTL. *(Turns round; sharply.)* But then it will also come out that you were in a Special Duty Squad, Herr Ziereis!

ZIEREIS. *(Stops as though struck by lightning.)* Me?

STEISSHÄUPTL. *(Rising.)* Forty-three–in Vilna.

ZIEREIS. In Vilna, yes, but never—

STEISSHÄUPTL. *(Goes toward him; cuttingly.)* And you can be sure there will be witnesses. Reputation plays a certain part too; everyone knows you're after my daughter; several times you have made indecent approaches to her. Do you think my fatherly heart is going to put up with that indefinitely? That's abusing your official position–do you think we're in Vilna?

(Ziereis stares at him.)

STEISSHÄUPTL. Right, now go ahead and arrest him.

ZIEREIS. *(In a low voice.)* I was never in a Special Duty Squad.

STEISSHÄUPTL. Go ahead!

(Ziereis does not move.)
(Burgerl comes downstairs.)

BURGERL. I've told her. She will be down in a minute. She's just
dressing. *(In front of Steisshäuptl; in an undertone.)* I've got
something important to tell you.

STEISSHÄUPTL. Stop bothering me.

ZIEREIS. *(Slowly.)* Now I should like a drink . . .

STEISSHÄUPTL. *(Contentedly.)* That's fine . . . You see,
everything can be arranged . . . *(To Burgerl.)* A double, and give
good measure, for the inspector. Bring it to the private room, and
look sharp!

*(Burgerl to the bar, pours out the drink, takes the glass to the table in the private
room; Ziereis follows with lowered head.)*

STEISSHÄUPTL. *(Alone.)* Yes, the past is a power . . .

(Sieglinde comes downstairs.)

STEISSHÄUPTL. My sunshine! *(Goes to meet her, puts his arm
round her, leads her front stage.)* There you are at last. I knew
I could rely on you–blood is thicker than water.

*(Burgerl, who has come back from the private room, comes to a stop in front of
Steisshäuptl.)*

STEISSHÄUPTL What the hell do you want now?

BURGERL. *(Intimidated.)* Nothing . . . *(Into the kitchen, off.)*

(Sieglinde and Steisshäuptl sit down.)

ZIEREIS. *(Who has drunk his schnapps standing.)* Vilna . . . forty-
three . . . *(Worried.)* I didn't give the order. . . *(Off.)*

STEISSHÄUPTL. *(Uneasily.)* What a face you're making–one might
imagine . . . Do you by any chance think I'm going to scold
you? It had to be done. *(Impatiently.)* Well, what is it?

(Sieglinde remains obstinately silent.)

STEISSHÄUPTL. *(Melancholy.)* My premonitions . . . I felt it–
he is going to be implacable about taking . . .

SIEGLINDE. Shall I tell you?

STEISSHÄUPTL. Everything! Spare me nothing.

SIEGLINDE. Well then *(Straightens up.)* I'm absolsutely crazy about
him—

STEISSHÄUPTL. What are you saying?

SIEGLINDE. I felt it from the first moment. He is a man, and the
special thing about it is that I can't forget it. It's not like with
the kids who come here in the summer–oh no, he is a great
man—

STEISSHÄUPTL. *(Jumps up.)* Didn't I impress upon you that it's a matter of life and death? I must know what he wants of me and how much–didn't you get it out of him in the forest?

SIEGLINDE. I never thought about it.

STEISSHÄUPTL. You didn't think–? Two hours in the hunting lodge and you found out nothing?

SIEGLINDE. I heard all the angels sing.

STEISSHÄUPTL. *(Furious.)* Shameless creature, what do I care about your angels!

SIEGLINDE. Careful . . . *(Jumps up.)* I'm under his protection! *(Steisshäuptl winces.)*

SIEGLINDE. *(In a low voice.)* Now things look different, don't they? *(To the stairs; quickly up; off.)*

STEISSHÄUPTL. *(Sinks onto a chair, rests his head on his hands.)* That's . . . inhuman . . .

(Burgerl appears, approaches.)
(Steisshäuptl does not move.)

BURGERL. You must pull yourself together. *(Shakes him.)* Zagl is a traitor; he wants to marry me and move to Stadlmeier's; he says they're stronger, and that we should get away from you–

(Steisshäuptl looks up.)

BURGERL. I don't know what it's all about and I don't care. I just want peace and quiet in the house.

STEISSHÄUPTL. To Stadlmeier's?

(Zagl appears in the entrance hall.)
(Burgerl nudges Steisshäuptl with her elbow, points to the back, withdraws into the kitchen and shuts the door.)
(Steisshäuptl turns round.)

ZAGL. Good evening, Chief.

STEISSHÄUPTL. *(Quietly.)* Come here.

ZAGL. Why?

STEISSHÄUPTL. For a chat.

Zagl sits down facing him.)

STEISSHÄUPTL. Is everything all right in the house?

ZAGL. *(Monosyllabically.)* Yes

STEISSHÄUPTL. Was anything wrong?

ZAGL. No.

(Pause)

STEISSHÄUPTL. It's strange.

ZAGL. What?

STEISSHÄUPTL. There are certain things that mustn't be forgotten, even if they're unpleasant.

ZAGL. *(Uneasily.)* What things?

STEISSHÄUPTL. For example, what would you say if Johann Suchanek in Ganselstadt suddenly found out who denounced him and his friend to the Gestapo in 1942?

(Zagl stares at him.)

STEISSHÄUPTL. Through a miracle, Suchanek came back alive, but his friend returned to his relations in a tin coffin. *(Leans forward.)* Why are you looking at me like that? *(Zagl chokes.)*

STEISSHÄUPTL. *(More sharply.)* You can't serve two different masters. If you try, there comes a day when you don't wake up; that's happened before now. *(Suddenly grabs him.)* Out with it!

ZAGL. *(Trembling.)* I'll tell you everything.

STEISSHÄUPTL. *(Holds him in an iron grip.)* What happened?

ZAGL. I was the victim of corruption. Burgerl is too fat for me, anyhow, Dr. Suppinger wants to defend the Raspberry Picker, Dr. Schnopf has been telling everyone, Ybbsgruber was here with Herr Stadlmeier, the gentlemen as so eloquest, they say that from today you are done for, Chief, and that they will come to an agreement about the gold over your head– you see, I'm firmly on your side again, I don't give a damn for it all!

(Steisshäuptl lets go of him.)
(Meanwhile the public bar has filled up with ordinary customers.)

ZAGL. There are customers in there, I must serve them. Life goes on, Chief. *(Off into public bar.)*

STEISSHÄUPTL. *(Elegaically.)* Surrounded by traitors, in my own house, in my own town . . . *(Rises, takes a bottle of liquor and a tumbler from a wall cupboard, fills the tumbler and drains it at one draft.)* And then one is not supposed to get downhearted. . . . *(Puts the bottle and glass on the table.)* One's own daughter stabs one in the back, goes shamelessy into the forest . . . and that Zagl, to whom I was never anything but kind, goes and opens the door to Stadlmeier, a deadly enemy . . . Dr. Schnopf . . . Dr. Suppinger . . . and they think they're educated men . . . and that underhand Ybbsgruber who has been boozing away my liquor free for years. *(Fills his glass again; empties it.)* When you think about it all, you feel like retiring into solitude, on a mountain, where there are no comrades, only cattle that at least don't talk . . . *(Fills the glass for the third time; drains it; after a pause, in a different tone.)* Yes, gentlemen, you seem to forget that we are in Brauning, at Steisshäuptl's. *(Throws the glass against the wall.)* I'm a force of nature, against me you're all nothing but a lot of fools! *(Leans with both hands on the table, leans forward.)* Or do you think I won't get the better of you? *(Straightens up, laughs a booming laugh.)* Oho, gentlemen, I shall cut you so deep your blood will spurt on the ceiling! *(Grimly.)* Bring the harness! Harness the horses! I'm mounting the dray, watch out! I turn the whip handle round–giddap– and slash you all to bits like I used to slash my horses. Come on–lets go! *(Marches across and kicks open the door of the public bar.)*

(As soon as the customers see him, conversation stops.)
(Steisshäuptl in the middle of the bar.)

ZAGL. *(Approaches with concern.)* Chief—
STEISSHÄUPTL. Shut your trap, now I'm going to speak!
(Zagl draws back.)
STEISSHÄUPTL. *(looks round.)* Listen all of you! *(To a man sitting alone at a table in the background.)* You there, pay attention– even if you're a stranger here! *(To Zagl.)* A schooner of beer! *(Bellows.)* Bring that schooner or else!
(Zagl runs; fills a tankard.)
STEISSHÄUPTL. Something regrettable has happened here, something dirty in our town that is otherwise so clean. I know there are a few gentlemen here who have an odd opinion of me *(Terrifying.)* but I know them all!

(Breathless silence.)

STEISSHÄUPTL. A hero came to me, a man with a pack of hounds on his heels–Ernst Meiche, the famous Raspberry Picker of Wüstenhofen concentration camp. It's an injustice that he should still be persecuted on that account; those were different times, and you can't make omelettes without breaking eggs– or is there anyone who thinks differently?
(The customers sit mute and motionless like wax dummies.)
STEISSHÄUPTL. Where was he to turn? Everyone knows that in out hearts nothing has changed, we can choose whom we want; inwardly we have remained just what we were; so one might have expected that in such a situation the comrades would stand together like one man, but no—

ZAGL. *(Puts the tankard of beer down beside him; beseechingly.)*
Herr Steisshäuptl—

STEISSHÄUPTL. Silence in the pigsty! But no: They conspire against me and try to turn my guest of honor against me, to take him away from me, cunningly to entice him away from me; and who is the first culprit? Why, Dr. Schnopf, of course. *(Takes a mighty draft from the tankard.)* Trust him. Does he by any chance imagine I have forgotten that back in those days he shortened a few unworthy lives in the Old Age Home? *(Makes the gesture of giving an injection.)* If that ever comes out, he can whistle for his pension—that's the least that will happen to him. And a man like that dares to challenge me. What do you think of that?

(No one moves.)

STEISSHÄUPTL. *(Puts the tankard down.)* Speak up—we have freedom of speech here! *(The silence is so intense that the grandfather clock can be heard ticking.)*

STEISSHÄUPTL. And his bosom pal, the headmaster—what the hell, I don't know who is a friend and who is an enemy any more— he went manhunting with a shotgun in the forests of his German homeland, going after fleeing foreign workers; he was acquitted, of course; dead men tell no tales. But times have changed—the case could be reopened, Herr Huett!

ZAGL. *(Beseechingly.)* Mr. Mayor—

STEISSHÄUPTL. Don't interrupt; everything must come out! *(Takes another deep draft; puts down the tankard, wipes his mouth.)* After a schnapps, a beer like that is the only thing . . . *(Straightens up.)* And Dr. Suppinger, who can't wait for them to catch the Raspberry Picker, because he wants to become famous by defending him at his trial. He'd do better to think of what he stole when Herr Hirsch was Aryanized—that's an endless tale. Millions and millions! By comparison I'm a smalltimer with my two boxes of dental gold. And if Hirsch turns up, or his heirs, we shall have to pay restitution out of our taxes— a dirty trick; how can we, who is going to give anything back to us? *(Silence.)*

STEISSHÄUPTL. *(Empties the tankard at one great draft.)* And now —irony of ironies—Herr Stadlmeier is trying to get the Raspberry Picker away from me, so that he can blackmail a pile of money out of me for his mineral water factory—when I think of it my stomach turns over—and his factory is full of old party stalwarts, holders of the Blood Order, who ought to have been denounced long ago along with Ybbsgruber and Stadlmeier. Yes, they ought to have been ruthlessly denounced to Herr Bricha in the capital, he would make a clean sweep of the factory —Herr Bricha the engineer! If I had his telephone number handy I'd ring him at once, so he could board a train and come down here and clear the place out, from top to bottom!

ZAGL. *(Almost weeping.)* Herr Group Leader!

(The Stranger rises without a sound and disappears into a corridor where a notice says "Toilets, Telephones.")

STEISSHÄUPTL. *(Who is suddenly completely drunk.)* Who is that shouting like a clap of thunder? *(Pulls himself together, stands to attention, swaying.)* Local Group Leader Konrad Steisshäuptl! The boxes of gold . . . yessir, all sold . . . But who could I have delivered it to at that time? . . . Those were turbulent days . . . what could I have done with it—sunk it in the Katzles? The value would have been lost to humanity . . . *(Holds himself up by the edge of the table.)* and humanity . . . means me!

ZAGL. *(Goes up to him; boldly.)* Behave yourself in front of the guests!

STEISSHÄUPTL. Hands off! *(Pushes him away.)* What is mine is mine, what matters is loyalty . . .If Hitler hadn't lost the war, he would still be my *Führer* . . . That was his only mistake and I can't forgive him for it—he was farsighted. *(Yells.)* Sieg Heil!

(Zagl has meanwhile run across to the kitchen door and thrown it open.)

ZAGL. The chief is ill! *(Burgerl immediately appears and hurries into the public bar, while Zagl races upstairs.)* Fräulein Sieglinde! *(Off.)*

BURGERL. *(Horrified.)* But Chief—?

STEISSHÄUPTL. *(Swaying.)* That's all . . . there's no more to be said . . . I'm going . . . No, I don't need any support! I'm going . . . of my own accord. *(Leans on Burgerl, who leads him across the room.)* Make way!

(A few customers inconspicuously leave the inn.)
(Zagl comes downstairs with Sieglinde.)

SIEGLINDE. *(Takes in the situation; vigorously.)* Upstairs! *(With
    Burgerl's help she drags Steisshäuptl upstairs; all three off.)*
(Zagl crosses over into the public bar.)
ZAGL. *(Goes from table to table collecting the money.)* Don't hold
    it against him, he was drunk . . . He doesn't really mean it,
    he just likes making political speeches. . . He was intoxicated
    by the thought of his old power; it happens from time to time.

*(The customers—apart from two sitting at the table nearest
    the front—leave in silence.)*
(The Stranger comes back from the corridor.)

THE STRANGER. *(To Zagl.)* I made a long-distance phone call–
    how much is it?
ZAGL. I can't think about that now, pay me tomorrow.
THE STRANGER. *(Hands him a hundred-mark note.)* I imagine that
    will cover it.
ZAGL. *(Puts the note in his pocket; absent-mindedly.)* Thanks,
    thanks very much.

(The stranger leaves.)

FIRST CUSTOMER. *(To second.)* I must say Steisshäuptl takes
    terrible chances.
SECOND CUSTOMER. *(In surprise.)* Why? Is he running any risk?
FIRST CUSTOMER. *(After a pause.)* No, that's true. Zagl, bill please!

(Zagl takes the money in silence.)
(Both customers leave.)

ZAGL. *(Alone.)* It's madness . . . *(Begins to clear up; after a
    pause.)* Heavens above, it isn't easy having a hero in the house!

(Curtain.)

ACT 3

(Next day, early morning. Zagl and Sieglinde in the private room.)

ZAGL. *(Spreads out the morning paper in the newspaper holder.)*
    No, Fräulein Sieglinde, I can't take the responsibility.

SIEGLINDE. What I am asking—I only want you to go up and call him out and tell him I'll be waiting for him at ten o'clock outside the cemetery—

ZAGL. *(Hangs the newspaper holder on a hook over the table in the private room.)* You have no idea who he is.

SIEGLINDE. I don't care who he is. I haven't asked him and I shan't ask him. *(Imploring.)* Be nice and go up, do me this favor, Zagl, please!

ZAGL. I've already told you: I'm not going to get involved. No one knows what may have happened by ten o'clock; things are in a flux and that's that.

SIEGLINDE. Have you no humanity?

ZAGL. No, I'm perfectly healthy.

SIEGLINDE. *(Stamps her foot.)* You'll never see me again! *(Through the back door out into the street, off.)*

ZAGL. *(Goes across to the private room.)* The Raspberry Picker, naturally, he would appeal to anyone . . .

(The inspector enters from the hall; he is pale and tired.)

ZIEREIS. The chief up yet?

ZAGL. He's sleeping off his binge.

ZIEREIS. An expensive binge. But if it's true what I've heard, it'll be your turn next!

ZAGL. It's no one's turn—we're in Brauning.

ZIEREIS. You don't know what has happened in the meantime, during the night—

(Steisshäuptl has appeared on the stairs, well rested and in the best of spirits.)

STEISSHÄUPTL. *(Calmly.)* What has happened, Inspector?

ZIEREIS. *(Turns round.)* Ah, good. *(Goes to him.)* I must speak to you urgently.

STEISSHÄUPTL. *(Moves to the front; to Zagl.)* Has the drayman been yet?

ZAGL. No, but—*(In a low voice.)* Your daughter has run away.

STEISSHSÄUPTL. Aha. *(After a pause.)* Fetch me when the drayman comes.

ZAGL. Very good, Chief. *(Goes into the hall.)*

ZIEREIS. *(Nervously.)* What has happened has happened. The fact is that yesterday evening some unknown man telephoned Engineer Bricha and told him to board a train and come straight down here, because of the Raspberry Picker and all the others.

What do you say to that?

STEISSHÄUPTL. *(Sits down at the family table.)* Where did you get that from?

ZIEREIS. The telephone operator, a certain Fiala, listened in and immediately told her colleague, until it reached me through an informant. Now we're in trouble. Bricha knows Meiche personally— he spent two years in the camp. If he comes down here— and that's to be expected—we shall all be in for it. It's ghastly!

STEISSHÄUPTL. *(Regretfully.)* Caught together, hanged together.

ZIEREIS. The engineer wasn't at home; the call was taken by his wife or his daughter, says Fiala, who said she would tell him when he got back from the café. *(Knocks over a chair.)* A catastrophe!

(Pause.)

STEISSHÄUPTL. Listen, Ziereis, I have an idea. Phone Bricha from the police station, it won't cost you anything, you've got the number; give some false name. Either he is already on his way —that'll be a blow—or he is at home or in his office; his wife or his daughter will tell you that; in the end you pretend you have got a wrong number and come straight here and report to me.

ZIEREIS. *(Looks up.)* It's a glimmer of hope.

STEISSHÄUPTL. Meanwhile I'll think the matter over.

(Ziereis rises; leaves without a word.)

STEISSHÄUPTL. *(Shouts.)* Burgerl! Breakfast!

(Burgerl in the kitchen doorway.)

BURGERL. Good morning. Are you feeling better?

STEISSHÄUPTL. What nonsense! When wasn't I feeling well? I was in high spirits and now I want my breakfast—hurry up with it.

BURGERL. With coffee?

STEISSHÄUPTL. No, without.

(Burgerl off.)

(Steisshäuptl goes to the shelf, chooses a bottle of wine, uncorks it, pours out four ounces of white wine.)
(Huett and Schnopf appear in the private room.)

HUETT. If only I knew what I had done; I'm all in.

SCHNOPF. I've been feeling just the same since six o'clock, and yet I usually sleep till nine.

HUETT. This accusation out of the blue–can you explain it?

SCHNOPF. Of course, alcohol . . . If I were an educationist I would warn the youth against alcohol; it's no use my being a doctor, because everyone says that teetotalers die too. By the way, about out little difference of opinion yesterday—

HUETT. Forgiven and fotgotten!

SCHNOPF. We must face up to the danger.

HUETT. One for all and all for one.

(They shake hands.)
(Burgerl brings breakfast.)

STEISSHÄUAPTL. *(With wine bottle and glass to the table.)* Zagl says Sieglinde has run away. Be so good as to see about her.

BURGERL. I'll go and fetch her at once, so we can have some peace and quiet.

(Fetches her coat and head-scarf from the kitchen; into the hall and off.)
(Steisshäuptl sits down to breakfast.)
(Ybbsgruber and Stadlmeier enter the private room.)

YBBSGRUBER. Aha, already on the job, gentlemen. Don't let us disturb you! We're on our way through to Steisshäuptl to settle accounts—

STADLMEIER. *(Angrily.)* I've told you before, I don't want to be ruined by your recklessness; we must come to an agreement with the man; either you get some sense into your head, or else—

YBBSGRUBER. *(Ill-humoredly.)* All right, all right; anyway I'm not deaf.

STADLMEIER. *(Subdued.)* That madman is the only person who can save us– therefore I suggest that I should talk to him in the name of the community. That's our only chance.

SCHNOPF. Yes, yes, very good.

HUETT. You will be performing an invaluable service.

YBBSGRUBER. But all the same, he's a pig–I mean Steisshäuptl.

STADLMEIER. Gentlemen–we must humble ourselves. Quick march!

(They goose-step across the stage; Steisshäuptl puts down his knife and fork and revels in the spectacle.)

STEISSHÄUPTL. I'm dreaming . . . a mirage . . . Managing
Director Stadlmeier, who ordinarily never honors me with his
company, surrounded by the intellectual elite. To think that I
should live to see this . . . What has happened, gentlemen?

STADLMEIER. *(With dignity.)* We will pass over that.

YBBSGRUBER. *(Roughly.)* You've got us in a nice mess! You ought
to be ashamed of yourself, instead of sitting there wolfing bacon
at this time of the morning.

STEISSHÄUPTL. *(Holds out the plate to him.)* Do you want a
piece?

YBBSGRUBER. I won't take anything from a traitor—

STADLMEIER. *(Imperiously.)* Keep quiet!

YBBSGRUBER. *(Daunted.)* All right . . . if you think so . . .
(Sits down.) Give us the bacon! *(Takes it and eats.)*

STADLMEIER. Let us avoid all emotionalism. You know what
threatens us if the engineer comes here. What do you intend
to do?

STEISSHÄUPTL. *(Gnawing a bacon rind; perfectly calm.)* Nothing.

STADLMEIER. Herr Steisshäuptl—

STEISSHSÄUPTL. Leave me in peace; breakfast is a sacred rite; I
don't see why I should be forever wearing myself out for the
so-called comrades. I've been doing it for years, with no
advantage to myself, and what thanks do I get?

STADLMEIER. But I beg you . . . Don't you see that you too are
in danger?

STEISSHÄUPTL. I'm touched that you should be so concerned for
my well-being. But don't worry, I shall get out of trouble–a
Steisshäuptl does not surrender.

STADLMEIER. I beg you—

STEISSHÄUPTL. When I have once said no, it is irrevocable. Do you
think I haven't suffered? Out of sheer anguish I got drunk; now
the effects of my drunkenness have fallen upon the guilty, that's
all.

STADLMEIER. Don't be stubborn, take a tolerant view of things.
You see, we are prepared for any sacrifice, like the burghers of
Calais. Isn't that right, gentlemen?

HUETT. A new trial–do you know what that means?

SCHNOPF. Think of my pension.

YBBSGRUBER. Ask what you like, but get us out of this mess.
(Pause.)

STEISSHÄUPTL. *(Thoughtfully.)* Calais . . . that's the place where
you cross the Channel and throw up . . . *(Straightens up.)* I

don't know whether I can overcome my reluctance, I'm only human. If I make the effort, gentlemen, it will be out of pure idealism! I won't take anything in return, but I shall make one condition–that the story about the two boxes will never at any time or in any way be mentioned again!

STADLMEIER. Of course.

STEISSHÄUPTL. Doctor?

SCHNOPF. That goes without saying.

STEISSHÄUPTL. Headmaster?

HUETT. Not a word will ever be said about it.

STEISSHÄUPTL. Ybbsgruber? Colonel!

YBBSGRUBER. *(Chewing.)* Word of honor.

STEISSHÄUPTL. Very well, then *(Rises, triumphantly.)* please sit down.

(Stadlmeier, Schnopf, and Huett sit down.)

STEISSHÄUPTL. You, Herr Huett, have nothing to fear from a retrial, even if new witnesses present themselves. I shall give you a statement in black and white that at the time in question you were here on a visit with friends. Some monster was mistaken for you–that can happen. I'm not worried about you either, Doctor. Your younger colleague passed away some years ago, and if anything really happened in the Old Age Home, then it was your late lamented colleague who shortened the old people's sufferings, and you are in the clear. As to the factory–listen closely, Herr Stadlmeier, and you, Ybbsgruber–it is child's play to find a solution. Why am I in charge of the Register Office? I shall obtain fresh papers for the wearers of the Blood Order and no one will bother them any more; I shall be performing an act of Christian charity. And now to our guest of honor, the Raspberry Picker–

(Lawyer Suppinger enters in a great hurry from the hall, a briefcase under his arm.)

SUPPINGER. *(In high spirits.)* Your servant, gentlemen! No doubt you've already heard, the engineer is on his way–that'll make headlines. Don't worry, Herr Steisshäuptl–the picture has changed; if they arrest him, I shall defend him so that the sparks fly—

STEISSHÄUPTL. *(Has come up close to him.)* Just a moment—

SUPPINGER. I've no time to spare, I must go to my client!

STEISSHÄUPTL. *(Barring his path.)* I've only got one thing to say to you: Make yourself scarce!

SUPPINGER. Oh, I see, you're afraid ... *(Smiling.)* I'm sorry, the Raspberry Picker has retained me; I was quicker, we have a verbal agreement; even if you don't like it, I must insist upon it—

STEISSHÄUPTL. —upon our reopening the Suppinger case, Hirsch and heirs?

SUPPINGER. *(Still smiling.)* You can't scare me with that; I know more than you think—

STEISSHÄUPTL. Watch out. I shall count to three–

SUPPINGER. Go ahead, count, count! Nothing can stop me. *(To the others.)* Help me, gentlemen, we have a sacred duty. Material considerations must take second place. The cause must not fail because of the bad conscience of a single individual—

YBBSGRUBER. Very true. *(Goes up to him.)* If you're still there at three, you can number your bones. *(To Steisshäuptl.)* Carry on counting.

STEISSHÄUPTL. One.

YBBSGRUBER. Two.

SUPPINGER. *(Retires into the entrance hall.)* The last word has not been spoken. *(Waving his briefcase.)* I've got something on all of you; you will be hearing from me.

(Off.)

STEISSHÄUPTL. *(Contemptuously.)* Idiot *(Turns round.)* The Raspberry Picker must leave at once; wait in the private room, but don't make a sound till the danger is past; I shall now summon all my strength! *(Upstairs and off. The gentlemen cross over to the table in the private room.)*

STADLMEIER. *(Enters last; closes the door.)* You'll see, he'll manage that too.

YBBSGRUBER. *(Worried.)* Suppose the Raspberry Picker refuses to play ball?

HUETT. *(Disconcerted.)* Do you think he might?

(Ybbsgruber shrugs his shoulders.)

SCHNOPF. Terrible ...

STADLMEIER. *(At the window, drums with his fingers on the pane.)* It is indeed ...

SCHNOPF. *(Takes the newspaper from the hook; sighing.)* If only it were over already ...

HUETT. *(Surprised.)* You're reading the newspaper at a time like this?

SCHNOPF. It's a habit, but you're right. *(Puts the newspaper on the table.)* I can't concentrate at the moment.

(Kerz comes down, followed by Steisshäuptl.)

STEISSHÄUPTL. No, let us speak frankly. The material question has been overtaken by events, there's no further point in discussing it; now I'm offering to save your very life–

KERZ. What are you talking about? I don't feel in any danger—

STEISSHÄUPTL. Because you don't know what has happened–let me finish! Since last night they are on your tracks—

KERZ. *(Stops still.)* Damnation!

STEISSHÄUPTL. Do you think I'm not furious too? Sit down and listen calmly.

KERZ. *(Sits down.)* Now of all times . . .

STEISSHÄUPTL. *(Sits facing him.)* Manly courage would be pure madness now; we must be realistic; you have no time to lose, in half an hour the engineer may be here—

KERZ. Who?

STEISSHÄUPTL. Bricha!

KERZ. Bricha . . . *(Shaking his head.)* I don't know any engineer called Bricha.

STEISSHÄUPTL. *(Impatiently.)* That's enough. With all due respect for your incognito, it's utter stupidity now; Bricha doesn't give a damn for your incognito, or do you by any chance suspect that I'm going to give you away, Herr Meiche?

KERZ. What–did you call me?

STEISSHÄUPTL. *(Relieved.)* Now it's out.

KERZ. *(Leaning forward.)* Meiche–?

STEISSHÄUPTL. I've told you a hundred times already that the water is up to your neck, and you act as though nothing has happened, and yet every child knows you are the Raspberry Picker–

KERZ. The Raspberry Picker–?

STEISSHÄUPTL. *(Angrily.)* Who else?

KERZ. Raspberries, haha–

STEISSHÄUPTL. What is there to laugh about?

KERZ. Even as a child I was allergic to them—

STEISSHÄUPTL. *(Jumps up.)* I've had enough of this. I'm not going to be made a fool of, not even by you, with all due respect! I'm racking my brains how to save you from this Old Testament vengeance and you laugh at me and treat me like a spy–is that worthy of your great past?

(Pause.)

KERZ. *(In a different tone.)* Great–in what sense?

STEISSHÄUPTL. Ah I see, you want to put me to the test. All right: During the war, as the Raspberry Picker you did in around eight thousand prisoners among the raspberry canes with a telescopic rifle in the stone quarry at Wüstenhofen–Herr Troup Leader Ernst Meiche!

KERZ. *(Has jumped up, trembling all over his body.)* Around eight thousand–?

STEISSHÄUPTL. Or six; I'm not reproaching you, those were other times, don't let's waste time on that. Your companion has nothing to fear, but you must disappear immediately, into the old hunting lodge; I'll organize everything; we will tell the engineer that you have fled, and tomorrow or some time we shall bring you across the frontier with first-class papers; in a few weeks you will be in Egypt, or South America, or somewhere, and who knows, in a few years we may see each other again in the Old Comrades Association; you will always find friends here. *(Kerz looks at him in horror.)*

STEISSHÄUPTL. Don't hesitate, think of your family. Upstairs!

(Kerz stands for a few seconds motionless; then he races upstairs; off.)

STEISSHÄUPTL. *(Takes out his handkerchief, wipes his brow.)* Where there's a will . . . *(To the private room; flings the door open.)* Victory is ours!

(The gentlemen come out and surround him.)

STADLMEIER. What's wrong?

STEISSHÄUPTL. *(Proudly.)* Nothing. The material question has been settled for all time; it will never be referred to again. The guest of honor is packing his things; in ten minutes we shall be rid of him, and we shall tell the engineer that he has fled, we don't know where.

STADLMEIER. Magnificent.

HUETT. A real miracle.

SCHNOPF. You are our salvation.

YBBSGRUBER. Steisshäuptl *(Slaps him on the back.)* You're a hell of a fellow!

STEISSHÄUPTL. *(Flattered.)* Such recognition makes up for a great deal.

(Ziereis comes running in.)

ZIEREIS. *(In front of Steisshäuptl.)* I've telephoned: Engineer
   Bricha isn't coming.
STEISSHÄUPTL. He isn't?
ZIEREIS. He was given the message yesterday, but he only laughed
   and said we must think him a fool if we imagine we can entice
   him away just now.

(Pause.)

YBBSGRUBER. He doesn't believe in our Raspberry Picker.
ZIEREIS. No, he doesn't believe in him.
STEISSHÄUPTL Well–I thought he was cleverer than that.
HUETT. The Semitic intelligence is generally overrated.
SCHNOPF. Well, the chief thing is we shan't be bothered with him.
STEISSHÄUPTL. *(In a low voice.)* Somehow it almost troubles me.
   ·. . . *(Straightens up.)* Well, however that may be, we will have
   a little farewell party for the Raspberry Picker. Come gentlemen,
   you too, Inspector; you have behaved very correctly, you are
   one of us.

(All go across to the family table.)
(Burgerl comes back.)

BURGERL. *(To Steisshäuptl.)* It's no use talking to Sieglinde, she
   is absolutely determined to run away–
STEISSHÄUPTL. Oh, she's just lovelorn–time heals all wounds.
   Bring us something to eat–salami, ham, liver pâté, and whatever
   else you can find for seven people, a bit of a feast. In a
   quarter of an hour there will be peace in the house again.
BURGERL. About time! *(Off into the kitchen.)*

(Outside the sound of a lorry starting up, then silence.)

ZAGL. *(in the hall.)* The drayman!
STEISSHÄUPTL. *(To the gentlemen.)* I'll be back in a minute. *(In
   front of Zagl.)* Fetch a bottle of champagne from the cellar,
   but no foreign stuff, the best we have–German Sekt!
ZAGL. Very good, Chief. *(To the cellar door beside the bar, down
   and off.)*

(Steisshäuptl disappears into the entrance hall.)
(The gentlemen sit down.)

YBBSGRUBER. You can say what you like: Steisshäuptl is a
personality.

STADLMEIER. *(Who in the course of the preceding scene has grown
very thoughtful.)* Yes, but . . . just think a minute: Was it
really necessary?

(Dark down below; light up above.)
(Kerz is leaning against the wall.)

GRAPPINA. *(In front of him.)* Aren't you pleased? Sasha! It's the
best thing that could have happened to us; they take you for
a mass murderer, splendid–murder is nobler than theft; if
you're clever now, you will string them along—

KERz.ᐧ Stop it!

GRAPPINA. Are you mad? Forward, Raspberry Picker, let them
hide you in the forest, let them stuff you with money; what
does it matter to you who they mistake you for? When you've
fleeced that gang, we'll flit and laugh ourselves silly. Don't
stand there staring–Downstairs, quick march!

KERZ. Around eight thousand . . .

GRAPPINA. Well, what of it? No one's going to pay you for your
long face, all we need now is for you to break into tears . . . .
What do the dead matter to you? Were they your brothers,
your relations? Grass is growing over them now, several feet
high; and anyway most of them were only Jews, Michel never
liked them, *les sales juifs qui font le commerce*——

KERZ. *(Shouts at her.)* Get out!

GRAPPINA. *(Flabbergasted.)* Me–?

KERZ. *(In a low voice, between his teeth.)* I never want to see you again.

(Pause.)

GRAPPINA. I see . . .

(Kerz does not move.)

GRAPPINA. The dead! *(Scornfully.)* What a petty crook you are,
Alexander Kerz . . . Admit it, you want to sleep with the
redhead. I was good enough for you in Marseilles, in the Rue
Tapisvert—

KERZ. Go! *(Pause.)*

GRAPPINA. *(Goes to the table, takes her beauty case; then to the
door, turns round.)* Take care you don't regret this, you . . .
you . . . *(Contemptuously.)* hero! *(Off.)*

KERZ. *(Motionless, in a low voice.)* Around eight thousand . . .

(Darkness, the pop of a champagne cork, then light down below.)

STEISSHÄUPTL. *(Fills the champagne glasses.)* It's always the same,
whether it's a drayman or a member of the better classes–they
all think they can exploit my good nature without limit, but in
the end I cry halt and emerge victorious . . . Have a glass too,
Zagl, I don't bear grudges.

(Grappina comes downstairs.)

ZAGL. *(Holds out a glass to him.)* It will be a lesson to me, Chief.

STEISSHSÄUPTL. *(Fills his glass.)* I'd like to know what's keeping him
so long. *(Turns round.)* Who is that?
ZAGL. *(Whispers to him.)* His woman.
STEISSHÄUPTL. Not a bad bit of stuff at all.
GRAPPINA. *(Approaches mockingly.)* Champagne for the Raspberry
Picker?
STEISSHÄUPTL. *(Reserved.)* This is a private party.
GRAPPINA. Don't worry, I'm not going to disturb the victory feast.
(Laughs loudly.)
STEISSHÄUPTL. *(Indignantly.)* Your laughter is out of place.
GRAPPINA. Laugh, landlord, laugh, gentlemen, laugh! That man up
there is nothing but a wretched crook who faints at the sight of
a chicken being killed–not a hero, a thief with eighteen
previous convictions in five countries—
YBBSGRUBER. *(Jumps up.)* What a dirty trick!
STEISSHÄUPTL. Take it easy! Ybbsgruber, sit down! *(To Grappina.)*
You're making a mistake, it's too crude; your jealousy is under-
standable, but even slander has to be credible; we weren't born
yesterday, we know what we know—
GRAPPINA. Like hell you do! If you don't believe me, then go
and fetch him, fetch him, messieurs—
STEISSHÄUPTL. That's enough! And speak German here! Zagl, go
up at once!

(Zagl hurries to the stairs.)

GRAPPINA. Zagl, stop!

(Zagl stops.)

GRAPPINA. Don't forget the case! The small leather case! *(Zagl goes up and off.)*

STEISSHÄUPTL. *(To Grappina.)* In your position I would beat it.

GRAPPINA. Not a bad idea, landlord. What have I got to lose here? A man? That's a laugh . . . *(Withdraws into the entrance hall.)* Have fun, gentlemen, and don't forget your hero's name: Kerz–Alexander Kerz! *(Quickly off.)*

ZIEREIS. *(Starts after her.)* Wait a moment, you–!

STEISSHÄUPTL. Forget it, let her go! We would only have trouble with that creature . . .

ZIEREIS. That's true. *(Comes back to the table.)* It shows you once again what a woman is capable of–terrible . . . *(Stops still; thoughtfully.)* Kerz . . Alexander Kerz? *(In a low voice.)* But we're looking for someone by that name too . . . *(Takes the list of wanted persons out of his briefcase; studies it.)*

(Kerz comes down followed by Zagl, who is carrying the case.)

ZAGL. *(Still on the stairs.)* The lady wanted it, we can't help it—

STEISSHÄUPTL. Shut your trap! *(Goes to meet Kerz, leads him to the table.)* The gentlemen . . . the comrades know you already. . . . And now *(Picks up his glass.)* Let us drink to our unshakable resolve to preserve our—

ZIEREIS. *(Raises his hand.)* One moment! *(Goes up to Kerz.)* May I have a look in your case?

STEISSHÄUPTL. *(To Ziereis.)* What the hell's got into you?

ZIEREIS. A routine check, just so the matter is settled once and for all. *(To Kerz.)* The key please, if you don't mind.

STEISSHÄUPTL. *(To Kerz.)* Don't take offense; he is a fanatic for duty.

(The gentlemen round the table laugh. Kerz slowly puts his hand in his waistcoat pocket, takes out the key, gives it to Ziereis. Ziereis takes it; puts the case on the table, opens it, takes out some pieces of jewelry, among them a gold watch.)

ZAGL. *(Pulls his sleeve.)* That's what he has collected. *(In a whisper.)* For the Odessa Organization. . .

ZIEREIS. *(Turns the watch round; reads.)* Ragnar Rosenberg, jeweler. *(Looks up; sharply.)* From the robbery–?

(The gentlemen jump to their feet.)

STEISSHÄUPTL. *(Bellows.)* What–?

ZIEREIS. *(Fearlessly.)* Relax, this is not political any more! *(To the gentlemen.)* I must inform you that I am now acting in an official capacity. *(To Kerz; energetically.)* You are identical with a certain Kerz whom the arrested men describe as an accessory?

ZAGL. No, no, he's the Raspberry Picker!

ZIEREIS. *(Thunders at Zagl.)* Silence! *(To Kerz quietly.)* Are you that Alexander Kerz? *(Kerz nods. Everyone stands dumbfounded.)*

ZIEREIS. *(To Steisshäuptl, regretfully.)* A mistake. A confusion of identity. *(Takes handcuffs from his briefcase and puts them on Kerz. Burgerl comes from the kitchen with a tray.)*

BURGERL. I've emptied the whole refrigerator, I'll bring bread in a minute, good appetite! *(Looks up; perplexed.)* Oh, what has the gentleman done?

YBBSGRUBER. *(Contemptuously.)* He stole.

SCHNOPF. In Ganselstadt, from Rosenberg's.

STADLMEIER. A shopbreaker. A thief.

STEISSHÄUPTL. To think there are people ... *(Shattered.)* It's like gazing into an abyss.

BURGERL. *(Sympathetically.)* Poor fellow ... *(Puts down the tray; goes quickly into the kitchen, leaving the door open.)*

(Sieglinde enters from the hall.)

SIEGLINDE. *(Very agitated.)* The woman is lying, it's not true, the bitch is simply jealous–no wonder, look at her bosom and mine. *(Goes to Kerz.)* Tell them at once that it isn't true; it's all a shameless lie! You're not a thief, I don't care what else you may be, but—

KERZ. *(Raises his handcuffed hands.)* –not a mass murderer!

SIEGLINDE. *(Backs away.)* It isn't true–it can't be true . . .

YBBSGRUBER. *(Disgusted.)* He is actually proud of it.

SIEGLINDE. I don't believe it, no . . .

(Burgerl comes back.)

BURGERL. *(In front of Kerz.)* Here. *(Gives him a small parcel.)* Two ham rolls, for the journey ...

STEISSHÄUPTL. *(Absent-mindedly.)* Eleven schillings fifty ...

STADLMEIER. Unbelievable.

SCHNOPF. *(To Burgerl.)* You're acting improperly.

YBBSGRUBER. Yes, there's a fool born every minute.

ZAGL. I'm glad I didn't marry you!

BURGERL. *(Steps back, looks from one to the other.)* What are you thinking of? I don't talk, but there comes a moment when my patience snaps. Don't you want peace and quiet? Are you only happy when you can attack someone? Who do you look up to? If a man murders a few thousand people, you'll lick his boots, but when you come across a poor fellow who hasn't done anyone any harm you stamp on him. You disgust me; I wonder if you're human at all! *(Into the kitchen, slams the door behind her.)*

ZAGL. What a beast.

(Ziereis motions to Kerz to walk ahead of him; the two men leave through the hall.)

HUETT. *(Who has not taken his eyes off the arrested man.)* So that . . . well, I never . . . extraordinary! *(Follows the two; off.)*

SIEGLINDE. *(In a low voice.)* The man . . . his manner . . . his appearance . . . No: It was lovely all the same. Of course it would have been better still . . . *(Sighs.)* A pity, an everlasting pity! *(Upstairs; off.)*

(Silence.)

STEISSHÄUPTL. *(Bitterly.)* Fine figures we cut . . . *(Looks up.)* If I only knew who got us into that mess . . .

STADLMEIER. As to that *(Sharply.)* You'd better ask Lieutenant Colonel Ybbsgruber!

YBBSGRUBER. *(Indignantly.)* What—me?

STADLMEIER. Yes, you! It was you who made the whole thing possible by acting on your own account—

YBBSGRUBER. That's a rotten lie! How can I help it if Dr. Schnopf came running up to me—

SCHNOPF. What—me?

YBBSGRUBER. Yes, you! You set the ball rolling—

SCHNOPF. So you're trying to pin it on me! Who recognized the Raspberry Picker at first glance? *(Points with outstretched hand at Zagl.)* Zagl! *(Turns on his heel, crosses over to the private room, and takes refuge behind the newspaper.)*

STEISSHÄUPTL. *(Menacingly.)* Zagl—come here . . .

ZAGL. *(Backs away.)* What do you want from me, you hyenas? *(Tries to run away, but is surrounded.)* . Leave me alone, he looked like him—he still looks like him, to err is human. *(All three fall upon him.)*

ZAGL. *(Yells.)* Let me go!

STEISSHÄUPTL. I'll kill him!

(At this moment Huett comes back.)

HUETT. *(In a stentorian voice.)* Let go of him this instant!

(The gentlemen let go of Zagl.)

ZAGL. *(Howling.)* I'll never again poke my nose into anything! *(Past Huett into the hall and off.)*

HUETT. Just think: Who was to blame for everything? *(Closer.)* The face struck me as suspicious right away: the hooked nose, the shape of the skull, the hair—everything points unequivocally to a member of the alien Semitic race that has through all the ages brought disaster upon our people—

YBBSGRUBER. What—a Jew?

HUETT. As an experienced racial scientist I consider there is absolutely no doubt.

STADLMEIER. So he's a Jew . . .

STEISSHÄUPTL. *(Downcast.)* Nothing but a common Jew . . .

(Schnopf is standing in the door of the private room.)

SCHNOPF. Gentlemen. *(Waves the newspaper.)* Sensation, sensation! *(Closer.)* Here is the morning paper, latest news. *(Reads.)* "Late last night the former Troop Leader Ernst Meiche, known as 'The Raspberry Picker,' whom the authorities had been seeking for twenty years, was arrested not far from the capital." *(Lowers the newspaper; to Steisshäuptl, ironically.)* My condolences.

STEISSHÄUPTL. *(Becoming serious.)* Why?

YBBSGRUBER. Do you ask? *(Scornfully.)* You didn't come to an agreement with the real Raspberry Picker—I wonder what he will have to say about your dental gold.

STADLMEIER. Yes, and about the other valuables!

STEISSHÄUPTL. *(Uncomfortably.)* I see . . . well, everyone knows I'm not unreasonable . . . it's always possible to come to terms . . . I'm no monster, am I?

SCHNOPF. *(Who has been studying the news, again raises his hand.)* One moment! *(Reads.)* "As we learned just before going to press, Ernst Meiche hanged himself in his cell before the first interrogation."

(The gentlemen stand as though struck by lightning.)
STEISSHÄUPTL. *(His face clears.)* Ah well, gentlemen, there is no
cure for death . . . *(Goes to the table; as he looks from face
to face his coarse face mirrors a whole gamut of emotions:
hypocritical melancholy, false condolence, gleeful delight, and
finally triumph at having got the better of everyone in the end.)*
Over and done with. *(Raises his champagne glass.)* With that in
mind . . . *(Beaming.)* In memoriam!

(The gentlemen go up to the table and drink more or less reluctantly to the victor.)

(Curtain.)